THE POLITICS OF
INTERNATIONAL POLITICAL ECONOMY

Europa Politics of ... Series

This major series from Routledge offers up-to-date surveys covering the politics of a wide variety of contemporary issues of interest to students, academics, professionals and general researchers. Expert editors and contributors provide a wealth of information in a format designed for ease of use.

Most titles contain some or all of the following sections, depending upon their relevance to the subject:

- Essay chapters and, where applicable, case studies, written by a wide range of academic and other experts selected by the volume editor.
- A–Z Glossary for reference containing entries on major issues, organizations, countries, regions, personalities, etc., cross-referenced for ease of use.
- Maps.
- Statistics.
- Select Bibliography.

The Politics of Religion
Edited by Jeffrey Haynes

The Politics of Oil
Edited by Bülent Gökay

The Politics of Migration
Edited by Barbara Marshall

The Politics of the Environment
Edited by Chukwumerije Okereke

The Politics of Climate Change
Edited by Maxwell T. Boykoff

The Politics of Gender
Edited by Yoke-Lian Lee

The Politics of the Olympics
Edited by Alan Bairner, Gyozo Molnar

The Politics of Water
Edited by Kai Wegerich, Jeroen Warner

The Politics of Conflict
By Vassilis K. Fouskas

The Politics of Maritime Power
By Andrew T.H. Tan

The Politics of Terrorism
Edited by Andrew T.H. Tan

The Politics of Space
By Eligar Sadeh

The Politics of Narcotic Drugs
Edited by Julia Buxton

The Politics of Fair Trade
Edited by Meera Warrier

The Politics of Development
Edited by Heloise Weber

THE POLITICS OF
INTERNATIONAL POLITICAL ECONOMY

A SURVEY

FIRST EDITION

Editor: Vassilis K. Fouskas

LONDON AND NEW YORK

First edition published 2015
by Routledge
2 Park Square, Milton Park, Abingdon, OX14 4RN, United Kingdom

and by Routledge
711 Third Avenue, New York, NY 10017, USA

Routledge is an imprint of the Taylor & Francis Group, an informa business

© 2015 Vassilis K. Fouskas for selection and editorial material; individual chapters, Routledge

The right of the editor to be identified as the author of the editorial material, and of the authors for their individual chapters, has been asserted in accordance with sections 77 and 78 of the Copyright, Designs and Patents Act 1988.

All rights reserved. No part of this book may be reprinted or reproduced or utilised in any form or by any electronic, mechanical, or other means, now known or hereafter invented, including photocopying and recording, or in any information storage or retrieval system, without permission in writing from the publishers.

Trademark notice: Product or corporate names may be trademarks or registered trademarks, and are used only for identification and explanation without intent to infringe.

Library of Congress Cataloging in Publication Data
The politics of international political economy : a survey / edited by Vassilis K. Fouskas.
    pages cm
Includes bibliographical references.
1. International economic relations. 2. International economic relations–Case studies. 3. International finance. 4. International finance–Case studies. I. Fouskas, Vassilis K., 1963- , author, editor of compilation.
    HF1359.P656 2014
    337–dc23
                2014010765

ISBN: 978-1-85743-638-9 (hbk)
ISBN: 978-0-203-14597-5 (ebk)

Europa Commissioning Editor: Cathy Hartley
Editorial Assistant: Lydia de Cruz

Printed and bound in the United States of America by
Edwards Brothers Malloy on sustainably sourced paper

Contents

List of illustrations	ix
List of contributors	xi
Foreword	xii
Acknowledgments	xiv
List of abbreviations	xv

ESSAYS

Global political economy and the separation of academic disciplines KEES VAN DER PIJL	3
Revisiting Bretton Woods, 1944–71 ALEX O. TACKIE	20
The failure of neo-liberal financialization (1971–91) VASSILIS K. FOUSKAS AND BÜLENT GÖKAY	38
Shock therapy and the political economy of the former Soviet space SABINE SPANGENBERG	57
Revisiting the 1992–93 EMS crisis in the context of international political economy DIMITRIS P. SOTIROPOULOS	78
Asia catches cold, Russia sneezes: the political economy of emerging market crises in 1997–98 MICHAEL F. KEATING	95
The rise of the *qi ye ji tuan* and the emergence of Chinese hegemony JAYANTHA JAYMAN	119
The global South: from dependency to convergence? RAY KIELY	146
The policy response to the great recession of 2008: is it the 1930s all over again? YIANNIS KITROMILIDES	165
Understanding the global financial crisis BÜLENT GÖKAY	178
The political economy of the Arab uprisings SHAMPA ROY-MUKHERJEE	188

The politics and economics of the Greek debt crisis 209
CONSTANTINE DIMOULAS AND VASSILIS K. FOUSKAS

A–Z GLOSSARY 249
Select bibliography 295

List of illustrations

FIGURES

7.1	GDP: World, G7 + Australia, China, India, Russia	122
11.1	MENA GDP growth, 1996–2011	195
11.2	GDP and per capita GDP growth by region, 2012	197
11.3	MENA fiscal balance (percentage of GDP), 1996–2011	198
11.4	Manufactured exports as a percentage of total merchandise exports	199
11.5	Tariff Reform Index (percentile ranking), 2000–07	200
11.6	FDI inflows into the MENA region, 2011	200
11.7	Unemployment rates in MENA countries in 2011	203
11.8	Unemployment in percentage among youth, women and educated in 2009	203

TABLES

3.1	Average profit rates in three sectors	50
3.2	Comparing average profit and unemployment rates, and average annual rates of change for real wages, in selected OECD countries	50
4.1	Selected economic indicators	69
4.2	Selected economic indicators	70
11.1	The original and augmented Washington Consensus	190
11.2	MENA region statistics	196
12.1	Sectoral structure of GDP at factor costs as a percentage of total	219
12.2	Balance of payments deficit and invisible receipts (1960–80) in US$ million, current prices	220
12.3	Some key economic indicators, 1974–89	222
12.4	EEC/EC transfers during PASOK's second term, 1985–89	223
12.5	Athens Stock Exchange: share price indices, 1980–2010	226
12.6	Evolution of the Greek public debt and its relation to GDP in US$	229
12.7	Exports over imports	231
12.8	Annual loans of the Greek state, state receipts, receipts from EC and expenditures	232

ILLUSTRATIONS

12.9 Annual change of exports over imports, the share prices in Athens Stock Exchange and GDP in market prices   233
12.10 Population over 15 years and employment in Greece in thousands, 1998–2010   236
12.11 Employed according to their occupational status in thousands, 1998–2010   238

List of contributors

Constantine Dimoulas is Assistant Professor in Social Administration and Evaluation of Social Programmes at the Department of Social Policy, Panteion University, Athens, Greece.

Vassilis K. Fouskas is a Professor of International Politics and Economics at the School of Business and Law and Director of STAMP (Centre for the Study of States, Markets and People), University of East London, UK.

Bülent Gökay is Professor of International Relations and Head of the School of Politics, International Relations and the Environment (SPIRE) at Keele University, UK.

Jayantha Jayman is Assistant Professor of Global Studies at St Lawrence University, USA.

Michael F. Keating is Professor of International Political Economy at Richmond University, the American International University in London, UK.

Ray Kiely is Professor of International Politics in the School of Politics and International Relations, Queen Mary University of London, UK.

Yiannis Kitromilides is Visiting Research Fellow at the Centre for International Business and Sustainability, London Metropolitan University, UK.

Shampa Roy-Mukherjee is Principal Lecturer in Economics at the Royal Docks Business School, University of East London, UK.

Dimitris P. Sotiropoulos is Senior Lecturer in Finance in the Department of Accounting and Finance at Open University, UK.

Sabine Spangenberg is Associate Professor of Economics and Finance at the School of Business and Economics, Richmond University, The American International University in London, UK.

Alex O. Tackie is Senior Lecturer in Economics in the School of Economics, Politics and History at Kingston University, UK.

Kees van der Pijl is Professor Emeritus of International Relations at the University of Sussex, UK.

Foreword

The Politics of International Political Economy is a contribution to post-Marxist and post-Keynesian understandings of international politics and economics, suggesting that social inequalities in the world today are the product of an unequal distribution of wealth and power, which pertains to a faulty suffusion of states, societies and markets under the superintending and intervening role of the USA, an empire-state *par excellence*. The volume is designed to assist students at all levels to understand how the post-1944 global economic system has been functioning, whether in periods of growth and prosperity or in periods of severe crisis.

The book is divided into parts. The first, Essays, begins with a reflective contribution by Kees van der Pijl looking at how useful a cross-disciplinary approach to political economy can be. Next, a jargon-free essay on the Bretton Woods system by Alex Tackie sets the historical context for the rest of the essays. Vassilis K. Fouskas and Bülent Gökay focus on the crisis of the 1970s and suggest that the core political economy of the world, that of the USA, has entered a long and protracted period of terminal decline.

Sabine Spangenberg examines the disintegration of the Soviet empire and the political economy of Eastern Europe after the domination of neo-liberal reforms, whereas Dimitris P. Sotiropoulos revisits the important juncture of 1992–93 during which the British pound and the Italian lira collapsed.

Michael F. Keating and Jayantha Jayman shift the frame of the discussion to the East, the former by examining the crisis of 1997–98 in South-East Asia and the latter by looking into the emergence of China as a new global hegemonic power.

Ray Kiely's wide-ranging essay focuses on the 'global South' suggesting that inequalities persist all along the global economic system and that there are limits to convergence between the 'core' and the 'periphery', or between the 'global North' and the 'global South'. Yiannis Kitromilides's essay then draws some parallels between the great recession of 2008 and the financial crisis of 1929, whereas Bülent Gökay offers a 'global fault-lines' perspective for understanding the global financial crisis. Shampa Roy-Mukherjee offers an exceptional reading of the Arab Spring as an affair with political economy origins that can be traced back to the 'Washington Consensus', whereas Constantine Dimoulas and Vassilis. K. Fouskas provide a bracing account on the Greek/eurozone crisis adopting a 'global fault-lines' perspective.

The next part of the book is the A–Z glossary on key concepts in international political economy, written by Vassilis K. Fouskas with the assistance of Zoe Lazaridis. A comprehensive bibliography concludes the book.

Vassilis K. Fouskas
Professor of International Politics and Economics
Director of the Centre for the Study of States, Markets and People (STAMP)
School of Business and Law
University of East London
June 2014

Acknowledgments

I am indebted to Cathy Hartley, Europa Commissioning Editor at Routledge, for her constant support for this project and for being nice to me after having missed the first deadline for the delivery of the manuscript.

I wish to thank all of the contributors to this volume, from whom I have gained a tremendous amount of knowledge and information by editing their excellent contributions. Thanks are also due to my former student, Zoe Lazaridis, for assisting me with the compilation of the A–Z glossary.

A version of the chapter by Dimoulas and Fouskas on the Greek debt crisis has appeared in the *Journal of Balkan and Near Eastern Studies* 14(1), March 2012. We thank the Routledge team managing the journal for facilitating the re-publication process, especially some sensitive quantitative data.

The Politics of International Political Economy: A Survey is dedicated to the new poor and deprived across Europe and to the migrant who gets drowned in trying to cross the Aegean and the Mediterranean Seas. This is a result of deliberate policies of which Europe's civilization should not, and cannot, be proud. This book is a contribution towards reversing these policies.

Abbreviations

ABS	asset-backed securities
AEA	American Economic Association
AFTA	Asian Free Trade Area
AMU	Arab Maghreb Union
ASE	Athens Stock Exchange
ASEAN	Association of Southeast Asian Nations
BIS	Bank for International Settlements
BRICs	Brazil, Russia, India, China
BRICS	Brazil, Russia, India, China, South Africa
BSEC	Black Sea Economic Cooperation
CAP	Common Agricultural Policy
CBR	Central Bank of Russia
CCP	Chinese Communist Party
CDO	collateralized debt obligation
CDS	credit default swaps
CEE	Central and Eastern Europe
CFR	Council on Foreign Relations
CIA	Central Intelligence Agency (USA)
CIS	Commonwealth of Independent States
Comecon	Council for Mutual Economic Assistance
CPI	consumer price index
DWSR	Dollar-Wall Street Regime
EBRD	European Bank for Reconstruction and Development
EC	European Community/European Commission
ECB	European Central Bank
ECOFIN	Economic and Financial Affairs Council (Council of the European Union)
ECSC	European Coal and Steel Community
ECU	European Currency Unit
EEC	European Economic Community
EEZ	exclusive economic zone
EFSF	European Financial Stability Facility
ELSTAT	Hellenic Statistical Agency
EMCF	European Monetary Cooperation Fund
EMS	European Monetary System
EMU	European Monetary Union

EOI	export-oriented industrialization
EPU	European Payments Union
ERM	Exchange Rate Mechanism
ESM	European Stability Mechanism
EU	European Union
EUROSTAT	European Statistics (Directorate-General of the European Commission)
FDI	foreign direct investment
FRB	Federal Reserve Board
FTA	free trade agreement
GAFTA	Great Arab Free Trade Agreement
GATT	General Agreement on Tariffs and Trade
GCC	Gulf Cooperation Council
GDP	gross domestic product
GNI	gross national income
GNP	gross national product
GPE	global political economy
GPN	global production network
GWP	gross world product
HIPC	Heavily Indebted Poor Countries initiative
IBRD	International Bank for Reconstruction and Development
ICA	international commodity agreement
ICBM	intercontinental ballistic missiles
ICSID	International Centre for Settlement of Investment Disputes
ICU	international clearing union
IDA	International Development Association
IFC	International Finance Corporation
IFI	international financial institution
IMF	International Monetary Fund
IPE	international political economy
IR	international relations
ISDA	International Swaps and Derivatives Association
ISI	import-substitution industrialization
IT	information technology
LIBOR	London Interbank Offered Rate
MENA	Middle East and North Africa
MEP	member of the European Parliament
MER	market exchange rate
MFN	most favoured nation
MIGA	Multilateral Investment Guarantee Agency
MNC	multinational corporation
MTFA	medium-term financial assistance
NAFTA	North American Free Trade Association
NATO	North Atlantic Treaty Organization
NCM	New Consensus Macroeconomics

ABBREVIATIONS

ND	New Democracy
NGO	non-governmental organization
NICs	newly industrialized countries
NIEO	New International Economic Order
OCA	Optimum Currency Area
OECD	Organisation for Economic Co-operation and Development
OEEC	Organisation for European Economic Co-operation
OPEC	Organization of the Petroleum Exporting Countries
PASOK	Pan-Hellenic Socialist Movement
PI(I)GS	Portugal, Ireland, (Italy), Greece, Spain
PPP	purchasing power parity
REE	Rare Earth Elements
RIIA	Royal Institute of International Affairs
RPLA	resource-poor, labour-abundant
RRLA	resource-rich, labour-abundant
RRLI	resource-rich, labour-importing
SALT	Strategic Arms Limitation Talks
SAP	structural adjustment programme
SASAC	State-Owned Asset Supervision and Administrative Commission
SDRs	Special Drawing Rights
SEA	Single European Act
SGP	Stability and Growth Pact
SMEs	small and medium-sized enterprises
SOE	state-owned enterprise
STMS	short-term monetary support
TNC	transnational corporation
TRIPS	Agreement on Trade-Related Aspects of Intellectual Property Rights
'Troika'	EU-IMF-ECB policy group formed in 2010 to supervise the debt crisis in the periphery states of the EU
UIP	uncovered interest parity
UK	United Kingdom
UN	United Nations
UNCTAD	United Nations Conference on Trade and Development
US(A)	United States (of America)
USSR	Union of Soviet Socialist Republics
VAT	value-added tax
VSTF	very short-term facility
WBG	World Bank Group
WTO	World Trade Organization
WWI/II	World War I/II

Essays

Global political economy and the separation of academic disciplines

KEES VAN DER PIJL

International, or preferably *global*, political economy (IPE, or GPE), is not just a matter of combining economics and politics, or just restoring the classical approach to the topic. 'The real achievement of IPE,' Robert Cox (1993: 79) writes, 'was not to bring in economics [into political science], but to open up a critical investigation into change in historical structures.' My argument in this chapter is that this is best understood in light of how the mainstream social sciences have been parcelled out into separate disciplines, beginning with the split between economics and sociology. This was a process finalized in the USA, where the academic division of labour in the form we know today acquired its particular profile. 'The departmental structure appeared only in American universities, although since mid-[20th] century it has gradually spread to Europe and elsewhere', writes Abbott (2001: 123). Global political economy, I argue, is the attempt to bring back a comprehensive social science, including history.

Classical social theory, and political economy as one subject within it ('political' referring to the scale of 'household' to which economy refers—that is, the state), in the age of Enlightenment leading up to the French Revolution produced a series of theories, each postulating the operation of an optimization principle. Through it individual freedom was supposedly translated into social harmony. Adam Smith, whose *Wealth of Nations* was published in 1776, argued that the market represents such a principle in the field of political economy. Otherwise Smith was a polymath who also studied other topics; his contemporary Immanuel Kant likewise covered every aspect of social thought. He also was the first to write about the evolution of the universe. That was what the Enlightenment was about: the sky, literally, was the limit.

The French Revolution revealed the dangerous aspects of Enlightenment optimism to the established ruling classes in Europe. The unrestrained investigation of the bases of social power and wealth carried risks that might destabilize the social order. Both sides—that is, the political structure of social power and the organization of social thought—had to be modified in order to prevent shock-like adjustments. As Edmund Burke argued in his famous *Reflections on the French Revolution* of 1790 (Burke 1934: 23), 'a state without the means of some change is without the means of its conservation', and the knowledge on which controlled change is based therefore must be tailored to serve that purpose.

In the Restoration following the defeat of Napoleon, a new period of great scientific progress opened up, marked by Hegel's dialectical understanding of history and Ricardo's theory of the distribution of wealth among different classes. At first haltingly and in Gramsci's phrase, 'molecularly', the forces of democracy were gathering strength again as well, leading to social explosions of 1830 and 1848 which furthered the spread of constitutional government. 1848 was also the year of the publication of the *Communist Manifesto* by Marx and Engels. Here for the first time the global sweep of the capitalist mode of production and the idea that history progresses through class struggles, were articulated in such a striking way that the need for a social science to back up a strategy of flexible adjustment became most urgent. In the process, the different areas of study were beginning to be separated into distinct fields, primarily to meet the challenge of historical materialism.

In this chapter, I address what I see as the key moments of this transition. First, the separation of an axiomatic, deductive economics from an empirical sociology (paradoxically, also covering the field of the economy as its prime concern). Second, a look at how the challenge of Marxism in Germany was met in the context of the *Staatswissenschaften*, in which economics and sociology were still combined. I then look at how in the English-speaking tradition and especially in the USA, philosophy was sidestepped altogether and a focus on epistemology and method adopted instead; thus the disciplinary organization of the social sciences was facilitated. Finally, I give some examples of how different IPE/GPE approaches can be understood as attempts to recapture the original post- or trans-disciplinary social science.

ECONOMICS AND SOCIOLOGY

Liberalism emerged triumphant in the slipstream of Britain's new global power after the defeat of Napoleon. As Wallerstein (2001: 191) writes, 'there followed a thrust to consolidate and justify this hegemony in the domains of culture and ideology'. Nowhere was this more evident than in political economy, in which British thinkers had made their name as the country became the 'workshop of the world', establishing a first-mover advantage unchallenged until the crisis of the early 1870s.

The political economy of Smith and Ricardo is based on the labour theory of value, in which labour time is the common measure to compare the value of good exchange in the market. The labour theory of value goes to the heart of bourgeois thought. It claims that wealth is obtained through work, rather than by privilege or inherited title as in the past. However, in Smith especially there are ambiguities in establishing what in the end constitutes value; he also claims that the 'ultimate' source of value must be traced to the different components of income, such as ground rent or profit. This contradictory understanding made it possible to see value as entitlement. Whether this 'slip' can be traced to the fact that Smith, like his mentor, David Hume, was close to the ruling class of Edinburgh, may be left aside here, but there is no doubt that this contradiction, to quote Marx, 'threw the door to vulgar economics wide open' (Marx and Engels 1956–71: vol. XXIV, 372).

'Vulgar economics' refers to an approach that abandons the investigative quest into economic processes for a justificatory one that legitimizes capitalist class society by leaving certain questions unanswered. John Stuart Mill (1806–73) is the major figure in shifting the ground in this respect. Mill, like many contemporaries, was concerned about working-class agitation against the appalling conditions created by the Industrial Revolution. Casting the factory owner as a benefactor to society who instead of keeping his wealth to himself, makes it available for use as capital in production and 'give work' (hence, the German term for employer, *Arbeitgeber*), Mill cleared the way for an entirely different approach to economics based on a new theory of value, marginalism.

Marginalism built on the ambiguities in Smith and Ricardo concerning the sources of wealth, reformulating political economy along utilitarian lines as a psychology of choice. W. Stanley Jevons (1835–82), a Manchester engineer who took up the chair in political economy at the University of London in 1876, also re-baptized the field 'economics', since 'erroneous and practically mischievous' ideas about political economy were gaining ground and 'becoming popular among the lower orders' (quoted in Meek 1972: 88 n.). Amidst a growing call 'to abandon Ricardo's theory of value because it leads to socialism' (Labriola 1908: 82), Jevons dropped the connection with labour time altogether and identified subjective (marginal) utility as the source of value, taking forward Mill's ideas on this issue. This approach places each claim to income on the same ethical level; a capitalist, a landowner, a worker, all seek a return on the 'factor' they supply, and are equally entitled to it. The labour theory of value, on the other hand, not only advances an explanation for the source of new wealth, but also implies that those who really work have a more fundamental claim.

Also, the labour theory of value seeks to uncover the inner workings of the economy, whereas marginal utility theory leaves in the dark the question *why* some people grow rich whereas others seem to lose out. This is instead interpreted as a quasi-natural phenomenon. Jevons's theory that sunspots are the cause of the business cycle instead aimed at naturalizing the capitalist mode of production, sealing it off from social criticism (Davis 2002: 222–23). Just as you cannot do anything about sunspots, you cannot change the economy either. Alfred Marshall at Cambridge then reworked the classical and the marginalist traditions into a single narrative ('It's all in Marshall'). Thus he 'defended' Ricardo by arguing that the latter's theory of value 'though obscurely expressed ... anticipated more of the modern doctrine of the relations between cost, utility and value than has been recognised by Jevons and other critics' (quoted in Meek 1972: 93). This of course pushed the crucial disagreement on the source of value (labour or 'utility') under the rug.

The growing power of the working class that added urgency to the revision of the labour theory of value had a different impact in the liberal, English-speaking

West and in late-industrializing countries on the European Continent. In Britain, working-class agitation in the 1790s had been met by ferocious repression and factory conditions owed a lot to the concern of employers to keep the workers under a tight discipline (Thompson 1968: 195 and passim). Organized in trade unions for each craft and long represented in politics by the Liberal Party, the conditions of its early emergence imparted a particular weakness to the British working class. The Labour Party inherited this legacy. Its intellectuals, organized in the Fabian Society, 'had, and were proud of having, no economic theory of their own. Instead they accepted "scientific" economics, that is the marginal theory' (Bernal 1969: 1099). In North America, attempts to build working-class strength faltered in the face of repression, geographical dispersion and mobility, and the ideological inclination to embrace possessive individualism (Davis 1980). 'Hegemony', Gramsci writes of the USA, ' ... is born in the factory and requires for its exercise only a minute quantity of professional political and ideological intermediaries' (Gramsci 1971: 285). Here too, marginalism became the established economic theory in the 1880s.

In Europe, the archaic, aristocratic façade of ruling-class power exposed it to popular agitation much more than in the USA; on the continent, there was the additional problem of maintaining social cohesion in the face of the competitive advantages enjoyed by British capitalism. Beginning in France, the need for social protection gave rise to what I call the contender state, and social science conformed to the need as well through the development of sociology. Auguste Comte, the secretary of Saint-Simon, in the 1850s formalized his master's progressive doctrine into a scientistic philosophy of history, Positivism. He saw it as a bulwark against communism which had reared its head in the revolutions of 1848. Indeed, sociology emerged to deal with the rifts in society that the French Revolution and Napoleon, Restoration and 1848 had left behind; Émile Durkheim's sociology intended to achieve the same in the aftermath of the Paris Commune of 1870–71. For Durkheim, the state must weigh in to dampen class antagonism and maintain social solidarity (Durkheim 1964: 379; Zeisel 1975: 122–23).

Durkheim's advocacy of class compromise rested on a comparison between the basis of solidarity in a traditional society and the objective characteristics of industrial society; he rejected the British concept of possessive individualism. From a French perspective, the freely choosing individual is a meaningless abstraction, it is the state that holds society together. Even when marginalism took hold in France, Léon Walras (who taught in Lausanne), constructed it from objective premises such as scarcity and equilibrium; as Watson (2005: 59) writes, 'the Walrasian framework bears none of the [utilitarian] underpinnings of Jevons' *Theory of Political Economy*'.

In the second half of the 19th century, the economic centre of gravity in Europe shifted more and more to Germany. Friedrich List's concept of a late industrialization (which he had developed in US exile in the 1830s) also required a strong, directive state; in the same spirit Heinrich von Treitschke, historiographer of Prussia, in 1864 argued that an ascendant country cannot afford to weaken its executive power and be satisfied with what he called 'a state of the English/Belgian type' (quoted in Kuczynski 1977: 171). Once the country's unification under Prussian leadership had been achieved in 1871, these ideas became part of what Wallerstein (2001: 192) identifies as a 'current of resistance' to liberal universalism, the *Staatswissenschaften*.

A contender state is compelled to entrench against British and, later, Anglo-American liberalism in order to avoid economic colonization and political subordination. Today the People's Republic of China and Iran find themselves in this position, as did the USSR during the Cold War. Such a state must also retain control of its own society as much as possible, just as the social sciences must remain part of a single discursive sphere. German social science ever since its inception in the days of Fichte and Humboldt in French-occupied Berlin had been state-oriented; it was also intimately connected to philosophy, in which German scholarship excelled. The title of PhD (Doctor in Philosophy), still used in English today, has its origin here. If German universities were not as directly geared to the recruitment of state personnel as the *grandes écoles* established by Napoleon, the privileged status of the civil service helped to sustain the attraction of public employment for graduates and enshrine the central role of the state.

THE CHALLENGE OF MARXISM

An additional reason why German (and to a lesser extent, Austrian and Russian) social science clustered around concepts of a strong state providing protection against British capital, was the labour movement. Along with rapid industrialization after 1871, German social democracy grew quickly too. It initially followed the state-socialist doctrine of Ferdinand Lassalle, but the crystallization of capitalist class relations in industry made it more receptive to Marx's version of the labour theory of value, which he historicized, with the help of Hegel's dialectics, into a theory of laying the foundations for socialism.

Ricardo's theory of profit sees its source in that part of the working day that is not needed to produce the equivalent of the reproduction costs of the worker's labour power. The proportions between necessary labour (covered by a wage) and surplus labour (profit) vary with overall social productivity. Marx instead argues that the historical compulsion of capital is to reduce the necessary labour time and increase the mass of what he calls surplus value, which is then distributed among the different capitalists as profit (Marx and Engels 1956–71: vol. XXVI.2, 407–8). In addition to the inference that the capitalist mode of production is not natural, but historical, bound to be superseded by another type of society (Marx only briefly mentions that this will rest on the 'associated mode of production': Marx and Engels 1956–71: vol. XXV, 485–86), he also stresses that this develops through class struggles. Wages, the length of the working day, the introduction and application of machinery, the tendency of the rate of profit to fall as a result of the competitive replacement of living power by machinery and other 'dead labour'—all this is subject to relations of strength between classes. So there is a lot be gained from working-class organization.

This powerful historical political economy exerted growing influence on the German (-speaking) labour movement. After the death of Marx, Friedrich Engels passed on its key tenets to a new generation of labour leaders, often giving it a didactic and schematic twist which tended to divide the historical materialist legacy back to its two constituent elements, (naturalistic) materialism and idealism. Materialism underpinned a positive theory of economic causation, of which Rudolf Hilferding's *Das Finanzkapital* of 1910 (Hilferding 1973), praised by Karl Kautsky as the 'fourth volume' of *Das Kapital*, is an example. Hilferding builds his analysis around the interpenetration of bank and industrial capital typical of the contender state entrenching against British liberal internationalism. This produces a power struggle among states turning into an imperialist contest over markets and colonies.

In 1925 Hilferding specified his historical perspective with the thesis of 'organised capitalism', which he claimed could be transformed into socialism under conditions of parliamentary government once a socialist majority had been achieved (Fülberth 1991: 19–20). Kautsky himself, the expert on agriculture and the grand old man of the Sozialdemokratische Partei Deutschlands (SPD, or Social Democratic Party of Germany) after the death of Engels, shared this perspective but also played down the dangers of imperialism to the working class. In 1914, on the outbreak of World War I, he even claimed that since imperialism results from 'the steady progress of the necessary agrarian inputs for industry' (Kautsky 1914: 911), it was only a matter of time before the imperialists would conclude that it was much more economical to look beyond imperialism ('ultra-imperialism') and exploit the periphery collectively (ibid.: 920). So the workers did not have to be too concerned about imperialism.

Within German social democracy the left critique of social democratic passivity in the face of imperialism came from Polish-born Rosa Luxemburg, whose *Akkumulation des Kapital* appeared in 1913. Like Hilferding, Luxemburg too sought to provide an 'update' of Marx's *Kapital*, arguing that capitalism forms and develops historically in a non-capitalist social milieu (Luxemburg 1966: 289). Imperialism in this light is the final competitive struggle, fought out on a world scale, over the remaining conditions for accumulation. By now, Russian revolutionaries such as Lenin, Bukharin and others had joined the fray. Lenin attacked Kautsky in *Imperialism, the Highest Stage of Capitalism*, stressing that imperialism exposes the weakest links of the rival imperialist blocs to revolutionary breakthroughs (Lenin 1917: 295–96).

In hindsight one would think that if there ever were an international/global political economy, here it was, but all these discussions took place outside the universities. After the Russian Revolution, they became taboo. Already in the 1870s, the rise of the labour movement in German academia had been responded to by embracing the social protection aspect of Bismarck's contender state policy (the other aspect was repression). In 1873 the *Verein für Sozialpolitik* was founded by academics in the *Staatswissenschaften*, the so-called socialists of the lectern (*Kathedersozialisten*), committed to social reform. Economists like Gustav Schmoller, the founder of the so-called Historical School, his student Werner Sombart, and others, largely abandoned theory for an evolutionist understanding of economic forms, successive stages of organizing the economy, from the household to the world economy. Schmoller from 1890 to 1917 was president of the *Verein für Sozialpolitik*, which also counted the political economist and sociologist Max Weber (1864–1920) among its active members.

Weber cast his ideas into the mould of the neo-Kantian, hermeneutic tradition to demarcate it from Marxism (and from his own initial materialism). In the *Protestantische Ethik* of 1904–05 and the posthumously published *Wirtschaft und Gesellschaft* he sought to explain why Germany had entered the contest with the liberal West so late, which remedies might help it to catch up, and how the working class could be integrated into the state. Returning from a trip to the USA in 1904 he became one of the first scholars to recognize that an American Century was in the making, but as Rehmann (1998: 20–28) highlights, the experience also left him deeply ambivalent about that prospect. Certainly the trip to the USA was one of the reasons for his recovery from a severe depression; the other was the editorship of the journal of the *Verein für Sozialpolitik* (Hughes 1958: 301, 294).

As with the French sociologists, the German scholars in the *Staatswissenschaften* were reformists who, unlike the British utilitarians, advocated a flexible, 'investigative' approach to social issues (Therborn 1976: 225). Whereas economics followed the British lead, sociology as a discipline followed that of France. In Germany, the disciplinary divide was not consummated; neither did marginalism catch on. The Historical School kept aloof from theoretical debates, and the attack on the labour theory of value in German-speaking Europe was launched from Austria-Hungary instead—significantly, by state officials. Carl Joseph Menger, a civil servant in the Dual Monarchy, and Eugen von Böhm-Bawerk, its finance minister in the 1890s and author of *Marx and the Close of his System* of 1896, made their names in the process.

DISCIPLINE AND METHOD

The turn from political economy to utilitarian economics in Britain, which no longer questions the inner workings of the economy, can be related to a long process of avoiding all substantive, speculative thought. Both on the British Isles and in North America, the original core of what I call the Lockean heartland, this agnostic, empirical (or in the case of utilitarian economics, deductive-axiomatic) approach followed from an agreement with the Anglican Church in the English Civil War. This agreement held that scholarly endeavour was permitted as long as God and the soul remained exempt. John Locke, the ideologue of the Glorious Revolution of 1688, was strongly committed to this doctrine, and based his theory of knowledge, laid down in his *Essay Concerning Human Understanding* of 1690, on this principle (Locke 1993: 273 and passim).

The priority for epistemology characterizing the English (-Irish) empirical tradition of Locke and Bishop Berkeley, found a powerful echo in David Hume (1711–76), who turned it into the basis for the moral sciences by claiming that people arrive at ideas by association, which they turn into habitual notions. Adam Smith was his protégé and took forward Hume's ideas on free trade.

Like so many other features of life in the North American colonies, intellectual development was a radicalized version of the original Lockean empiricism. This included the Anglican proscription on transgressing into metaphysics, the domain of the Church. In North America, this latter arrangement was applied under the auspices of a far more militant, Puritan clergy for which agnosticism was not enough. Universities in the USA were long under the control of Protestant fundamentalists and as a result systematic philosophy as the common anchorage of science was and remains largely absent from academic life in North America. On the basis of his own detailed investigation of the composition of university administrations, Clyde Barrow concludes that well into the 1890s, the aim of education was to transmit the Protestant ethic and 'moral character through the development of mental discipline' (Barrow 1990: 39, cf. 36–38, Tables 2.3–2.5).

It took until the 20th century for businessmen and bankers to displace clergymen from their seats on university boards, imposing their own limits to what could be legitimately taught. The notorious academic freedom cases that brought home these constraints also worked to force a degree of inward-looking specialization on social scientists, fostering the separation into disciplines. 'In case after case of university pressure brought against social scientists in the 1880s and 1890s, the conservative and moderate professional leaders … [made] clear the limited range of academic freedom … *A degree of professional autonomy was achieved by narrowing its range*' (Ross 1991: 118, emphasis added). The original moralistic, missionary impulse resonated in the Social Gospel movement which aimed to purify society from sin. In the words of Jean Bethke Elsthain (2001: 44), the Social Gospel movement was the attempt 'to define an American civil religion and bring a vision of something akin to the Peaceable Kingdom to fruition on earth, or at least in North America'. Its adherents included the philosophers who in the same period were advocating the further reduction of British empiricism to pragmatism, encapsulated in William James's famous aphorism, 'An idea is true if it works'. With James's *Pragmatism* of 1907, writes Hughes, 'the intellectual horizon suddenly seemed to clear: everything became simple, direct, unequivocal. No longer was it necessary to break one's head over Kantian metaphysics and Teutonic hair-splitting' (Hughes 1958: 112).

With the simultaneous rise of the foundations spun off from the fortunes of the founders of the big corporations of the period—the Carnegie institutions and the Rockefeller Foundation and its offshoots, later the Ford Foundation—the emphasis on 'method' became all-pervasive (Parmar 2012: 7). Through funding strategies and dismissals a macrostructure crystallized in the period from the 1880s to the 1920s, with an academic labour market in which the supply lines are disciplines and jobs are exchanged at national disciplinary meetings (Abbott 2001: 126). With methods declared universally valid, the disciplines only differ in terms of the objects to which the method is applied (Barrow 1990: 140, 160). In the absence of philosophy as the common grounding of social science, a confusingly termed 'inter-disciplinarity' takes its place as a common methodology, unifying both the academic and the practitioners' worlds through common methods. This was also what the large foundations wanted: no 'ivory tower' knowledge, but knowledge in the hands of certified experts which could be mobilized for the exercise of power (Parmar 2012: 63).

Taking the insights pioneered by the British in the previous century into the realm of academic elaboration, US class strategists like Elihu Root and Walter Lippmann elaborated a class discipline for academia closely attuned to the wider needs of the West, incorporating parts of the intellectual heritage of Germany (notably, Weber's) into the academic division of labour uniquely created in the USA. Decentralization and the absence of philosophical anchorage thus gave the US academic system, which after World War II would become the gold standard world-wide, its specific characteristics. 'In England an aristocratic class resisted university innovation and expansion, and in France and Germany centralized state authority controlled growth and made appointments in new subjects adjunct to traditional fields', writes Dorothy Ross:

> In contrast, American capitalists, modernizers, and politicians quickly recognized the economic and social benefits of modern knowledge and supported a rapid expansion of higher education ... The decentralized American colleges, competing for students and prestige, allowed the new disciplines to multiply quickly and establish their independence.
>
> (Ross 1991: 161)

Economics and sociology had separated formally already in the 1880s in the struggles around the newly founded American Economic Association (AEA). The AEA was the first of a line of 'specialized, functionally oriented professional organizations' which together with the universities sought to monopolize 'control over access to specialized knowledge', whilst offering stable careers from which claims to professional authority could be mounted (Ross 1991: 63). Initially, the AEA was the bulwark of progressives exposed to the *Staatswissenschaften* during their studies in Germany; William Graham Sumner, who stayed out of it and attacked it as too radical, became the founder of sociology in the USA, whilst the AEA in due course reverted to neo-classical orthodoxy too.

The final component of the disciplinary division of labour was the belated establishment, in the slipstream of the Versailles peace conference, of the groundwork for a discipline of international relations (IR). A body of more than 100 experts, nicknamed 'The Inquiry', accompanied President Woodrow Wilson to provide him with materials on European nationality issues, borders and related matters; Lippmann was its secretary. Out of informal discussions between The Inquiry and British imperial strategists at Versailles emerged the Council on Foreign Relations (CFR) in the USA and the Royal Institute of International Affairs (RIIA) in Britain. Meanwhile, the 10-year prison sentence for the leader of the American Socialist Party, Eugene Debs, for a speech in which he characterized the conflict as a 'capitalist war' (quoted in Burch 1980: vol. II, 227), served as a warning to those adhering to the theory of imperialism whilst highlighting the challenge a political economy approach poses to both class and academic discipline (Krippendorff 1982: 25–27).

IR was to be part of the new social science landscape of which Lippmann drew the contours in *Public Opinion* of 1922. Here he argues how the social sciences should be re-engineered from historical enquiry to providing expert advice, so that a new type of social scientist would emerge who would 'take his place in front of decision instead of behind' (Lippmann 2010: 246). Lippmann mused about having 'a central agency' channelling university research to Washington, and vice versa, since 'except a few diplomatic and military secrets', all government information should freely percolate back to academia. Mutual exposure and actual circulation of personnel between government and academia would produce a political science 'associated with politics in America'.

To orient foreign policy expertise more narrowly to the US national interest, academic IR in 1930 was placed under the surveillance of a dedicated committee on the Social Science Research Council headed by one of the founders of the CFR, James Shotwell, and stacked with international financiers like Owen Young of General Electric. At the CFR itself, Allen Dulles, another Inquiry veteran and future director of the Central Intelligence Agency (CIA), took over at the same juncture. Even so, it would take until the exodus of intellectuals from Nazi Europe later in the decade before this academic infrastructure became truly operational (see van der Pijl 2014: Ch. 2).

TOWARDS A POST-DISCIPLINARY GLOBAL POLITICAL ECONOMY

'Early students of political economy were polymaths who wrote on economics, politics, civil society, language, morals and philosophy', write Bob Jessop and Ngai-Ling Sum (2001: 90). The reconstitution of what they term a *post-*disciplinary social science has found a major lever in GPE. In this concluding section, let me give a few examples of attempts to integrate particular disciplines into a more or less comprehensive political economy (a more complete overview is in van der Pijl 2009).

First, Institutionalism. The rift between the founders of the AEA around Richard Ely, steeped in the *Staatswissenschaften*, and the critics around Sumner not only caused the split between economics and sociology. After Ely had been removed from his position in the AEA and the association had been brought under the control of mainstream economists, it also left a divide between deductive marginalist economics and an American version of the German Historical School, re-baptized (evolutionary) Institutionalism. In the separation, the Institutionalists also took forward the pragmatist principles of straightforward empirical observation, just as they embraced Social Darwinism and Herbert Spencer's thesis of the 'survival of the fittest'. This was a popular thesis in a frontier society in which the native Amerindians were slowly pushed back by the advancing capitalist society.

The label 'Institutionalism' was applied to this current at the 1918 AEA conference, where its main representative was Norwegian immigrant Thorstein Veblen (1857–1927). It was the umbrella uniting those who wanted to counter the 'abstract theories of market exchange and price equilibration' by investigating the real variety of economic practices and their embeddedness in society. Dismissing the abstractions of neo-classical economics as sterile, they claimed that this was caused, as one of them put it, by the fact that 'the classical schools were without the benefit of modern anthropology, which has revealed so many varieties of communal life and economic mores' (quoted in Brick 2006: 69). Veblen studied anthropology and sociology (actually with Sumner, the original critic of Ely and the most prominent representative of the Social Darwinism of Spencer in the USA). In *The Theory of the Leisure Class* of 1899 Veblen argued that all societies are characterized by a class that is exempt from work and dictates the tastes and many of the habits of society, since in every society people emulate what others do, especially those who lead enviable lives. What people do today become the habits and the encrusted 'institutions' of tomorrow (Veblen 1994: 118).

In the modern capitalist economy, Veblen sees two main habits that have become fossilized into institutions: the institution of *acquisition*, and that of *production*. With the former, he associates a pecuniary interest, imbricated with a sentiment of rivalry; with the latter, an industrial one. Or, using different terms again, we have industry proper, understood in the literal, mechanical sense, and 'business'. Business is the domain of capitalists who manipulate markets and 'sabotage' what might be produced by industry (which he understands in terms of honest workmanship) because of their single-minded concern with profit. Social Darwinism was a powerful force among the first generation of Institutionalists. Thus E.R.A. Seligman borrowed his economic determinism from the Italian vulgar Marxist Achille Loria, but gave it a biological twist by arguing that social change was determined by 'the inexorable law of nature, which is the struggle for existence through natural selection' (quoted in Ross 1991: 188). Both Veblen and another prominent Institutionalist, John R. Commons, became the victims of academic repression and had to move to other universities, and in the case of Commons, also adjust their views. Commons's chair at Syracuse University was closed down under pressure from corporate donors after he gave a speech in which he praised Marx (Barrow 1990: 193).

Karl Polanyi (1886–1964), who was born in Hungary and emigrated to escape the Nazis, is one the most-read Institutionalists today. In his work the connection with anthropology is particularly prominent; indeed, Polanyi is an example of studying the economy from a post-disciplinary angle. Commons identified large organizations as a key institution of the inter-war years; Polanyi saw large-scale planning as such an institution, a habit that spreads in society. In *The Great Transformation* of 1944 Polanyi provided the argument for a mechanism that he called 'The Double Movement', which is the involuntary effect of the attempt to impose the self-regulating market on society, destroying the non-market arrangements in which it has been hitherto embedded, as well as the natural environment on which it rests. Thus, the assumption that 'labour' is a commodity—i.e. that labourers are produced for the market and will therefore appear on the market in quantities required—vitiates the actual process of human reproduction.

Labour, writes Polanyi, is a *fictitious* commodity and if we think otherwise, humanity as a species will be degraded and its life made hell (Polanyi 1957: 73). Therefore, in practice, attempts to extend the self-regulating market to labour relations and supply, will always at some point be accompanied/compensated by *socially protective* measures (no child labour, maternity leave, paid holidays, working hours legislation, compulsory education, etc.). Otherwise a society will destroy its human foundations. The same applies to *land* and to *money*, neither of which are produced for the market either and hence must be protected if nature, or the monetary system, respectively, are not to be destroyed completely.

Of course these fictitious commodities are not just a random selection; they are, one for one, the *factors of production* on which the entire marginalist argument revolves. This does not mean that Polanyi was a radical anti-capitalist, or intent on abolishing the market as a social institution. His point is rather that throughout history, markets have existed (he himself did many detailed studies on the earliest forms of market economy), *but always embedded in society*. This also means that a particular economic system, market economy or better, capitalism (a term that Polanyi avoids), always exists in a variety of social settings. Hence the 'Varieties of Capitalism' school, a widely adopted version of contemporary Institutionalism.

The student protest movements of the late 1960s, against the war in Viet Nam and against racism and imperialism generally, in the universities worked to break the mainstream monopoly except perhaps in economics, which still today remains a bulwark of orthodoxy. Indeed, in the 1980s, in the neo-liberal conjuncture associated with Thatcher and Reagan, a radicalized version of axiomatic utilitarianism was propagated which as 'Rational Choice' is also colonizing adjacent disciplines.

In most fields, however, rigid dividing lines drawn by adherence to positivist-empiricist method were removed as a consequence of student and staff activism. The result was that approaches like Institutionalism could break out of the quarantine imposed on them in the Cold War, but also a host of hitherto marginalized or proscribed strands of thought. At the heart of this was historical materialism, which was a key reason for the disciplinary reorganization of academia at the turn of the 20th century. In the case of international political economy, the theories of imperialism more specifically were declared taboo in the inter-war years.

Now the historical materialist tradition did not survive its exclusion from academia unscathed. Unlike the Nazi attempt to remove Einstein from physics (documented in Poliakov and Wulf 1989: 102–3 and passim), which was too short-lived to produce an 'Einsteinism' reproducing itself in isolation, the century-long exile of Marx engendered sectarianism and formulaic retrogression. That Marxism after Marx largely failed to assimilate his philosophical revolution too, lapsing into a materialist theory of economic causation again, triggered further internal discord whilst reducing its overall plausibility. In the 1960s student revolt, the study of imperialism returned in new versions through the work of the authors of the *Monthly Review* group such as Harry Magdoff (1969) and André Gunder Frank (1971), or writers like Samir Amin (1971) and Pierre Jalée (1973), to name only a few. The critique of transnational corporations by Klaus Busch (1974) or Christian Palloix (1973) was another angle from which the analysis of imperialism was approached.

At the same juncture the writings of Antonio Gramsci were republished as well (Gramsci 1971). Gramsci was one of the generation of Marxist theoreticians of imperialism, but had not contributed a work on the topic. Once he was imprisoned by the fascist regime of Mussolini, Gramsci's primary concern was why the Russian Revolution had failed to be replicated by a successful workers' revolt in Western Europe, a region where according to the standard reading of Marx, the conditions for such a transformation were much more favourable. Hence in his *Prison Notebooks*, Gramsci began to reflect on what could have caused this miscarriage, studies that produced an original, unorthodox take on how the state connects to society and what allows the ruling classes to maintain power largely through consensus, *hegemony*. Gramsci's analysis did not conform to Stalinist orthodoxy (a rigid materialist theory of economic causation) because in a cruel paradox, he was 'protected' from Stalinist discipline by the fascist prison from which he was only released when he was about to die. However, in the 1960s conjuncture his explorations inspired a range of authors to begin to rethink the problematic of imperialism in new terms.

Nikos Poulantzas (1936–79), a Paris-based scholar of Greek origin, combined Gramsci's concepts with the structuralism of Louis Althusser. In a series of works on fascism and dictatorship (Poulantzas 1974), and on the state and classes (Poulantzas 1971), Poulantzas disentangled himself from the Althusserian legacy without entirely breaking with it. In one of his key writings on international political economy, 'Internationalization of Capitalist Relations and the Nation-state' (originally of 1973), he argues that the power of US capitalism turns all states into its relays: 'The states themselves assume responsibility for the interests of the dominant imperialist capital in its extended development actually within the "national" formation' (Poulantzas 2008: 245). This is why 'Europe' (the integrated Europe, today's European Union, or EU) cannot (or could not at the time) become a real rival of the

USA, because it must, in order to compete, *internalize* the power relations and technical organization of production developed by the dominant US capitals operating in Europe. In adjusting its own society to the needs of transnational capital, it *disorganizes* its own internal class and productive structure.

> The capital that transgresses ... national limits does indeed have recourse to the national states, not only to its own state of origin but also to other states. This produces a complex distribution of the role of the states in the international reproduction of capital under the dominance of American capital. This distribution can have as effects off-centrings and displacements in the exercise of these functions *among their supports*, which remain essentially the national states.
> (Poulantzas 2008: 253)

This same problematic, covered by what has been called 'transnational historical materialism' (Overbeek 2000), was also taken up by Canadian scholar and labour diplomat Robert W. Cox (b. 1926). In extending Gramsci's categories to the global political economy, Cox takes up the distinction between the advanced states of the West with their developed civil societies, and latecomer states which have a 'gelatinous' society lacking the complexity of their Western counterparts—a difference on which Gramsci's distinction between 'war of position' (the slow build-up of a hegemonic position) and 'war of manoeuvre/movement' (the surprise seizure of power) is based. A society of the latter type will tend to adjust to the hegemonic structures through which the West exerts its power, by *passive revolution*. This concept, in its application to international and transnational relations, refers to the absorption of certain structural features of the hegemonic West whilst resisting any revolutionary transformation from below.

Gramsci already theorized how the transformations that force societies into passive revolution mode, radiate across borders. In Cox's words:

> The French Revolution was the case Gramsci reflected upon, but we can think of the development of US and Soviet power in the same way. These were all nation-based developments which spilled over national boundaries to become internationally expansive phenomena. Other countries have received the impact of these developments in a more passive way ... This effect [i.e., passive revolution] comes when the impetus to change does not arise out of 'a vast local economic development ... but is instead the reflection of international developments which transmit their ideological currents to the periphery'.
> (Cox 1993: 59, quoting Gramsci)

These few examples highlight contemporary attempts to recover the original unity of the social sciences. The challenges facing humanity today can no longer be addressed by narrowly specialized technocrats, if they ever could.

GPE and the separation of academic disciplines

The need to recover the cohesion of theory, social and natural, which was lost in the second half of the 19th century and enshrined in the US academic division of labour currently sweeping the globe, is mandatory. Global political economy in this light must be viewed not as another discipline, but as a programme for reintegration.

REFERENCES

Abbott, Andrew (2001) *Chaos of Disciplines*, Chicago, IL: University of Chicago Press.
Amin, Samir (1973) *Le développement inégal. Essai sur les formations sociales du capitalisme périphérique*, Paris: Minuit.
Barrow, Clyde W. (1990) *Universities and the Capitalist State. Corporate Liberalism and the Reconstruction of American Higher Education, 1894–1928*, Madison, WI: University of Wisconsin Press.
Bernal, J.D. (1969 [1954]) *Science in History*, 4 vols, Harmondsworth: Penguin.
Brick, Howard (2006) *Transcending Capitalism. Visions of a New Society in Modern American Thought*, Ithaca, NY: Cornell University Press.
Burch, Philip H., Jr (1980) *Elites in American History*, 3 vols, New York: Holmes & Meier.
Burke, Edmund (1934) *Reflections on the Revolution in France* [1790] and *Thoughts on French Affairs* [1791], Vol. IV of the *Works of Edmund Burke*, Oxford: Oxford University Press; London: Humphrey Milford.
Busch, Klaus (1974) *Die multinationalen Konzerne. Zur Analyse der Weltmarktbewegung des Kapitals*, Frankfurt: Suhrkamp.
Collins, Randall (1998) *The Sociology of Philosophies. A Global Theory of Intellectual Change*, Cambridge, MA: Harvard University Press.
Cox, Robert W. (1993 [1983]) 'Gramsci, Hegemony and International Relations: An Essay in Method', in Stephen Gill (ed.) *Gramsci, Historical Materialism, and International Relations*, Cambridge: Cambridge University Press.
Davis, Mike (1980) 'Why the US Working Class is Different', *New Left Review* I (123): 3–16.
——(2002) *Late Victorian Holocausts. El Niño Famines and the Making of the Third World*, London: Verso.
Durkheim, Emile (1964 [1933, 1893]) *The Division of Labor in Society*, 5th edn, trans. G. Simpson, New York: Free Press; London: Collier-Macmillan.
Elsthain, Jean Bethke (2001) 'Why Public Intellectuals?', *The Wilson Quarterly* 45(4): 43–50.
Frank, André Gunder (1971 [1965]) *Capitalism and Underdevelopment in Latin America. Historical Studies of Chile and Brazil*, rev. edn, Harmondsworth: Penguin.
Fülberth, Georg (1991) *Sieben Anstrengungen, den vorläufigen Endsieg des Kapitalismus zu begreifen*, Hamburg: Konkret.
Gramsci, Antonio (1971) *Selections from the Prison Notebooks*, trans. and ed. Q. Hoare and G.N. Smith, New York: International Publishers (written 1929–35).
Hilferding, Rudolf (1973 [1910]) *Das Finanzkapital*, Frankfurt: Europäische Verlagsanstalt.
Hughes, H. Stuart (1958) *Consciousness and Society. The Reorientation of European Social Thought 1890–1930*, New York: Vintage.
Jalée, Pierre (1973) *L'impérialisme en 1970*, Paris: Maspero.
Jessop, Bob and Sum, Ngai-Ling (2001) 'Pre-disciplinary and Post-disciplinary Perspectives', *New Political Economy* 6(1): 89–101.

Kautsky, Karl (1914) 'Der Imperialismus', *Die Neue Zeit*, 1913–14, 2. Band: 908–22.
Krippendorff, Ekkehart (1982 [1975]) *International Relations as a Social Science*, Brighton: Harvester.
Kuczynski, Jürgen (1977) *Gesellschaftswissenschaftliche Schulen*, Vol. 7 of *Studien zu einer Geschichte der Gesellschaftswissenschaften*, Berlin: Akademie-Verlag.
Labriola, Antonio (1908 [1896]) *Essays on the Materialistic Conception of History*, trans. C.H. Kerr, Chicago, IL: Charles H. Kerr & Co.
Lenin, V.I. (1917) *Imperialism, the Highest Stage of Capitalism*, in *Collected Works*, vol. XXII, Moscow: Progress.
Lippmann, Walter (2010 [1922]) *Public Opinion*, n.p.: BNPublishing.com.
Locke, John (1993 [1690]) *An Essay Concerning Human Understanding*, abridged and ed. J.W. Yolton, London: Dent; Vermont: Tuttle.
Luxemburg, Rosa (1966 [1913]) *Die Akkumulation des Kapitals. Ein Beitrag zur Ökonomischen Erklärung des Imperialismus*, Frankfurt: Neue Kritik.
Magdoff, Harry (1969) *The Age of Imperialism. The Economics of U.S. Foreign Policy*, New York: Monthly Review Press.
Marx, Karl and Engels, Friedrich (1956–71) *Marx-Engels Werke*, 35 vols, Berlin: Dietz. Vols. 23–25 contain *Capital*, I–III.
Meek, Ronald (1972 [1956]) 'The Marginal Revolution and its Aftermath', in E.K. Hunt and Jesse G. Schwartz (eds) *A Critique of Economic Theory*, Harmondsworth: Penguin.
Overbeek, Henk (2000) 'Transnational Historical Materialism', in R. Palan (ed.) *Contemporary Theories in Global Political Economy*, London: Routledge.
Palloix, Christian (1973) *Les firmes multinationales et le procès d'internationalisation*, Paris: Maspero.
Parmar, Inderjeet (2012) *Foundations of the American Century. The Ford, Carnegie and Rockefeller Foundations in the Rise of American Power*, New York: Columbia University Press.
Polanyi, Karl (1957 [1944]) *The Great Transformation. The Political and Economic Origins of Our Time*, Boston, MA: Beacon.
Poliakov, Léon and Wulf, Joseph (eds) (1989 [1959]) *Das Dritte Reich und seine Denker*, Wiesbaden: Fourier.
Poulantzas, Nikos (1971) *Pouvoir politique et classes sociales*, 2 vols, Paris: Maspero.
——(1974 [1970]) *Fascisme et dictature*, 2nd edn, Paris: Le Seuil/Maspero.
——(2008 [1973]) 'Internationalization of Capitalist Relations and the Nation-state', in J. Martin (ed.) *The Poulantzas Reader. Marxism, Law, and the State*, London: Verso.
Rehmann, Jan (1998) *Max Weber: Modernisierung als passive Revolution: Kontextstudien zu Politik, Philosophie und Religion im Übergang zum Fordismus*, Berlin: Argument Verlag.
Ross, Dorothy (1991) *The Origins of American Social Science*, Cambridge: Cambridge University Press.
Therborn, Göran (1976) *Science, Class and Society. On the Formation of Sociology and Historical Materialism*, London: Verso.
Thompson, E.P. (1968 [1963]) *The Making of the English Working Class*, Harmondsworth: Penguin.
van der Pijl, Kees (2009) *A Survey of Global Political Economy*, PDF web-textbook, version 2.1. www.sussex.ac.uk/ir/research/gpe/gpesurvey.
——(2014) *The Discipline of Western Supremacy*, vol. III of *Modes of Foreign Relations and Political Economy*, London: Pluto.

Veblen, Thorstein (1994 [1899]) *The Theory of the Leisure Class*, New York: Dover.
Wallerstein, Immanuel (2001 [1991]) *Unthinking Social Science. The Limits of Nineteenth-Century Paradigms*, 2nd edn, Philadelphia, PA: Temple University Press.
Watson, Matthew (2005) *Foundations of International Political Economy*, Basingstoke: Palgrave Macmillan.
Zeisel, Hans (1975 [1933]) 'Zur Geschichte der Soziographie', in M. Jahoda, P.F. Lazarsfeld and H. Zeisel, *Die Arbeitslosen von Marienthal. Ein soziographischer Versuch*, Frankfurt: Suhrkamp.

Revisiting Bretton Woods, 1944–71

ALEX O. TACKIE

INTRODUCTION

The Bretton Woods agreement 'represented an unprecedented experiment in international rule making and institution building—rules and institutions for post-war monetary and financial relations' (Ikenberry 1993: 155). As an example of international economic policy co-ordination the system established was a qualified success. The system's success, however, was neither due to any consistent internal blueprint nor clinical implementation. It was conceived as a response/reaction to the bitter economic experiences of the inter-war period—a period during which nationalistic interests paralyzed the expansion of world trade: bilateral trade, competitive devaluations and currency inconvertibility were the order of the day.[1] At the same time, political elites in Western Europe were being challenged by a growing popular labour movement. The political and economic turmoil of the time helped to promote an intellectual consensus which harnessed the economic insights of the work of John Maynard Keynes.

The Bretton Woods system—the design of which commenced in advance of the end of World War II (WWII)—was supposed to be a blueprint for a new international monetary order, i.e. one that would avoid the negative sum game that evolved during the inter-war years.[2] The preparations for the meeting at Bretton Woods, New Hampshire, began in April 1944. In May of the same year, the US Treasury Secretary Henry Morgenthau invited 44 countries to participate in the Bretton Woods conference of 1 July 1944. Prior to this, 17 countries attended a preliminary meeting in Atlantic City, New Jersey, in June of the same year. The outcome of the Bretton Woods conference was the agreement of a system characterized by four main features: fixed but adjustable exchange rates; current account convertibility; capital controls; and the elimination of restrictions on payments for current account transactions. The 'system' came into operation in 1945, to a large extent, held together by the consensus that full employment and domestic agendas were paramount. Initial concerns about how the dollar shortage of the time might harm the prospects for resurrecting world trade were circumvented by other institutions. A mounting series of crises from the late 1960s into the early 1970s proved fatal to the system and its end was marked by President Nixon rescinding the gold convertibility of the US dollar in 1971.

This chapter considers the nature of the Bretton Woods system: its successes and failures and its legacy as one of the biggest projects in international economic policy co-ordination since WWII. The plan of the chapter is as follows. First, to understand the motivation for Bretton Woods and the International Monetary Fund (IMF) articles of agreement that emerged from the meeting, a bridge to the preceding period is required. Consequently, some brief discussion of the run up to the Bretton Woods period provides relevant economic background and also serves to highlight the power relationships and geopolitics that shaped the agreements and their aftermath. Second, the Bretton Woods conference itself is considered: the rules that were agreed and the institutions that would supervise and promote those rules. Third, the 'Bretton Woods period' is discussed. This is dated here as running from 1945 to 1971, and is considered as two sub-periods: 'The Bretton Woods system (1945–58)' and 'The Bretton Woods system (1959–71)'. The distinction essentially reflects the relative lack of convertibility for current account transactions in the first sub-period and its widespread existence in the second. Though the system required convertibility to achieve its goals, there was some inherent tipping point at which convertibility (of currency into gold) started to rebound on the system. Fourth and finally, a brief consideration of the aftermath of the Bretton Woods period is integrated with some concluding comment and summary.

THE RUN UP TO THE BRETTON WOODS AGREEMENT

In the run up to Bretton Woods, the two plans considered—the US and British plans—were characterized by very different thinking. Other countries—notably France and Canada—presented plans: logistically, however, there was only ever time to consider two plans given the complex issues involved. Moreover, the weight of economic and political might at the time dictated that the final construct would be little influenced by other nations (Mikesell 1994: 3). Whilst the US government was outward looking the British government—like many European governments—had become very inward looking. This difference in outlooks was accounted for by the differing fortunes of the USA and many European countries during WWII and its consequent implications. At the end of WWII, Britain was the world's leading debtor country on account of its debts to WWII creditors and had a deficit on its balance of payments of the order of £1,250 million (Newton 1984: 392). It therefore placed a premium on conserving its reserves (mainly of gold and US dollars) and protecting its fragile economy.[3] WWII ended with the USA relatively unscathed and advocating international multilateralism, i.e. unrestricted international trade along with the currency convertibility required to achieve it. After WWII not only was there a manifest shortage of food, commodities and capital equipment in Europe, but also of US dollars. This shortage of reserves was one of the main reasons why a significant proportion of European trade had come to be based on restrictive practices by the end of WWII. Britain was at the centre of the sterling area which comprised the Commonwealth countries and a handful of non-Commonwealth countries.[4] These countries held sterling reserve assets in London, and used sterling as a medium of exchange in transacting with each other and Britain.[5] Within the sterling area capital controls and trade restrictions were minimal, and during the war the gold and dollar pool was introduced, whereby the members of the sterling area pooled their gold and dollar reserves and restricted their dollar expenditures during times of shortage. The reduction in dollar expenditures was achieved through discriminatory trade practices much to the frustration of the USA. With European countries now more dependent on North America for their supplies of resources, one of the important issues was the source of the dollars required to pay for imports from the USA.

John Maynard Keynes's persuasive explanation of the causes, consequences and policy implications of the very large and prolonged unemployment of the inter-war years was instrumental in providing an intellectual focus to which most could subscribe. Indeed, the pursuit of full employment and high gross domestic product (GDP) were cited as the overriding economic objectives in the run up to 1 July 1944.[6] However, as Cesarano points out, 'the details of the Bretton Woods architecture were driven more by the tactical moves of the two sides than by strategic design; and tactics were dictated by politics' (Cesarano 2006: 164)—the two sides being the Americans and the British as a proxy for the European wartime allies. Whereas under the Gold Standard, the objective had been for the internal economic values to be consistent with achievement of the exchange rate target, i.e. the par value of the currency, priorities had now been reversed so that there was some scope for the exchange rate target to be altered to fit internal values arising from domestic policy. Standard economic models as personified by the Mundell-Fleming model suggest a policy 'trilemma' in which only two of the three policy choices—a fixed exchange rate, the pursuit of internal stabilization through monetary policy, and an unfettered flow of financial capital across borders—can be realized because the chosen two will always be in conflict with the third.[7] Consequently, capital controls were to be used as instruments to help preserve an independent monetary policy for the pursuit of domestic economic stability.

THE BRETTON WOODS CONFERENCE

The Bretton Woods system was conceived as a framework of international monetary co-operation. In an attempt to expand trade against a backdrop of stable currencies, it moved a large part of the world economy towards a system of fixed exchange rates and created the IMF to help bridge temporary imbalances in international payments. To complement the IMF as part of the USA's drive for freer trade and multilateralism, the General Agreement on Tariffs and Trade (GATT) was subsequently created in 1947. GATT was created as a vehicle for the reduction of obstacles to trade and worked on the basis of non-discrimination and reciprocity.[8] The World Bank (formally the International Bank for Reconstruction and Development) was also created to provide long-term assistance for the reconstruction of war-torn member economies.

Its formal existence began in December 1945 when 29 countries became members by signing its articles of agreement. The framing of the Bretton Woods system originally included the USSR but the onset of the Cold War and the consolidation of the Eastern Bloc at the end of WWII led to its withdrawal (Schenk 2011: 28).

In principle, the fixing of exchange rates would create certainty and help avoid the 'beggar-thy-neighbour' practices of the inter-war years, whereby countries devalued their currency to alter the terms of trade in their favour, with subsequent rounds of retaliatory devaluations. The IMF was to create a buffer stock by pooling contributions from member central banks. These contributions would be based on the economic importance of the members and 25% of each contribution would be in gold or US dollars: the remainder would be in the domestic currency. This buffer would then be used to provide short-term loans of currency to assist countries with balance of payments deficits. Some of the most relevant aspects of the articles agreed at Bretton Woods are:

1 Exchange rates were to be fixed but adjustable, i.e. fixed in the medium term but adjustable in the long term.
2 A par value for each country's currency would be expressed in terms of the US dollar, whilst the US dollar would both be expressed in terms of gold and be convertible to gold.
3 Countries on proposal and with the approval of the IMF could make changes to this par value in circumstances of 'fundamental disequilibrium'.
4 The social or political contexts of the proposing member states were not to be a factor in the IMF's deliberations.
5 Each member would be assigned a quota and its subscription would be equal to its quota.
6 The IMF would provide a short-term credit facility to help countries overcome temporary balance of payments imbalances (non-fundamental disequilibrium).
7 Members could exercise the controls they regarded as necessary to regulate international capital movements, but not in a manner that would restrict payments for current transactions.
8 Article XIV, in recognition of the impossibility of moving straight to the new arrangements, made provision for a transitional period[9] during which members were to be released from their obligations as laid out in Article VIII.[10]

In (1) above, 'adjustable in the long term' refers to the changes allowed by the fundamental disequilibrium provision, whilst the par value in (2) would be subject to a band of ±1%. It is this par value system that is known as the 'Bretton Woods system'. 'Fundamental disequilibrium' was left undefined, though there was a proviso that during consultation, the IMF's satisfaction that there was a need to correct a fundamental disequilibrium would be required. (7) refers to the importance of the use of capital controls in a way that would not restrict convertibility of foreign-held currencies if the objective of expanded multilateral trade on the current account was not to be compromised. In a par value system, the central bank uses reserve currencies to intervene in the foreign exchange market, to maintain the par value or peg. Consequently, the presence or otherwise of convertibility is usually dictated by the needs of the central bank. Its absence leads to bilateral trades and these are typically less efficient.[11] (6) above refers to the adjustment mechanism for temporary balance of payments disequilibria. (2) is a reflection of the concerns about the sufficiency of international liquidity: doubts had grown about the use of gold as international money because of its inelastic supply relative to the growth of international trade over time.[12] The price of an ounce of gold was fixed at US$35. The intention was to promote confidence in the dollar and encourage its use as a reserve currency: other things being equal, the US dollar would be as good as gold. It was further hoped that the pound sterling would also serve as a reserve currency. Hence, the unqualified inflow and outflow of gold along with (largely) dollar reserves but also sterling reserves would be directed towards correcting temporary imbalances, and changes in par values of exchange rates by the IMF would be a last resort.[13]

Clearly then, to achieve the objective of easing the strain on gold as a reserve asset, such a system of international finance required the USA and Britain to run deficits on their balance of payments. Though the British position—existing deficits from the war effort and the prospect of accumulating further deficits in resurrecting its economy—was consistent with contributing to international liquidity, it was unclear how things would work in the context of the USA. Keynes in his capacity as the British team's chief negotiator settled for this outcome in the end, though his proposal had been for an international clearing union with the ability to issue an international currency. Keynes was keen to see a system in which the onus was on both debtor and creditor nations to make adjustments. It is commonly held that the return to the Gold Standard following World War I, allied to the banking crises, caused the Great Depression and the sustained deflation experienced at that time. Thereafter, the damage caused by this deflation was etched on the psyche of policy makers and they subsequently sought to avoid deflation at all costs. This reaction was evident in the design of the Bretton Woods system as implemented. Under the Gold Standard the symmetry inherent in the adjustment mechanism was thwarted by creditor nations sterilizing gold inflows and thereby avoiding the increase in prices that would have been a concomitant and disciplining mechanism.[14] Keynes's proposal was the creation of an international currency to enhance international liquidity and a multilateral clearing system to facilitate multilateral trade. He reasoned that in a system where surplus balances were retained (within the system) and recycled to deficit countries, there would be a tendency towards balance. Keynes wanted to achieve this symmetry by setting limits on both deficits *and* surpluses. The key to Keynes's proposal was an international bank (international clearing union—ICU) which would have the ability to create the 'bancor'— Keynes's international currency. The bancor would be converted into national currencies at a predetermined rate and would be used as a unit of account in balance of payments accounting. Each country would have a bancor account at the ICU: deficit countries would have a predetermined overdraft limit with which to service their imbalance, and surplus countries would receive bancor credits. Countries with a large trade deficit would be charged interest on their account, whilst countries with a large trade surplus would also face an interest charge.[15] Further, deficit countries would have to devalue their currency whilst, importantly for Keynes, surplus countries would be obliged to pay interest on the value of their surpluses. In this way, there would be incentives for both deficit and surplus countries to address their imbalances over time.

The rival plan—the White Plan—which largely won out was by comparison conservative. Both plans had similar goals: to promote multilateral trade, fixed exchange rates and facilitate adjustment, whilst minimizing disruptions to internal balance (full employment and buoyant prices). In contrast to Keynes, who wanted to relegate the importance of gold in the international monetary system, White's plan was for a gold exchange standard—eventually personified by (2) above. The treasuries of countries would contribute their currencies and gold and White's International Stabilization Fund would provide the currencies needed by deficit countries. Gold would therefore maintain a role as unit of account. The bancor would not only have been a unit of account but also an international currency.[16] Keynes's plan would clearly have been more in keeping with multilateral clearing. The US negotiating team believed that the US Congress would not approve the decoupling of gold from the international monetary system that the ICU implied, and that it would generally be difficult to bring the US public and politicians into the fold. Whilst Keynes's plan had made provisions for devaluations (for deficit countries) and revaluations (for surplus countries) against the bancor, the final provisions of Article IV reflected the White plan and the undefined notion of fundamental disequilibrium.

In the White plan, quotas and subscriptions paid in (in the form of gold, foreign exchange reserves and the domestic currency) would form the basis of the line of credit countries could draw on to settle their payments imbalances. Keynes's plan only intended for quotas to be used as a reference point in setting 'the ceilings on the countries' debit and credit positions purportedly to satisfy the property of symmetry' (Cesarano 2006: 134). In principle, the 'scarce currency clause' of White's plan could have brought about this symmetry: when the Americans rejected Keynes's clearing union plan, the scarce currency clause was inserted into the IMF articles at the behest of the British. In the event that the IMF ran out of stocks of a creditor country's currency, the clause would allow the widespread use of capital controls and trade discrimination against the country in question. In the event, the scarce currency clause was never used. Given the economic dominance of the USA, it was assumed that other things equal, a dollar shortage might ensue. The British had hoped that as and when this was the case, it would be able to take advantage of the clause. That there was not a dollar shortage in the early years of operation of the Bretton Woods system was largely owing to bilateral loan arrangements, the Marshall Aid Plan and the European Payments Union.

In summary, when set against the objectives, the system agreed was one of political compromise: Keynes sought a symmetrical system partly to protect the interests of the British but also because the active involvement of surplus countries could help stimulate the kind of private capital movements that helped sustain the Gold Standard.[17] Whilst Keynes saw surplus or creditor countries as holding the key to the solution of imbalances, the eventuality was White's plan which subjected surplus members to far less scrutiny.[18]

The economic hegemony enjoyed by the USA after WWII equated to political hegemony. This hegemony led to final arrangements that produced a system in which the USA was handed the privilege of being able to pursue its foreign and domestic policy aims whilst the other countries shouldered the burden of the fixed exchange rate system. With the dollar as the main reserve currency, it was clear that US deficits would be a necessity: within the Bretton Woods scheme of things, it was not clear how they would come about. Both plans lacked a check on inflation and this provoked some concern about global inflation as economies were reconstructed and reserves were run down. Further, the model adopted at New Hampshire gave the USA the power of seigniorage.[19] The USA was able to pay for some of its purchases of foreign assets and imports through this seigniorage, derived from the expansion in US dollars that other countries held as reserves. These benefits which accrued (and continue to accrue) to the USA because of the pivotal role of the dollar as the key reserve currency were bitterly resented by the French, who frequently complained during the 1950s and 1960s.

THE BRETTON WOODS SYSTEM (1945–58)

There is no consensus about whether or not the Bretton Woods agreement lived up to the aspirations of its founding fathers. However, it does seem that during the early years of its implementation, the faith placed in the agreement per se to secure a stable international monetary environment was misplaced. Payments imbalances were all too common, the liquidity that the IMF could supply to assist countries with imbalances was too small and the use of capital controls as a policy instrument was insufficient. Furthermore, although the World Bank was geared towards reconstruction, in practice its resources and hence its capacity were too modest.

Analyses of the life of the Bretton Woods system conventionally divide it into two sub-periods: the period up to 1958 (when full current account convertibility was largely achieved); and the period from 1959 to 1971, when the system effectively broke down. The progress of the world economy in this first period owed far more to other institutions than to the Bretton Woods system. Cesarano summarizes thus:

> The extremely difficult situation at the end of WWII was dealt with outside the institutions created at Bretton Woods, in that post war problems were not the responsibility of the International Monetary Fund and the World Bank. To keep from distorting the essential purpose of those institutions, therefore, other instruments were used. In addition to the Marshall Plan, which helped restore stability and growth in Europe, the European Payments Union paved the way to multilateralism, thus facilitating the return of convertibility.
>
> (Cesarano 2006: 1–2)

The conjunction of economic, social and geopolitical circumstances that existed at the end of WWII fostered the development of the Marshall Plan and the European Payments Union. At the geopolitical level, important parallel developments were the division of the war Allies into two hostile camps: the Western capitalist industrial countries and Eastern socialist countries, the former led by the USA and the latter dominated by the USSR. In addition, the process of decolonization had been set in motion: defeated countries like Japan and Italy lost their colonies and victor countries like Britain, France and the Netherlands started to withdraw from theirs (Pollard 1997: 8–9).

Economically and socially, the health of European nations failed to revive. The ill health of Europe's economies put at risk the liberal multilateral economic system to which the Americans aspired. The threats posed to America's economic and political hegemony arose from the possibility of European economies reverting to some of the types of bilateral agreements that had supported their acquisition of resources during the wartime effort. That Britain and other European countries might resort to these closed off economic arrangements which ran counter to the Bretton Woods project and that social unrest arising from Europe's economic woes might benefit communist parties spurred the Truman Administration to promote the Marshall Plan (Clark 1997: 173).

From 1947–48 onwards, the World Bank was pushed aside to a large extent by the Marshall Aid Plan. Sixteen countries received assistance under a plan that was tailored to their individual needs. It involved aid in the form of shipments of fuel, food and other staples, as well as equipment, thus helping Western Europe to restore and grow its industrial capacity. The oft-quoted outlay by the USA for the period of the Marshall Plan (1948–51) is $13 billion. There are many competing hypotheses about the motives of the USA for taking on this responsibility, but it seems clear that the Marshall Plan has to be regarded as more than just a bargaining chip to induce other countries to participate in an open and multilateral economic system (Clark 1997: 136).

Following WWII, Britain needed to find a way of balancing its internal commitment to full employment and the creation of a welfare state, with its large debt and balance of payments deficits.[20] If Britain was to avoid deflation and unemployment and eventually balance its trade, then this was to be achieved through a global expansion of aggregate demand with the USA as the bulwark. In keeping with Keynesian economic thinking, Britain sought and secured a long-term loan of $3,750 million to finance its dollar gap. The loan was neither as large nor on terms as favourable as it had hoped. This Anglo-American loan agreement was signed in July 1946 and was conditional on Britain reducing its debts and achieving full current account convertibility within one year of signing the agreement. The size and the terms of the loan from the USA reflected the American aversion to the discriminatory trade practices of the sterling area which they saw as an obstacle to their goal of expanding global trade and multilateralism. Accordingly, Britain attempted to lift currency controls on 5 July 1947, precipitating a run on its reserves of foreign currency. From this 'sterling crisis', it became clear that full currency convertibility at this stage was premature and that it would have to be delayed until conditions were more favourable.

In 1949, there was a co-ordinated effort to correct global imbalances by devaluing sterling against the US dollar. In line with this devaluation of sterling, the currencies of the sterling area and Europe devalued too. However, the effects of the devaluation were ineffectual in persuading countries to relinquish exchange controls and hence achieve current account convertibility as required by Bretton Woods. This failure, the preceding events and the geopolitical environment caused the USA to relax its stance on discriminatory trade agreements. It settled for second best to the extent that by aiding the establishment of regional trade areas in Western Europe, it facilitated a limited form of multilateral trading through European economic integration.[21] The Eastern Bloc countries looked towards the USSR and were 'excluded from western trading systems by strategic embargoes' (Schenk 2011: 37), as was the People's Republic of China after its formation in 1949.

The European Payments Union (EPU) was established in 1950 under the auspices of the Organisation for European Economic Co-operation (OEEC), designed to smooth Europe's transition to full convertibility within the Bretton Woods system.[22] The mechanics of the EPU were not dissimilar to Keynes's ICU and the bancor: the mechanism involved using the balances of surplus countries to provide credit for deficit countries. The EPU required participating countries to make their currencies convertible for intra-EPU trade. In 1958, countries were able to assume their Article VIII convertibility obligations and the EPU ceased to exist. The 1950s were a period of growth, during which the EPU effectively served its purpose of helping to alleviate payment problems and pave the way for convertibility.

The Schuman plan of May 1950 led to the establishment of the European Coal and Steel Community (ECSC) in April 1951, whilst the Treaty of Rome in 1957 led to the establishment of the European Economic Community (EEC) in 1958. These institutions, together with the EPU, by improving convertibility locally and therefore helping to expand markets and production locally, eventually helped close the gap between US exports and European exports, and hence to alleviate international payment problems, thereby making a significant contribution to the achievement of convertibility more widely.

THE BRETTON WOODS SYSTEM (1959–71)

During the 1960s, the Bretton Woods system faced further challenges, arising from a conjunction of factors, not least of all (paradoxically) the fact that the USA had gone from being a surplus country to a deficit country on the balance of payments. The 1960s was a period during which US domestic expansion had significantly increased the supply of dollars whilst America's holding of gold reserves decreased. First, President Johnson's Great Society programme and then the Viet Nam War swelled US domestic expenditures. In addition, a number of civil incidents and political scandals took place and these raised question marks about the internal political stability of the country. Second, the resulting dollar inflation caused a credibility gap as the supply of dollars in external hands rose so that the actual ratio of dollars to gold started to outstrip the ratio of $35 per ounce. Third, in anticipation of a dollar devaluation (i.e. an increase in the dollar price of gold), countries started to sell dollars in exchange for gold, thus pushing the system towards a crisis that proved irreversible.

Though official convertibility provided for the conversion of dollars to gold at the gold dollar peg of $35 per ounce of gold, an open market in gold existed outside the USA.[23] Discrepancies between the official price and the market price could therefore be exploited to the advantage of countries with internal problems, unless the gold peg against the US dollar could be varied or the open market price stabilized at the official rate. The London gold pool[24] which existed from 1961 to 1968—proposed by US Treasury Undersecretary Robert Roosa—tried to stabilize the price of gold at $35 per ounce. The central banks of the participating countries (the USA, Britain, West Germany, France, Switzerland, Italy, Belgium, the Netherlands and Luxembourg) pooled their gold reserves—the USA supplied 50% of the gold—and used these to intervene in the market, preventing the price of gold from rising above the peg. Over time, operations became increasingly difficult for the participants due to the continual flood of US dollars during this period. The French under De Gaulle broke ranks, scuppering the pool by selling dollars for gold.

The Belgian-American economist Robert Triffin first pointed out the tension between America's role as the supplier of liquidity to the international monetary system and the long-term survival of that system (Triffin 1961). The mechanics of the system involved central banks guaranteeing to convert their currencies freely into each other's currency at the same time that the US Federal Reserve guaranteed to convert these currencies into dollars at the established par values. Hence, as the volume of world trade increases, central banks increase their demand for dollars to hold as reserves. The Bretton Woods agreement had put a two-tier system into place in order to lessen the reliance on gold. For this two-tier system to work effectively, the US economy (and to a lesser extent, the British economy) had to run deficits on the balance of payments, otherwise international liquidity would dry up as in the problems of the 'early Bretton Woods' period. Excessive balance of payments deficits, however, would lead to a situation in which the ratio of gold held by the US Federal Reserve significantly outstripped $35 per ounce. The resulting inflation might trigger a mass conversion into gold if the true worth of the US dollar were questioned. As dollars leave the system in this manner, international liquidity is reduced. So, the essential tension Triffin was pointing to was that between the supply of the key reserve currency through continued deficits and the potential for these deficits to undermine confidence in the value of the reserve currency. The flip side, of course, was the deflationary pressure that would have been generated had the USA curtailed deficit balances. In Triffin's view, this was avoidable through the creation of an external reserve asset, the supply of which would expand and contract with the pace of growth in world trade.

The introduction by the IMF of Special Drawing Rights (SDRs) in 1969 was an attempt to supplement international reserves and hence ease the pressure on the US dollar. The design of SDRs involved countries receiving a quota according to their economic importance. This quota effectively augments the international reserves of a member country. It facilitates international payments and liquidity through voluntarily exchanges of SDRs for hard currency and vice versa with other countries: if a country purchases SDRs to the extent that it holds more SDRs than its allocated quota, it receives interest payments on the excess; if a country sells SDRs to the extent that it holds fewer SDRs than its allocated quota, it pays interest on the shortfall. The IMF could additionally decree that exchanges take place between countries with balance of payments surpluses and those with deficits. Despite the introduction of SDRs, both the US deficit and purchases of gold continued to grow. It has been suggested that the purchase of gold was (unnecessarily) exacerbated by the conservative outlook of central bankers and their reluctance to drop their old habits and beliefs (Despres *et al.* 1966: 526–27).

The system's par values became too rigid and were not adjusted as often as they perhaps should have been. The system had primarily intended full currency convertibility for current account transactions: the early 1960s onwards saw activity involving capital flows. This was possible partly because of the removal of some restrictions on capital movements and partly because in practical terms, once there was full convertibility for current account transactions it became difficult to make the separation between international investment flows, currency flows for trade purposes and other capital flows. Financial innovations such as the beginnings of the Eurodollar market at the end of the 1950s and the advent of Eurobonds and other financial activity associated with the rise of multinational corporations simply compounded this difficulty. Consequently, adjustments to par values carried the risk of attracting destabilizing speculative flows that central banks would find extremely difficult to deal with. In addition, without a symmetric system such as Keynes had provided for in his plan, there would be a tendency for surplus countries to avoid bearing some of the burden of adjustment. This was indeed part of the experience of the 1960s. As countries like Japan and Germany recovered from the devastation of WWII, their economies were propelled into rapid rates of growth based to a significant extent on the development of export industries. Such countries were reluctant to revalue their currencies because of the effect it would have on their export industries (de Vries 1995b: 129).

The system fell into disarray during the period 1968 to 1971, when the pressure that had been mounting on the US dollar came to a head. Between 1964 and 1967, the British pound had been under continual pressure from speculative flows because it was thought to be overvalued against the US dollar—i.e. Britain had been experiencing persistent balance of payments deficits. The danger for Britain arose from two related factors: first, its reserve currency status meant that if it were devalued, there would most likely be subsequent pressure on the US dollar (given its similar circumstances); and second, if the sterling area decided to flee sterling by converting its sterling balances to dollars, this would wipe out the UK's reserves (Schenk 2010). Once doubts arose about reserve currencies, a run on gold would complete the sequence of events. Despite co-ordinated institutional attempts to save the pound, the wolves could not be kept at bay, and in 1967 the pound was devalued. There followed a speculative run on gold in 1968 and this forced the USA to suspend convertibility of gold.[25] With assistance from the Federal Reserve, the new sterling parity of $2.40 was held. Britain started to show a balance of payments surplus in 1969 and the attention shifted to the Deutsche mark, French franc and the Canadian and US dollars. On 15 August 1971, as part of an economic package—sometimes referred to as the 'Nixon Shock'—to address the increasing size of its budget and growing trade deficits, the USA unilaterally suspended dollar convertibility into gold and imposed, amongst other things, a 10% surcharge on all imports. The Bretton Woods system had effectively come to an end. The short-lived Smithsonian Agreement of 18 December 1971 was the ultimate attempt to preserve the system of fixed exchange rates. Under the agreement, the parities in the system were realigned. However, since the US dollar was still inconvertible and it did not commit itself to defending the new parity, doubts arose the following year. Meanwhile, the 'snake in the tunnel' was born on 24 April 1972, as part of the movement by the EEC towards a single European currency. The Smithsonian Agreement allowed currencies to fluctuate by ±2.25% around their par values against the US dollar. However, this opened up the possibility of two currencies pegged to the US dollar moving against each other by a much larger margin. The 'snake', as it was commonly known, imposed a limit of ±2.25% on the margin of fluctuation between the currencies of any of the EEC member countries. Britain joined on 1 May 1972. However, sterling quickly returned to crisis again: domestic high inflation, prolonged labour disputes and the re-emergence of trade deficits pushed the pound down. Despite co-ordinated efforts to support the pound, Britain withdrew from the snake and announced a temporary float of sterling. In the interim, other countries had opted to float their currencies and more followed.

CONCLUSION

The Bretton Woods system helped to take the tension out of international economic relations. Between 1948 and 1960, the total value of merchandise exports of non-communist countries rose from $53 billion to $112.3 billion, at an average growth rate of more than 6% per year. Growth was even faster in the 1960s, when the average annual rate of export volumes increased to more than 8% (Kenwood and Lougheed 1992: 286). This begs the question of whether the Bretton Woods system was a catalyst in providing the conditions that contributed to this expansion of trade. Though one might initially look to the impact of institutions such as GATT and other conventional economic explanations of trade growth, doubts have been raised about the contribution of both in this context. The doubts about the contribution of GATT arise because its impact has been largely of a cumulative, longer-term nature. The EEC was mainly a consequence of the desire to find a more effective alternative to GATT, as a solution to Europe's complex trade issues (Irwin 1995). The conventional economic explanations in terms of transport advances, communication technologies, income growth and trade models receive little support in empirical work (Rose 1991; Irwin 1995). The early Bretton Woods system was propped up by bilateral arrangements, the Marshall Plan and the European Payments Union. It therefore seems that the Bretton Woods system cannot be credited for the return to convertibility towards the end of the 1950s.[26] The period of convertibility under Bretton Woods was one of low exchange rate variability: I discussed earlier the reluctance to alter the exchange rate peg because of susceptibility to speculative capital flows. Using market exchange rates, Bordo (1993) found statistical evidence to support this low exchange rate variability, whilst Reinhart and Rogoff (2002), using market exchange rates, found support for exchange rate stability in the period post-1960. The system was not credible in the long run and the tensions in the latter part of the 1960s can be attributed squarely to the lack of an effective adjustment mechanism on two levels: first, the refusal of the USA to alter its domestic policy stance or devalue the US dollar meant that world price-level stability was no longer assured; and second, the problems of realigning the peg because of the threat posed to reserves by speculative capital flows. As long as US policy was consistent with a gold price of $35.00 per ounce, world price-level stability would be assured. To the extent that in the 1960s the system worked as it was supposed to, and this period coincided with the rapid growth of trade, the Bretton Woods system may well have played a significant role.[27]

Some have put the demise of the Bretton Woods system down to a fundamental ambivalence of US policy. According to this view, on adoption of the White plan, the USA effectively became the *de facto* world banker: it continued to be able to exercise its monetary sovereignty but also accepted the responsibility of supervising the international monetary system. Its preoccupation with furthering its own aims whilst it was custodian of the system precipitated the end of that system. The other view can be seen through the lens of the Triffin dilemma, which pointed to the dynamic instability of the system. The added problem of restricted capital mobility meant that at the same time as capital did not flow sufficiently freely across borders to ease the pressure on central bank reserves, it flowed sufficiently freely to make speculative capital flows a real threat to the reserves of central banks.

The system when set against its objectives has notable pluses: the prevention of the kind of destructive devaluations experienced in the 1930s and the establishment of a platform for national macroeconomic policy autonomy in the context of a positive sum game.[28] Two important aspects of the Bretton Woods system—the key reserve currency status of the US dollar which effectively turned the system into a dollar exchange standard, and the way in which votes were assigned to the members—have had a lasting legacy in terms of US economic strength, despite the cessation of the system in 1971. The increasing global integration that has taken place in the post-Bretton Woods era and the lack of a conscious design or system of international monetary order has been pointed to as a factor in the great recession of 2007–08. Consequently, some have argued for a Bretton Woods II to help restore stability in international economic affairs.

It is clear from the discussion above that whilst some of the factors that militated against the system were owing to design flaws, others owed more to the system being operated in a flawed way. The lack of onus on surplus countries to make adjustments was quite apparent. In principle, the surplus countries of Western Europe could have redressed the balance by revaluing their currencies, thereby making US imports more expensive and US exports more competitive. This would have moved both their surpluses and the USA's deficits downwards. This did not happen and instead the EEC countries prevailed upon the USA to find internal policy initiatives to solve the problem. This was probably an expression of the desire of Western European countries to see the power of the USA curbed, by dethroning the US dollar as the most important asset (Grubel 1977).

International monetary arrangements will invariably be compromised by the ebb and flow of international political power. The special circumstances that existed in Europe at the end of WWII promoted the USA to the role of the world's banker. The downfall of the system can be accounted for by its flaws, combined with the way in which it was operated. The relatively faster rates of growth in Western Europe and the domestic disturbances in the USA during the 1960s served to undermine the position of the USA. During this period, some European nations—France in particular—questioned the role of the USA as the world's banker. Since a devaluation of the US dollar would have undermined the foundations of the system and there was no inbuilt mechanism to curb 'excessive' US deficits, it was incumbent on the USA to keep its monetary expansion in alignment with the system. When it failed to do so, and the surplus nations were unwilling to contemplate revaluation of their currencies, the system could no longer survive.

NOTES

1 These were symptoms of the failure to agree/achieve an orderly return to the Gold Standard.
2 'Negative sum game' refers to the sum of the losses and gains of the different countries being negative and, hence, world trade contracting overall due to the attempts of countries to improve their trade balance through devaluations and restrictions.
3 The IMF (2010) *Balance of Payments Manual* defines reserve assets as: 'those external assets that are readily available to and controlled by monetary authorities for meeting balance of payments financing needs, for interventions in exchange markets to affect the currency exchange rate, and for other related purposes. Typically they include a country's holding of foreign currency and deposits, securities, gold, IMF special drawing rights (SDRs), reserve position in the IMF, and other readily available claims.'
4 Of these, India and Egypt, in particular, had accumulated large amounts of sterling assets: assets which by far exceeded the foreign exchange reserves available to liquidate them.
5 London acted as a banking centre for these countries and there was full convertibility of balances into dollars.
6 The Bretton Woods conference ran from 1 to 22 July 1944.
7 See for example, Mankiw (2012: ch. 12) for a good undergraduate-level exposition.
8 Reciprocity meant that tariff reductions were applied to all members.
9 The length of the transitional period mooted was three to five years; *ex post*, it turned out to be 10 years.
10 Article VIII detailed 'general obligations' and amongst other things included 'Avoidance of discriminatory current practices', 'Avoidance of restrictions on current payments' and 'Convertibility of foreign-held balances'.
11 In the absence of convertibility, country A may be able to sell a larger dollar volume of goods to country B than it imports. If country A can convert its *net* export earnings into dollars, it can use those dollars to import goods from another country. In the absence of convertibility, country A can restrict its exports to country B and thus avoid holding its net export earnings in country B's currency. Alternatively, it might take additional goods from country B in payment when ordinarily it would prefer to obtain those from another country. Alternatively, country B might restrict imports of goods from country A so that it does not face the problem of how to pay for its *net exports*. Whichever the case, it prevents the multilateral expansion of trade.
12 International liquidity refers to the resources available to a central bank for the settlement of a domestic balance of payments deficit. In the Bretton Woods context these were initially US dollars: SDRs were added at a later stage.
13 Unqualified in the sense that (in contrast to the Gold Standard) no concomitant changes in the monetary base and, hence, in the price level were required.
14 This involved making sales of government bonds in order to neutralize the increase in the money supply which was the counterpart of gold inflows under the Gold Standard.
15 The predetermined overdraft limit would be equivalent to half a country's average trade value over five years.
16 The accumulation of gold 'locked up' effective demand and therefore exerted deflationary pressure.
17 A good undergraduate-level account of the principles and practical working of the Gold Standard can be found in de Grauwe (1996).
18 The term of a loan for a temporary payments imbalance was 18 months to five years. The larger the loan, the more stringent was the attached conditionality. The

conditions and cost of borrowing would therefore fall more heavily on borrowers of large sums.
19 In a fiat money economy, seigniorage represents the difference between the face value of a currency and its marginal printing cost: the conferment of a monopoly in the printing of money can therefore gives rise to a significant command over resources.
20 A debt of £3,000 million and 'a prospective cumulative balance of payments deficit of £1,250 million between 1945 and 1950' (Newton 1984: 392).
21 With currency convertibility within an area, it becomes a question of balances between areas. Hence, the degree of multilateralism *within an area* is increased.
22 The OEEC originally came into existence on 16 April 1948 for the purpose of working on a joint recovery programme for European countries and managing the distribution of aid from the Marshall Plan.
23 From 1933 to 1975, gold could not be legally traded in the USA.
24 So called because of the market's location in London.
25 Between 1962 and 1968, France and, to a lesser extent, Germany were the largest official purchasers of gold.
26 See Eichengreen (1996: 109).
27 Terborgh (2003) has explored empirically the impact of the Bretton Woods system on credibility and exchange rate volatility and hence trade growth.
28 A scenario in which one country's gain is not at the expense of other countries.

REFERENCES

Borchardt, K. and Buchheim, C. (1992) 'The Marshall Plan and Key Economic Sectors: A Microeconomic Perspective', in C.S. Maier and G. Bischof (eds) *The Marshall Plan and Germany*, Oxford: Berg, 410–51.
Bordo, M. (1993) 'The Bretton Woods International Monetary System: A Historical Overview', in M.D. Bordo and B. Eichengreen (eds) *A Retrospective on the Bretton Woods System: Lessons for International Monetary Reform*, Chicago, IL: University of Chicago Press, 3–108.
Cesarano, F. (2006) *International Monetary Theory*, Leiden: Cambridge University Press.
Clark, I. (1997) *Globalization and Fragmentation*, New York: Oxford University Press.
de Grauwe, P. (1996) *International Money*, New York: Oxford University Press.
Despres, E., Kindleberger, C. and Salant, W. (1966) 'The Dollar and World Liquidity: a Minority View'. *The Economist* 218 (5 February): 526–29.
de Vries, M.G. (1995a) 'The Bretton Woods Conference and the Birth of the International Monetary Fund', in O. Kirschner (ed.) *The Bretton Woods-GATT System: Retrospect and Prospect After 50 Years*, New York: M.E Sharpe, 3–18.
——(1995b) 'Bretton Woods 50 Years Later', in O. Kirschner (ed.) *The Bretton Woods-GATT System: Retrospect and Prospect After 50 Years*, New York: M.E Sharpe, 128–42.
de Long, J.B. and Eichengreen, B. (1993) 'The Marshall Plan: History's Most Successful Structural Adjustment Program', in R. Dornbusch, W. Nolling and R. Layard (eds) *Postwar Economic Reconstruction and Lessons for the East Today*, Cambridge, MA: MIT Press, 189–230.
Eichengreen, B. (1993) *Reconstructing Europe's Trade and Payments: The European Payments System*, Manchester: Manchester University Press.
——(1996) 'Institutions and Economic Growth: Europe after World War II', in N. Crafts and G. Toniolo (eds) *Economic Growth in Europe since 1945*, Cambridge: Cambridge University Press, 38–70.

Foley, D.K. (2007) 'The Economic-Historical Roots of U.S. Foreign Policy', New York University series—*Critical Issues in Global Affairs*, 18 November.

Garber, P.M. (1993) 'The Collapse of the Bretton Woods Fixed Exchange Rate System', in M.D. Bordo and B. Eichengreen (eds) *A Retrospective on the Bretton Woods System: Lessons for International Monetary Reform*, Chicago, IL: University of Chicago Press, 461–94.

Gilbert, M. (2000) *The Second World War*, London: Phoenix.

Gimbel, J. (1976) *The Origins of the Marshall Plan*, Stanford, CA: Stanford University Press.

Grubel, H. (1977) *The International Monetary System*, Harmondsworth: Penguin.

Harberler, G. (1953) 'Reflections of the Future of the Bretton Woods System', *American Economic Review* 43(2): 81–95.

Hogan, M.J. (1987) *The Marshall Plan, Britain, and the Reconstruction of Western Europe, 1947–1952*, Cambridge: Cambridge University Press.

Ikenberry, J.G. (1993) 'The Political Origins of Bretton Woods', in M.D. Bordo and B. Eichengreen (eds) *A Retrospective on the Bretton Woods System: Lessons for International Monetary Reform*, Chicago, IL: University of Chicago Press, 155–82.

International Monetary Fund (2010) *Balance of Payments and International Investment Position Manual*.

Irwin, D. (1995) 'The GATT's Contribution to Economic Recovery in Post-War Western Europe', in B. Eichengreen (ed.) *Europe's Postwar Recovery*, Cambridge: Cambridge University Press.

Kahn, R.F. (1950) 'The European Payments Union', *Economica* 17(67): 306–16.

Kenwood, G. and Lougheed, A. (1992) *The Growth of the International Economy, 1820–2000*, London: Routledge.

Krugman, P. (1995) 'Growing World Trade: Causes and Consequences', *Brookings Papers on Economic Activity* 1: 327–62.

Krugman, P. and Obstfeld, M. (2008) *International Economics*, Boston, MA: Pearson.

Mankiw, N.G. (2012) *Macroeconomics*, New York: Worth.

Mikesell, R.F. (1994) 'The Bretton Woods Debates: A Memoir', *Essays in International Finance*, No. 192, Princeton, NJ: International Finance Section.

——(1995) 'Some Issues in the Bretton Woods Debates', in O. Kirschner (ed.) *The Bretton Woods-GATT System: Retrospect and Prospect After 50 Years*, New York: M.E Sharpe, 19–29.

Mikesell, R.F. and Furth, J.H. (1974) 'The Behavior of Foreign Dollar Holdings', in R.F. Mikesell and J.H. Furth (eds) *Foreign Dollar Balances and the International Role of the Dollar*, Cambridge, MA: NBER, 58–84.

Milward, A.S. (1984) *The Reconstruction of Western Europe, 1945–1951*, London: Methuen.

Mundell, R. (1961) 'A Theory of Optimal Currency Areas', *American Economic Review* 51 (September): 657–65.

Newton, C. (1984) 'The Sterling Crisis of 1947 and the British Response to the Marshall Plan', *The Economic History Review*, New Series, 37(3): 391–408.

Obstfeld, M. (1993) 'The Adjustment Mechanism', in M.D. Bordo and B. Eichengreen (eds) *A Retrospective on the Bretton Woods System: Lessons for International Monetary Reform*, Chicago, IL: University of Chicago Press, 201–56.

Pollard, S. (1997) *The International Economy*, London: Routledge.

Reinhart, C. and Rogoff, K. (2002) 'The Modern History of Exchange Rate Arrangements: A Reinterpretation', *NBER Working Paper*, No. 8963.

Rose, A.K. (1991) 'Why Has Trade Grown Faster than Income?', *The Canadian Journal of Economics* 24: 417–27.

Schenk, C.R. (2010) *The Decline of Sterling: Managing the Retreat of an International Currency, 1945–1992*, Cambridge: Cambridge University Press.

——(2011) *International Economic Relations Since 1945*, Abingdon: Routledge.

Solomon, R. (1977) *The International Monetary System, 1945–1976: An Insider's View*, New York: Harper and Row.

Terborgh, A.G. (2003) 'The Post-War Rise of World Trade: Does the Bretton Woods System Deserve Credit?', LSE Working Paper No. 78/03.

Triffin, R. (1961) *Gold and the Dollar Crisis*, Yale, CT: Yale University Press.

The failure of neo-liberal financialization (1971–91)

Vassilis K. Fouskas and Bülent Gökay

We view financialization as a policy process initiated by the decision of the Nixon Administration in August 1971 to opt out of the gold fetter, thus deliberately placing the international political economy (IPE) on a pure dollar standard. However, financialization did not come out of the blue. It is part of the imperial strategic culture of the USA that goes under the name of 'open door' (Williams Appleman 1959/1972; Bacevich 2002; Layne 2006). Open-door imperialism has been the broader strategic matrix of US policy-making elites since the 1890s, indicating a preference for a global capitalist market freed from state interference. When the fundamentals of US capitalism rest on the global expansion of the real economic sector, then open door is geared towards policies that sustain and expand that sector globally (this was, for instance, the Bretton Woods era). However, when it is geared towards financial (or 'fictitious') activities (derivatives trading, insurance, portfolio management, mergers and acquisitions), then open door is concerned with opening up the financial and banking sectors of other countries. This is the era that has begun with the end of the Bretton Woods system.

Financialization would have been impossible without state participation in facilitating it. The aim of this state-driven process has been the dismantling of the Keynesian pillars of the post-war economy (welfare state, high wages, deficit spending, state ownership of public utilities), forging supply-side economics and structural changes that meet the needs of financial capital and, above all, the financialized transnational corporations (TNCs). If financialization applies primarily to the external environment of the state, then what we have described above as privatizations, liberalization of the banking and financial sector, welfare state retrenchment, etc., can be termed as *neo-liberalism* and applies primarily to the internal environment of the state. Both processes feed each other and, importantly, are superintended by the US state. *Neo-liberal financialization* meets open-door requirements in that it constitutes the policy response of American capitalism for expansion and new forms of profit making in the wake of the *stagflation* (stagnation accompanied by high inflation) of the 1970s and the fall in profitability in the real economic sector of the Western core. This chapter argues that these policies and processes failed to turn the global political economy around towards sustainable development, growth and prosperity and that the crisis of the 1970s still lingers on unresolved over the policy-making circles of Washington, London and Berlin. Neo-liberal financialization is defensive in form and substance and is therefore unable to provide an alternative to the long-term historical, structural and protracted decline of the Anglo-American imperium that began in the 1970s. Herein lies our key disagreement with Leo Panitch, Ray Kiely and other scholars (Panitch 2012; Kiely 2010), who argue that the 'Volcker Revolution' and Clinton's 'globalization' got the US-led global capitalist system on the move again.

First we concentrate on the strategies adopted by Anglo-American political and business elites to deal with stagflation. We pay particular attention to the recycling of petro-dollars and the contribution of the US defence industry to generate global surpluses which return to the USA itself. We then explain why neo-liberal financialization failed to restore profitability and growth in the Anglo-American economies, creating instead a vulnerable global economic environment based on the shaky grounds of finance.

BUSINESS STRATEGIES AND THE US EXECUTIVE

Stagflation was a typical manifestation of an *over-accumulation* crisis inherent in industrial capitalism: great masses of capital could not be profitably invested, as capital owners had no confidence that their investment would generate new, high rates of profit. Thus, the mass of industrial workers created during the years of rapid development, were now becoming increasingly redundant and obsolete as direct producers/agents of capital valorization. The tendency of a protracted class situation of over-accumulation and stagnation is to concentrate poverty on one pole, and wealth on the other. Both poles are *under-consumed/under-utilized*—which is what distinguishes over-accumulation and stagnation from a virtuous period of capitalist development led by the industrial sector, whether in state or private hands, or both. Over-accumulation and stagnation in industry led business classes to diversify their class strategies *well before the Nixon Administration broke away from the gold fetter.* For our purposes here, two of these, organically interlinked, strategies employed by the business interests are important. Both, it should be noted, combined with the US Federal Reserve and the Nixon Administration, initiating the new phase of globalization/financialization and the dismantling of the Keynesian/Fordist/welfarist nexus.

The first was capital's 'flight' to the realm of finance via its transformation into a 'new multinational/transnational corporation', involving cross-cutting equity ownership, joint ventures, cross-licensing, diversified portfolio investment, etc. (Dicken 2011). Capital assumed new flexible dimensions, cutting on cumbersome bureaucracies by taking advantage of technological advances. Galbraith's 'technostructure' could no longer hold (Galbraith 1967). Secondary sourcing and the development of subsidiaries knitted together capital from different nations, the aim being to withstand competitive pressures, compensate for inflationary constraints, and find favourable tax regimes and cheap—and ideally, skilled—labour. As Ernest Mandel described in 1969, productive capital was transforming itself into financial capital; in other words capitalists were gradually trying to become *rentiers* in pursuit of hot money (Mandel 1969). Rentiers are basically money makers who acquire their assets/income by way of extracting royalties from *future* production. As money and dollars could move around the globe unfettered—see, for instance, the so-called abolition of 'capital controls' by the USA in 1974—capitalists could re-invent all sorts of ways to extract profit from future production of values, without guarantees that the assets acquired from speculative activity would be, all or in part, re-invested for the creation of new values in material production. This happens because certain capitalists want to invest their money-capital in ways that bring them the highest yields with the minimum possible risk. This is how 'stock' and 'security' markets in the Anglo-American world began developing anew, whose key function was buying and selling products representing claims on future economic activity. Thus, the creation of bubbles and 'boom and bust' cycles was unavoidable. Wall Street and the City of London began assuming a major global position as leading financial and banking centres, with investment banks, asset management and consulting companies, and a huge shadow banking sector, such as hedge funds, playing a key role. Bonds, shares and, later, derivatives, mortgage-backed securities, credit default swaps and so on, were all forms of rentier activities with no guarantees of re-investment of profits in real value-creation.[1] Yet, these capitalist strategies that emerged in the 1960s in the wake of the first signs of stagflation were obstructed by the fixed exchange rates regime of Bretton Woods. This means that new profiteering outlets for capital in the realm of finance and a renewed *financialization* via *dollarization* could only come about in a post-Bretton Woods era. It should also be noted that this type of business activity is something that distinguishes the present-day Anglo-American capitalism from German, French and Japanese capitalisms. From this perspective, the thesis developed by Poulantzas—following Hilferding and Lenin—according to which financial capital is 'the mode of amalgamation of industrial capital and money capital in the reproduction of social capital' (Poulantzas 1974: 114) as a whole, may be true in a European continental or Japanese context, but it fails to grasp the real development of Anglo-American capitalism. For example, whereas in Germany a bank will become an active and even leading participant in any new business to which it lends money, so as to diminish risks on future extraction of profits, in Britain a bank will lend money to a new business on the grounds of what assets are possessed by the capitalist who wants to borrow. In this context, German capitalism is more cautious and risk-averse; Anglo-American capitalism is more adventurous and risk-friendly. This is crucial and it should not be confused with the pressure exercised bilaterally on European continental capitalisms by the USA in order to adopt this new form of open door applied to the financial and banking sectors.

The second related strategy pursued by Anglo-American business interests was to engage directly with the state machine in order to adopt a new type of intervention, effecting anti-Keynesian, supply-side policies. The main target

The failure of neo-liberal financialization

was presumably inflation. Since the late 1960s, Paul Volcker had been a key player within the US executive advocating this strategy at least as persistently as pushing for the abandonment of the gold fetter.

With the rates of profitability in tatters, the economic elite began to put pressure on the Keynesian executives to abandon protections for workers. These policies in the West began making headway first in the USA and the UK. They involved the purest forms of class exploitation and subordination of labour to capital: the retrenchment of the welfare state, the lowering of wages accompanied by mass lay-offs, waves of privatization of state enterprises and public utilities, and the introduction of flexible labour schemes. All these policies disregarded the need for sustained aggregate demand. Time and again, and contrary to a neo-Smithian and neo-Weberian tradition which see the state as a bureaucratic machine that stands alone, separate from economic and social relations, there is clear evidence that the state is, first and foremost, a representative of the socioeconomic class (or fraction of a class) that dominates the relations of production and class exploitation. The Anglo-American open-door policy and dollar-sterling class interests set the tone for the actions which other, subaltern states had to follow.

In this sense, the post-World War II capitalist state in Europe and Asia had been an active participant, even a protagonist, in the shaping and reproduction of the global economic system, structured along the line of contradictions and antagonisms between and among various capitals and class interests in the global chain of interests rattling under the supremacy of the USA.[2] The US empire-state had dominated the chain of its vassal capitalisms, without always being able to direct and control the class antagonisms manifested across the domestic environments of them in the way it wanted. The inherent contradictions of the global economic system manifest themselves in the disintegrative logics of open door, leading to its historical demise.

Both strategies had to rebuild a functional class regime of *co-operative interpenetration* in order to alter the terrain of class antagonisms, by replacing the 'bygone era' of the fixed exchange rates/Keynesian regime with that of financialization and neo-liberalism. In this context, US business and political interests, working closely with other Organisation for Economic Co-operation and Development (OECD) elites, were aiming to open up the jurisdictions of the financial and banking regulations of European and South-East Asian capitalisms. The aim was to transfer streams of real and fictitious value in order to finance the decline of the USA as it was (and is) reflected in its federal budget and current account deficits. North Atlantic Treaty Organization (NATO) and US power in the European and Pacific theatres would oversee and guarantee this flow of income from the 'periphery' to 'metropolises'. From this perspective, the USA is an imperial state in the very classical sense of the word, in that it appropriates international value while this process is accompanied by its guarantor: military power. All in all, financialization (globalization) and neo-liberalism had to merge, in the final instance, for a twin purpose: to restore the (average) rate of profit by defeating the advances of labour power achieved under the previous accumulation regime, and to undo the constraint imposed on the USA-UK by the global competition of Germany and Japan. Let us see how the US empire-state attempted to achieve that.

RECYCLING 'PETRO-DOLLARS' AND 'WEAPON-DOLLARS'

There was an inherent contradiction in the Bretton Woods system. On the one hand, there was the privileged position of the dollar as the main global transaction currency and, on the other, the difficulty the USA had to devalue its dollar in order to offset balance of payments difficulties and deal with its debt problem. It was contemplated that, had the USA done that, it would have resulted in a parallel devaluation of all other major currencies (the mark, the yen, the British pound, etc.) in order to offset the US advantage. However, increasing competition from the other capitalist centres (Western Europe and Japan), the escalation of the Viet Nam War in the late 1960s, the massive outflow of gold and the Great Society programme pushed US policy makers to print more dollars, inflating the global economy, yet without solving an increasing balance of payments deficit and its connection with the US debt. The USA also began accumulating large amounts of foreign dollars coming to the USA from the gold buying of France and other countries that followed the French lead. Under these conditions, the gold-dollar equivalence could not hold. By the late 1960s the dollar was completely out of tune with all other major international currencies, a tendency that was articulated in asymmetrical fashion with the rates of inflation across the world creating unsustainable disequilibria in exchange rates regimes. However, this did not cause US policy makers to lose sleep. When, on 15 August 1971, President Nixon cut the Gordian Knot by 'closing the gold window', as Joanne Gowa (1983) put it, he knew that this move was representing a massive increase of economic freedom and action for the USA, since the entire IPE now would have to turn into a pure *dollar standard*. The dollar was becoming the sole standard against which other currencies could be measured. Now, under floating conditions, the US Treasury could devalue the dollar at will, thus reducing foreign-debt obligations and boosting exports. As the USA was the sole power that could print dollars, it could be argued that the move represented a fully fledged transition from *commodity* money to *fiat* money, a situation unique in the monetary history of the last 200 years. *Fiat* money is a different name for *seigniorage*, which means that the dollar seigniorage can bring royalties to the USA and its business classes by spending or investing money abroad (e.g. portfolio investment) without the need to earn or produce anything abroad, or without the need to bother very much about changes in the dollar exchange rate. The same goes for setting up a military base abroad: the USA is not constrained by any foreign exchange constraint.

Strictly speaking, the USA was not interested in just shifting the IPE from pegged to floating exchange rates: in essence, the USA was seeking to restore its economic and political leadership in the capitalist world, using multilateral political means and acting under the international political umbrella of *détente*, a foreign policy seeking co-operation and mutual nuclear disarmament with the USSR (see, for instance, the SALT initiatives).[3] Thus, in December 1971, at the Smithsonian Institution of Washington, all major industrialist countries agreed to a significant devaluation of the dollar against all major currencies. This was deeply resented by the Japanese and the Europeans alike, but the response by John Connally was sarcastic: 'the dollar is our currency but it's your problem' (Volcker and Gyohten 1992: 81).

From then on, the road had opened to financialization, as speculators, like post-1971 tourists, could move their money and assets around the world, without major restrictions, capitalizing on favourable exchange rate regimes and playing on the strong/weak currencies ratios and interest rates regimes. Nixon ensured, despite serious objections from other countries of the capitalist core, that financial relations would progressively be taken out of state control, centred instead on private financial operators and asset managers. Yet, from that point on, the USA had to find a way to convince the world to continue to accept every devalued dollar in exchange for all sorts of services and goods the USA needed to get from Asian, European and other producers. A partial solution to this was found in US oil policy, although this should not be seen separately from weapons procurement and the centrality of the Arab–Israeli conflict, which Jonathan Nitzan and Shimshon Bichler called the 'weapon-dollar/petro-dollar coalition'. Especially after the Six-Day Middle East War in 1967, the USA began simultaneously a massive internationalization of the arms industry and a conspicuous politicization of the oil sector (Nitzan and Bichler 2002). Let us take the thread of the story from the beginning.

From 1969 to 1974, Paul Volcker, a former financial economist for Chase Manhattan, had served as Under-secretary of the Treasury for international monetary affairs. He had been instrumental in pushing for the decisions leading to the US suspension of gold convertibility in 1971, which ended the Bretton Woods system. Volcker, a Democrat, was nominated by the Carter Administration in August 1979 as head of the US Federal Reserve ('Fed'), a position he kept under Ronald Reagan and until August 1987. When he became chairman of the Fed, inflation was running at 9% and in 1980 it hit 11%. Since monetarist logic has a natural aversion to inflation and dictates that inflation ruins savings and devalues bond holdings, Volcker's response was to limit the money supply and lead a spectacular rise in the basic interest rate of the Fed: from 8% in 1978, to 19% in 1981 (Panitch 2012). By 1983, the inflation rate had decreased to less than 5%, while bondholders and Treasury bill holders, chief among whom were the Japanese and the Saudis, benefited greatly. However, the ultimate beneficiary was the US Fed system, as it could divert foreign Treasury liquidity to the financing of the Cold War. Moreover, high interest rates sent Latin American debt sky high, with growth plummeting: the debt crisis hit Argentina in 1981, Brazil in 1983, and Chile and

Mexico in 1982. Overall, Latin American debt soared to US$315 billion in 1983 from $75 billion in 1975. This 'debt dollarization' of Latin American countries resulted in enormous returns of capital for the US Treasury, dealing a devastating blow to the assets and industrial potential of those countries.[4]

The real response of the US empire-state to stagflation was financial statecraft along the new forms of embeddedness of a petro-dollar/weapon dollar regime topped by Volcker's interest rates hike. However, as we shall see, this financial statecraft also failed to reverse the historical and structural decline of Anglo-American world centrality. This is a major oversight in the work of Leo Panitch, Leonard Seabrook, Ray Kiely and others (Panitch 2012; Kiely 2010; Seabrook 2001).

Now let us turn back to the role of international energy markets in sustaining the USA's unique role as supplier of the world's reserve currency. As we have maintained elsewhere (Fouskas and Gökay 2005), the Nixon Administration realized that if oil trade and reserves were denominated in dollars, then oil-producing states would find it impossible to spend those dollars on domestic projects alone, due to the large amounts of money generated by oil's international transactions. One possible outlet would be to invest these oil-produced dollars—hence their nickname 'petro-dollars'—in US shares and bonds. This, in turn, could finance the US twin deficits, including US military undertakings, with the USA alone holding the privilege, as we noticed earlier, to print dollars by fiat.[5] The advantageous position gained by the USA was more than obvious. Given the dependency of both Europe and Japan on Gulf oil, any disturbance either in the flow of oil from the Gulf to their markets or in the price of oil would cause havoc to them, while leaving the USA virtually unaffected. In fact, when the Organization of the Petroleum Exporting Countries (OPEC) increased the oil price fourfold in the wake of Yom Kippur War in October 1973, Western European states and Japan were the countries that felt the heat the most. The increase in the price of oil was not the result of the anger of the Saudi oilmen exhibiting solidarity to Arab brothers and sisters due to the Yom Kippur War; it was the result of Washington's careful financial statecraft in the Gulf states, at least two years before the eruption of the Arab–Israeli war in October 1973. As Peter Gowan argued, petro-dollar recycling and a crippling blow to Japanese and European economies were the principal political objectives of the Nixon Administration's drive for an OPEC oil price rise (Gowan 1999: 20–21). US hegemony via petro-dollarization in the Gulf was formalized in June 1974, when US Secretary of State Henry Kissinger established the US-Saudi Arabian Joint Commission on Economic Cooperation, with the specific purpose of stabilizing oil supplies and prices. The Japanese and the Europeans had no option but to bandwagon, albeit grudgingly. As far as Europe was concerned, its plans, under France's lead, to follow up the completion of a customs union in the late 1960s with a monetary union, were severely punished. The so-called Werner Report—named after the prime minister of Luxembourg, Pierre Werner—which described 'a process by which monetary union could be achieved by 1980' (Eichengreen

2008: 151) was shelved. Europe suffered a massive loss of competitiveness due to the dollar fall.

The *de facto* breakdown of the Bretton Woods regime in 1971 was formalized in 1976 during a conference meeting of key International Monetary Fund (IMF) members in Kingston, Jamaica. The conference increased the IMF quotas, especially those of OPEC countries, legalized floating exchange rates, reduced the role of gold, and left the states free to determine to which currency they wished to peg their currency—an essentially pretentious stipulation, as most countries would peg their currencies to the dollar *anyway*, not least because the USA was the dominant power, both politically and militarily. The IMF and the World Bank, both under the paramountcy of the US Treasury, had also changed tack:

> Both [the IMF and the World Bank] began to engage in new forms of lending. The IMF moved from short-term to medium-term lending, and the nature of conditionality changed: instead of insisting primarily on changes in macroeconomic policies aimed at rather rapid external adjustment, it began to insist on changes in microeconomic policies aimed at extensive domestic reforms ... The World Bank moved from project lending with disbursements tied to actual spending on the corresponding project, to various forms of structural adjustment lending, with an urgent emphasis on rapid disbursement.
>
> (Kennen 1994: 93)

This is a rather polite way to say that the two Bretton Woods institutions were changing under the leadership of the USA in order to meet the new requirements of the post-1971 US-led IPE. These changes included, among others, the liberalization of the internal accumulation regimes of the subaltern states by way of emphasizing supply-side economics, following the lead of the US empire-state. Conditionality now meant enforcement upon the world of neo-liberal restructuring programmes and labour discipline, something which also directly undermined the so-called policies of 'import substitution industrialization', a policy generally pursued by Latin American and other periphery states—such as petro-states under the influence of Nasserite Arab nationalism. That is how the beginnings of 'globalization' met the beginnings of 'neo-liberalism' in an organic intra-suffusion. However, there is more to the affair than meets the eye.

The *politicization* of the oil business went hand in glove with the *commercialization* and *globalization* of the arms industry. As underscored previously, they both had as their backbone the dollar standard. In the 1950s, some 95% of US armament exports had been provided as foreign aid, whereas by 1980 the figure had fallen to 45% and by 2000 to one-quarter. From the early 1970s onwards, US defence production shifted to a high degree of privatization and internationalization, followed by an unprecedented degree of mergers, acquisitions and consolidations according to the pattern of 'new multinational corporations'. The so-called 'privatization of defence industry' should be seen in the context of a US empire-state whose centrality in the arms industry and procurement does not depend on who has legal ownership of companies, but on the *political direction and control* the empire-state can exercise through security institutions and political agencies, thus determining policy outcomes. From the early 1970s onwards, the Middle East became the world's chief importer of weaponry, overtaking South-East Asia. Tensions in the Middle East created the necessary requisite for a type of dollar recycling based on weapons sales. Since the 1940s, Nitzan and Bichler argue convincingly, the Middle East's role in world accumulation was intimately linked to oil exports, but from the 1960s onwards, this significance was further augmented by a newer flow of arms imports. These two flows provided a powerful response for the USA to its profitability crisis, inasmuch as the combination of these two flows was associated with the generation of substantial profits for the US defence industry, Anglo-American oil companies and the Treasury Department. Furthermore, it should not be forgotten that the two flows were *dollarized*. Thus, for example, in 1974 Saudi Arabia's arms imports amounted to $2.6 billion, whereas between 1985 and 1992 it spent $25.4 billion. Throughout the 1970s and 1980s the USA increased its arms sales to Middle Eastern states, particularly during the Iraq–Iran War of 1980–88. In 1988, 'the Administration suggested increasing US arms exports by $3.3 billion, to a level exceeding $15 billion—with proposed shipments worth $3.6 billion to Israel, $2.7 billion to Egypt, $950 million to Saudi Arabia, and $1.3 billion to other Middle Eastern countries' (Nitzan and Bichler 2002: 261). Intensified conflict and rising tensions in the Gulf region and, later, in Central Asia and North Africa, which included the Pakistani/Indian orbit, meant greater involvement of the USA in the region, greater militarization of the region and the USA, and greater consolidation of the alliance between US military and energy interests. The USA and Israel as 'garrison-prison states'—a concept put forward by Harold Lasswell in 1939–44 and largely ignored by Marxism and critical theory—were in full swing (Lasswell 1997).

Perhaps the best example of the way in which US military and energy interests became locked into US domestic politics and grand strategy, is the notorious 'state-of-the-art' US military base of Camp Bondsteel in Kosovo (Fouskas 2003). It was built between July and October 1999 in the wake of Milosevic's capitulation and was financed by Kellogg Brown & Root under a $33.6 million contract. It also needs some $180 million annually to operate. Kellogg Brown & Root was at the time one of the largest oil services corporations, whose managing director was Dick Cheney, later vice-president of the USA under President George Bush Jr. Meanwhile, the same company—as well as a number of other US-led companies—was interested in getting involved in the trans-Balkan pipeline project from the Bulgarian port of Bourgas to Durres, Albania's Adriatic port. In this context, and taking into account that US strategy in the Balkans and Central Asia was and is to control the complex network of (new and old) oil and gas pipelines so as to eliminate Russian influence, the merger of US politics and its energy interests and military undertakings is obvious.[6] In the event, this weapon-dollar/petro-dollar alliance, coupled with royalties drawn from dollar seigniorage, brought the USSR to its knees in the 1980s, when the Reagan Administration was able to finance its 'star wars' project with the recycling of petro/weapon-dollars, while the USSR had no such arrows in its quiver.

Did any of these policies reverse the long-term relative historical decline of the USA? Did the 'Volcker shock' restore the industrial dynamism of the USA and its global creditor status? Did it produce or initiate a period of monetary and financial stability? In other words, did US financial statecraft at both domestic and international levels rebuild US global supremacy? The answer to all those questions is plainly no.

After the collapse of the dollar's powerful role in international finance, the USA entered into a long period of economic instability, including a recession in 1971, an even deeper and longer recession from 1973 to 1975, a period of hyperinflation from 1979 to 1980, followed by a severe recession in 1981–82, a real estate bubble and stock market panic in 1987, and finally another deep recession in 1992–93. Altogether, nine of the 22 years from 1971 to 1993 could be characterized as 'economically troubled', with the years in between reflecting uneasy transitions from one crisis to another. The only constant event that marked this period was an unsteady attempt by the USA to restore the role of the dollar and its own economic power by linking the dollar to two commodities: petroleum and weapons. The reasons behind the functionality of this petro-dollar/weapon-dollar regime were twofold. The first was *economic*, in that the Bretton Woods system never found a way successfully to recycle the huge profits and widespread speculation it generated (Varoufakis 2013); the second was *political*, in that the regime shifted the focus of global politics to weapons procurement and build-up, as well as to the Middle East and other areas of petroleum production and conflict. Understanding how that system developed with those contradictions offers important insights into the present crisis, underpinning the thesis developed in our previous work, namely that the wars conducted by the USA since the fall of the USSR have been wars of an economically weak power.

THE PROTRACTED DECLINE OF THE ANGLO-AMERICAN SOCIOECONOMIC SYSTEM

The efforts to recreate the dollar's dominant position in global finance began almost immediately after 15 August 1971, based on the emerging role that oil was already playing in the early 1970s as a strategic commodity for industrial production. This made oil a logical choice because, unlike gold, it had a central role in modern economies that could further underpin its value. This advantage was put on dramatic display during the oil embargo that followed the 1973 Arab–Israeli War, when a denial of significant amounts of oil drove the advanced economies of the Bretton Woods system into panic. Linking the dollar to oil, however, was a work of diplomatic art conducted between the USA and Saudi Arabia, which was then the leader of the oil embargo and the principal source of oil for Bretton Woods countries; it was not an effort on behalf of the Bretton Woods system itself.

Since the US-Saudi agreements of 1972–74, Saudi Arabia, which was and remains the world's largest oil producer, has become one of the most reliable US allies, enjoying a privileged status within OPEC that exempts it from allotted production quotas as the proxy representative of the USA.[7] After the mid-1970s it used its position as OPEC's 'swing producer' to 'manage' oil prices in order to increase or decrease oil production and bring about oil scarcity or glut in the world market, according to US interests. The US-Saudi agreements implicitly created a global petro-dollar economic system that not only put a floor under the value of the US dollar, but also allowed the USA once again to manage international trade on terms that disadvantaged its European and Japanese competitors. This, coupled with the importance of arms sales and build-up, worked by making these commodities a *de facto* replacement for the pre-1971 dollar-Gold Standard, thereby guaranteeing a demand for dollars, whose value was ultimately linked to oil and weapons trade and production. In this scheme, the OECD bloc had to purchase oil either from OPEC or from one of the smaller oil producers, but they could conduct these purchases only by pricing and buying oil and weapons in dollars, thus restoring the dollar's role as a required reserve currency.

It did not take long for the contradictions of the system to implode. The entire model kept demand for dollars artificially high, and as the price of oil went up following the 1973 Arab–Israeli War, the demand for dollars increased, raising the value of the dollar even further and once again subsidizing US domestic and military spending. This form of dollarization boosted further the inflationary trends in the USA, Europe and Japan, deepening the stagnation of the global economic system.

The creation of the petro-dollar system also once again provided a double loan to the USA, first by allowing it to set the terms for the international oil trade, and second by subsidizing the value of the dollar and exempting it from the burden of internal US monetary and economic policies. This allowed the USA to print dollars to pay for its oil imports without giving up goods and services in exchange, as the value of those dollars was supported by the demand created for them by the petro-dollar/weapon-dollar regime. The yin and yang of this petro-dollar/weapon-dollar economy, however, also meant that US benefits were offset by costs imposed on other capitalist economies—particularly those emerging from post-colonialism and other periphery states—as the USA exported its economic problems. Thus, when the 1973–75 recession began, the USA could shift its effects onto its capitalist partners, which then bore the greater burden as oil prices rose after 1974. Similarly, the hyperinflation of the late 1970s and the sharp global recession of 1981–82 (which were also linked to the petro-dollar economy and caused dollars to pile up once again in an international banking system) became global crises

The failure of neo-liberal financialization

as Bretton Woods institutions struggled to recycle the dollars into for-profit investments. This led depositor banks in the advanced capitalist economies to look to less developed countries for profits, because oil-exporting economies were unable to absorb the huge oil revenues that were generated in US dollars (Greider 1989).

The tragic results of the crises of the 1970s and early 1980s were, once again, exacerbated by a failure by the USA to exercise leadership within the OECD bloc. Rather than promoting sensible social investments (whether in its own economy or in those of the developing world), the USA chose in the mid-1970s to use the petro-dollar/weapon-dollar overhang as an opportunity to promote the purchase of US Treasury bonds and bills, which would act as yet another subsidy for the US economy, especially its increasing current account deficit. The short-term benefits this solution provided, however, were more than offset by its long-term costs, as the USA increasingly came to rely on foreign investors as the primary source of finance for US investments. This had the effect of artificially increasing prices through speculation, leading to an inflationary outburst that undermined the perceived value of the dollar, causing a decline in demand for dollars and a corresponding upward spike in US interest rates which found expression in Volcker's policy. This in turn forced depositor banks to scramble to find new ways to invest the growing hoard of petro-dollars, leading to further attempts to dump excess petro-dollars in developing economies (e.g. Latin America), which merely fed the inflationary spiral there by adding to the mix a rapid increase in the price of basic commodities. In this case, however, the vast amount of liquidity that flowed into the banking system was accompanied by a disregard for the underlying financial problems that it masked. The banks, which were making huge profits on loans, had little incentive to blow the whistle, and the US executive, which was using the situation to create an illusion of prosperity, had little incentive to self-critically examine a system for which it was ultimately responsible. As Volcker stepped in to raise interest rates radically to cool inflation and protect the dollar, a growing number of the economies of developing countries sank into a deep depression.

These crises might have brought down the entire Bretton Woods institutions, except for massive new spending by the USA as part of a new Cold War initiative. Generally identified as 'star wars', this initiative by President Ronald Reagan poured huge amounts of money into military spending, presumably in an effort to drive the USSR into bankruptcy. However, the reasons were not systemic, as mainstream international relations (IR), and especially its old-fashioned realist IR branch, want us to believe. The reasons lie in the domestic stagflation of the US economy—that is, the over-accumulation crisis of the core, which employed all policy means possible to fight over-accumulation and regain the global initiative. Capitalism, though, is a beast that imperial policy, whether monetary/neo-liberal or Keynesian, cannot tame. For example, the 'star wars' project, never really carried out, helped to dry up the petro-dollar surplus temporarily by channelling it into military development, but it also touched off another burst of speculation within the USA which centred on commercial and residential real estate. While much smaller than the present speculative bubble, the collapse of this real estate speculation was at the time the most serious financial crisis to hit the USA since the Great Depression, sparking the largest single-day decline in US stock prices and shaking confidence in the economy which continued through the 1992–93 economic recession (Black 2005).

Volcker's neo-liberal financial statecraft provided no solution to the issue of stagnation and low rates of growth, and it did not solve the problem of unemployment across the core, despite the introduction of flexible labour schemes (part-time work, fractional contracts, etc.) and other devastating measures for labour. Importantly, neo-liberal policies and the dismantling of the Keynesian state apparatus, personified in Margaret Thatcher and Ronald Reagan, did not restore the rate of profit, especially in manufacturing. This happened despite a substantial fall in real wages (see Tables 3.1 and 3.2).

During the decade 1979–89, average Japanese annual real gross domestic product (GDP) growth fell by half (it was 10%) and that of OECD-Europe to 2.3%. Denmark, the Netherlands, Greece, Sweden and West Germany were the countries mostly hit by the long downturn. Between 1950 and 1973 average world GDP growth was at 4%, whereas between 1973 and 1996 it fell to 2.9%. Between 1965 and 1980 the average annual growth rate in the Middle East and North Africa was 6.7%, but it fell to 0.5% between 1980 and 1990 (for Latin America and the Caribbean the numbers were 6% and 0.5%, respectively). Post-1971 neo-liberal financialization failed spectacularly to deliver real growth, welfare and prosperity.

Table 3.1 Average profit rates in three sectors

	1948–69	1969–79	1979–90
Manufacturing	24.8	15.05	13.0
Non-farm non-manufacturing	11.1	10.3	9.1
Non-farm private	20.5	17.1	15.0

Source: Adapted from Robert Brenner, *The Boom and the Bubble*, p. .21.

Table 3.2 Comparing average profit and unemployment rates, and average annual rates of change for real wages, in selected OECD countries

	Net profit rate		Real wage		Unemployment rate	
	1950–70	1970–93	1950–73	1973–93	1950–73	1973–93
US	12.9	9.9	2.7	0.2	4.2	6.7
Germany	23.2	13.8	5.7	1.9	2.3	5.7
Japan	21.6	17.2	6.3	2.7	1.6	2.1
G-7	17.6	13.3			3.1	6.2

Source: Adapted from Robert Brenner, *The Boom and the Bubble*, p. 8.

WHY THE RATE OF PROFIT MATTERS

Capitalism, as a social and global system, rests upon the search for profit and accumulation of capital. What stimulates investment is, however, not just the absolute level of profit, but the 'rate of profit', which is the ratio of profits to investment. Most observers of capitalism consider the rate of profit as one of the most important indicators of the 'robustness' of the economic system. Classical economists, especially Adam Smith, David Ricardo and Karl Marx, believed that the rate of profit in a capitalist economic system would tend to fall over time. The rate of profit is an essential indicator that determines, as well as exposes, conditions of accumulation, in other words, the 'health' of a particular economic body. In the world economy, the rate of profit stayed more or less steady, and even rose, all through the late 1940s, the 1950s and the early 1960s. As a result, these years witnessed a steady rise in the levels of investment, and a continual boom. However, from the late 1960s onwards, profit rates fell continuously, especially in manufacturing, with the global economy witnessing a real decline in the rate of global GDP growth: as we saw earlier, growth slowed, profits dropped, inflation and unemployment rose and a fiscal crisis of the state stepped in.

We also outlined the responses: governments, under the lead of the USA and its central bank, introduced a series of measures which later came to be known as neo-liberalism. Neo-liberal response(s) to the recession took the form of 'Reaganism' in the USA and 'Thatcherism' in Britain, with their policies spreading in most of the developed economies of the West and also in the so-called 'emerging markets' of Asia and elsewhere. Under pressure from the leading capitalist agencies (primarily the USA) and the US Treasury—via the IMF and the World Bank—core European and Asian economies have adopted structural adjustment programmes along the same lines. As a result, global growth averaged 1.4% in the 1980s and 1.1% in the 1990s; however, it was 3.5% in the 1960s and 2.4% in the 1970s (Harvey 2005). Global growth was no more.

Let us now look at profits. Net profit rates in manufacturing in the USA were 10% in 1980—the lowest point ever—and went up to 15% in 1989, the best Reaganite year, and then hit 19% in 1997–98, the best years under Clinton, before starting to fall again.[8] What caused this partial recovery in US manufacturing? The argument put forth here by Brenner is very convincing:

> What mattered most, though, was the value of the currency. Between 1985 and 1990, and then between 1990 and 1995, the exchange rate of the yen and mark appreciated against the dollar at the extraordinary average annual rates of 10.5% and 12.7%, respectively, and then 9.1% and 2.5% respectively. The way was thus prepared for an enormous gain in US manufacturing competitiveness. Between 1985 and 1995 US nominal wages expressed in dollars rose at an average annual rate of 4.65%, while those of Japan and Germany rose respectively at an average annual rate of 15.1% and 13.7%. Over the same ten-year period, manufacturing unit

labour costs expressed in dollars rose at an average annual rate of 0.75% in the US, compared to 11.7% and 11.3% in Japan and Germany respectively. By 1995, therefore, hourly wages for manufacturing production workers were $17.19 in the US, $23.66 in Japan, and $31.85 in Germany. On the basis of such extraordinary advances in relative costs, US producers could make major gains in overseas sales.

(Brenner 2006: 206–7)

Thus, what had been essential in this partial recovery of the rate of profit in the USA had been currency devaluation and the increase of the share of total profits in the total national income at the expense of wages. This meant increased pressure for people to work harder, especially migrant and unskilled labour, and all kinds of attacks and cuts on welfare services. It meant a fall in the real wages and a massive increase in working hours. Almost everywhere in the world, the proportion of the wealth produced that went back to the workers had decreased since the 1970s. However, despite the fact that this approach is methodologically flawed as an aggregate factor, one should also add the role of US consumer debt in stimulating the partial recovery of the 1990s.

Still, as seen in the figures above, the profit rates never recovered more than about half their previous decline. The US Federal Reserve and the Bank of England began cutting interest rates and promoting lending in order to deal with periodic mini-recessions and encourage investment. At the same time, money became very cheap for the average consumer, who was encouraged to borrow. An active state-led process of 'deregulation' began. This included, among other things, the elimination of robust oversight of financial institutions, investment banks, hedge funds and all sorts of operators and new financial instruments. Such measures were able to encourage spending to some extent and thus to extend the booms, but one can now firmly conclude that these practices simply delayed the bursting of the bubble for a few years, inasmuch as the growth registered was fictitious and debt-led. This was a clever way on the part of the Anglo-American elites to pass the debt from the state to society, yet this proved a temporary measure, offering only a short breathing space for the already declining US hegemonic system.

The Carter Administration initiated industrial deregulation in airlines, trucking, the landmark being the bailout of Chrysler in 1980. This set the tone for what was to follow. Tax reform acts reduced taxes on individuals, disproportionately placing the burden on the weak and the deprived, as the Social Security Tax—corresponding to National Insurance contributions in the UK—increased by 25%. As far as the transformation of industrialists into financial operators and rentiers was concerned, this took on an entirely exceptional form: huge amounts of liquidity were financialized into shares, bonds and other instruments, including participation in interest-bearing schemes of non-manufacturing firms, the aim being easy profiteering in any business environment conducive to it. 'Manufacturing corporations' interest payment as a proportion of profits', Brenner observes, 'having grown to 15%

during the years 1973–79 compared to just 3.8% for the years 1950–73, increased to 35% between 1982 and 1990 and 24% between 1990 and 1996' (Brenner 2006: 215). Mergers and acquisitions continued apace (during the Reagan years in the 1980s, their total value was *circa* $1.40 trillion, the result of some 31,200 mergers and acquisitions). With active government encouragement, during the period 1975–90, the proportion of total investment on plant and equipment in the private business economy annually devoted to finance, insurance and real estate, doubled from about 12%–13%, to about 23%–25%. All this resulted in a substantial increase in the share of financial services in the GDP of the USA, which surpassed that of industry in the mid-1990s. From 1973 to 2008 the portion of manufacturing in GDP fell from 25% to 12%. The share represented by financial services rose from 12% to 21%. In parallel to this, borrowing at all levels was encouraged by new financial structures, which were re-shaped and relaxed to allow high levels of risky borrowing. This is how General Motors had been displaced by Wal-Mart and Goldman Sachs as the USA's 'business template'. Meanwhile, defence spending continued. The US military share as a percentage of the world total in 1996 increased by 20% compared to a peak Reaganite year, 1985. Whereas in 1985 the USA was spending only 65% as much on defence as did the Soviet bloc, the People's Republic of China and Cuba, just a few months before the terrorist attacks on the USA on 11 September 2001 it was spending more than twice as much as did all these former communist threats. Clearly, this spending was partly financed by the US debt that Saudi, Japanese and, later, Chinese and other Asian producers were buying.[9] Paying attention to the debt dimension of the US economy in the 1990s and after is significant, because it is directly linked to deindustrialization, the position of the dollar and, eventually, to financialization and neo-liberal policy making.

The over-accumulation crisis of the 1970s led the USA and other core economies to embrace complex forms of financialization and neo-liberalism in order to restore 'profitability without producing', as Costas Lapavitsas (2013) put it. However, this undermined the growth of the real economy while increasing the growth of debt relative to GDP. Outstanding consumer debt as a percentage of disposable income in the USA rose from $1,450 billion in 1981 to $6,960.6 billion in 2000 and $11,496.6 billion in 2005 (Arrighi 2007; Hudson 2003). In the end, total debt in the US economy—that is, debt owed by households, investment and commercial banks, non-financial business as well as government—amounted to 'three and a half times the nation's GDP ... and not far from the $44 trillion GDP for the entire world' (Foster and Magdoff 2009: 46). This has also contributed to growth, as measured by national accounting practices with which we methodologically disagree, as it gives a false and rather misleading image about economic development, welfare and modernization. Thus, the truth of the matter remains as put forth by Robert Brenner: whereas financial profits rose from 15% in 1960 to 40% in 2005, profits in manufacturing fell from about 50% in 1960 down to 13% in 2003. However, we need to go a step further—namely, to point to the outsourcing to the global East, especially of manufacturing and labour-power, processes that should be seen as a result of the failure of financialization and neo-liberalism to put the USA's and the UK's political economies back on a developmental track.

CONCLUDING REMARKS

In this chapter, we have tried to describe the way in which Anglo-American political and business elites confronted the stagflation of the 1970s and the crisis of the dollar. We have showed that the devaluation of the dollar and the collapse of the Bretton Woods system was a deliberate attempt on the part of the US executive to restore competitiveness and address the problem of the falling rate of profit, especially in the real economic sector, thus arresting the overall decline of Anglo-American capitalism as a social system. This is the context in which one could consider the twin strategy of business elites in North America and Britain: on the one hand, they began moving to the sphere of corporate and global finance to compensate for the loss of profitability in manufacturing; on the other, they put enormous pressure on state traditional elites to restructure the state-economy nexus by abandoning Keynesian policy making. Despite being relatively successful with the recycling of petro-dollars and the general recycling of global surpluses through the US Treasury, this twin strategy has proven extremely vulnerable to 'boom and bust' crisis cycles, eventually culminating in the global financial crisis of 2008. Both financialization and neo-liberalism have failed to address the issue of real economic growth and the rate of profit, escaping instead to the realm of finance and thus to the terminal macro-historical decline of US global hegemony.

NOTES

1 It should be noted that this business strategy was not new at all. In fact, it was precisely this unfettered function of the Anglo-American markets the led to the collapse of the credit system in the late 1920s, an event rehearsed in 2007–08; see, among others, Andrew Glyn, *Capitalism Unleashed: Finance, Globalisation, and Welfare*, Oxford: Oxford University Press, 2007, a work also indispensable for understanding the evolution of 'rentier capitalism' since the 1970s; and Robert Kuttner, 'Testimony before the Committee on Financial Services', Washington, DC: US House of Representatives, 2 October 2007. Kuttner looks at the 'alarming parallels', as he calls them, between 1929 and 2007.

2 From Mandel and Poulantzas (particularly in his last theoretical statement, *State, Power, Socialism*), to Arrighi, Panitch, van der Pijl, Brenner, Harvey, Rosenberg, Callinicos and Gowan, there seems to be a solid agreement on this very point within neo-Marxist and Marxisant discourses. Constructivists, such as Alexander Wendt, have a very flippant definition of the state, whereas realists, such as Gilpin, typically defined the state as a political unit separate from economic and social relations.

3 The Johnson Administration had started the SALT (Strategic Arms Limitation Talks) but had given them very low priority. Thus, Nixon and Kissinger were, in effect, starting them anew. The SALT I agreement was finally signed in 1972,

freezing the deployment of ICBM (intercontinental ballistic missiles). As is well known, the SALT agreements, in practice, came to naught because the USA disagreed on a number of issues. The advent of Reagan in office in 1981 destroyed the entire SALT structure.
4 Some of the issues we tackle here are well presented in Dominick Salvatore, James W. Dean and Thomas Willett (eds), *The Dollarisation Debate*, Oxford: Oxford University Press, 2003. The same thesis is also found in Joseph Stiglitz, *Globalisation and its Discontents*, London: W.W. Norton, 2002, p. 239.
5 See David E. Spiro, *The Hidden Hand of American Hegemony: Petrodollar Recycling and International Markets*, Ithaca, NY: Cornell University Press, 1999.
6 We do not wish here to give the impression that the war between NATO and Yugoslavia in 1999 was because of US energy and military economic interests in the Balkans. This is certainly one factor but, as we have explained elsewhere, US objectives in the region included, significantly, matters regarding European security and the assertion of US primacy in Europe via NATO's eastward enlargement. The USA, simply, could not allow Serbia, a client state of Russia, to be in its underbelly a hostile force, at a moment when NATO and the USA were incorporating Hungary, Poland and the Czech Republic into their security policy.
7 In 1982, OPEC adopted the 'quota system' to limit its oil supplies and thereby keep oil prices from falling below certain levels. Under this system, each OPEC country is allocated a specific quota for oil production. This did not prevent the 1986 oil price collapse, however, because most OPEC countries did not respect their quotas (Gökay 2006).
8 See Brenner (2006: 7, Figure 0.3, and 198 ff).
9 See Fouskas and Gökay (2005: 59–60); the findings of Arrighi (2007); and Hudson (2003).

REFERENCES

Arrighi, G. (2007) *Adam Smith in Beijing*, London: Verso.
Bacevich, A. (2002) *American Empire*, Cambridge, MA: Harvard University Press.
Black, W. (2005) *The Best Way to Rob a Bank*, Austin, TX: University of Texas.
Brenner, Robert (2002) *The Boom and the Bubble: The US in the World Economy*, London: Verso.
——(2006) *The Economics of Global Turbulence: The Advanced Capitalist Economies from Long Boom to Long Downturn, 1945–2005*, London: Verso.
Dicken, P. (2011) *Global Shift*, 6th edn, London: Sage.
Eichengreen, B. (2008) *Globalizing Capital*, London: Princeton University Press.
Foster, John Bellamy and Magdoff, Fred (2009) *The Great Financial Crisis: Causes and Consequences*, New York: NYU Press.
Fouskas, V. (2003) *Zones of Conflict*, London: Pluto Press.
Fouskas, Vassilis and Gökay, B. (2005) *The New American Imperialism*, Westport, CT: Praeger.
Galbraith, J.K. (1967) *The New Industrial State*, Harmondsworth: Penguin.
Glynn, A. (2007) *Capitalism Unleashed*, Oxford: Oxford University Press.
Gökay, B. (ed.) (2006) *The Politics of Oil*, Abingdon: Routledge.
Gowa, J. (1983) *Closing the Gold Window*, Ithaca, NY: Cornell University Press.
Gowan, P. (1999) *The Global Gamble*, London: Verso.
Greider, W. (1989) *The Secrets of the Temple*, New York: Touchstone.
Harvey, D. (2005) *A Brief History of Neo-liberalism*, Oxford: Oxford University Press.
Hudson, M. (2003) *Super-Imperialism*, London: Pluto Press.

Kennen, Peter B. (ed.) (1994) *Managing the World Economy*, Washington, DC: Institute for International Economics.
Kiely, R. (2010) *Rethinking Imperialism*, London: Palgrave.
Lapavitsas, C. (2013) *Profiting without Producing*, London: Verso.
Lasswell, H. (1997) *Essays on the Garrison State*, New Brunswick, NJ: Transaction Publishers.
Layne, C. (2006) *The Peace of Illusions*, Ithaca: Cornell University Press.
Mandel, E. (1969) 'Where is America Going?', *New Left Review* 54.
Nitzan, Jonathan and Bichler, S. (2002) *The Global Political Economy of Israel*, London: Pluto Press.
Panitch, L. (2012) *The Making of Modern Capitalism*, London: Verso.
Poulantzas, N. (1974) *Les classes sociales dans le capitalism aujourd'hui*, Paris: Maspero.
Seabrook, L. (2001) *US Power in International Finance*, London: Palgrave.
Varoufakis, Y. (2013) *The Global Minotaur*, London and New York: Zed Books.
Volcker, Paul and Gyohten, T. (1992) *Changing Fortunes*, New York: Times Books.
Williams Appleman, W. (1959/1972) *The Tragedy of American Diplomacy*, New York: Norton.

Shock therapy and the political economy of the former Soviet space

SABINE SPANGENBERG

INTRODUCTION

Over the past 25 years the former USSR underwent a complete political change with the creation of independent states. The former Soviet bloc contained communist nations which were closely allied to the Soviet Union; this included satellite states Bulgaria, Czechoslovakia, the German Democratic Republic (GDR), Hungary, Poland and Romania, all members of the Warsaw Pact. The foreign policies of these nations followed closely the directive from Moscow, but excluded countries likes China, Yugoslavia (aligned until 1948) and Albania (aligned until 1960), which pursued independent foreign policies. The USSR collapsed in 1991, and out of the 15 Soviet republics the Commonwealth of Independent States (CIS) was formed later that year. The CIS contains 12 of the former Soviet republics: the Baltic nations of Estonia, Slovenia and Lithuania separated from the CIS and became members of the European Union (EU), with Estonia adopting the euro. All former Soviet allies of the USSR space are now members of the EU, with one former ally, Slovakia, having adopted the euro in 2009.

The political change was accompanied by extreme structural alterations. The changes that followed from what we commonly refer to as 'the collapse of communism' or 'the collapse of really existing socialism' have had implications on society and economy that we have been witnessing for a while. Today, we observe amongst the states of the former Soviet space vast differences in quality of life and large imbalances in the distribution of income and wealth. This observation poses questions as to who has gained from the transformation and whether it was successful in achieving the set objectives. Any reform works towards a set of targets, with a successful reform policy achieving these. The transformation of communist countries in Eastern and Central Europe followed the principles of the Washington Consensus and in particular the neo-liberal construction of shock therapy. The Washington Consensus was a term coined by Williamson (1990) to describe the policy instruments of market-based economic systems as a healing force for developing low-income countries as well as post-communist nations. These nations would adopt market-based economic structures and follow economic-political advice of international Western institutions such as the International Monetary Fund (IMF) and the World Bank. The policy instruments in post-communist nations adopted various forms of structural adjustment programme, market liberalization and privatization. The debate surrounding the Washington Consensus has been extensive, particularly relevant to the former Soviet bloc focused mainly on the neo-liberal shock therapy with its main economic protagonist Jeffrey Sachs and its critic Peter Gowan.

The institutional change observed in the former Soviet space was exogenous, indeed classified as *fundamentalist-institutional*. Institutions were chosen by international political decision makers and partly imposed on the respective nations. The reform process was not gradual, but sudden and profound in the fashion of a big bang. The former Soviet bloc underwent fundamental political and economic transformation. The newly formed nations widely adopted market-based economic systems and therewith replaced the structures of a planned economy. The replacement of the centrally planned economic system occurred both in the Central and Eastern European area (CEE) as well as in the newly formed CIS. In view of these fundamental system changes within those areas, attention will be paid to the economic system change alongside the changes of the political system. To evaluate the process of transformation and its effects, the origins of and motivation for change will have to be understood. This will subsequently lead to an assessment of the institutionalized transformation in post-communist nations. Attention will be paid to the assumed non-existence of social norms or aims within a nation or a region: instead, the neo-liberal school follows the neo-classical orthodox view that competitive markets in combination with competitive forces and private property rights will lead to welfare maximization. The interconnectedness of political decisions and economic outcomes becomes highly apparent when economic-political recommendations are followed by very little consultation with society. The institutions-focused neo-liberal school recommends market-based structures irrespective of the aims of society.

THE CASE OF THE INSTITUTIONALIZED TRANSFORMATION

Economic transformation is the fundamental alteration of the structures of the economic system. The economic system is a partial social system, as are the legal and policies systems. System transformation is synonymous with institutional change, which can be initiated and exercised in different ways. A top-down approach can be juxtaposed to a bottom-up approach, an evolutionary approach to a revolutionary one, and a gradual to a sudden shock approach. The structural changes that occurred in the CEE and CIS followed a top-down, sudden shock approach which arguably succeeded evolutionary political changes but might have been unrelated to those. The process of change is often motivated by structural needs and followed by political decisions. The political changes followed the reform years of Gorbachev and Walesa, but the economic structural changes were radical rather than gradual and the process of change was orchestrated through institutionalized shocks to economy and society.

The institutionalized transformation follows a goal function, mostly constructed through political decisions. However, these political decisions do not necessarily constitute civil consensus, as they might be influenced or required by globalized Western institutions. As will be argued in this chapter, in most cases the political decisions were not taken by the citizens of the respective nations, but rather were conceived by international political decision makers. In this case it becomes relevant to assess whether the imposed social goal function is indeed commensurate with the objectives of the individuals/citizens. These societal goal functions can be used as a yard stick to identify whether the process of transformation and the adaptation of new structures have been successful. However, the nature of success would be dependent on the individuals' behavioural adjustment to the structural changes as well as the evaluation of people's individual functions of well-being.

This chapter uses an inductive approach to identify the structural changes. It is factually based and investigates the economic features and outcomes since the adoption of the new system. The method of inductive inference is often utilized by historical schools of economic thought; however, it must be noted that institutional change is often linked with value or norm changes, so that it remains debatable to what extent such an analysis could ever be truly value-free. The identification of the substantive social goal function is the biggest problem when we aim to assess the effects, desired or undesired, of structural changes. Here, we are concerned with underlying norm changes rather than a paradigm change. However, the question remains whether these norm changes are logically substantiated.

It is widely believed that the norm changes in the CEE and CIS were due to the comparative differences in liberty and material well-being between the West and the East. These differences, which occurred alongside a gradual democratization of the political system, would assume the creation of new values that necessitated the construction of new structures. It needs to be investigated whether the structural changes were indeed based on such value creation, whether the new elements of the system were internalized into the individual behavioural economic functions and whether there is thus harmony between values and institutions. Here the inductive method will be used to show the phenomena of the transformation. The constraints of the deductive methodology lie in the lack of evolutionary economic theories and it is beyond the scope of this chapter to assess their respective validity, hence they will largely be ignored and deductive conclusions will be confined to the standard economic theory. The approach is scientific and discusses value without value judgements (Myrdal 1969; Weber 1947).

Any dissonance between values and institutions can logically create resistance, discontent and opposition which possibly hinder the transitional phase and delay gradual adjustment and reform responses. Reform responses become more difficult, if not impossible, as the shock approach relies on orthodox neo-classical assumptions and the ex-ante identification of the generic end goals and objectives, namely the integration of post-communist countries into the Western system of capitalism and thereby maximizing global welfare. It also relies on the ex-ante design and architecture of the institutions that are deemed best to achieve these goals. The institutionalized transformation approach disallowed scrutiny and reform responses. It ignored the hazards of not integrating the people into the reform through worker ownership models when advocating human freedom and accountability. It ignored the hazards of employing autocratic systems allied to Western powers when advocating a rise in living standards through democracy.

STRUCTURES IN SOVIET BLOC ECONOMIES

The socialist Soviet bloc organizational framework was one of centralization, hierarchy and lack of formal liberties. The co-ordination of economic plans and the decision-making structure were centralized with co-ordination following the system of order rather than agreement, as apparent in social production, consumption and price policies. Economic decisions were centrally made and constructed in plans that aimed at the creation of a developed socialist society. These plans covered long time periods, were relevant for all parts of the economy and most economic activities, and identified a unity between economic and social policy. In a didactic approach it aimed at the improvement of the cultural and material living standards and further development of socialist production and growth of labour productivity. Plans were constructed centrally with little or no peripheral influence. Authority was centralized to the extent that there was little room for plan modification; instead, a system was in place that rewarded successful plan implementation.

The Soviet motivation structure can be described as one of intrinsic values, which Weber describes as value rational. Here intrinsic or extrinsic values are attached to forms of behaviours, i.e. value is existent or created by a form of behaviour. This differs from the instrumental-rational form of motivation where the individual defines a utility function; here the variables inside the function are tools to achieve the specific objective in a rational manner. This forms the basis of the neo-classical assumption of *homo oeconomicus*. The purpose is defined as utility value, cardinal or ordinal. Instead, the socialist economy prohibited the exchange of products or production factors on markets; as a result, neither goods markets nor factor markets were existent in their pure sense. The allocation of resources and the distribution of goods and services followed the central authority's decision. State ownership had the effect that incentives could not originate from private property ownership. It was impossible due to the lack of markets to ensure efficiency and maximization of output per worker (Bergson 1992). The socialist structure imposed immense costs (not only) due to the need for information collection and the creation of widespread economic inefficiencies. In terms of technical comparative productivity, the lag became apparent in terms of the relation between outputs and inputs, capital, land, technology, but also labour.

Historic events must be considered with care. Had the financial crisis in 2007 happened 20 years earlier, would there still have been the belief in market forces and superiority of market economies? For the second half of the 20th century, the Western market economies prospered with growth rates far outstripping the states that followed the communist-planned model supporting the Hayekian view of a planned economy's road to serfdom (Hayek 1935). Economies that followed the decentralized approach effectively overtook the centrally planned ones in terms of all major economic indicators. As a result the newly formed states of the CEE and CIS largely followed the Western economic framework in the design of the new economic order.

POLITICAL CONSENSUS OR WESTERN STRATEGIC DOMINANCE: REFORM OR DESIGN

Observing the various system changes in post-communist states one cannot disregard the reform processes within. Here, the process of transformation of the Polish economy is used as an example of the creation of a fundamentalist-institutional approach that was employed or imposed on post-communist Eastern European states. Poland has had a long history of freedom movements and stands out as the nation to which shock therapy was brought by Western economists such as Sachs and Lipton.

The Polish civil movement largely found its voice through the labour federation Solidarnoz, founded in August 1980, which won increasing support during the early 1980s, fighting for the rights of workers in particular and social change in general. This human rights movement that represented the apparent fall of the communist government was legalized in 1989 and subsequently won the free elections later that year. The Solidarity-led government with a communist president created a pragmatic approach based on Polish patriotism. Poland was considered a more open and liberal communist state than the rest of the Soviet bloc and thereby is believed to have led the way for other bloc nations. Despite these advancements, it soon became apparent that not only had the political system changed, but the economy had collapsed, the socialist economic plan was dead and price inflation followed severe market shortages.

During this first year of post-communism, Harvard economist Jeffrey Sachs was approached to assist with the Polish reform process and visited Poland in April 1989, soon after the legalization of Solidarnoz. Some of Sachs's visits were funded by the investor George Soros, who also paid for Sachs's Harvard colleague David Lipton's advisory trips to Poland (Lipton worked for the IMF and later for the US Treasury under Clinton). Together these two individuals embarked on devising a stabilization programme for the Polish economy. The design was such that Poland should become a member of the European community with a Western-style capitalist economy. The design of a mixed economy followed the structural blueprint of Western Europe with its laws and institutions. The proposed transformation of the Polish economy was one that was founded on an institutional basis, which relied on opening markets and borders, allowing free movement of products and production factors and the essential prospect of integrating Poland within the European community. It is noteworthy to witness that Sachs and Lipton 'began to write a plan about the transformation of Poland from a socialist economy in the Soviet orbit to a market economy within the European community'—a plan that was a 'leap across the institutional chasm' (Sachs 2005: 114).

The evidence is clear: there has been little, if any, gradual transition from central planning to decentralized decision making; instead, the transformation was designed and imposed, a planned design for a decentralized unplanned economic system. The two dominant features of the transformation of the CEE and CIS are institutional design and speed. The institutional transformation followed the Western scheme with a focus on liberal markets, free trade, complete and private property rights, and international institutional integration. The ownership structure was to be the same as the one in Western Europe, physical capital was to be owned predominantly by private units, shares owned by households, firms or financial institutions. The transformation was to happen quickly and the structures were to be established with speed. Speed was believed to be an 'administered therapy', whereby the patient is shocked into a particular reaction. Clinical economics attempted the resuscitation of post-communist states through the sudden administering of a multitude of fundamental body function-changing medicines along the lines of the Washington Consensus. These medicines focused on establishing:

- price stability (internal and external);
- price liberalization and securing commercial transactions through a legal framework;
- converting state ownership into private ownership (as part of the concept of the mixed economy a welfare system had to be introduced which allowed the unemployed, elderly, etc. to be protected); and
- institutions in Polish society which would eventually allow Poland's entry into the EU.

The concept of sudden price liberalization was not entirely innovative. The removal of price controls was historically inspired by the German post-war economic reforms under Ludwig Erhard, then minister for economic affairs, who later became German chancellor (1963). The sudden liberalization was expected initially to create vast price differentials in similar markets, which were therefore forced to adjust, hence a shock adjustment, framing the applied approach 'shock therapy'.

In Poland itself, Finance Minister Lescek Balcerowitz supported the transition from centrally planned to free market economy by opening the borders to international trade, removing price controls and introducing price liberalization with deflationary measures. External price instability was a serious issue due to the lack of a single currency market that could result in one currency rate; instead, the official rate stood next to a black market rate. The imbalance on the foreign exchange market and the price differential motivated currency arbitrage, which accelerated the destabilization of the Polish currency. This hindered the allocation of funds as the currency value was not believed to represent Poland's monetary situation comparative to the rest of the world. To overcome this problem and create a convertible currency and foreign exchange reserves, the Zloty Stabilization Fund with a value of 1 billion zloty was established by January 1990, all price controls were abolished and the Polish currency was pegged to the US dollar at 9,500 zloty. During the Soviet era, products' respective scarcity were shown by queues of consumers rather than increasing prices. The queues outside shops were now replaced by price inflation. Shortages on the goods markets initiated an adjustment that first year students can find in any economics textbook—namely, increasing prices signalling that more products would be bought if they were supplied. Cross-border trade made up for the shortages in certain markets, also introducing new goods such as bananas to Polish customers, which received a lot of publicity.

The motivation to integrate Poland into market-based Western Europe resulted from belief in New Growth Theory and the accredited relationship between trade, growth and geography, a model for which Paul Krugman (1991a, 1991b) much later (in 2008) received the Nobel Prize. The position of Poland was extremely fortunate, bordering highly developed European countries that were closely integrated in international trade. The geographic position (even if peripheral) and the country's endowment with a highly literate and well-educated workforce were conceived to allow Poland's entry into international competition away from the previous trade dependency within the Soviet bloc (the area of the Council for Mutual Economic Assistance, or Comecon).

Previously, within the socialist system, industrial output in socialist Poland was produced largely for Soviet planned demand, with the USSR supplying energy cheaply. The rise in energy prices following the collapse of the socialist model caused Polish manufacturers initially to reduce their output, and with limited factor substitutability this meant that factory labour combined with energy and old capital had to be laid off, so unemployment rose. The gradual replacement of old capital with new and the comparative Polish wage advantage attracted foreign companies to start up production sites, bringing in further foreign financial and real capital, raising productivity rates. This coincided with the end of state subsidization, leading to a reduction in wages and a drift in social power (Gowan 1995).

The neo-classical narrative assumes that once the institutional framework had been established, obsolete capital equipment was replaced by new production factors. Rational investors would naturally consider the risk of asset allocation, which was institutionally addressed via the institutional private property rights structure and through investment funds which were often managed by Western accountancy companies. Here the risk of institutional default had to be eliminated—once again the emphasis was placed on creating the institutional framework similar to those prospering nations in the West. Alongside foreign direct investment, infrastructure investment was an immediate requirement. For this, the public finances needed to be put into order, which was problematic given the large budget deficit, but aided through the stabilization fund.

In summary, shock therapy had two main aspects: institutional reform, and speed with stabilization. The institutional reforms to the Polish economy were focused on the establishment of: a price mechanism that would reflect scarcities through the market mechanism of demand and supply; a Polish economy that was integrated in the world economy with a convertible currency; and private property rights, and free entry and exit of firms into and out of markets. Stabilization was conceived as a process that alleviated hyperinflation and an adjustment instrument that was financially assisted to prevent longer-term instability. Despite the swift institutional set-up, it became apparent during the first years of Polish transformation that the remaining problems were its obsolete production status and the slow process of privatizing the large state-owned enterprises (SOEs).

PRIVATIZATION OF SOES

The privatization of state-owned enterprises is not only relevant to post-communist states—it spread across a wide spectrum of economies. The respective privatization strategies are centralized, decentralized or mixed. The centralized approach makes use of a single body that has decision-making authority and responsibility of implementation. This approach usually employs a government agency, a privatization body or a holding company. The decentralized model instead relies on the respective sectoral ministries to hold responsibility. The mixed approach uses fragments of the two approaches in a combined form. Privatization of SOEs in post-communist states followed the centralized approach (OECD 2003). However, the practice of selling SOEs was highly influenced by the experience of the opening of monopolistic markets and the practice of floating previously state-owned utilities in Western Europe (British Telecom, Deutsche Telekom AG). Here, the concept was to restructure the corporations and then sell their shares on the stock market. This was seen by the Sachs team as far too time-consuming, so instead they recommended a faster privatization process. Small and medium-sized enterprises (SMEs) would be offered to employees as a management buy in and larger corporations would quickly be put into private hands. The approach used was that of trade sales. A trade sale is usually considered if the government wants to keep ownership in a relatively small number of hands, where initial public offerings would not necessarily fulfil this objective. Trade sales can be completed more quickly than floatation on the stock market and are seen as more advantageous for practical reasons, such as coherent management and guarantees of employment. In Poland, by 2001 trade sales accounted for 86% of companies that used an indirect capital method, either through public invitation or public tender (OECD 2003). This shows the comparatively small number of worker-owned enterprise sales and the large number of privatizations that aimed for a more concentrated ownership structure.

In line with the main approach of the therapy, the privatization emphasis was on speed. Western economists widely agreed that a speedy privatization would benefit the transition and avoid long-term inflexibility and deadlock. It was believed that a case-by-case approach, i.e. restructuring the enterprise and gradually selling off the shares, could lead to paralysis due to political obstacles, and this expectation, which is considered as non-hypothetical, was founded on the experiences of previous privatization strategies (Lipton and Sachs 1990).

Eastern reformers were less confident that a speedy privatization of large state-owned enterprises would generate a socially acceptable ownership structure. These critics saw the fundamental error in that the therapy's alleged workings were based on experience in countries in completely different circumstances. Even moderate reformers, such as Hungarian critic of neo-classical economics Janos Kornai, warned that the private sector should be developed from the bottom up rather than from the top down. This would entail securing behavioural changes throughout society, which were necessary for long-term economic growth and successful transformation (Kornai 1990).

The centralized privatization approach and the conversion of large state-owned enterprises into treasury-owned joint-stock companies in Poland were similar to the process adopted during the East German privatization process. Here, the enterprises were transferred to the privatization agency Treuhand, which then subsequently restituted or sold them to the highest bidder. The conversion into treasury-owned company shares provided the institutional basis according to the standard theory of the firm, whereby the corporate form of private ownership is expected to lead to the efficient allocation of resources. The Polish privatization process allowed for only a few shares of SMEs to be distributed freely to workers and to financial institutions such as commercial banks and mutual funds for further distribution to the public.

Evidently, the privatization process did not place emphasis on the final distribution of property and was therefore inconsiderate of social acceptability and justice. The creation of a financial market system lay at the core of the privatization process, and of the transformation process in general. The involvement of the financial sector and commercial banks in particular were reflected upon positively by the transformation designers. The fact that 'institutional investors now hold more than half the value of shares in the United Kingdom, Italy, and Japan, as well as more than half the value of the New York Stock Exchange' (Lipton and Sachs 1990: 294) was seen as the example and pattern that post-communist transformational economies should follow. Financial market institutions were not only considered to facilitate the necessary capital requirements for the purchase of enterprise shares, but these institutions were also silently given the role of buying these shares. The financial injection was considered vital but the resulting ownership structure was hardly a consideration for the Western economists. The privatization approach generated government revenue which was needed to keep a balanced public budget; in Poland foreign debt to Western states and international organizations was substantial, exacerbated by the high and rising inflation. Eventually, Polish debt repayment was deferred until 2001 and half of the debt was cancelled.

Other post-communist states adopted similar approaches. Hungary's privatization process was also based on the shock approach, causing an initial influx of foreign capital with a later slow-down, with ownership often being transferred to those who had close links with the government, influencing political decisions rather than changing the production structure of the companies, allowing production to start. Instead the political influence and focus on their own pockets gained priority. Historically, Hungary adopted, after initial protests in 1956, Soviet foreign policy with limited discretion over home affairs. However, domestically it introduced a new economic mechanism in 1968 which allowed a gradual transition to the Western model; it was a third way between central planning and the free market. This went alongside some degree of political freedom, which resulted in the opposition parties winning the elections in 1990, forming the new pro-market government.

In contrast to these nations, other former socialist states disintegrated or ceased existence in their previous form. Czechoslovakia split in 1993 into two separate states, which postponed the privatization process. The privatization of enterprises in the Czech Republic followed a system whereby each citizen was given a voucher with which they could buy shares in investment funds. In Slovakia, the process of large-scale privatization was divided into two waves to speed up the whole process, also making use of voucher privatization. These nations formed new specialized institutions, such as the Slovak National Property Funds, which was an independent legal entity with the purpose of realizing and approving privatization projects, concluding buyer-seller contracts, organizing public competitions and public auctions and temporarily administering state property shares in transformed or partially privatized enterprises. Once again, the privatization approach is one of centralized authority.

Similarly, the GDR was incorporated in the Federal Republic of Germany after economic and monetary union between the two states on 3 October 1990. The unification followed a mass exodus of East Germans in 1989 via Hungary and Czechoslovakia, and concluded with the conversion of the ostmark into the Deutsche mark. The conversion rate was 1 ostmark to 1 DM, although it is estimated that the real exchange rate was closer to 1:6–12. The favourable conversion rate accentuated the citizens' support for the Western model as their monetary wealth improved consequently. However, the main effect of the currency conversion was that wages and salaries increased dramatically so that East German production became wage expensive despite the capital disadvantage of East German factories. Like other post-communist production functions, East German production relied on capital equipment that was obsolete and a process that was wage expensive. The dramatic surge in unemployment that followed drained the federal budget alongside the

Shock therapy and the former Soviet space

massive infrastructure investment that was needed in the East, partly financed through a solidarity tax-surcharge.

It has been suggested that the political fall of the Soviet bloc was due to the 'economic debility' of the USSR (Cameron and Neal 2003: 395). The failure of Gorbachev's programmes of *perestroika* (restructuring) and *glasnost* (opening) to implement sustainable reforms eventually led to the separation of the Union and the creation of independent states. Gorbachev's vision involved the state retaining political control within a democratic system that allowed economic freedom in the form of accountability, profitability and self-management. The reforms were subtle gestures compared to the radical structural change to move from a centrally planned to a market economy. However, these reforms meant that some products could be manufactured privately and the transactions could take place without state intervention. Within the agricultural sector, land could be leased privately and co-operatives could be formed upon initiative. The Yeltsin presidency (1991–99) instead opposed the reforms that were spearheaded by Gaidar and applied a policy of counter-freedom and counter-constitutionality (Gowan 1995). The economic hardship in terms of debt, unemployment and a reduction in living standards, in particular, and the economic unsustainability in general, culminated in the Russian default in 1998 whereby bonds owned by Russian citizens were not paid out. Putin has since exercised a policy of maintaining power by force instead of allowing market forces to operate fully; here we find a capitalist structure in singular sectors and markets. Overall, during the 1990s East European formerly centralized countries lost 30% of their gross domestic product (GDP).

MORE THAN 20 YEARS LATER

More than 20 years after the transformation of post-communist states began, some results have become obvious. The tables illustrate some economic indicators which can be used to highlight the main results of transition. All former Soviet bloc nations experienced increases in the Human Development Index and raised their per capita incomes (in comparison to 1995). For example, for Poland, which became a member of the EU in 2004, per capita income increased from £8,360 in 2006 to £17,776 in 2012. However, it is apparent that economic development in post-communist countries has been uneven with regards to macroeconomic and transition indicators. In terms of macroeconomic indicators, Kyrgyzstan and Azerbaijan lead with substantial public deficits of 5.3% and 4.9% of GDP, respectively. Although Azerbaijan has repeatedly announced deficit reduction plans through further privatization, it has shown reluctance to follow the IMF's recommendation to privatize the International Bank of Azerbaijan, the majority of which is owned by the government. As a petro-state the country is highly dependent on its gas and oil exports but suffers from corruption and structural economic inefficiencies. However, the degree of inequality in Azerbaijan is considerably lower than that of a country with a similar gross national income (GNI) per capita, such as Turkmenistan (Table 4.1).

In comparison, the industrial sector-based economy of Belarus records one of the lowest public deficits, the second highest per capita income and the lowest degrees of income inequality (recorded here as Gini coefficient) among CIS nations (Table 4.2). Of all its industry and banks, 80% and 75%, respectively, remain in state hands. The state continues to play a dominant role despite privatization efforts such as the recent sale of Betrazgas to Russian state-owned Gazprom.[1] Belarus records the second highest government expenditure as a share of GDP (26.3%). In contrast, Russia, Georgia and Turkmenistan have the highest inequality ratios. Russia's private sector holds the largest part of the industrial sector in private hands, with the exception of the energy and defence-related sectors. Steel factories, in particular, were sold to a small group of individuals with an informational advantage and close to the elite, again via trade sales, which resulted in the creation of an oligarchy. Often these assets were sold for far less than their market values or shares were transferred in return for loans, as was the case in the privatization of Sibneff during 1996–97. Russia has held a number of the world's top exporter positions: first in natural gas, second in oil, and third in steel and aluminium; it has acceded to a be a middle-income country and records the highest per capita income amongst the 12 CIS republics. The income growth is a result of trade integration (World Trade Organization membership in 2012), but Russia is also pursuing stronger trade links with the former Soviet space. It created a customs union with Belarus and Kazakhstan, and is working toward the Eurasian Economic Union with states of the former Comecon.

Russia's income distribution is highly unequal with a Gini coefficient of 42.3. The degree of inequality has remained high throughout the process of transformation, which has been argued to be a result of the inequality on earnings within the labour income sector. It has been shown that this inequality is not linked to differences in skills and human capital, and instead remains largely unexplained and contributes to the high working poverty in Russia (Denisova 2012). Former Soviet republics Georgia and Kyrgyzstan suffer from corruption issues. In the latter the World Bank (2012) expects a further increase of the public deficit by 6.4% in 2013 due to a reduction in non-tax income and increases in planned expenditure. Georgia's economy is agriculturally based and depends on energy imports despite the recent investment in hydro-electric power. Tax administrative issues remain problematic. Similarly, Turkmenistan suffers from a largely bureaucratic economy and an inefficient public sector despite its large reserve capital from natural gas sales. In contrast to Georgia, Moldova and Kyrgyzstan, Turkmenistan's gas reserves have allowed investment in the construction sector, but little of this activity takes place within the private sector. The large state sector has not yet been able to invest enough in more labour-intensive sectors alongside the less labour-intensive gas sector, which according to estimates employs 60% of the labour force (World Bank 2012). Ukraine has the most evenly distributed

Table 4.1 Selected Economic Indicators

Country	HDI 1995	HDI 2011	GNI per capita, PPP (2012), US $	Unempl.% (2012)	Below poverty line %, less than $1.25 per day
Former Soviet republics, non EU members					
Armenia	0.595	0.716	5385	17.3	1.3**
Azerbaijan	n.a	0.731	7911	5.2	0.4
Belarus	n.a	0.756	12245	0.7	0.1***
Georgia	n.a	0.733	4235	15	15.3
Kazakhstan	n.a	0.715	10451	0.6****	0.1
Kyrgyzstan	0.545	0.615	2009	8.4	6.2
Moldova	0.585	0.649	3319	5,6	0.4**
Russia	0.675	0.755	14461	5.5	0
Tajikistan	0.528	0.607	2119	2.5****	6.6**
Turkmenistan	n.a	0.686	7782	4*****	N/A
Ukraine	0.665	0.729	6428	4.1	0.1
Uzbekistan	0.611	0.641	3201	0.4	N/A
Former Soviet republics, Baltic States					
Estonia (euro)	0.716	0.835	17402	10.2	0.5
Latvia	0.693	0.805	14724	14.9	0.1
Lithuania	0.696	0.810	16858	17.8	0.2
Former USSR-allied nations, Eurozone-members					
Hungary	0.737	0.818	16088	10.9	0.2
Czech Rep.	0.788	0.865	22067	7.3	N/A
East Germ.*	0.895	0.905	35431	7	N/A
Former USSR-allied nations, EU members					
Bulgaria	0.698	0.771	11474	7	0
Poland	0.791	0.813	17776	10.1	0.1
Romania	0.687	0.781	11011	10.1	0.4
Slovakia	0.752	0.834	19696	14	0.1

Source: ILOSTAT ILO (2012), UNDP (2012), World Bank (2014), IMF (2013) World Economic Outlook Database. IMF (2013).
* Gesamtdeutschland, **2009, ***2003, ****defined as registered unemployed, *****three criteria: without work, currently seeking and available for work.
Public budget as % of GDP is defined as net borrowing/lending as % of GDP.

Table 4.2 Selected Economic Indicators

Country	GNI per capita, PPP (2012), US $	Public budget **** (% of GDP, 2011, IMF)	Income GINI	Government Expense as % of GDP
Former Soviet republics, non EU members				
Armenia	5385	-2.1	30.9	22.6
Azerbaijan	7911	-4.9	33.7	15.0
Belarus	12245	-0.6	27.2	26.3
Georgia	4235	-2.1	41.3	24.3
Kazakhstan	10451	-4.8	30.9	15.1
Kyrgyzstan	2009	-5.3	33.4	21.7
Moldova	3319	-2.6	38	32.8
Russia	14461	-0.7	42.3	25.2
Tajikistan	2119	-2.8	29.4	N/A
Turkmenistan	7782	1.8	40.8	N/A
Ukraine	6428	-4.2	27.5	38.2
Uzbekistan	3201	1.2	n.a	N/A
Former Soviet republics, Baltic States, EU members				
Estonia (euro)	17402	0.3	30.1	31.7
Latvia (euro)	14724	-1.4	35.7	30.6
Lithuania	16858	-2.9	37.6	34
Former USSR-allied nations, Eurozone-members				
Hungary	16088	-2.7	31.2	46
Czech Rep.	22067	-2.9	31	35.4
East Germ.*	35431	-0.4	28.3	29.5
Former USSR-allied nations, EU members				
Bulgaria	11474	-1.8	45.3	31.5
Poland	17776	-4.6	34.2	34.3
Romania	11011	-2.5	31.2	33.9
Slovakia	19696	-3.0	26	35.3

Source: ILOSTAT ILO, (2012), UNDP (2012), World Bank (2014), IMF (2013) World Economic Outlook Database. IMF (2013).
* Gesamtdeutschland.
Government expense is cash payments for operating activities of the government in providing goods and services. It includes compensation of employees (wages and salaries), interest and subsidies, grants, social benefits, and other expenses such as rent and dividends.

income amongst the CIS states. However, the considerable current deficit (8% of GDP) might push Ukraine toward closer trade integration with the EU. It is particularly noteworthy that the association agreement with the EU was suspended in November 2013, possibly under the influence of Russia, which is working towards tighter Eurasian trade integration.

The lowest levels of transition were achieved by Belarus, Turkmenistan and Azerbaijan, followed by Tajikistan (EBRD 2011). The European Bank for Reconstruction and Development (EBRD) report classifies indicators into the categories of privatization, price liberalization, trade and foreign exchange policies, and competition policy. All of these indicators relate to the structural changes as part of the process of privatization. It becomes clear yet again against which yard stick the achievements are measured—namely, structural transformation. In terms of privatization indicators, Turkmenistan has made little progress in large-scale privatization and Belarus and Azerbaijan lag behind the other post-communist republics with a substantially privatized share but an incomplete privatization process, which has been highlighted as announcements have been made to reduce the deficit through further privatization. Overall, the private sector share of GDP lies between 60% and 90% (EBRD 2007). For most former Soviet bloc countries, issues of governance remain difficult; the exceptions are Hungary and Poland with governance structures of industrialized societies, followed by Bulgaria, the Baltic states and the former Yugoslavia. All nations have achieved price liberalization, with some poorer indicators for Belarus, Turkmenistan and Uzbekistan. Trade and foreign exchange policies similar to those of industrialized nations have been implemented greatly, again with some lags in Belarus, Russia, Tajikistan, Turkmenistan and Uzbekistan. Competition still remains weak in all republics, with the exception of Hungary, the Baltic states and Slovakia.

It has become apparent that the structural transformation has been the fastest in those nations that acceded to or propose accession to the EU, as they adopted already existing structures. The EBRD transition report's findings on privatization can be supplemented further with the results from Estrin *et al.* (2009), who identified that not only the scale of privatization matters, but also the type of new owner. In fact, privatization to foreign owners has been claimed to have had positive or insignificant effects in microeconomic terms, such as efficiency, productivity, profits and revenue. In contrast, privatization to domestic owners only has had a negative or insignificant effect. This has been accredited to the degree of firm restructuring dependent on the type of owners. Djankov and Murrell (2002) found that foreign ownership led to faster restructuring. It can be suggested that a time-lag exists and that inertia and behavioural lags contribute to the less successful performance. The results show that weak institutions result in relatively poorer economic performance. The current data suggest that post-Soviet bloc nations which adopted the framework of the EU swiftly acceded to comparatively better economic performance. However, it remains to be seen whether this trend will continue in the long term. Behavioural considerations play a large part in this.

INSTITUTIONS AND BEHAVIOUR

The fundamental reform rationale lies at the heart of institutional economics. A changed framework and the regulations therewith will cause behavioural changes soon to follow suit. Shock therapy set all its belief in the mechanism of incentives, motivation and rational behaviour. For instance, once the consumer identified that s/he could choose, s/he would simply turn into a marginal rate of substitution conscious economic agent, amongst other basic behavioural adjustments.

Privatizing SOEs implied substantial behavioural adjustments. SOEs' decision-making structure was usually organized through worker councils. The centralized privatization strategy of trade sales, in particular, went alongside a removal of decision-making authority from councils and placed the authority in the hands of new owners. A worker ownership structure was rejected, essentially stripping the worker or resident of the previously given right of corporate governance unless they were allocated a stake or were successful in winning such during auctions or sales. In the case of privatization through auction, asymmetric attitude situations must not be neglected. It is obvious that it would be more difficult for an entrepreneurial citizen successfully to secure the finances for a purchase than any Western corporate counterpart.

These sociological and behavioural asymmetries were largely ignored by the big-bang approach which worked to the disadvantage of Eastern European citizens. In East Germany, it soon became apparent that former state property concentrated in the hands of West German companies and families (Spangenberg 1998). The fast privatization approach relied heavily on the belief that outside ownership would maximize performance, which was used against a direct allocation of ownership rights to workers. Another argument used against direct worker ownership was the equity argument. It would be unjust to disadvantage a worker of an unsuccessful firm with an assigned share of the company in which s/he coincidentally worked, while a worker in a successful firm would be assigned a share value that was higher. However, to use this argument and simply deprive the worker of ownership is ethically questionable.

EVALUATION

The design of the transformation of the CEE and CIS can be evaluated empirically and conceptually. On the one hand, the empirical evidence shows that more than 20 years later, most of the transition countries have not yet achieved economic situations comparable to industrialized nations. On the conceptual level, the non-gradual institutional approach must be assessed.[2] It appears that a desire for political reform and material freedom in Central and Eastern Europe was hijacked by those in support of the Washington Consensus, and the ransom paid was the self-governance of the economic reform process. On the side of the opponents of the root-and-branch approach sits Burke's critical approach to a top-down reform in the sense that reform seeks the gradual improvement of the state. This concept of preservation and improvement and the verdict of 'everything else is vulgar in the conception' and 'perilous in the execution' (Burke 1790: 231) sits alongside the Austrian rejection of an institutional-fundamentalist approach. Popper's gradual or piecemeal approach relies on engagement with people rather than a radical approach that would disengage in a dictatorial style. The Hayekian focus on decentralization is based on informational sub-optimality and knowledge inefficiencies (Popper 1973; Hayek 1945, 1979). These notions of a critique of utopian social engineering were ignored and instead a shock therapy-engineered capitalist structure was pursued. The therapy used the drugs sold by the Washington Consensus.

In the case of the Eastern European transformation, the pre-existent norms were replaced by a void of economic policy. Instead, political objectives such as democracy, free speech and free markets were adopted as new aims. However, what these new objectives did not specify were the desirable parameters. What degree of competition was acceptable? What kind of distribution of income and wealth should follow? The consensus was based on the notional superiority of the capitalist outcome over the planned one. Even the planning of economic policy to achieve the desirable outcome appeared to involve too much planning. Instead, a neo-classical approach was adopted, one that followed the rationale of the root-and-branch approach of the Washington Consensus. Not only did this consensus ignore the institutional rigidities, it also ignored the psychological factors, which Tinbergen (1952) had already identified 50 years prior to the transformation and called personal inertia. Personal inertia existed due to asymmetrical information and the inherent fear of uncertainty. As a result, the transformation in its non-gradual form required the exact design of the institutional change by Western academics. The focus was a swift solution to the dire economic situations in Eastern European countries after the fall of the wall. This solution focused on a political solution more than a reform solution designed for and specified by the individual nation. The political solution encompassed the reshaping of the economic system and hence followed the top-down approach of shock therapy.

The end result is a regional separation by EU membership: those that are EU members achieve higher material living standards, whilst those that are not members have comparatively lower material living standards, with the exception of Russia! Amongst the CIS states, four states remain low middle-income countries (Kyrgyzstan, Moldova, Tajikistan and Uzbekistan); all other states are high middle-income countries, with the exception of Russia with a high GNI per capita of $14,461. All nations that joined the EU achieved high-income country status except for Bulgaria and Romania, which are both at upper middle-income level. The devastating result is the lag of the majority of former Soviet republics: the orphans of the late USSR. Their fortune depends largely on the future of the Eurasian Economic Union in 2015, strongly pushed for by Russia. This economic union is geo-strategically intended, with possible expansions into Turkey, India, Syria and other states of the Middle

East. Ukraine's position will be crucial; the recent U-turn by the EU towards the Eurasian Economic Union might be the result of Russian support (expected bailout in early 2014). It seems unlikely that Ukraine will now follow the example of Uzbekistan, which suspended its membership in the Eurasian Economic Union in response to security support from the USA in 2008. What has become clear, is that the CIS states did not gain independence but became puppets held by two strings, pulled in opposite directions. The Central Asian Economic Organization might be the only alternative: a free trade agreement with no Russian involvement.

CONCLUSIONS

The societal change of the former Soviet bloc was largely masterminded by the Washington Consensus. Eastern Europe was structurally adjusted to fit into the institutional requirements of the EU. The transformation was more successful for some states than for others. The tragedy of the transformation was the lack of a gradual approach, which would have offered the possibility of reaction to current outcomes, initiating debate and reform. This can lead to the establishment of better institutions. Large-scale privatization and price liberalization allowed a large concentration of wealth in Russia, Georgia and Turkmenistan, in particular. Institutional rigidity is mostly presented through the concentration of power and corruption, and pursuit of individual self-interest and a concentration on short-term goals. Institutional rigidity will fail any system and produces sub-optimal welfare outcomes. Russia stands today as the nation with the highest inequality of wealth distribution, with 35% of Russia's wealth owned by 110 people. The norms that were adhered to in the shock approach are those of political liberalization, autonomy and individualism; they clearly ignored the potential negative externalities of market systems. As a result, oligopolistic markets, ownership concentration and uneven income distribution appear to be among the dominant performance outcomes. Economic liberalization without institutional restraints paved the way at high social costs. It follows from an institutional conceptualization that a gradual reform process could prevent such sub-optimal outcomes with inherently high social transformation costs. In disagreement with Polterovich (2012), who proposes that any reformer should identify the final desirable institution when designing interim institutions, it has here been argued that no such grand design should be possible. The construction of an efficient sequence of interim institutions is fallacious—the concept ignores the dynamic nature of human and economic behaviour. Any society at a given point might be able to construct a set of values and derive norms of behaviour as rules. As long as these values remain unchanged and the decentralized dispersion of information is given, the construction of efficient institutions should be possible. An institution is considered efficient if it reinforces behaviour that is considered to be just and good and does not allow behaviour that is unjust and bad. Instead, anything goes and as long as the market allows the behaviour, it is acceptable. The role of the state is circumcised and the role of the market enforced. The reform process ignored questions of immediate justifiability of inequality. Power concentration in the former Soviet bloc, in particular the CIS, is a result of the dramatic failure to address behavioural reform.[3] The designer of institutional reforms must scrutinize the institutional parameters against the 'behavioural norms (that are) standard in society' (Sen 2010: 78).

Shock therapy is an institutionally fundamentalist disaster, even more so from a political-economic perspective and a notion of justice. Institutions were not chosen to promote justice in post-communist states, but instead were introduced as institutions that themselves were considered to be manifestations of justice. The outcomes of the transformation are a result of the Washington Consensus. The consensus assumed a transformation model that was based on the notion that the behaviour of economic and political agents could be predicted. This neo-classical model ignored the fallibility of systems which resulted in more-or-less authoritarian regimes, wealth concentration, corruption and imperfect market structures. It is possible to make assumptions about the performance of different institutions; however, none of these predictions is infallible. Human behaviour cannot be predicted in a scientific way. This being so, there cannot be 'a just institution'. Some institutions might appear to promote greater justice than others, but no ultimate just institution exists. It has become apparent that institutions must be open to adjustment. A market can be assumed to lead to Pareto-efficient welfare outcomes, but it does not have to. Institutional fundamentalism must be rejected; instead, the institutional design should conceive every institutional creation as an intermittent feature which deserves continuous scrutiny against the values of society. Values and norms vary in time and space and are often unique to particular societies. Hence, there is no ultimate institutional framework that possesses superiority.

NOTES

1 Russian Prime Minister Dmitry Medvedev was chairman of the board of directors of Gazprom until 2008.
2 Please see Polterovich (2012) for further thought on the development of a theory of reform.
3 If one accepts that people do not voluntarily act for the common good, social ethics have to be given scope for development. Sen (2010) highlights the interrelationship of institutions and behavioural forms in their relevance to modern economics and political philosophy.

REFERENCES

Bergson, A. (1992) 'Communist Economic Efficiency Revisited', *The American Economic Review* 82(2): 27–30.
Burke, E. (1790) *Reflections on the Revolution in France*, London: Dodsley.

Cameron, R. and Neal, L. (2003) *A Concise Economic History of the World*, New York: Oxford University Press.
CIA (2012) *The World Factbook*, Washington, DC: CIA.
Denisova, I. (2012) *Income Distribution and Poverty in Russia*, OECD Social Employment and Migration Working Papers, No. 132, Paris: OECD Publishing.
Djankov, S. and Murrell, P. (2002) 'Enterprise Restructuring in Transition: A Quantitative Survey', *Journal of Economic Literature* 40(3): 739–92.
EBRD (2007) *Transition Report 2007: People in Transition*, London: European Bank for Reconstruction and Development.
——(2011) *Transition Report 2011: Crisis and Transition. The People's Perspective*, London: European Bank for Reconstruction and Development.
Eckstein, A. (ed.) (1971) *Comparison of Economic Systems: Theoretical and Methodological Approaches*, Berkeley: University of California Press.
Eggertsson, T. (2004) *Economic Behaviour and Institutions*, Cambridge: Cambridge University Press.
Estrin, S., Hanousek, J., Kocenka, E. and Svejnar, J. (2009) 'The Effects of Privatisation and Ownership in Transition Economies', *Journal of Economic Literature* 47(2): 699–728.
Fouskas, V. and Gökay, B. (2012) *The Fall of the US Empire, Global Fault-Lines and Shifting Imperial Orders*, London: Pluto Press.
Gowan, P. (1995) 'Neo-liberal Theory and Practice for Eastern Europe', *New Left Review* 213: 1.
——(1999) *The Global Gamble*, London: Verso.
——(2010) *A Calculus of Power*, London: Verso.
Hayek, F.A. (1935) *Collectivist Economic Planning*, London: Routledge.
——(1945) 'The Use of Knowledge in Society', *American Economic Review* 25(4): 519–30.
——(1979) *Law, Legislation and Liberty Vol. 3: The Political Order of a Free People*, Chicago, IL: University of Chicago Press.
ILO (International Labour Organization) (2012) 'ILOStats: Statistics and Databases', ilo.org/global/statistics-and-databases/lang-en/index.htm.
IMF (International Monetary Fund) (2013) *World Economic Outlook Database*, www.imf.org/external/pubs/ft/weo/2013/02/weodata/index.aspx.
Koopmans, T.C. and Montias, J.M. (1973) 'On the Description and Comparison of Economic Systems', in A. Eckstein (ed.) *Comparison of Economic Systems: Theoretical and Methodological Approaches*, Berkeley: University of California Press.
Kornai, J. (1990) *The Road to a Free Economy. Shifting from a Socialist System: The Example of Hungary*, New York: W.W. Norton.
Krugman, P. (1991a) *Geography and Trade*, Cambridge, MA: MIT Press.
——(1991b) 'Increasing Returns and Economic Geography', *Journal of Political Economy* 99: 483–99.
Lipton, D. and Sachs, J. (1990) 'Privatisation in Eastern Europe: The Case of Poland', *Brookings Papers on Economic Activity* 2: 293–341.
Myrdal, D. (1969) *Objectivity in Social Research*, London: Pantheon Books.
North, D. (1990) *Institutions, Institutional Change and Economic Performance*, Cambridge: Cambridge University Press.
OECD (2003) *Privatising State-Owned Enterprises. An Overview of Policies and Practices in OECD Countries*, Paris: OECD.
Pineda, J. and Rodriguez, F. (2006) 'The Political Economy of Investment in Human Capital', *Economics of Governance* 7(2): 167–93.

Polterovich, V. (2012) *Institutional Reform Design*, paper presented at ESHET Conference, St Petersburg, 19 May.
Popper, K. (1973) *The Open Society and its Enemies*, London: Routledge & Kegan Paul.
Sachs, J. (1993) *Poland's Jump to the Market Economy*, Cambridge, MA: MIT Press.
——(2005) *The End of Poverty*, London: Penguin,
Sen, A. (2010) *The Idea of Justice*, London: Allen Lane.
Spangenberg, S. (1998) *The Institutionalised Transformation of the East German Economy*, Heidelberg: Physica Verlag.
Tinbergen, J. (1952) *On the Theory of Economic Policy*, Amsterdam: North-Holland.
UNDP (2010) *Human Development Report*, Washington, DC: World Bank.
——(2012) *Human Development Indicators*, Washington, DC: UNDP.
Weber, M. (1947) *The Theory of Social and Economic Organisation*, London: Free Press.
Williamson, J. (1990) 'What Washington Means by Policy Reform', in J. Williamson, *Latin American Adjustment: How Much has Happened?*, Washington, DC: Peterson Institute for International Economics.
World Bank (2012) *Data and Statistics*, such as: Krygyz Republic, web.worldbank.org/WBSITE/EXTERNAL/COUNTRIES/ECAEXT/KYRGYZEXTN/0,menuPK:3057 86~pagePK:141132~piPK:141109~theSitePK:305761,00.html.
——(2014) *Data and Statistics*, web.worldbank.org.

Revisiting the 1992–93 EMS crisis in the context of international political economy

DIMITRIS P. SOTIROPOULOS

INTRODUCTION

This chapter revisits the sequence of events that led to the well-known 1992–93 crisis in the Exchange Rate Mechanism (ERM) of the European Monetary System (EMS) in the context of international political economy. The EMS was the forerunner of the eurozone and the crisis to some extent laid the foundation for the emergence of the subsequent institutional European framework. From this point of view, the 1992–93 crisis of the EMS was part of the long European movement towards economic and political integration.

In the early 1990s the EMS was surrounded by optimism and widely considered to be 'the most ambitious experiment in the international monetary and exchange rate cooperation of the post-Bretton Woods era' (Buiter *et al.* 1998: 1). Its crisis in 1992–93, which came just two years before the Mexican currency and financial crisis, led to a series of academic and political debates followed by numerous research outputs. These discussions were subsequently sent into oblivion as part of the unpleasant history of the European Monetary Union (EMU) project, and only revisited in order to draw lessons for the feasibility of a fixed exchange rate system in East Asia.

This chapter reconsiders the 1992–93 crisis, trying to make a general point about the workings of monetary unions and contemporary financial markets. It must not be seen as an ex-post contribution to a lifeless debate, but as an approach from the perspective of international political economy to put forward a proper reasoning for the understanding of recent economic trends in capitalism. The lessons to be drawn could also help enhance an understanding of the contemporary crisis of the eurozone.

The second section briefly revisits the historical background that led to the inauguration of the EMS in the late 1970s. The third section describes its economic characteristics. The analysis does not recycle mainstream economic ideas but puts forward economic reasoning emerging from the standpoint of political economy. The fourth section touches upon the workings of modern finance, focusing on the exchange rate market. In contemporary financial markets, foreign exchange is widely viewed and treated as a distinct class of asset; it will also become clear that the scope of a monetary union is necessarily based on the unrestricted and uncontrolled operation of the exchange rate market. Section five revisits the density of events that built up to the wide-range speculative attacks in September 1992. It also explains the reasons that necessitated the abandonment of the 'hard' version of the EMS. Section six attempts to draw a general lesson, useful not only for interpretation of the past but also for analysis of the most recent developments in the European Union (EU).

THE HISTORICAL BACKGROUND OF THE EMS

The EMS was an intermediate point in the long route towards European integration. This route was by no means smooth, but full of contradictions, tensions and crises. The idea of a common market with exchange rate stability has always been a major priority and concern.

The Treaty of Rome in 1958 created the European Economic Community (EEC), with the basic aim of gradually moving towards a common market for goods, services, labour and capital. During this period, exchange rate stability was secured by the Bretton Woods regime (until its demise in the early 1970s).[1] Nevertheless, the tensions in this regime in the late 1960s threatened the coherence of the international monetary system and led the EEC to hold a summit in The Hague in December 1969. This summit acknowledged once more that a monetary union was the major long-term goal of the Community. The German and French governments firmly supported this plan, the terms of which were made more concrete in the so-called Werner Report, which put forward a three-stage approach to monetary union:

> The first stage would foster policy coordination; in the second stage, realignments of exchange rates would require agreements among the countries participating in the plan; in the third stage, a unique central bank, similar to the Federal Reserve System in the United States, would take control over European monetary policy.
>
> (Buiter *et al.* 1998: 22)

Monetary integration was also seen as a 'vehicle for pushing forward political integration' (Eichengreen 2000: 4). The geopolitical aspect of European unification as a process that might challenge US neo-imperial hegemony must not be underestimated; this was a target to be pursued by insisting on agendas for strong economic performance and co-ordination. However, the interplay between economy and politics was dialectical: the economic process of unification was always based less on strict economic reasoning and more on straightforward political determination. Economic integration and convergence were in most cases conceived not as prerequisites but as *results* of European-wide institutional reforms. In other words, the institutional project of European unification must be seen as one of guiding, disciplining and shaping economic behaviour in line with particular economic strategies (which favour austerity-type policy regimes). We shall come back to this issue in the next section.

The *stagflation* (high inflation accompanied by stagnation) of 1970s and the unsuccessful attempts to establish a stable exchange rate system brought the European Monetary System to life at the end of 1978. After a short period of negotiation, this plan attained Community-wide consensus. In brief, there were three main features.[2] First, according to the European Exchange Rate Mechanism, each EEC country committed itself to limit the fluctuation of its exchange rate within a band of ±2.25% around its bilateral central parity against other members of the ERM (the corresponding limit was ±6% for Italy, as well as for Spain, the UK and Portugal, which did not initially join the ERM). Second, a new European Currency Unit (ECU)—a weighted basket of the ERM currencies due to each country's economic importance—was the new means of settlement among EEC central banks. Third, extensive financing mechanisms were created to ensure that each member state had the necessary resources to meet temporary difficulties in financing balance of payments deficits and in defending bilateral exchange rate parities. For this purpose 'twenty percent of the member countries' gold reserves had to be deposited with the European Monetary Cooperation Fund (EMCF) in exchange for the equivalent value in ECUs' (Volz 2006: 6). Moreover, 'three kinds of credit facilities were created: the very short-term facility (VSTF), the short-term monetary support (STMS), and the medium-term financial assistance (MTFA)' (ibid.).

The start was uneasy, with a great deal of pessimism about the fate of the newly established exchange rate system. Until the first half of the 1980s cumulative realignments exceeded the narrow band limits, allowing inflation differentials to reproduce themselves across the EEC. In addition, the existence of controls in the movement of capital relaxed to some extent the discipline of fiscal austerity and anti-inflation priority targets. The 'new' or 'hard' EMS that was inaugurated with the Single European Act (SEA) of 1986 attempted to enhance the credibility and the disciplining character of the system to anti-inflationary policies by removing capital controls and creating a single market for financial services until 1990. Financing facilities supporting the role of European central banks were further enhanced by the Basle-Nyborg Agreement in 1987. 'This so-called New EMS was set for a relatively long period of European exchange rate stability. No realignment took place between January 1987 and September 1992 ... Meanwhile, as the idea of complementarity between a single market and a single money received widespread political (but little analytical) support, proposals for a European Monetary Union were back on the European agenda' (Buiter *et al.* 1998: 29).

This mini success of the 'hard' version of the EMS rekindled the three-stage approach to monetary union of the Werner Report. Jacques Delors chaired the committee of representatives from European Community (EC) central banks which set forth the well-known 'Delors Report'. The latter suggested that the decision to enter the ongoing union process should be regarded as a commitment to pursue the goal of a final monetary union. This report was adopted as an official blueprint by the Madrid Summit in June 1989. The summit launched a political process that led two years later to the Maastricht Treaty in December 1991.[3]

As we shall see below, this European optimism was curtailed but not destroyed by the EMS crisis of 1991–93, which revealed the weakness of the exchange rate system without undermining either the final target of the common currency or the priority to fiscal austerity and price stability. It prepared, thus, stage III of the EMU, which began in 1999 by irrevocably locking exchange rate parities and making for the introduction of the euro.

THE ECONOMIC CHARACTER OF THE EMS: A GENERAL OUTLINE

The idea of a European monetary union gained solid ground at least from the late 1960s in the wake of the declining Bretton Woods regime and marked all subsequent institutional developments that led at the end of the 1980s to the Delors Report.

There is no doubt that the Optimum Currency Area (OCA) paradigm[4] was at the heart of the discussions about a European monetary union. The roots of this approach lie in the neo-classical conception of money. This, and all innovations attached to it, are to be understood as genuine (private sector) inventions that reduce transaction costs faced by market participants. This simple idea 'has led numerous economists to construct models showing how the private sector could evolve towards a monetary economy as a function of a search for cost minimisation procedures within a private sector system, within which government does not necessarily enter at all' (Goodhart 1998: 410). The OCA can be seen as a natural extension of this analytical approach into the spatial dimension. The gradual replacement of national currencies by a common one would accordingly minimize a class of transaction and adjustment costs.

In the above context, the process of European unification was more or less explicitly dominated from its very beginning by the pronounced *aversion to exchange rate fluctuations.*

> One after the other, the political initiatives undertaken to strengthen the process of European integration have led to attempts to lock European currencies into systems and mechanisms that limit the flexibility of their conversion rates. Even during periods when the tide of European integration was at a low ebb, the idea and ideal of exchange rate stability never completely disappeared from the institutional architecture of the Community.
>
> (Buiter *et al.* 1998: 19)

From this point of view, the long history of European unification can be summarized as the 'quest for exchange rate stability in Europe' (this widely used expression was initially coined by Giavazzi and Giovannini 1989). Nevertheless, this quest is the epiphenomenon of another long-term quest for low inflation (competitiveness) and for fiscal discipline linked to policies of austerity. This point was implicitly made at an early stage by Fischer (1987): participation in the ERM was welcomed as an institutional mechanism for 'importing' disinflation and 'borrowing credibility' from the Bundesbank through the stability of the exchange rate.

To understand the nature of the argument, let us suppose that there are two kinds of economies: a peripheral one which is inflation prone and less competitive in the global market, and a central one which is more competitive and able to control inflation to relatively low levels. Why do they come to a monetary union or to a pegged exchange rate system? A first answer is given by the following passage, which reflects the mainstream line of reasoning:

> An asymmetric system where the low-inflation country sets the pace of system-wide monetary policy was suddenly seen as an opportunity for monetary and fiscal authorities in inflation-prone countries to make an explicit and publicly verifiable commitment to contain and overcome the forces making for domestic inflation (high monetary growth fed ultimately by fiscal deficits) and loss of international competitiveness.
>
> (Buiter *et al.* 1998: 27)

In the context of political economy we can reconsider this argument as follows. Within an internal conflicting social formation there are classes that favour expansionary economic policies. These policies boost domestic demand, making room for wage increases and welfare state services (with both these tendencies likely to create inflationary pressures). For sustainable economic development, the burden of these policies falls necessarily on capital. Hence, capitalists would be unhappy with expansionary policies and they will demand price stability and fiscal discipline—an austerity mix of economic policies. The above passage indicates that for a peripheral economy, joining the fixed exchange rate system will secure fiscal discipline and competiveness. It will expose domestic firms to international competition, putting the adjustment pressures solely upon labour. It will also undermine the welfare character of the state. It will therefore embed a form of discipline on domestic labour with exploitation strategies favourable to capital.[5] In other words, open economic borders and exchange rate pegs create an economic milieu that benefits the interests of capital. This is the basic incentive for the ruling classes of a peripheral economy to join a fixed exchange rate system similar to the ERM. For a competitive economy of the centre, the reasoning is pretty much the same. Now the pegged exchange rate system ensures not only discipline to austerity and competitiveness but also exporting markets purged of protectionist biases.

There is one issue in the above mechanism which must not go unnoticed. *The austerity character of the whole setting depends on the insistence of the core on deflationary policies.* Otherwise there will be some room for expansionary policies both in the centre and in the periphery. The system has a heart (core) and this heart must not run contrary to the rules of the game. Let us see why.

During the 1980s the German mark was considered the key currency in the EMS, and Germany itself as the most important core economy (with a 'strong' currency and a tendency to generate trade surpluses). On the other hand, inflation-prone Italy could be regarded as an example of a peripheral economy (a 'weak' currency with a tendency for trade deficits). In this setting, the Italian lira would have a clear tendency to depreciate against the German mark. What must be the nature of the response in order to defend the exchange rate parity?

A symmetric response (by both Italy and Germany) as a rule would tend to negate the austerity character of the monetary union. The low inflation core economy would have to embark upon domestic expansionary policies (a reduction in interest rates), not to mention the necessary interventions in the exchange market to counteract the revaluation of its currency. However, this type of reaction would undermine the need for austerity in the periphery. From the viewpoint of the capitalist classes in both countries, this would not be an attractive scenario. As we shall see below, this reluctance will make the symbiosis vulnerable to unexpected events, but this is pretty much the cost to be paid for securing the long-term interests of capital. The character of the adjustment must thus be asymmetric (Italy's sole responsibility is to defend its currency peg) with an option of symmetric intervention in the extreme case of financial distress. Otherwise, the idea of the monetary union will not be an appealing strategy for ruling classes (of course, this is the description of the general mechanism, which cannot capture other contradictions that may arise in the event of a crisis).

THE WORKINGS OF FINANCIAL MARKETS

Uncovered interest parity and cross-border capital flows

Speculative attacks indeed played a crucial role in the crisis of 1992–93. We must therefore take into consideration the workings of modern finance and the way it fitted into these events. This section will not exhaust the issue. It will just put forward some basic ideas which will be part of the interpretation in section five.

The so-called uncovered interest parity (UIP) condition from international finance is the benchmark model. The idea is simple. In an economic region with fixed exchange rate parities, similar assets with the same maturity must have similar yields regardless of the currency denomination. Therefore, interest rate differentials on similar assets cannot be consistent with the assumption of equal yields unless there is an expected currency depreciation over the period.[6] The following equation can help us clarify the point:

$$r - r_f = S^e - S$$

r is the domestic interest rate for a single country (say Italy), while r_f is the interest rate on a similar asset in another (foreign) country of the union (say

Germany). S is the logarithm of the current exchange rate of the domestic currency in terms of the foreign currency (e.g. the price of lira in units of marks), and S^e the logarithm of the expected price of the same exchange rate at the time of asset maturity. Note that the expected price is usually reflected in the forward and futures exchange rate market, but we shall leave derivative markets out of our exposition. The message of the above equation is straightforward: interest rate differentials ($r - r_f$) measure the expected (probable) shift in the exchange market (appreciation or depreciation: $S^e - S = 0$). If market participants believe in the pegged exchange rate between the two countries, then $S^e - S = 0$ means that there would be a tendency towards negligible interest rate differentials: $r - r_f = 0$. Otherwise, a relative higher domestic interest rate ($r - r_f > 0$) is a signal of an expected exchange rate depreciation in the near future ($S^e - S > 0$).[7]

We can understand this as follows. If the interest rate in Italy is 15% and in Germany is 10%, then the Italian lira is expected to depreciate against the German mark by approximately 5%. Put simply, as the Italian lira depreciates, higher domestic yields will not make a stronger investment case there, as opposed to Germany. However, uncovered interest parity has also another implication when read inversely: if market participants expect a depreciation of the domestic currency in the near future, an exchange rate peg can only be sustained by a rise in the domestic interest rate r (or, alternatively, by a fall in r_f; nevertheless, this interest rate is out of the control of domestic authorities). In practice this presupposes a policy mix of higher short-term borrowing costs, fiscal austerity and intervention in the foreign exchange market (the maintenance of a proper amount of international reserves and credit lines by resorting to the VSTF). It also presupposes a loss in the control of monetary policy, since it is subsumed to the exchange rate peg. This result is in line with the general rule of international macroeconomics, the so-called 'policy trilemma'.[8] According to the trilemma, for an economy that allows free movement of capital across its borders, exchange rate stability can only be satisfied if monetary policy is the 'variable' to be adjusted. Practically, this implies loss of traditional monetary policy tools.

The gradual liberalization of European financial markets increased cross-border capital flows. Economies less competitive than Germany, but with higher growth prospects and interest rate yields, like Spain and Italy, experienced significant capital inflows. There were two factors promoting this development (or alternatively, two sets of financial strategies[9]). The first is *portfolio diversification*. International investors and hedge fund managers could include assets in their portfolios from a wider range of choices encompassing now the countries of the so-called European 'periphery'. The second factor concerns the profit opportunities from intra-ERM yield differentials in the context of fixed exchange rates. In plain terms, investors could exploit different interest rates between EMS participating economies, betting on the stability of exchange rates. While there are many different ways to implement a bet like that, we can understand it as a simple case of *carry trade*. This is a widely established investment practice in contemporary exchange rate markets, which involves borrowing in a currency with a low interest rate and simultaneously investing in another currency with a higher interest rate.[10] If market participants anticipate a credible ERM, then the condition of uncovered interest parity does not hold: interest rate differentials can persist in the absence of exchange rate realignment. An investment in Italian assets will have higher expected returns than a similar investment in German assets, and this difference will not be offset by exchange rate depreciation, since the economies of the EMS are determined to defend the pegged ERM system.

The functioning of financial markets is, in reality, much more complex, but the above-mentioned strategies capture fundamental tendencies that have played important roles in the frame of the ERM.

On the trade off between 'flexibility' and 'credibility'

From the viewpoint of a country with a weak currency, defending the exchange rate peg is theoretically possible but it comes with a social cost, since it is conditioned upon a policy mix of austerity and higher borrowing costs (for both private and public sectors). Within limits, this policy mix is welcomed by capitalist power since it disciplines state governance in line with neo-liberal strategy: this was, after all, the fundamental incentive for European economies to join the ERM. Nevertheless, the safe 'limits' of austerity can easily be challenged by unpredicted events due either to internal class conflicts or to international conjuncture. Mainstream economic theory categorizes these two sets of unexpected events as 'shocks' external to the economic system in order to model them statistically. This is a rather misleading definition: it mystifies the substantive economic and political roots of the processes.

There is a certain threshold beyond which a pegged exchange rate loses its 'credibility' because defending it comes at too high a cost. For instance, a sustained rise in domestic interest rates to defend a weak currency can threaten the viability of the banking sector and can easily dampen aggregate demand and investment activity.[11] This development in its own right may easily derange public finances. At the same time, a speculative attack in the absence of capital controls can only be met by resorting to significant amounts of foreign exchange. In practice, this is hardly ever the case. However, even under the ERM facility that enabled inter-central bank credit lines, the strong currency country would be unwilling to provide unlimited credit since this would accordingly cause, first, losses for the central bank in the face of a possible exchange rate realignment, and second, a probable liquidity inflow to the economy which would endanger the anti-inflationary policy framework.

In other words, there is a certain trade off between the credibility of a fixed exchange rate system and the inherent sustainability or flexibility to deal with unfavourable developments. The commitment to defend the peg therefore cannot be considered unconditional. In this sense, the policy costs it imposes both upon the centre and the periphery of the EMS is the necessary condition for a possible speculative attack: speculators, being aware of the 'costs', can bet against the peg.

This is why the ERM left some room for adjustment by implicit escape clauses. In fact, it was a fixed exchange rate system with a limited option to realign. The flexibility of the peg is well verified by the data. For instance, in the period between 1979 and 1985, the cumulative devaluation of the Italian lira and the French franc against the ECU turned out to be 20.25% and 9.25%, respectively, while the cumulative revaluation of the German mark against the ECU was 22.25%.[12] The real question involved is how to make room for possible realignments without sacrificing the credibility of the system along with its disciplining austerity character. In practice, this is a difficult equation to be solved. A government must devalue without signalling to the market that inflationary anti-austerity policies have been adopted, but this is not an easy and manageable target to hit.

Strategic sequential trading in the context of political economy

Financial markets, well aware of the above trade off, can set up speculative attacks. A mechanism was suggested above for betting on the credibility of a pegged exchange rate mechanism, but what if private sector investors anticipate a devaluation or loss of faith in the credibility of the system?

Let us take the example of the British pound sterling, which joined the ERM in October 1990.[13] The UK had inflation three times higher than Germany, much higher interest rates, double-digit public deficits and, most importantly, a financial system full of home mortgages, the great majority of which had floating rather than fixed interest rate conditions. It is obvious that interest rate differentials suggested a forthcoming devaluation of sterling. Anticipating some realignment in the near future, exchange market speculators borrowed in British sterling and invested in German marks or other strong currencies. This line of transactions is identical to selling the weak currency (sterling) and buying the strong one (Deutsche mark) in order to take advantage of the coming devaluation in the short term. As we mentioned above, this profit-seeking incentive could only be counteracted if the British government had decided to raise short-term interest rates. Given the economic data, the UK government's position was vulnerable because the economic and social costs of defending the peg would be extremely high. Higher short-term interest rates could put the economy into a recession, threaten the stability of the banking sector, increase the debt burden to households, cause a deterioration in public finances and curtail demand. Private sector investors were well aware of all these events and came up with proper strategies (selling the pound) to take advantage of the government's predictable behaviour.

This is exactly what happened after the summer of 1992. On 16 September, so-called 'Black Wednesday', a group of speculators, on the basis of an evaluation of the state of the UK economy and a series of other events in the context of the EMS which had wounded its credibility, launched an (uncoordinated) attack to force the withdrawal of British sterling from the ERM. They anticipated that the British government would not be in a position to defend the peg. The route of events is fairly well known:

> in the morning the Bank of England raised the minimum lending rate from 10 percent to 12 percent. A few hours later, a new increase to 15 percent was announced but never implemented. Sterling closed below its ERM floor in London. In the evening, the Bank of England announced the 'temporary' withdrawal of sterling from the ERM. A few days later, on September 19, return to ERM was postponed indefinitely.
> (Buiter *et al.* 1998: 59)

The day after the crash, the Bank of England brought its interest rate back to 10%, validating ex post the expectations of the market and justifying the speculative attacks.

This strategic sequential type of trading is just one example of how financial markets work. Investors try to anticipate the pattern of events several steps ahead, forcing the counterparty to commit an 'error'. Their move hinges upon the analysis of the economic and political conjuncture and of relevant past moves and behaviour. It looks like a game of chess.[14] Nevertheless, *this strategic game was crucial for the organization of the EMS as a system that disciplines government policies to neo-liberal austerity.* It may sound contradictory, but without the threat of 'speculative' attacks, the rules of the EMS could not be implemented and reproduced. In fact, markets take into account the likelihood of a negative development (and try to make a profit out of it), and impose the terms on governments for dealing with it. Governments, being aware of the workings of the markets, organize their policies in a precautionary manner in order to avoid these negative attacks. Governments address the dilemma of 'austerity or economic instability' to the society and win consensus to the austerity agenda. This means that market attacks in line with the interests of capital are by and large a fundamental mechanism for organizing consensus on austerity.

The above setting is not, of course, shielded against crises and unfavourable developments, but even crises are extreme moments within the very same disciplining mechanism. What followed the September crisis of the ERM was not the break-up of the ERM system but the quest for a tighter fiscal policy in the economies affected by the exchange rate crisis. Very illustrative is the case of Italy, which experienced an attack similar to the one against sterling. The first serious tensions for the Italian lira appeared in the summer of 1992. The ongoing outflow of reserves reinforced consensus to further austerity and wage reductions. At the end of July, 'employers, unions, and the government signed a historic agreement on income policy, disinflation, and labour costs, which reformed the system of industrial relations, abolishing what was left of the *scala mobile*, that is, the automatic indexation of wages and salaries' (Buiter *et al.* 1998: 55). After the severe attacks of September, Italy took further steps 'toward an ambitious project of economic reform, which hinged on containment of the budget deficit, privatizations of state enterprise, and stabilization of lira. The emergency budget for 1993, approved by the cabinet on October 1 and presented to the Parliament three weeks later, involved spending cuts (including a freezing of salaries in the public sector) and tax increases for 1993 amounting to 5.8 percent of GDP' (ibid.: 61). From this point of view, financial markets do not cause states to fade away but their policies are in line with a particular form of state governance: the one which tends to dissolve the welfare aspect of it.

A (RE)INTERPRETATION OF THE EVENTS

This section will revisit some of the events that contributed to the 1992–93 crisis of the ERM in light of the above discussion.[15] Initially it will focus on the developments that made the ERM vulnerable as a system. Then it will describe the speculative attacks, their results, and how the 'hard' version of the ERM came practically to an end.

Towards the summer of 1992–93

German reunification was a major event in the history of the 20th century. It also proved a painful economic event not only for the German economy but also for the stability of the ERM as a system. For the newly unified German economy there were two striking economic results: a boost in domestic demand and in inflationary pressures. Both were unusual for the western part of the country and both tended to derange the export-orientated structure of the economy. While the first reaction of the Bundesbank was rather cautious and completely subordinated to the political priorities of reunification, by the beginning of 1992 it became clear that this modest attitude was over. The target of price stability became again an unambiguous priority and monetary authorities were ready to use interest rate instruments regardless of possible international consequences to the credibility of the ERM. From the end of 1991 until the summer of 1992, interest rates in Germany were steadily increasing. This made the asymmetric defence of weaker currencies an even more difficult task.

This difficulty was combined by some other conjectural economic developments. The UK economy was mired in a severe recession (then considered the worst recession in the post-war history of the country), accompanied by relatively high unemployment. The pressures for expansionary domestic policy (lower interest rates and inflation to alleviate the symptoms of the crisis) were in contradiction with the goal of defending the exchange rate peg, especially in the wake of the unusual increases in German interest rates. The same wave of recession was also felt by other European economies with lag in 1992: France, Italy, Spain and Germany. The position of the Italian government was particularly difficult. A deterioration in economic activity was associated with serious fiscal problems and a noticeable reduction in international reserves. Given all the above facts, it is not difficult to understand why market attacks focused mostly on the Italian lira and the British pound.

There are three more unexpected events which eroded investors' faith in the overall credibility of the ERM. First, the economic recession caused a deterioration in public finances and widened the gap between the Maastricht fiscal criteria and the economic performance of the EU as a whole. This was considered a negative development, curtailing the optimism in the whole project. At the same time, the credibility of the ERM was further wounded by the result of the national referendum in Denmark. The Maastricht Treaty was rejected, contrary to expectations. We have to underline the fact that although the Danish people said no by a narrow margin (50.9% to 49.4%), all main political parties had campaigned for the Treaty. This result boosted the confidence of the anti-EU political groups all over Europe and weakened the future prospects for European economic integration especially among market participants. It also functioned as a catalyst for subsequent events, adding to the mood of speculation in the markets against the credibility of the ERM. Finally, on 8 September 1992, for the second time in one year, the Finnish Central Bank was running out of international reserves to defend the currency, all the while reluctant to raise short-term interest rates above their current already high level of 14%. Hence, it let the Finnish markka freely float and the new exchange value embodied a 13% depreciation against the German mark. This was a clear sign of a significant mismatch between official targets on the one hand, and real economic trends and market expectations on the other.

In brief, the above events of the first half of 1992 weakened confidence and the overall credibility of the ERM project. While interest rate differentials throughout the EMS suggested that markets expected devaluations vis-à-vis the German mark, economic conditions both in the centre and the periphery raised serious doubts about the ability and willingness to defend the current exchange rate peg. The stage was ready for the first severe speculative attacks, betting against the credibility of the ERM and the overall stability of the exchange rate pegs.

The speculative attacks and the dawn of 'Black Wednesday'

The aforementioned developments made it rather clear to both market participants and state officials that the existing currency parities in the ERM were unsustainable. The first signs of speculative bets were already in place from the beginning of the summer, especially against the Italian lira. In the official meeting of the EEC in Bath on 5–6 September 1992, ministers of finance and central bank governors expressed their worries, mostly complaining about the high levels of German short-term interest rates. These high numbers made the defence of the currencies under attack much harder, both in technical and social terms. The German side communicated its unwillingness to shift its restrictive monetary policy radically and instead came up with a compromise proposal: it could consider lowering interest rates only if there were a general realignment (devaluation) of all other currencies. This trade off would reverse the inflationary pressures in the German economy that would be caused by lower interest rates. The proposal indicated Germany's willingness to come to an arrangement that did not involve aborting its overall monetary policy. Nevertheless, it was not supported by any other participant in the meeting.

The lack of co-ordination, which was widely reported in the press, further boosted the speculative mood. Bets anticipating a near-future depreciation of the lira intensified after the Bath meeting. In the following week, the Bundesbank and the Bank of Italy offered a similar proposal for intra-ERM co-ordination, officially acknowledging the unsustainability of the current parity of lira: only a few days after the Bath meeting, the defence of the lira required interventions of 24 billion German marks in Frankfurt and approximately 60 billion German marks across Europe. The proposal suggested a general realignment: a 3.5% revaluation of the German mark and a 3.5% devaluation of the lira against all other currencies in the ERM. In practice, this was equal to a 7% devaluation of the lira against the mark. The proposal also suggested a significant cut in German interest rates, but presupposed co-ordinated actions which other ERM parties refused to pursue. This second co-ordination failure in such a short period evidently evaporated any remaining faith in the credibility of the ERM. Nothing could convince even the most bona fide investor that exchange rate parities would remain unaltered and the current interest rate differentials would persist intact.

In the following days, policy reactions across Europe were in the right direction but were unable to alter market beliefs. Initially the Italian lira was the only currency to be devalued against the German mark, by 7%, while the Bundesbank, for the first time in five years, lowered the central bank discount rate by 0.5%. British sterling also depreciated, while the lira could not be stabilized even at its new parity levels. The selling of British sterling was further boosted by the anticipation that, given the fragile condition of the British economy, no serious defence could be implemented for long. The Bank of England reported a loss of about half of its international reserves (around US $15 billion). The president of the Bundesbank in a public statement confirmed the market sentiment, arguing that despite Germany's efforts no one could exclude the fact that some currencies might experience huge pressures. The setting was ready for the final act. Economies that appeared unable to defend their currencies at any cost were the first to experience the final attack: the Italian lira, the British pound and the Spanish peseta.

16 September is known in history as 'Black Wednesday'. The Bank of England raised its interest rate from 10% to 12% and, when this proved insufficient, it announced a further rise to 15%. The latter never materialized, since the volume of currency sales was so great that nothing could prevent the coming devaluation. In the evening of the same day, the Bank of England

'temporarily' withdrew the sterling from the ERM; the British pound never again joined the mechanism. The very same night was no less difficult for the lira and peseta as well. Italy followed Britain out of the ERM. Spain devalued its currency by 5% but it did not abandon the ERM. During the following days Italy declared its unwillingness to rejoin the ERM, while the Bank of England cut its interest rates to 9%.

From the day after to the final collapse of the 'hard' ERM

It did not take much time for the speculation to reach more 'central' economies. The French franc was the next target. This came as a surprise, since the macroeconomic condition of the French economy did not indicate strong vulnerabilities. The puzzle was even bigger because the attacks intensified after the positive result of a French referendum on the Maastricht Treaty on 20 September. These attacks were finally unsuccessful because of overwhelming interventions in the exchange rate. The losses of the Bank of France reached the extraordinary amount of 80 billion francs in one single month, while short-term interest rates significantly increased. Drastic also was the intervention of the Bundesbank in support of the franc. Other more 'unorthodox' forms of interference in the market were put in motion: implicit controls in both capital movements and domestic lending rates. Similar anti-market controls were also introduced by other currencies under pressure (those of Spain, Ireland and Portugal).

The answer to the French puzzle is that when confidence in the ERM as a system is lost and policy co-ordination seems untenable, 'weak' and 'strong' currencies are by and large on the same page: both are candidates for speculative attacks. It is not as important to go through all the events that followed 'black' September. The credibility of the ERM was irrevocably wounded. Market attacks continued in waves through all of the next year but not at the same level of intensity. Financial markets were wavering between periods of tension and relaxation, triggering state interventions and parity realignments.

The last act of the ERM was to be written in August 1993, when the whole setting came once more under systemic pressure. After a period of six months, French short-term interest rates were again above those of Germany, signalling an expected devaluation. Similar tensions caused the Central Bank of Denmark (the second referendum on 18 May had supported the Maastricht Treaty) to raise interest rates. On 30 July most of the ERM currencies were expected to depreciate against the German mark, while the Bundesbank refused to adjust its interest rate and change its monetary policy. The drastic reorganization of ERM rules was decided in an emergency meeting which took place in Brussels on 1 August 1993. From this day, currency rates were allowed to fluctuate 15% on either side of the central parity. This new commitment was not far from a free float. The German mark and Dutch guilder were excluded from this rule, remaining in the old narrow fluctuation bands. Before the end of the year all currencies except the Dutch guilder had depreciated within their new enlarged bands. The maximum depreciation was 6.95% for the Belgian franc, 8.93% for the Danish krona, 5.7% for the French franc, 4.37% for the Irish pound, 4.94% for the Portuguese escudo, and 5.77% for the Spanish peseta.

This silent break-up of the ERM did not negate the maintenance of a common target for European unification. It rather made quite clear to all sides that the project would be non-functional in the absence of a common currency and proper institutional arrangements to safeguard it from a similar wave of speculative attacks. The new system, which lasted until the decision to lock the exchange rates in 1999 and replace them in the near future with the euro, was not used for implementation of demand-side expansionary policies. On the contrary, European states remained loyal to the austerity-type policies and used the wider bands only as protection against speculation in order to recalibrate market expectations to the stability of the system.

CONCLUDING REMARKS

It is evident that fixed exchange rate regimes have two basic moments in their general design. They are peculiar economic unions made up of different societies and states, with different institutional settings and growth patterns. All participants share a common strategic target: emphasis on fiscal austerity and competitiveness (exposure to international competition). This is a policy mix that favours the upper classes of the society and is against the interests of labour. At the same time, this *sui generis* form of symbiosis hinges upon the workings of financial markets. In brief (and obviously abstracting from other important tendencies in modern finance), the strategies involved in the latter can take two extreme opposite versions: betting on the stability of the exchange rate pegs or against it. In the first case, we have the so-called 'convergence plays', which generate persistent capital inflows to fast-growing economies, resulting in financial account imbalances within the whole system. In the second case, speculative attacks tend to make the economic symbiosis quite vulnerable, given the economic interconnectedness.

The above summary sketches the main tendency to be developed within a system of fixed exchange rate symbiosis. The two moments are interlinked. The basic message is straightforward: the system is favourable to the long-term strategic interests of capital but it comes with a cost, because it is quite vulnerable to unexpected events or internal developments. Nevertheless, the whole setting would be more stable and not so hostile to the interests of labour if it were based on the condition of symmetric policy responses. In that case, the adjustment would be an obligation of the system as a whole, while the disciplining role of finance would be significantly undermined, making room for social welfare policies. This is the basic lesson from the EMS crisis. By and large, the very same patterns in a quite different institutional context can also explain the recent predicament in the EU. The lesson from the earlier crises can be used to help understand the more recent catastrophic events.

NOTES

1 Buiter *et al.* (1998: 19); Eichengreen (2007: 163–97); see also Chapter 2 on the Bretton Woods system, in this volume.
2 See Garber (1998); Volz (2006); Gros and Thygesen (1998).
3 See Eichengreen (2007: Ch. 11); Buiter *et al.* (1998: 29–31).
4 This is a standard topic in international macroeconomics textbooks; see Goodhart (1998) for a comprehensive account of the relevant discussions.
5 For an analytical description of this strategy of exposing capital to international competition, see Milios and Sotiropoulos (2009, 2010); Bryan and Rafferty (2006: Ch. 5).
6 We have implicitly assumed that exchange rate risk premiums are zero. For the argument see Svensson (1992); Volz (2006); Buiter *et al.* (1998).
7 When $S^e > S$, one unit of the foreign currency is expected to correspond to more units of domestic currency in the future. This is practically a depreciation of domestic currency.
8 See Bryan and Rafferty (2006: Ch. 5); Obstfeld *et al.* (2008).
9 For the development of this point see Buiter *et al.* (1998: 69).
10 For a general account of contemporary foreign exchange investment strategies including carry trade, see Gyntelberg and Schrimpf (2011).
11 See Volz (2006: 2); Krugman (2008).
12 See Buiter *et al.* (1998: 25).
13 For this example, see Easley *et al.* (2012: 7–8); Buiter *et al.* (1998: 57–58).
14 See Easley *et al.* (2012: 8).
15 All these events have been widely discussed in the relevant literature. In what follows I shall just attempt a synopsis in the line of the reasoning of the above sections. I will not use any references or quotations. Further discussion on the same events associated with the crisis of 1992–93 can be found in: Buiter *et al.* (1998); Eichengreen (2000, 2007); Krugman (2008); Gros and Thygesen (1998); Steinherr (2000).

REFERENCES

Bryan, D. and Rafferty, M. (2006) *Capitalism with Derivatives. A Political Economy of Financial Derivatives, Capital and Class*, New York and London: Palgrave Macmillan.

Buiter, W.H., Corsetti, G. and Pesenti, P.A. (1998) *Financial Markets and European Monetary Cooperation: The Lessons of the 1992–93 Exchange Rate Mechanism Crisis*, New York: Cambridge University Press.

Easley, D., López de Prado, M.M. and O'Hara, M. (2012) 'The Volume Clock: Insights into the High Frequency Paradigm', working paper, ssrn.com/abstract=2034858.

Eichengreen, B. (2000) 'The EMS Crisis in Retrospect', *NBER Working Papers*, no. 8035, www.nber.org/papers/w8035.

——(2007) *The European Economy Since 1945*, Princeton, NJ and Oxford: Princeton University Press.

Fischer, S. (1987) 'British Monetary Policy', in R. Dornbusch and R. Layard (eds) *The Performance of the British Economy*, Oxford: Oxford University Press.

Garber, P.M. (1998) 'Notes on the Role of Target in a Stage III Crisis', *NBER Working Paper Series*, No. 6619, www.nber.org/papers/w6619.

Giavazzi, F. and Giovannini, A. (1989) *Limiting Exchange Rate Flexibility: The European Monetary System*, Cambridge, MA: MIT Press.

Goodhart, C. (1998) 'The Two Concepts of Money: Implications for the Analysis of Optimal Currency Areas', *European Journal of Political Economy* 14: 407–32.

Gros, D. and Thygesen, N. (1998) *European Monetary Integration*, Harlow: Addison Wesley Longman.

Gyntelberg, J. and Schrimpf, A. (2011) 'FX Strategies in Periods of Distress', *BIS Quarterly Review*, December issue.

Krugman, P. (2008) *The Return of Depression Economics and the Crisis of 2008*, London: Penguin Books.

Milios, J. and Sotiropoulos, D.P. (2009) *Rethinking Imperialism: A Study of Capitalist Rule*, London and New York: Palgrave Macmillan.

——(2010) 'Crisis of Greece or Crisis of Euro? A View from the European "Periphery"', *Journal of Balkan and Near Eastern Studies* 12(3): 223–40.

Obstfeld, M., Shambaugh, J.C. and Taylor, A.M. (2008) 'Financial Stability, the Trilemma, and International Reserves', emlab.berkeley.edu/~obstfeld/OSTreserves.pdf.

Steinherr, A. (2000) *Derivatives: The Wild Beast of Finance. A Path to Effective Globalization*. Chichester: John Wiley and Sons Ltd.

Svensson, L.E.O. (1992) 'The Foreign Exchange Risk Premium in a Target Zone with Devaluation Risk', *Journal of International Economics* 33: 21–40.

Volz, U. (2006) 'On the Feasibility of a Regional Exchange Rate System for East Asia: Lessons of the 1992/93 ERM Crisis', Working Paper: The Whitney and Betty MacMillan Center for International and Area Studies at Yale.

Asia catches cold, Russia sneezes

The political economy of emerging market crises in 1997–98

MICHAEL F. KEATING

Cassandra: Already I prophesied to my countrymen all their disasters.
Chorus: How came it then that thou wert unscathed by Loxias' wrath?
Cassandra: Ever since that fault I could persuade no one of aught.
(Agamemnon by Aeschylus)

ECONOMIC CRISES, INTERNATIONAL FINANCIAL CAPITAL AND CONTAGION

An economic crisis caused by a bursting property bubble; fuelled by international speculative and short-term capital flows; facilitated by under-regulation; resulting in rapid contagion across interdependent economies, currencies in crisis, runs on banks and government bailouts of the private sector; International Monetary Fund (IMF) interventions (which go badly); regimes collapsing ... The reader might be forgiven for thinking of the global economic crisis or 'credit crunch' that began in 2007. However, this is in fact the story of the 'Asian economic crisis', which began 10 years earlier, in 1997, and quickly spread to emerging economies outside of the region. The similarities between these two economic crises beg the question of why no broader lessons for the global economy were learnt from the Asian economic crisis. In part, as Sachs and Woo (1999) note, this was because the 1997/98 economic crisis was seen as particularly 'Asian' in character, hence there *were* no lessons to be learned. Yet, nothing could be further from the truth: the Asian economic crisis is the Cassandra of modern economic times, an unheeded warning of the broader financial crisis of global capitalism which erupted in 2007.

The Asian economic crisis of 1997/98 and the Russian economic crisis of 1998 together provide an introduction to some of the most important ongoing themes of political economy in an era of globalization, particularly in terms of the political consequences of economic crises, the problem of contagion and the limitations of the existing architecture of global governance. Moreover, these crises bring some of the central claims of the discipline of international political economy (IPE) into sharp relief (Keating *et al.* 2012: 3–5).

First, as the overtly socio-political consequences of the IMF's 'technical' economic rescue packages demonstrate, it is necessary to take an interdisciplinary approach to the study of these crises. Second, although states, and interstate actors such as the IMF and World Bank, are central players in the story of emerging market crises in the late 1990s, so are non-state actors. Analysis requires the transcending of state-centric approaches, so as to engage directly with the role of global financial markets and market actors in both causing and exacerbating economic crises. Third, addressing these crises requires the systematic identification of 'interlinked and interdependent global, regional and domestic' causes and consequences. Fourth, and finally, analysis of these crises contributes to crucial normative debates in IPE, regarding financial liberalization, the international financial institutions (IFIs), the IMF and the World Bank, and state-led development strategies, national regulatory responsibilities and strategic interventions.

Economic crises appear as a central and recurrent feature of the global capitalist system. The neo-classical position that economic crises are rare 'externalities' to the functioning of the global economy is increasingly difficult to maintain. Furthermore, the rise of a financial form of capitalism has clearly increased the scope for systemic crises. The pegged exchange rate regime that crisis-afflicted states in Asia utilized helps to demonstrate this point. In the contemporary global economy, the financial power of markets massively outweighs the level of currency reserves that a state might be able to amass. Consequently, attempts by a central bank to defend a pegged currency regime are inherently self-defeating (Krugman 1979; see also Chapter 5 in this volume, on the 1992 ERM crisis). Furthermore, increasing economic interdependence within the global economy exacerbates the potential for 'contagion', the spreading of economic crises across states. Contagion is one of the major themes of the emerging market crises of the late 1990s, with obvious and direct relevance to the global financial crisis that began in 2007.

Three different types of contagion effects can be identified (see Ocampo *et al.* 2008: 8–9). *Real contagion* occurs when one state's exchange rate devaluation causes their exports to become more competitive, increasing the chance of speculative attacks against economies with similar industrial and trade profiles. *Financial contagion* is caused when economic problems with an international dimension are deemed likely to affect multiple states or financial systems ('clustered risk groups'), either on the basis of geographic proximity, trade or financial ties, or similarities in macroeconomic conditions or policy regimes. Here, expectations of contagion are causal: an economic crisis in one state triggers self-fulfilling expectations of crises in other states. Given global economic interdependence, financial contagion can be even wider in scope: financial actors hedging across states and regions may be required to draw liquidity from otherwise unrelated sectors of the global economy. If liquidity shortages are severe, this can lead to the underselling of assets or the liquidating of illiquid assets, with losses exacerbating financial problems and leading to further liquidations—a vicious circle of liquidation and losses.

Market failure (information asymmetry) can also cause *informational contagion*. Here, moral hazard drives international speculators to irrational 'herding', panic buying or selling, in markets that are perceived to have risks relating to markets in crisis, whether those risks are real or not. Benchmarks, best practices or other standardized procedures designed to reduce risk may well exacerbate this form of contagion.

All three forms of contagion are evident in the Asian economic crisis of 1997/98 and the Russian economic crisis of 1998. This chapter is not, however, a narrow study of contagion, but rather it shows how the issues that contagion raises directly engage with the broadest themes of political economy—development, economic crises, global finance, global governance, and the dangers and opportunities of globalization. The aim is also to demonstrate the continuing significance of a study of these crises to students of IPE today. The chapter begins with a discussion of the Asian economic 'miracle', then engages with the major causes and events of the 'meltdown' of 1997/98. The IMF's interventions are detailed, and the social, political and economic consequences of these are explored. Contagion to Russia in 1998 and the economic crisis that followed are then explained. Finally, conclusions are drawn, with particular emphasis on lessons not learned, and on comparison to the global financial crisis that began in 2007.

THE ASIAN MIRACLE

Part of the significance of the Asian economic crisis of 1997/98 is that the affected East and South-East Asian states constituted the most successful example of rapid economic growth and improvements in human development in the post-war era. The 'first wave' in East Asia—Hong Kong, Singapore, Taiwan and the Republic of Korea (South Korea)—is possibly the most rapid economic transformation in history, while the 'second wave' in South-East Asia—Malaysia, Indonesia, Thailand and the Philippines—also experienced impressive returns. While this rapid growth and development has been explained with reference to 'Asian values' (Dore 1987) or the power of 'free markets' (Lal 1983), the most coherent explanations focus on the 'developmental state' (Johnson 1982). In this latter approach, the facilitative role of the state in promoting a form of capitalist development, and in particular on the role of strategic trade and industry policy, is paramount. Perhaps most importantly, the developmental state constituted a *model of development*, in effect exported from Japan to East Asia, and then on to South-East Asia, which might be further emulated by other states (see Chang 2006; Wade 1990: 345–81).

In practice this 'model' applied far more to South Korea and Taiwan than it did to the island city-states of Singapore and Hong Kong, or indeed to the second wave tigers. In fact, in South-East Asia interventions were likely to be more neo-patrimonial in character and less successful in economic terms (Beeson 2007: 166–73). Nevertheless, in order to understand the Asian economic crisis of 1997/98 it is necessary to appreciate how states in East and

South-East Asia sought to promote internationally competitive manufacturing industries. Practices varied from state to state, but representative examples include infant-industry protectionism, targeting export-oriented manufacturing industries for special incentives and subsidies ('picking winners'), and 'getting the prices wrong', for example through interest rate manipulations which distorted the cost of capital. The subsidization of industries was tempered by the export-orientation of overall industry policy, such that world markets were the judge of success. Failed interventions were discontinued, though even in such cases there were often 'positive externalities' or 'spill-over' effects in technology and skills that benefited related industry sectors (see Amsden 1993; Applebaum and Henderson 1992; Evans 1995; MacIntyre 1994).

In essence, East and South-East Asian states pursued mercantilist strategies of 'competitive advantage' that prioritized industrialization rather than liberal, free market strategies based on 'comparative advantage'. Industry policy interventions were funded largely through domestic savings, rather than foreign investment, and this approach went hand in hand with constraints on domestic consumption patterns, particularly of luxury commodities. Crucially, the state controlled both inflows and outflows of capital, and particularly of the direction of investment capital. Control of the banking and financial sector enabled these states to discipline their productive private sector, and ensure that productivity gains were made and export targets met. Foreign corporations' investments into these states were also heavily regulated, so as to ensure the development of national corporations (often through joint-venture requirements), and to promote technological, financial, management and productive spill-over effects (Chang 2006: 1–46).

In political terms, East and South-East Asian states were illiberal and quasi-authoritarian, ranging from military to electoral dictatorships, and labour movements, student groups, and any other civil, political or religious organizations that voiced dissent or opposition, including business interests, were heavily repressed. Industrial policy was designed and implemented by a competent, technocratic and relatively corruption-free (more so in East than South-East Asia) bureaucratic elite, committed to national developmental goals. The lack of democratic accountability might be seen as allowing for the 'relative autonomy' of these elites, which could then design and implement industrial policy without having to pander to populist, sector-specific or electoral interest groups (Jenkins 1991). Alternatively, elites may have derived capacity from their 'embedded autonomy', or systematic formal and informal inter-linkages with domestic political actors, particularly the industrial and financial sectors (Evans 1995). These regimes were also remarkably stable during the period of transformation, as they were able to maintain a form of legitimacy, in what might be termed a 'national development consensus'. Illiberalism was, in essence, acceptable, as long as states continued to deliver economic growth and human development improvements. This legitimacy was furthered by 'growth with equity'—that is, the relative equality that developmental state policy interventions explicitly fostered (see Carroll 2010: 54).

These 'developmental state' explanations of Asian economic growth were initially completely rejected by the IMF and the World Bank. Throughout the 1980s, these IFIs advocated neo-liberal, free market-based development strategies based on a belief in the efficiency of the market's price mechanism in resource distribution, and on the distorting and sub-optimal role of forms of government intervention—particularly in developing states (Williamson 1993). However, in the landmark document *The East Asian Miracle* (1993), the World Bank admitted the existence of widespread government interventionism in Asia. Nevertheless, the World Bank largely dismissed any causality, preferring to highlight the importance of 'globalization' in creating the underlying conditions that made Asian rapid economic growth possible (World Bank 1993: 24–25). Certainly, as Cold War allies, East and South-East Asian states were able to free-ride on post-war US hegemony, protecting their markets from foreign (and US) competition, whilst dumping their goods on open US markets (see Stubbs 2005).

The USA was by far the largest market for Asian manufactures, but this free-rider strategy became increasingly problematic post-1989. The IFIs argued that accelerating globalization also meant that it was no longer possible for other developing states to emulate the Asian model. State-led development models and interventionist policies had therefore become anachronistic and obsolete, and needed to be replaced with a free market-oriented policy framework (free trade, capital account liberalization and the deregulation of foreign investment) in order to make economic growth sustainable (IMF 1994: 72–73; World Bank 1993: 24–25). Then Managing Director of the IMF Michel Camdessus was particularly vehement in arguing that the scope for states to use interventionist economic policies was 'greatly reduced in the contemporary context of globalisation' (Camdessus 1997). From the mid-1990s the IMF increased its emphasis on financial liberalization, through amendments to its Articles of Agreement which required member states to remove capital controls and adopt full capital convertibility. Financial liberalization in a globalized world would, for the IMF, massively increase the opportunities for developing states to attract capital investment, thereby improving their levels of economic growth. The mechanism of conditional lending was used to promote this liberalized trading and investment regime (Camdessus 1996; IMF 1990: 6–19; World Bank 1991: 4–11).

FROM MIRACLE TO MELTDOWN

In the early 1990s East and South-East Asian states pursued rapid financial liberalization, moving away from the developmental state model and towards a free market, foreign investment-based development strategy. It is debatable whether this was directly due to increased pressure from the IFIs and the US Treasury in a post-Cold War context, domestic pressures for liberalization and democratization, or some combination of these two (Ravenhill 2009: 23). Certainly, the USA has historically pursued an 'open-door' policy towards the region (Williams 1972; see Fouskas and Gökay 2012). Whatever the cause, this shift was seen as amounting to a 'subversion of effective financial governance' (Jomo 2000: 25–26), undermining the capacity of developmental states to control and co-ordinate capital flows (Weiss and Hobson 2000: 62). Consequently, rapid financial liberalization is central to explanations of the Asian economic crisis of 1997/98.

As a consequence of liberalization, East and South-East Asia was awash with enormous capital inflows by the mid-1990s. As these states had relinquished control over capital inflows, financial intermediation was poor. Asian states, and particularly Asian central banks, struggled to manage and regulate the newly liberalized sector and the increasing number and type of different financial actors. They also struggled to implement global rules and standards in banking and financial supervision, either because of a lack of capacity, or due to negative political or economic consequences for key social coalitions (Ravenhill 2009: 26–27). As a consequence, over-investment in (often unproductive) assets resulted, particularly in real estate. As asset prices rose, generating the appearance of high returns, this encouraged further borrowing and investment in an 'asset price inflationary bubble' (Edison *et al.* 1998: 1–3). Investment strategies also became increasingly high risk, resulting in large numbers of non-performing loans (Akyüz 1998: 35).

Asian states 'pegged' their exchange rates to the US dollar throughout the 1990s in order to maintain competitiveness in key export markets, and to provide certainty for international trade and foreign investment. This practice, however, may have contributed to a perception amongst investors that East and South-East Asian states guaranteed exchange rates. Indeed, combined with implicit guarantees for financial sector actors, severe moral hazard problems were created, exacerbating risk-taking and suppressing incentives to hedge external borrowings. Pegging also caused underlying region-wide economic problems, such as slowly appreciating currencies, the subsequent weakening of exports, and a relative slowing of economic growth.

'Financial mismatches' building up in the 1990s were particularly problematic, as they threatened otherwise economically viable investments. The first was a foreign vs. domestic currency debt denomination mismatch, in which investors would borrow foreign currency to finance projects which would return on investments in domestic currency. Consequently, abandoning the peg, if this led to exchange rate realignment and a sudden devaluation, would cause massive economic adjustment problems. The second was a short-term borrowing vs. long-term investment mismatch, wherein investors borrowed from short-term money markets to finance long-term investment projects. As short-term debt matured, it was rolled over with other short-term loans. This meant that any liquidity shortages in investment markets could be disastrous for these economies. Short-term foreign borrowing in fact constituted more than 50% of foreign investment into Asia in the 1990s. By 1996, European Union (EU), US and Japanese banks had US$ 625 billion in outstanding, un-hedged short-term loans to Thailand, the Philippines, Malaysia, South Korea and

Indonesia alone (Jomo 2009: 36–38; Ravenhill 2009: 16–29). As a consequence of these mismatches, East and South-East Asian states became increasingly vulnerable to sudden reversals in investor sentiment in the 1990s.

Thailand in particular suffered from a property bubble, based largely on short-term foreign financial investment. Indeed, in June 1997 the Asian economic crisis began with international speculators attacking the Thai currency, the baht. Speculation on a Thai devaluation vastly outweighed the estimated $4 billion the Thai government spent attempting to buy the baht back up to its pegged value. The Thai Central Bank also sought to limit the offshore tradability of the baht through the introduction of currency controls. On 1 July 1997, the Thai prime minister refused to contemplate a devaluation, stating that if this happened ' … We will all become poor'. Yet, the very next day, the Thai finance minister introduced a 'managed float', and within two weeks the baht had suffered a severe devaluation, from 26 to 32 to the US dollar. This devaluation indeed caused extensive financial and commercial sector collapses inside Thailand, as underlying economic problems were revealed— asset inflation, unproductive investments, non-performing loans and both forms of financial mismatch (Hewison 2000: 201–3; Lauridsen 1998).

However, these problems may better explain the economic crisis in Thailand than they do other East and South-East Asian states. Consequently, contagion in and of itself must be seen as a serious cause of the Asian economic crisis (Jomo 2009: 39–40). First, *real contagion* is evident: the devaluation of the Thai baht caused Thai exports to become more competitive, enough of a reason for international speculators to begin to attack other states in the region that constituted Thailand's competition. Second, and consequently, *financial contagion* is evident, as a large degree of trade, economic and financial interdependence was evident in the region. Consequently, Thailand's economic problems were always likely to have knock-on effects on the regional economy. Crucially, Thailand's failure to protect its currency meant that there was no confidence that neighbouring states would be able to defend their pegs either. Finally, *informational contagion* is evident: as fears about corruption and weak regulation in the region surfaced and fed investor panic, it is no surprise that the next state to be affected was Indonesia (Allen and Gale 1999; Krugman 2000: 89–98).

In July 1997 Malaysia and the Philippines joined Thailand and Indonesia in abandoning their pegs, and watching their currencies collapse; South Korea followed in November of that year. Further to the *informational contagion* position, international investors and capital markets clearly evinced behaviour such as 'herding', 'irrational pessimism' and 'overshooting'. Financial liberalization turned out to be a 'double-edged sword'—at first facilitating massive inwards investment, but now facilitating massive and rapid capital flight (Taylor 1997: 150; Wade 1998: 693–94). Rapid financial liberalization, taking place without building appropriate regulatory frameworks and capacity, was therefore seen a major cause of the problems in East Asia. By contrast, states that avoided financial deregulation, such as China and Singapore, survived relatively unscathed (Felker 2009: 63–64).

THE IMF: GOOD GOVERNANCE AND STRUCTURAL ADJUSTMENT

During the 1990s, the IFIs had increasingly sought to explain Asia's economic success stories with reference to the concept of 'good governance'. This amounted to a political system that was able to uphold the rule of law, create a 'business-friendly' investment, legal and regulatory environment, eliminate rent-seeking behaviour and fight corruption, and establish a neutral and streamlined civil service. The lessons of good governance in Asia were, for the IFIs, explicitly to be emulated by other developing states (World Bank 1993: 14; World Bank 1997: 73; IMF 1997a). The IMF, ironically, had particularly praised Asian states and central banks for their prudential supervision of the banking system and financial sector (IMF 1997: 56–92). The IFIs maintained this position right up until the economic crisis struck in 1997; then, in a sudden about turn, the IMF sought to explain the 'crisis of Asian capitalism' with reference to the 'poor governance' in these Asian states (Bello 2010: 194; Moschella 2010: 101–6).

Poor governance was held by the IMF to have caused international investors, first, severely to underestimate risk and overestimate both returns and asset values, and second, severely to under-value assets and engage in mass capital flight. Any apparent irrationality in the behaviour of investors could therefore be laid at the door of the inappropriate domestic policy choices of the East and South-East Asian states. These states had, through their poor governance, allowed the 'risks of globalization' to manifest. The IMF specifically focused on 'lack of transparency' in the region, embodied by the co-operative relations that had formed between government and the business, banking and financial sectors in East and South-East Asian states. Consequently, Asia's developmental state was now recast as 'crony capitalism'.

In this view, too much government intervention had led to corruption and nepotism, and in particular to the perception of implicit government guarantees for the banking and financial sector. Developmental state-style industry policy, such as directed credit programmes, served only to distort resource allocation. This, in turn, caused excessive risk-taking, fuelled short-term foreign loans, and drove poor investment decisions. Once the crisis was under-way, poor governance caused *informational contagion* by compounding investor doubts, exacerbating the severity of asset under-valuations and the extent of the capital flight. This was on top of the role of poor governance in causing *financial contagion*, as problems revealed in one Asian state were easily transformed into doubts about other states in the region with similar political and economic structures (Camdessus 1999; IMF 1998: 24–35, 1999: 26–36).

Their conversion to good governance in the 1990s therefore enabled the IMF to take a neo-liberal reading of the Asian economic crisis. This allowed states that had previously been lauded as prime examples of the success of neo-liberalism now to be castigated for failing to be neo-liberal at all (Carroll 2010: 52; see Pauly 1994). Prior to the crisis, the IMF had also augmented its structural adjustment loans with governance-related policy conditions (IMF 1997a). Consequently, the balance of payments difficulties the crisis caused in Indonesia, Thailand, South Korea and Malaysia were viewed by the IMF as an opportunity to promote deep, ambitious and comprehensive structural reforms. In economic terms, the bailout packages sought to abolish the economic distortions of the developmental state, and promote a neo-liberal, free market-based development strategy. Macroeconomic orthodoxy (tight monetary policy to stabilize exchange rates, and tight fiscal policy to ensure budget surpluses) was required, along with further liberalization of foreign trade and investment. Exchange rate flexibility (abandoning pegs), it was held, would restore investor confidence. In terms of political, governance-related conditions, the packages focused on the banking and financial sectors, emphasizing enhanced transparency and accountability and improved legal and regulatory institutions, and ending the corrupt, nepotistic and non-transparent relations between governments and the private sector. The IMF also strongly promoted global 'best practices', such as the Basle Accords. The resulting increases in transparency would, according to the IMF, lead to a more appropriate pricing of risk, inhibit herd behaviour, and ensure financial stability and economic recovery (Camdessus 1997, 1999a; IMF 1998: 23–38, 1999: 5–37).

THE BACKLASH

The IMF's advocacy of further financial liberalization as a *solution* to the crisis was unsurprisingly viewed as problematic by analysts who argued that rapid liberalization without regulation had *caused* the crisis. The focus on dismantling 'crony capitalist' state-led development models, furthermore, would only make sense if the IMF's explanation of the causes of the crisis— that Asia's flawed economic institutions had all simultaneously reached breaking point—was accurate (Beeson and Robison 2000: 14; Sachs and Woo 1999). In practice, the IMF's structural adjustment programmes were widely held to have greatly exacerbated the economic crisis, causing job losses, business failures, bank failures, deposit losses, and further stock market collapses and capital flight. The extent of IMF conditions, in the first instance, had the opposite effect to restoring investor confidence. The economic policies the IMF advocated, furthermore, were heavily pro-cyclical, and a combination of higher interest rates and cuts to government spending predictably caused further economic contraction. The 'one-size-fits-all' structural adjustment programme the IMF promoted reflected the solutions designed for sub-Saharan Africa in the 1980s, where (the failures of these measures notwithstanding) serious macroeconomic problems were evident. East and South-East Asian states, by contrast, featured relatively low inflation and debt levels, and were running budget surpluses (see Moschella 2010: 97–101). By 1998 the IMF had as much as conceded many of the critics' positions, and sought to moderate its programmes significantly, with an increased emphasis on social safety nets to mitigate the adverse socioeconomic impact of both the crisis and the

IMF's adjustment programme (Camdessus 1999; IMF 1998: 27–32, 1999: 6–43).

The IMF programmes also resulted in a political backlash. An important element of this was the so-called 'fire sale' of Asian assets that was held to result from simultaneous devaluation of asset values and exchange rates. Meanwhile, the IMF programme ensured that Asian companies and assets, particularly in the financial sector, were made available for sale to foreign ownership. The IMF argued that foreign ownership might substitute for domestic financial reform, and contribute to restoring economic confidence in the Asian newly industrialized countries (NICs) (Camdessus 1998; IMF 1998: 31–32). Although the extent to which US multinationals and financial interests benefited from this process may have been overstated (Robertson 2007, 2008), perceptions of a 'new imperialism' certainly contributed to widespread political resentment (Higgott 2000: 274–75; Khor 2008: 207).

To find examples of serious political consequences resulting from IMF programmes one need only look at the case of Indonesia. The failure of the initial IMF programme to address Indonesia's economic problems led to then-President Suharto rejecting the programme, and to difficulties in reaching a subsequent agreement. The primary area of disagreement related precisely to governance concerns, with the IMF advocating an extensive list of structural reforms aimed at abolishing cronyism and corruption. Such policies were opposed by Suharto as they were clearly aimed at the 'New Order', the government-business relations that enriched President Suharto's family and political allies, and so underpinned the regime's political and economic power base (Dalrymple 1998: 234–35; Robison and Rosser 2000: 175–79; Smith 2001: 85; Vatikiotis 1998). The IMF package that was eventually negotiated, furthermore, required the Indonesian government to take on the extensive private sector debts—effectively a bailout for foreign banks paid for by struggling Indonesians (Jomo 1998: 20; Lal 1999: 6). The photo of a crossed-armed IMF Managing Director Camdessus standing over Suharto as he signed the IMF agreement, almost looking like he was kow-towing towards the West, was front page news in the region. The neo-imperialist overtones of this image were devastating for the image of the Suharto regime, which soon collapsed amidst widespread riots and ethnic violence, in part attributable to the IMF loan conditions (Beeson 2007: 208; Case 2009: 102; Ito 2007).

The IMF programme for South Korea featured trade-related reforms which Japan and the USA had been pressuring South Korea to adopt in bilateral trade negotiations for over a decade. These included allowing foreign investors to buy up South Korean firms, and further liberalization of the banking and financial sectors. The South Korean government reportedly viewed the IMF conditions as 'politicized', and as an abuse of power (Chang 1998: 229–30; Wade 1998a: 1547). Meanwhile, the then Deputy US Treasury Secretary Lawrence Summers was reported as claiming that the IMF programme in Korea did more to promote the trade agenda of the US government than decades of bilateral negotiations had achieved (Hale 1998).

Malaysia's structural adjustment loan conditions cut to the heart of the United Malays National Organization (UMNO)/Mahathir regime (Malaysia Inc.), and the ethnic settlement that had underpinned Malaysia's political economy since the 1960s, and so also Malaysia's stability, rapid economic growth and development. Rather than follow Indonesia (and indeed Suharto), and watch the structure of state-social coalitions be torn apart by structural adjustment, then President Mahathir backed out of the programme completely. The leadership of the Finance Ministry (Deputy Prime Minister Anwar Ibrahim) and Central Bank were replaced, and despite fervent criticism from international capital and the IMF, capital controls and a range of other restrictive policy measures to protect the Malaysian financial sector and economy were put in place (Beeson 2007: 209–10; Moschella 2010: 108–9; Tiek 2003: 52–56). The IMF warned that capital limitations would cause greater panic amongst investors, but Malaysia in fact recovered far quicker than other states in the region, and has far outpaced them in climbing up the Human Development Index since 1997 (Khor 2008: 220–27; Stiglitz 2000: 1080).

Critics of the IMF in this period were far-ranging (see Moschella 2010: 106–7), but one of the main voices was in fact the IMF's sister organization, the World Bank. The World Bank's senior staff and publications in this period openly cast doubt on the idea that the Asian economic crisis could be explained through poor governance in domestic economies. Rather, the World Bank took the view that international financial markets and foreign investors were pivotal in both creating the pre-crisis boom, and in causing and exacerbating the crisis, as they had failed to price risks adequately or properly evaluate potential investments (Stiglitz 1998; Wolfensohn 1999; World Bank 1998). The World Bank explicitly implicated the rapid financial market liberalization which took place in the 1990s, arguing that this usually leads to financial crises when states have weak legal and regulatory institutions. Short-term capital flows, in particular, were held to make little contribution to economic growth while dramatically increasing 'economic instability' and 'financial market vulnerability' (World Bank 1998: 38, 1999: 97).

The idea that a lack of transparency in the region had caused the crisis was dismissed by the World Bank, which held that markets were well aware of the many political and economic problems in pre-crisis East and South-East Asia, but had chosen to ignore this information. Furthermore, where poor governance was evident in East and South-East Asia, this was largely a result of liberalization, which had occurred without ensuring adequate regulatory capacity, supervision or management of capital flows. The extent of divergence between these institutions in this period is most evident in the World Bank's questioning of the core neo-liberal assumption, central to the IMF's position, that the market mechanism, free from the distorting effects of government intervention, would successfully generate development. The World Bank instead pointed to the crucial role of the state in promoting development, particularly in terms of regulating financial markets (Stiglitz 1998a; World Bank 1998: 32–42, 1999: 81–82).

THE RUSSIAN ECONOMIC CRISIS OF 1998

By 1998, Russia had finished its widespread post-Soviet privatization programme, brought inflation under control and for the first time since 1989 was (just) registering positive economic growth. Oil prices were high, the stock market was booming and significant financial support from the IMF and the World Bank was being arranged. Russia had begun financial liberalization in January 1997, allowing foreign participation in the stock market and in the ruble Treasury bill market (GKOs). In the first half of 1997, Russia experienced significant increases in the scope and scale of capital inflows (Chiodo and Owyang 2002: 10–11; Woods 2006: 126–27). Russia, like the East and South-East Asian states, had also engaged in rapid economic liberalization without building appropriate regulatory institutions or financial oversight capacity. Consequently, this investment was poorly mediated. Private Russian banks accumulated large financial mismatches by borrowing in foreign currency, and investing in ruble-denominated government debt. The Russian economic crisis of 1998 therefore constitutes a further example of how financial liberalization in emerging markets has failed to generate improved resource allocation and faster economic growth, and has instead led to economic crises (Perotti 2002; Pinto and Ulatov 2010: 2–20).

Russia had limited economic, trade and financial relations with East and South-East Asia, such that *real contagion* would appear an unlikely explanation for the economic problems Russia faced in 1998. However, a number of factors point to other forms of contagion as significant causes of Russia's economic crisis. *Informational contagion* may have been a factor, in that the Asian economic crisis directly caused investors to become increasingly risk averse. Russia's declining economic fundamentals (particularly in fiscal terms) may have been sufficient to cause a capital exit after, but not before, the Asian economic crisis (Feridun 2004: 121). The Asian economic crisis may also have led investors to consider the hitherto unthinkable as possible: a Russian government default (Chiodo and Owyang 2002: 16).

Financial contagion is more clearly evident, in that the Asian economic crisis led to a slowdown in global production, and a commodity price crash. This was particularly significant with regard to energy and metal prices, Russia's most valuable sources of revenue and capital flows. Russia's fiscal deterioration revealed Russia's level of dependence upon a healthy global economy, and vulnerability to exogenous shocks. Indeed, 43% of Russian exports in 1998 came from oil and gas alone (Chiodo and Owyang 2002: 12; Feridun 2004: 114–17; Perotti 2002; Woods 2006: 128). The Asian economic crisis also caused global interest rates to rise from November 1997 onwards. Furthermore, in 1996, South Korean financial institutions seeking high return investments had bought a massive 40% of Russia's first Eurobond sale. When the Asian economic crisis struck in 1997, to resolve liquidity problems at home, South Korean firms began to liquidate these assets, as well as exiting the GKO market, and in October 1997, as prices dropped, a widespread sell-off of

Russian assets was instigated (Allen and Gale 1999; Pinto and Ulatov 2010: 2–7). Finally, using international sources to refinance Russia's short-term government debt—which kept Russia's economy functioning—became more difficult as the Asian economic crisis caused global liquidity problems (Perotti 2002). In November 1997, speculators had turned their attention not only to South Korea, but also to Russia. The Central Bank of Russia (CBR) lost nearly $6 billion in foreign exchange reserves defending the ruble peg, while billions more in debt was racked up by selling short-term Russian government bills. In the final quarter of 1997, capital flows to Russia dramatically reversed, as they had in Asia (Pinto and Ulatov 2010: 18; Woods 2006: 127–28).

Domestic and idiosyncratic causes clearly contributed to Russia's economic woes. The tax system in Russia was burdened by a non-payments crisis, and failed to generate any real revenue, further deteriorating the Russian state's fiscal position (Perotti 2002). Statements by Russian officials, and the IMF leaving Russia in October 1997 without securing an agreement, almost certainly damaged the confidence of international investors, and led to the widespread belief that a devaluation of the ruble was inevitable. This also contributed to the selling of Russian government bonds and securities in late 1997. Despite President Yeltsin firing his government in March 1998, tensions between the different branches of government in Russia continued to cause delays and uncertainty (Pinto and Ulatov 2010: 18–22; Woods 2006: 124–28). While Russia's ruble was pegged as part of the inflation-fighting economic priority of this period, this peg was in fact massively overvalued (Chiodo and Owyang 2002: 12–16; Feridun 2004: 113).

Other international factors in Russia's crisis must also be taken into account. The support the IFIs had provided to Russia, largely explicable in terms of maintaining a pro-Western Yeltsin regime, allowed Russia to maintain an overvalued and otherwise unsustainable ruble peg. Russia's unmanageable fiscal and debt problems were also, initially, sustained by the capital inflows financial liberalization enabled. Even when falling oil prices, deteriorating foreign exchange reserves and fiscal weakness made a crisis widely apparent, Russian state debt continued to build up thanks to international support, and foreign portfolio investment inflows generated through the Eurobond market. Consequently, when the crisis eventually broke out, the external debt burden was far larger than might otherwise have been the case (Perotti 2002; Pinto and Ulatov 2010; Woods 2006: 128–30).

By May 1998, however, even with 47% yields, Russian bonds could not sell. Continuing falls in commodity prices and a lack of confidence in international markets was compounded by a liquidity crisis at home—ironically caused by the Russian state's attempts to raise more tax revenue and crack down on corruption (Pinto and Ulatov 2010: 12; Feridun 2004: 113). In June, foreign exchange currency reserves, already low, were drained by another $5 billion in further attempts to defend the ruble, and the oil price slump meant that Russia could not generate enough revenue to pay its massive short-term debts, both private and public, maturing in September—of which markets were keenly aware. Yet, in July 1998, the IMF lent Russia $11.2 billion. This was nevertheless unable to resolve the liquidity crisis, as the sum was balanced by continuing capital flight and lost oil revenue. The IMF's package also failed to address default concerns, having little effect on market evaluations of sovereign risk in Russia. Indeed, the IMF bailout only served to exacerbate 'moral hazard'—the expectation of international investors that Russia was 'too big to fail', and that further IMF, World Bank, G-7 or even German/European bailouts would be forthcoming (Chiodo and Owyang 2002: 12–14; Hale 1998; Perotti 2002; Pinto and Ulatov 2010: 24–28; Woods 2006: 128–31).

The government switched from ruble-denominated debt to issuing US dollar-denominated Eurobonds, but increased borrowing and growing revenue problems only furthered default fears (Feridun 2004: 113–14). On 13 July a GKO-Eurobond swap was announced by the Russian government: the swap largely failed, and the demonstrable investor nervousness about the swap, indicating fears of a default, may well have triggered a default (Pinto and Ulatov 2010: 26–29). Russia was unable to roll over its maturing short-term debt, and as gross domestic product (GDP) sank and unemployment skyrocketed, global investors liquidated Russian holdings. Between 10 July and 14 August 1998, the CBR lost a net $4.5 billion as portfolio capital exited the equity and GKO markets. On 13 August Russian stock, bond and currency markets collapsed to 25% of their January value, again reflecting investor fears of a ruble devaluation and/or debt default (Chiodo and Owyang 2002: 14; Feridun 2004: 114).

The Russian government was in fact forced to default on both its public debts (valued at around $45 billion on the peg), and private external debt, on 17 August. Some $3 billion more was lost before the Russian government abandoned the peg, and floated the ruble, which massively devalued, on 2 September 1998. Russian debt, $36 billion at the start of the year, had leapt by $16 billion between 1 and 24 July alone. Although exports recovered, economic growth collapsed along with remaining foreign exchange reserves following the exit from the GKO market. Russian financial sector actors had accumulated large amounts of ruble-denominated assets, causing massive domestic economic problems in the wake of the devaluation. If devaluation did not cause a run on the Russian domestic banking system, as private depositors moved to the state bank (Sberbank), it certainly did not prevent it. There was no private bank bailout in Russia, unlike in Asia, but while this may have helped keep a lid on state debt levels, it also exacerbated Russia's liquidity crisis (Chiodo and Owyang 2002: 14; Feridun 2004: 113–14; Perotti 2002; Pinto and Ulatov 2010: 18–30).

The Russian economic crisis of 1998 had global ramifications: international markets rocked, and the hedge fund Long-Term Capital Management (LTCM), which lost $550 million in one day in August 1998, had to be bailed out to the tune of $3.6 billion. LTCM was deemed 'too big to fail', having acquired trillions of US dollars in debt (Hale 1998; Jorion 2000; Pinto and

Ulatov 2010: 3; Stiglitz 2000: 1082). In January 1999 *financial contagion* from Russia spread to Brazil, another country that had engaged in rapid financial liberalization, accumulated growing deficits and pegged its exchange rate—a mechanism which international investors had little reason to view as credible. Supporting the peg throughout 1997 and 1998 had caused Brazil to increase its foreign debt massively, not least by borrowing $41.5 billion from the IMF in 1998. With South Korea underselling its government bonds to raise liquidity, and following the market instability caused by the Russian default, Brazil, like so many countries before it, was forced to float its currency, the real. The real then massively devalued (Allen and Gale 1999; Evangelist and Sathe 2006).

As economic crises spread to Turkey and Argentina in 2000/01, the failures of the IMF in both the Asian economic crisis of 1997/98 and the Russia economic crisis of 1998, may have caused further *informational contagion*, by generating doubts among investors about whether IMF support would even be forthcoming for Argentina ('reverse moral hazard') (Calvo and Talvi 2008: 126). The Russian crisis also caused *informational contagion*, as international speculators began to view government bonds in emerging markets in general as potentially problematic. Indeed, it is argued that international investors were far more risk averse as a consequence of the Russian economic crisis of 1998, than of the Asian economic crisis of 1997/98 (Evangelist and Sathe 2006; Pinto and Ulatov 2010: 3). While international factors such as the Enron collapse certainly did not help Latin American states, it was the Russian economic crisis of 1998 that caused global interest rate rises and the collapse of capital flows in the region (and in emerging markets in general). Only Mexico, which had suffered a currency crisis of its own in 1994, where regional contagion was termed the 'Tequila effect' (Germain 2010: 59), was relatively unharmed. There were no economic ties between Russia and Latin America to cause *real contagion*, but in terms of *financial contagion*, the Russian default had hit the balance sheet of international investors hard, in effect causing a liquidity crunch (Calvo and Talvi 2008: 120–26).

CONCLUSIONS

One of the main lessons of emerging market crises in the late 1990s, therefore, is the extent to which states are vulnerable to contagion effects, as economic problems spread rapidly across the East and South-East Asian region, and then to states such as Russia, Brazil and Australia (Beeson and Bell 2000: 301–4). From the beginnings of the revival of international political economy in the 1970s, IPE scholars have struggled with questions of growing economic interdependence between states and its consequences (see Keohane and Nye 1977). However, in this case, important lessons about vulnerability and risk were not learned, as the global financial crisis that struck in 2007 demonstrated. Part of the problem, as intimated above, is that the 'crony capitalism' explanation put forward by the IMF, in particular, and widely picked up on in the news media, led to the Asian economic crisis being viewed as a particularly 'Asian' phenomenon, with no broader lessons for Organisation for Economic Co-operation and Development (OECD) states or other states outside the region.

The events of the late 1990s lead to questions about financial liberalization per se. Scholars question the capacity of financial market liberalization to promote development in both theoretical and empirical terms, arguing instead for the utility of controls on international capital markets and on required capital flows for small, open economies and developing states (Jomo 2009: 35; Stiglitz 2000). Financial liberalization, far from leading to an optimal allocation of economic resources, appears to be inherently pro-cyclical, causing a 'contagion of optimism'—asset inflationary spirals, or bubbles—followed by a 'contagion of pessimism'—financial panic and crashes. This creates a problematic stop-go investment pattern, and in overall terms slower economic growth and productivity growth results. Furthermore, investment seems to flow into states with obviously unsound economic positions, such as Russia in 1998, and within these states, investments appear to be diverted into consumption and high-return/high-risk investments (Ocampo *et al.* 2008: 1–25; Prasad *et al.* 2003; Rodrik 1998). One clear empirical observation from these crises is the apparent success of the capital controls utilized by Malaysia (Moschella 2010: 107–9), despite direct opposition to this strategy from the IMF (Camdessus 1997; IMF 1997: 91, 1999: 36). The 'Chilean model' of dampening short-term capital flows consequently became an acceptable strategy for dealing with an economic crisis, especially for particularly vulnerable small open economies, and even the IMF eventually came round to this position (Sachs and Woo 1999).

Indeed, as rapid financial liberalization clearly constituted a departure from the developmental state model, and crucially involved the abandonment of key elements of the industrial policy that characterized the developmental states—particularly control over the banking and financial sector—this must be seen as a main cause of the Asian economic crisis of 1997/98 (Chang 2006: 53; Jayasuriya 2000: 328–30). The IMF interventions, furthermore, must be understood as a direct attempt at dismantling remaining elements of Asia's developmental states. As the development states remain the only successful post-war development model, the clash between this and neo-liberal models of development is crucial for international political economy. Indeed, the Asian economic crisis spawned debates concerning the end of 'Asian capitalism', and of neo-liberal convergence (Beeson and Robison 2000: 17; see Bello 2010: 196–98). In addressing this debate, the significance of the failure of the IMF's 'good governance' interventions in crisis-ridden Asia should not be underestimated, as the dominant development paradigm of the time was revealed as a depoliticized, 'technicist' fallacy (Leftwich 2000).

Unfortunately for states in East and South-East Asia, this revelation took the form of severe socioeconomic and political crises. With their legitimacy grounded in their ability to deliver economic gains to broad swaths of their population, the very fact of the crisis undermined key social coalitions that supported regimes—with key lessons for China in particular (Holbig and Gilley 2010). Some reasserted themselves (South Korea and Malaysia), others slipped into a strange combination of failed state and re-legitimization through democratization (Indonesia and the Philippines), while Thailand has vacillated between these two poles (Case 2009: 100–4). The failure of democratic consolidation in Thailand is itself an important question of political economy in post-crisis Asia, and particularly for liberal theories of democratization. Overall, the future of Asia's 'illiberal democracies' remains both complex and opaque. In economic terms, the crisis of 1997/98 rendered it necessary for Asian states to restructure, refinance and consolidate their banking and financial sectors, including through forced closures and mergers, as well as to move to a flexible exchange rate, improve regulatory capacity, reduce numbers of non-performing loans, and improve their fiscal positions. Most significantly, they reduced their dependence on short-term loans and financing, and as a consequence, were well placed to weather the storm of the 2007 global economic crisis (Ee and Zheng 2009: 93–100; Fazio 2010: 103).

The IMF also suffered political consequences: effectively an opaque organization prior to the crisis, it was by 1998 publically and widely criticized for exacerbating the crisis. All IMF interventions between 1997 and 1999 failed, some within a matter of weeks. Demanding compensation for international speculators for their losses and assisting states in defending pegged exchange rates are certainly amongst the worst examples of IMF decision making in this period (Sachs and Woo 1999). Managing Director of the IMF Michel Camdessus now proclaimed that the IMF's job was to be 'responsive to the cries of the poor' (Gray 1999), and in the medium term, the IMF drastically reduced the scope and scale of its policy conditions, and moderated its position on a range of different development-related issues (Woods 2006: 3). By the time the global economic crisis struck in 2007, the IMF was out of clients, and at its lowest ebb in terms of intergovernmental support: closing the IMF down was under serious discussion. Furthermore, given the range of new clients and the recent recapitalization of the IMF, it is fair to observe that the 'credit crunch' has saved the IMF (Moschella 2010). Nevertheless, with senior IMF staff commenting that Asia's economic recovery since 1998 is evidence that the IMF's response to the crisis had been right all along (Grenville 2009: 204–10), Stiglitz's 2002 comment that the IMF is not a 'learning organization' seems increasingly apt. Evidence of the failures of the IMF in this regard are made explicit, ironically, in a former IMF staffer's list of 'lessons' the IMF had purportedly learned from the Asian economic crisis (Neiss 2009: 254). In response to the 2007 global economic crisis, the IMF and its partners have pursued opposite policies to these supposedly learnt lessons—particularly with regard to 'austerity' (Wolf 2010).

The institutional divisions between the IMF and the World Bank over the neo-liberal development paradigm are also significant: given dual responsibility for international development, they in fact reveal the faults, fracture lines and tectonic shifts in how development is to be understood and promoted. Practical problems result for developing states in negotiation with the IFIs, bilateral donors and the non-governmental organization (NGO)/charity sector. Setting aside internal divisions over the costs and benefits of competing development strategies, there are clearly numerous competing pressures, and often contradictory policy advice and objectives (Calderisi 2006). At a critical juncture—that of region-wide economic crises—policy coordination mechanisms failed or were absent, and policy or ideological divisions solidified within what turned out to be, in essence, competing IFIs (see Keating 1999). The entire architecture of global governance, unable to manage financial globalization or effectively respond to the resultant economic crises, clearly failed, and reform was needed. However, as long as contagion did not affect the USA or the EU, wider lessons were ignored. Reforms—modest as they are—have only followed from the 2007 global economic crisis (Mosley and Singer 2011: 226–27; Moschella 2010: 126–27).

The 'elephant in the room' for the political economy of the East and South-East Asian region is China. Chinese industrialization is very much reliant on regional trade and investment patterns, but it also constitutes a direct and continuing challenge to the competitiveness of its regional partners (Felker 2009: 64; Ba 2009: 196–97). The Chinese devaluation of 1994 has therefore been seen as directly contributing to the economic crisis (Jomo 2000: 26; Winters 2000: 42). Another key regional issue for IPE scholarship pertains to regional institution building, which had been a significant focus of research prior to the 1997/98 crisis (Katzenstein 1997). Any questions concerning the function and significance of existing institutions were answered definitively by the economic crisis, in the sense that these institutions were conspicuous in their absence. However, it is crucial to note that in late 1997 the Japanese government offered to manage the economic crisis through an 'Asian Monetary Fund', potentially injecting $100 billion into the region. The USA and the IMF, unwilling to loosen their grip on global financial governance, rejected this proposal (Jomo 2009: 58; Moschella 2010: 101; Tiek 2000: 228). Post-crisis Asia, then, has been characterized by new forms of regional co-operation, including non-institutional forms of financial co-operation such as the Chiang-Mai initiative (Okfen 2003). Most importantly, the post-crisis East and South-East Asian region was in financial terms primarily driven by the desire to avoid the possibility of future IMF intervention. This took the form of reducing external debts, and generating large financial surpluses, which in turn contributed to the global financial imbalances that were partly responsible for the global financial crisis that struck in 2007 (Germain 2010: 79; Cafruny 2010: 122; Nesvetailova 2010: 74–78).

Finally, the neo-liberal model of capitalism that underpinned the financial liberalization of the last 25 years appears to have vindicated Karl Polanyi's 1944 thesis in *The Great Transformation* (Polanyi 2001), regarding the inherent instability and socially pernicious consequences of an unregulated market economy. This was made apparent in the emerging market crises of 1997/98, and the similarities of these crises with the ongoing global financial crisis that began in 2007 are sufficient to raise the question of why reforms to the global financial system did not take place; why the Asian economic crisis has served as the Cassandra of modern economic times. Failure to learn lessons regarding asset-inflationary spirals, liberalization and under-regulation, the role of international financial capital and of course the speed and breadth of processes of contagion resulted in a Western economic crisis. Failure to learn the lessons of past IMF interventions has led to the contemporary repetition of the socioeconomic and political consequences of the Asian economic crisis across much of Europe. If anything, the threat of contagion in the global political economy has grown more serious in the intervening decade. *Real contagion* possibilities grow with increased real economic interdependence. *Financial contagion* possibilities grow with increased financial interdependence and with the financialization of the global economy. *Informational contagion*, in particular, appears an unavoidable consequence of the longstanding problem of the irrationality of economic actors, an observation which certainly does not exclude those in international finance (Keynes 2011 [1921]; Veblen 1994 [1899]).

REFERENCES

Akyüz, Y. (1998) 'The East Asian Financial Crisis: Back to the Future', in K.S. Jomo (ed.) *Tigers in Trouble: Financial Governance, Liberalisation and Crises in East Asia*, London: Zed Books, 33–43.

Allen, F. and Gale, D. (1999) 'The Asian Crisis and the Process of Financial Contagion', *Journal of Financial Regulation and Compliance* 7(3): 243–49.

Amsden, A.H. (1993) 'Asia's Industrial Revolution: "Late Industrialisation" on the Rim', *Dissent* 40 (Summer): 324–32.

Applebaum, R. and Henderson, J. (eds) (1992) *State and Development in the Asian Pacific Rim*, Newbury Park, CA: Sage Publications, 33–70.

Ba, A.D. (2009) 'A New History: The Structure and Process of Southeast Asia's Relations with a Rising China', in M. Beeson (ed.) *Contemporary Southeast Asia*, Basingstoke: Palgrave Macmillan, 192–207.

Beeson, M.K. (2007) *Regionalism and Globalization in East Asia: Politics, Security, and Economic Development*, Basingstoke: Palgrave Macmillan.

Beeson, M.K. and Bell, S. (2000) 'Australia in the Shadow of the Asian Crisis', in Richard Robison *et al.* (eds) *Politics and Markets in the Wake of the Asian Crisis*, London: Routledge, 297–312.

Beeson, M.K. and Robison, R. (2000) 'Introduction: Interpreting the Crisis', in Richard Robison *et al.* (eds) *Politics and Markets in the Wake of the Asian Crisis*, London: Routledge, 3–24.

Bello, W. (2010) 'States and Markets, States Versus Markets: The Developmental State Debate as the Distinctive East Asian Contribution to International Political Economy', in M. Blyth (ed.) *Routledge Handbook of International Political Economy (IPE): IPE as a Global Conversation*, Abingdon: Routledge, 180–200.

Cafruny, A.W. (2010) 'The Global Financial Crisis and the Crisis of European Neoliberalism', in L.S. Talani (ed.) *The Global Crash: Towards a New Global Financial Regime?*, Basingstoke: Palgrave Macmillan, 121–39.

Calderisi, R. (2006) *The Trouble with Africa: Why Foreign Aid is Not Working*, New York: Palgrave Macmillan.

Calvo, G.A. and Talvi, E. (2008) 'Sudden Stop, Financial Factors, and Economic Collapse in Latin America: Learning from Chile and Argentina', in N. Serra and J. E. Stiglitz (eds) *The Washington Consensus Reconsidered: Towards a New Global Governance: Towards a New Global Governance*, Oxford: Oxford University Press, 119–49.

Camdessus, M. (1996) 'Is the New Bretton Woods Conceivable', Address to the Société d'Economie Politique, Paris, 19 January, Washington, DC: International Monetary Fund.

—— (1997) 'The Agenda for Global Financial Cooperation', Address to the Association of Japanese Business Studies, Washington, DC, 13 June, Washington, DC: International Monetary Fund.

—— (1998) 'The IMF and Good Governance', Address at Transparency International, Paris, France, 21 January, Washington, DC: International Monetary Fund.

—— (1999) 'Governments and Economic Development in a Globalized World', Remarks at the 32nd International General Meeting of the Pacific Basin Economic Council, Hong Kong, 17 May, Washington, DC: International Monetary Fund.

—— (1999a) 'Looking Beyond Today's Financial Crisis: Moving Forward with International Financial Reform', Remarks to the Foreign Policy Association, New York, 24 February, Washington, DC: International Monetary Fund.

Carroll, T. (2010) *Delusions of Development: The World Bank and the Post-Washington Consensus in Southeast Asia*, New York: Palgrave Macmillan.

Case, W. (2009) 'The Evolution of Democratic Politics', in M. Beeson (ed.) *Contemporary Southeast Asia*, Aldershot: Palgrave Macmillan, 91–110.

Chang, H.-J. (1998) 'South Korea: The Misunderstood Crisis', in K.S. Jomo (ed.) *Tigers in Trouble: Financial Governance, Liberalisation and Crises in East Asia*, London: Zed Books, 222–31.

—— (2006) *The East Asian Development Experience: The Miracle, the Crisis and the Future*, London: Zed Books.

Chiodo, A.J. and Owyang, M.T. (2002) 'A Case Study of a Currency Crisis: The Russian Default of 1998', *Federal Reserve Bank of St. Louis Review* (November/December): 7–18.

Dalrymple, R. (1998) 'Indonesia and the IMF: The Evolving Consequences of a Reforming Mission', *Australian Journal of Political Science* 52(3): 233–39.

Dore, R. (1987) *Taking Japan Seriously—A Confucian Perspective on Leading Economic Issues*, London: The Athlone Press.

Edison, H.J., Luangaram, P. and Miller, M. (1998) 'Asset Bubbles, Domino Effects and "Lifeboats": Elements of the East Asian Crisis', *CEPR Discussion Paper No. 1866*, London: Centre for Economic Policy Research.

Ee, K.H. and Zheng, K.W. (2009) 'Ten Years From the Financial Crisis: Managing the Challenges Posed by Capital Flows', in R.W. Carney (ed.) *Lessons from the Asian Financial Crisis*, New York: Routledge, 84–111.

Evangelist, M. and Sathe, V. (2006) 'Brazil's 1998–99 Currency Crisis', unpublished paper.

Evans, P.B. (1995) *Embedded Autonomy: States and Industrial Transformation*, Princeton, NJ: Princeton University Press.

Fazio, G. (2010) 'Emerging Markets and the Global Financial Crisis', in L.S. Talani (ed.) *The Global Crash: Towards a New Global Financial Regime?*, London: Palgrave Macmilllan, 100–20.

Felker, G. (2009) 'The Political Economy of Southeast Asia', in M. Beeson (ed.) *Contemporary Southeast Asia*, Aldershot: Palgrave Macmillan, 46–73.

Feridun, M. (2004) 'Russian Financial Crisis of 1998: An Econometric Investigation', *International Journal of Applied Econometrics and Quantitative Studies* 1(4): 113–22.

Fouskas, V.K. and Gökay, B. (2012) *The Fall of the US Empire*, London: Pluto Press.

Germain, R. (2010) *Global Politics and Financial Governance*, Basingstoke: Palgrave Macmillan.

Gray, J. (1999) 'IMF Suddenly Hears the Poor', *The Australian Financial Review*, 4 October.

Grenville, S. (2009) 'Ten Years After the Asian Crisis: Is the IMF Ready for "Next Time"?', in R.W. Carney (ed.) *Lessons From the Asian Financial Crisis*, New York: Routledge, 198–221.

Hale, D.D. (1998) 'The IMF, Now More than Ever: The Case for Financial Peacekeeping', *Foreign Affairs* 77(6): 7–13.

Hewison, K. (2000) 'Thailand's Capitalism Before and After the Economic Crisis', in Richard Robison et al. (eds) *Politics and Markets in the Wake of the Asian Crisis*, London: Routledge, 192–211.

Higgott, R. (2000) 'The International Relations of the Asian Economic Crisis: A Study in the Politics of Resentment', in Richard Robison et al. (eds) *Politics and Markets in the Wake of the Asian Crisis*, London: Routledge, 261–82.

Holbig, H. and Gilley, B. (2010) 'Reclaiming Legitimacy in China', *Politics & Policy* 38(3): 395–422.

International Monetary Fund (IMF) (1990) *Annual Report 1990*, Washington, DC: IMF.

——(1994) *Annual Report 1994*, Washington, DC: IMF.

——(1997) *Annual Report 1997*, Washington, DC: IMF.

——(1997a) *Good Governance: The IMF's Role*, Washington, DC: IMF.

——(1998) *Annual Report 1998*, Washington, DC: IMF.

——(1999) *Annual Report 1999*, Washington, DC: IMF.

Ito, T. (2007) 'Asian Currency Crisis and the International Monetary Fund, 10 Years Later: Overview', *Asian Economic Policy Review* 2(1): 16–49.

Jayasuriya, K. (2000) 'Authoritarian Liberalism, Governance and the Emergence of the Regulatory State in Post-Crisis East Asia', in Richard Robison et al. (eds) *Politics and Markets in the Wake of the Asian Crisis*, London: Routledge, 315–30.

Jenkins, R. (1991) 'The Political Economy of Industrialisation: A Comparison of Latin America and East Asian Newly Industrializing Countries', *Development and Change* 22: 197–231.

Johnson, C. (1982) *MITI and the Japanese Miracle: The Growth of Industrial Policy, 1925–1975*, Stanford, CA: Stanford University Press.

Jomo, K.S. (1998) 'Introduction: Financial Governance, Liberalisation and Crises in East Asia', in K.S. Jomo (ed.) *Tigers in Trouble: Financial Governance, Liberalisation and Crises in East Asia*, London: Zed Books, 1–32.

——(2000) 'Comment: Crisis and the Developmental State in East Asia', in Richard Robison et al. (eds) *Politics and Markets in the Wake of the Asian Crisis*, London: Routledge, 25–33.

——(2009) 'Causes of the 1997/1998 East Asian Crises and Obstacles to Implementing Lessons', in R.W. Carney (ed.) *Lessons from the Asian Financial Crisis*, New York: Routledge, 33–64.

Jorion, P. (2000) 'Risk Management Lessons from Long-Term Capital Management', *European Financial Management* 6(3): 277–300.

Katzenstein, P.J. (1997) 'Introduction: Asian Regionalism in Comparative Perspective', in P.J. Katzenstein (ed.) *Network Power: Japan and Asia*, New York: Cornell University Press, 1–45.

Keating, M.F. (1999) 'Divergence and Convergence between the IMF and the World Bank's Conceptions of Development during the 1990s', in *Proceedings of the 1999 Conference of the Australasian Political Studies Association*, Volume II: Refereed Papers, Sydney: University of Sydney, 429–38.

Keating, M.F., Kuzemko, C., Belyi, A.V. and Goldthau, A. (2012) 'Introduction: Bringing Energy into International Political Economy', in C. Kuzemko, A.V. Belyi, A. Goldthau and M.F. Keating (eds) *Dynamics of Energy Governance in Europe and Russia*, Basingstoke: Palgrave Macmillan, 1–22.

Keohane, R. and Nye, J. (1977) *Power and Interdependence: World Politics in Transition*, Boston, MA: Little, Brown.

Keynes, J.M. (2011 [1921]) *A Treatise on Probability*, La Vergne, TN: Lightning Source.

Khor, M. (2008) 'The Malaysian Experience in Financial-Economic Crisis Management: An Alternative to the IMF-Style Approach', in J.A. Ocampo and J.E. Stiglitz (eds) *Capital Market Liberalization and Development*, Oxford: Oxford University Press, 205–25.

Krugman, P. (1979) 'A Model of Balance-of-Payments Crises', *Journal of Money, Credit, and Banking* 11(3): 311–25.

——(2000) *The Return of Depression Economics*, London: W.W. Norton & Co.

Lal, D. (1983) *The Poverty of Development Economics*, London: The Institute of Economic Affairs.

——(1999) *Renewing the Miracle: Economic Development and Asia*, Melbourne, Victoria: Institute of Public Affairs.

Lauridsen, L.S. (1998) 'Thailand: Causes, Conduct, Consequences', in K.S. Jomo (ed.) *Tigers in Trouble: Financial Governance, Liberalisation and Crises in East Asia*, London: Zed Books, 137–61.

Leftwich, A. (2000) *States of Development: On the Primacy of Politics in Development*, Cambridge: Polity.

MacIntyre, A. (ed.) (1994) *Business and Government in Industrialising Asia*, St Leonards: Allen and Unwin.

Moschella, M. (2010) *Governing Risk: The IMF and Global Financial Crises*, Hampshire: Palgrave Macmillan.

Mosley, L. and Singer, D.A. (2011) 'The Global Financial Crisis: Lessons and Opportunities for International Political Economy', in N. Phillips and C. Weaver (eds) *International Political Economy: Debating the Past, Present and Future*, Abingdon: Routledge, 223–30.

Neiss, H. (2009) 'Conclusions', in R.W. Carney (ed.) *Lessons from the Asian Financial Crisis*, New York: Routledge, 249–56.

Nesvetailova, A. (2010) *Financial Alchemy in Crisis: The Great Liquidity Illusion*, London: Pluto Press.

Ocampo, J.A., Spiegel, S. and Stiglitz, J.E. (2008) 'Capital Market Liberalization and Development', in J.A. Ocampo and J.E. Stiglitz (eds) *Capital Market Liberalization and Development*, Oxford: Oxford University Press, 1–47.

Okfen, N. (2003) 'Towards an East Asian Community? What ASEM and APEC Can Tell Us', *CSGR Working Paper No. 117/03* University of Warwick, Centre for the Study of Globalisation and Regionalisation, June.

Pauly, L.W. (1994) 'Promoting a Global Economy: The Normative Role of the International Monetary Fund', in Richard Stubbs and Geoffrey Underhill (eds) *Political Economy and the Changing Global Order*, London: Macmillan.

Perotti, E. (2002) 'Lessons from the Russian Meltdown: The Economics of Soft Legal Constraints', *International Finance* 5(3): 359–99.

Pinto, B. and Ulatov, S. (2010) 'Financial Globalization and the Russian Crisis of 1998', *Policy Research Working Paper Series No.5312*, Washington, DC: World Bank.

Polanyi, K. (2001 [1944]) *The Great Transformation: The Political and Economic Origins of Our Time*, Boston, MA: Beacon Press.

Prasad, E., Rogoff, K., Wei, S.J. and Kose, M.A. (2003) 'Effects of Financial Globalisation on Developing Countries: Some Empirical Evidence', *IMF occasional Paper No. 220*, Washington, DC: International Monetary Fund.

Ravenhill, J. (2009) 'From Miracle to Misadventure: The Political Economy of the 1997–98 Crises', in R.W. Carney (ed.) *Lessons from the Asian Financial Crisis*, New York: Routledge, 15–32.

Robertson, J. (2007) 'Reconsidering American Interests in Emerging Market Crises: An Unanticipated Outcome to the Asian Financial Crisis', *Review of International Political Economy* 14(2): 276–305.

——(2008) *Power and Politics after Financial Crises: Rethinking Foreign Opportunism in Emerging Markets*, Basingstoke: Palgrave Macmillan.

Robison, R. and Rosser, A. (2000) 'Surviving the Meltdown: Liberal Reform and Political Oligarchy in Indonesia', in Richard Robison *et al.* (eds) *Politics and Markets in the Wake of the Asian Crisis*, London: Routledge, 171–91.

Rodrik, D. (1998) 'Who Needs Capital Account Convertibility?' in S. Fischer *et al.* (eds) *Should the IMF Pursue Capital Account Convertibility?* Essays in International Finance No. 207, Princeton, NJ: Princeton University Press.

Sachs, J.D. and Woo, W.T. (1999) 'Executive Summary: The Asian Financial Crisis: What Happened, and What is to Be Done', *World Economic Forum (Asia Competitiveness Report 1999)*.

Smith, A.L. (2001) 'Indonesia: Transforming the Leviathan', in J. Funston (ed.) *Government and Politics in Southeast Asia*, London: Zed Books, 74–119.

Stiglitz, J. (1998) 'The Role of International Financial Institutions in the Current Global Economy', Address to the Chicago Council on Foreign Relations, Chicago, 27 February. Washington, DC: The World Bank.

——(1998a) 'Sound Finance and Sustainable Development in Asia', Keynote Address to the Asia Development Forum, Manila, 12 March, Washington, DC: The World Bank.

——(2000) 'Capital Market Liberalization, Economic Growth, and Instability', *World Development* 28(6): 1075–86.

——(2002) *Globalization and its Discontents*, London: Penguin.

Stubbs, R. (2005) *Rethinking Asia's Economic Miracle: The Political Economy of War, Prosperity and Crisis*, New York: Palgrave Macmillan.

Taylor, L. (1997) 'The Revival of the Liberal Creed—the IMF and the World Bank in a Globalized Economy', *World Development* 25(2): 145–52.

Tiek, K.B. (2000) 'Economic Nationalism and its Discontents: Malaysian Political Economy after July 1997', in Richard Robison *et al.* (eds) *Politics and Markets in the Wake of the Asian Crisis*, London: Routledge, 212–37.

——(2003) *Beyond Mahathir: Malaysian Politics and its Discontents*, London: Zed Books.

Vatikiotis, M. (1998) *Indonesian Politics Under Suharto: The Rise and Fall of the New Order*, third edn, New York: Routledge.

Veblen, T. (1994 [1899]) *The Theory of the Leisure Class*, New York: Penguin.

Wade, R. (1990) *Governing the Market: Economic Theory and the Role of Government in East Asian Industrialisation*, Princeton, NJ: Princeton University Press.

——(1998) 'From "Miracle" to "Cronyism": Explaining the Great Asian Slump', *Cambridge Journal of Economics* 22: 693–706.

——(1998a) 'The Asian Debt-and-Development Crisis of 1997–? Causes and Consequences', *World Development* 26(8): 1535–53.

Weiss, L. and Hobson, J.M. (2000) 'State Power and Economic Strength Revisited: What's So Special about the Asian Crisis', in Richard Robison *et al.* (eds) *Politics and Markets in the Wake of the Asian Crisis*, London: Routledge, 53–74.

Williams, W.A. (1972) *The Tragedy of American Diplomacy*, New York: W.W. Norton.

Williamson, J. (1993) 'Democracy and the "Washington Consensus"', *World Development* 21(8): 1329–36.

Winters, J.A. (2000) 'The Financial Crisis in Southeast Asia', in Richard Robison *et al.* (eds) *Politics and Markets in the Wake of the Asian Crisis*, London: Routledge, 34–52.

Wolf, M. (2010) 'The IMF's Foolish Praise for Austerity', *Financial Times*, 30 September.

Wolfensohn, J.D. (1999) 'Remarks at the International Conference on Democracy, Market Economy and Development', Seoul, 26 February, Washington, DC: The World Bank.

Woods, N. (2006) *The Globalizers: The IMF, the World Bank and their Borrowers*, New York: Cornell University Press.

World Bank (1991) *World Development Report 1991: The Challenge of Development*, New York: Oxford University Press.

——(1993) *The East Asian Miracle: Economic Growth and Public Policy*, Oxford: Oxford University Press.

——(1997) *World Development Report 1997: The State in a Changing World*, New York: Oxford University Press.

——(1998) *East Asia: The Road to Recovery*, Washington, DC: The World Bank.

——(1999) *World Development Report 1998–9: Knowledge for Development*, New York: Oxford University Press.

The rise of the *qi ye ji tuan* and the emergence of Chinese hegemony

JAYANTHA JAYMAN

INTRODUCTION

By all accounts China is now awake, having risen from the ranks of the ancient Middle Kingdom to be considered a potential hegemon to succeed the USA. Some accounts of 'China's rise' focus on Chinese exceptionalism— mainly suggesting that China has a unique form of 'state capitalism' (Halper 2010). Other accounts suggest a large and diverse space with many systems that continue to evolve.[1] Yet others suggest that China's arrangements can be seen as providing a developmental model for other states with paths that differ from the Western histories underlying the Washington Consensus. However, a broader historical view provides important insights. Attention to List's (1928 [1841]) interest in protectionism and championing of strategic industries and nationalism following Alexander Hamilton informed industrialization elsewhere, including in Germany and Japan, and this vantage point suggest China's rise is consistent with other major powers in the modern era. China's form of nationalist capitalism in the current era of globalization is consistent with Marx's insight into the importance of the modern nation over provincialism which heralds bourgeois victory (Marx and Engels 1975: vol. VI, 486, 519; vol. VIII, 161). The broader historical view taken in this chapter, attentive to both List's prescription and Marxist critique, suggests the need for caution in assessing China. The chapter questions both China's differences from and similarities to the capitalist powers to which it has so often been contrasted by those concerned with hegemony. In the current political economic climate, debate over China's role is often dominated by those who are fearful, given the importance of hegemony historically and concern for the future. Yet, when it comes to assessing China's trajectory and hegemonic potential, simple answers cannot do justice to the complex—and sometimes contradictory—forces evident in the historical circumstances that surround capitalism.

Hegemonic power is both contested and fluid. If we consider the Western-dominated global system from as early as the 15th century, there have been several hegemonic powers and contenders that have attempted to create the world order in their own images. Indeed, it is possible to identify a succession of hegemons dominant on the world stage for varying periods of time, with dominance based on pre-eminence in a variety of areas:

- Portugal 1494 to 1580 (end of Italian Wars to Spanish invasion of Portugal). Based on Portugal's dominance in navigation. Hegemonic pretender: Spain.
- Holland 1580 to 1688 (1579 Treaty of Utrecht marks the foundation of the Dutch Republic to William of Orange's arrival in England). Based on Dutch control of credit and money. Hegemonic pretender: England.
- Britain 1688 to 1792 (Glorious Revolution to Napoleonic Wars). Based on British textiles and command of the high seas. Hegemonic pretender: France.
- Britain 1815 to 1914 (Congress of Vienna to World War I). Based on British industrial supremacy and railroads. Hegemonic pretender: Germany.
- United States 1945 to 1971. Based on petroleum and the internal combustion engine. Hegemonic pretender: the USSR.

(Ferraro 2012)

With much at stake—not just the twin goals of capitalism and democracy, but also 'Western' culture itself—the identity of the world's next hegemon is understandably a key concern in the interregnum, the period between hegemonic orders. If we consider the last transfer of hegemonic power, from Great Britain to the USA, it is apparent that this was realized only after calamitous events. The hundred-year peace ended with World War I, which eventually forced Britain off the Gold Standard, and the Great Depression confirmed the end of British hegemony. Unused to being the key major power over two world wars, the USA only established its hegemony with a late entry into World War II. Historical experience suggests the present interregnum is not only a period of concern over capitalism and democracy, but also one of concern for issues of war and peace, given that hegemonic decline in the past has been marked by economic turmoil and war.

The work of Charles Kindleberger (1973) posited that a stable liberal global system needed a hegemon. Kindleberger (1973: 291) suggests that 'the 1929 depression was so wide, so deep and so long because the international economic system was rendered unstable by British inability and United States unwillingness to assume responsibility for stabilizing it ... '. The USA eventually led the way in setting up the Bretton Woods system and rebuilding Europe and Japan, creating a world that suited itself. It was in the 1970s that its excesses began to show with a departure from the Gold Standard itself. The rise of Japan in the 1980s seemed to herald a new regional hegemon, and one that suggested peaceful transition by providing the necessary regional public goods for developmentalism to succeed in the region, given that the country was the only industrialized nation without projectable military power (Jayman 2004). Yet Japan, to all intents and purposes, also sustained US hegemony in what has come to be known as the *nichibei* economy (Gilpin 1987). This collaborative hegemony, which included Western powers, allowed alternative views of managing the world economy via the G-7 nations led by

The rise of the qi ye ji tuan

the USA, but relied on US power when it mattered most. Thus hegemony—the ability to lead (the world) in the hegemon's own long-term interests—has been a key concern for the Western academy ever since the US share of the world economy began to decline after the 1970s.

The late scholar Susan Strange (1987: 552) once observed:

> In its extreme form, the myth that the United States today is just a little old country much like any other and has, in some sudden and miraculous way, lost its hegemonic power may seem more plausible than do some of these other myths. But when it is subjected to close and searching scrutiny, it is just as far from truth. And unless cool and rational analysis undermines its power to move minds and shape attitudes, it can be every bit as dangerous.

While in the 1980s Strange's sentiment seemed reasonable, particularly given the role of the USA in maintaining the G-7 nations via informal and formal treaties to assist with a broad hegemonic programme of free markets and a governance system labelled 'democracy' that managed to allow the deepening inequity of the markets systems, 30 years later the question of US decline has re-emerged in the face of the rapid and sustained rise of China, but also the deepening chaos in the post-war American project in Europe (Fouskas and Gökay 2012; Fouskas and Dimoulas 2013). The relative decline of the 'West' that shares a broadly similar vision of 'democracy' and capitalism has caused alarm in many Western capitals, but it is US power that has been of most concern.

In the realm of structure and capability, deemed essential for sustained hegemony, the US share of world gross domestic product (GDP) shrunk from about 25% in the years after World War II to less than 20% after the terrorist attacks on the USA of 11 September 2001, with much of the decline due to Asian re-emergence. When expressed in purchasing power parity (PPP) terms, as in Figure 7.1, the decline in the US share of world GDP has been a telling 23% to 18% from 1980 to 2000, a 5% decline in 20 years with an increase in the rate of decline in the first decade of the 21st century.

In estimates by the IMF (2012), by 2017 China will have the largest economy in the world. The share of the G-7 plus Australia, though, has managed to keep up with China, suggesting a crucial role of the club for the USA in the years ahead, particularly with the emergence of India and also the re-emergence of Russia. Thus, when considering relative US decline, one cannot also overestimate Chinese power, given other actors in the global political economy with which China had experience in the late 19th and early 20th centuries.

In less than 75 years a nationalist China has emerged from being dominated and occupied by Western powers and Japan to being a state that is now dominant in economic terms, but also in other areas pertinent to the role of global hegemon. Against the background of the relative decline of US power, this chapter considers China's potential for world hegemony, focusing on the

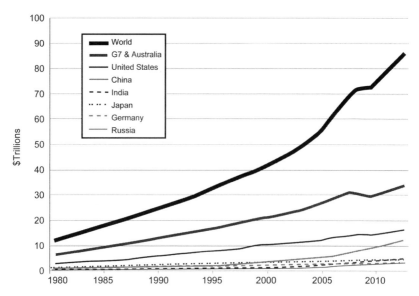

Figure 7.1 GDP: World, G7 + Australia, China, India, Russia
(US$ trillion PPP, Source: World Bank)

historical development of the large transnational corporation (TNC) from China as the bearer of daily hegemonic interests. It does so by considering how developments of nationalist capitalism speak to tensions between the ideas of Friedrich List and Karl Marx, both critics of imperialism, but not capitalism itself, a sense best conveyed in 1845 by Marx when he noted of List: 'The German idealising philistine who wants to become wealthy must, of course, first create for himself a new theory of wealth, one which makes wealth worthy of his striving for it' (Marx and Engels 1975: vol. IV, 265).

By critically considering the historical failures and successes that have coloured China's present-day authoritarian capitalist project that is now in contact with the rest of the world through the rise of China's large firms, it is possible better to understand the potential repercussions both within China and beyond its borders. In the development of these firms, the Western (Hegelian) notion of the end of history thesis that informs the Washington Consensus is challenged by what some see as a Beijing Consensus, an entirely different way of conducting capitalism alongside a very different conception of international community.[2] By considering the history of China's failures to achieve bourgeois capitalism (that is, via the well-worn path of oligarchic parliaments gradually yielding power to fractions of classes just below to gain what we now term 'democracy' and the emergence of the joint stock firms owned by the bourgeoisie that now encompass the world), we can better understand the specific trajectory that has led to China's 20th-century brand of capitalism without democracy and consider the implications for its hegemonic potential (Tsai 2007).

The rise of the qi ye ji tuan

THE HISTORICAL EMERGENCE OF CHINA

China's historical geography—an isolated landmass, east of the Himalayas and south of the cold Siberian spaces, contained on the east and south by the Pacific Ocean—shaped its emergence as an empire and then a modern national state. Historically preoccupied with developments in the eastern region of the Asian continent, over 2,000 years China has emerged as the dominant power of the region, contributing much to world technology in the process.[3] The regional preoccupation of leaders and bureaucrats did, however, minimize China's overseas trajectory in marked contrast to seaborne trajectories of relatively tiny countries such as Portugal, Holland and Great Britain, all of which were historically characterized by an outward orientation born of necessity. This meant that China encountered the West's early trading firms much later than it otherwise might have done, and not on its own terms. Driven by internal imperial and bureaucratic struggles that carried on for centuries, China, despite the presence of traders, had not developed the firm as a means to incorporate the wealth and ideas of others in distant lands. This presents a contrast to the West, where the role of the joint stock firm can be seen as central in the development of early capitalism and extending hegemony overseas. Jealous of Arab traders' control of East–West trade, Portuguese seafarers, who sought a route to Asian riches, were succeeded by highly organized Dutch firms which had the benefit of experience in the Hanseatic League, which predated the idea of the nation itself. With modernity and the establishment of the nation-state, the Dutch were in turn surpassed by the British, whose firms succeeded with increasingly powerful naval forces capable of projecting power far, thus being able to convert trading ports, even those extracted from major entities, such as India and China, into new colonies. Underpinned by the irony of using the Chinese discovery of gunpowder to maintain British dominance, the British firms dominated coastal areas of many parts of the world at a time when Britain's GDP was less than 10% of the world, and when China and India each had over 20% of world GDP (*The Economist* 2010).

While China and the Indian princely states influenced Europe through their technology and goods from a distance, absent an overseas commercial class, their power and interests remained regional. In this context, with its controllable pool of cheap labour at home, abundant resources from colonies and readily accessible global markets, as ports of land masses such as India took goods inland, capitalist accumulation in the classic Marxian sense of exploiting a proletariat matured first in Great Britain. With the British Parliament increasingly dominated by the *nouveau riche* of the time, the joint stock firm was accompanied by British naval power to further extend power all the way to China. The resulting warfare led to rapid advances in developing and adapting technology for military purposes.[4] With profits hard to come by in tough trading conditions, well-positioned British firms notoriously exploited China, creating drug dependency in seeking to gain Chinese silver coin, leading to the Opium Wars.[5] The Chinese government was forced to sign unequal treaties which gave Western firms access to its massive market, with this leading to the destruction of central authority and an unravelling of the state, encouraging the emergence of warlords that ensured the fragmentation of the Middle Kingdom.

In this historic context, Sun Yat Sen, the first leader of republican China, was influenced indirectly by the nationalist ideas of German thinker Friedrich List via Meiji-era Japan, and directly by his visit to Germany (Jansen 1954: 19). In his writings, List (1928 [1841]) drew attention to the importance of catch-up development and of protecting territorial space. Yet his nationalism as a reaction to imperialism had to be complemented by an understanding of class relations in contributing to the development of capitalism in national contexts, something well understood by Karl Marx.[6] It was Mao Tse-tung (1926) who managed to put things together eventually to develop a communism that was also nationalist. Mao termed Sun Yet Sen a *comprador* for encouraging the interests of foreigners in China. Averse to Sun Yet Sen's reactionary nationalist vision of favouring an emergent bourgeoisie at the expense of peasants, Mao considered the proper form of nationalism to be communist in nature, and so China was united into one entity with the help of the working classes and peasants. Mao presided over rapid development of basic industries, a monumental task accomplished via totalitarian control of society in a process that sacrificed some 45 million people.[7]

With Mao's death, subsequent leaders have used nationalism to preside over an orderly move away from Chinese communism, embracing the state *and* market to organize the economy with China's own open-door policy—a contrast to the US open-door policy of the 19th century constrained only by the 1890s Gold Standard and the Bretton Woods system which slowed US imperialism for brief periods (Fouskas and Gökay 2012).[8] Similar to US open-door policies that managed to use the departure from the Bretton Woods system to expand overseas via dominance of global finance, the Chinese version has allowed China to force the handover of technology, export goods and run surpluses, suggesting greater emphasis on a nationalistic model more consistent with List's priorities. China's growth rates noted by *The Economist* (2012) averaged around 9% from 1980 to 2010 to become the subject of much interest and speculation, but all of this came on the backs of an exploited working class and ecosystem.

China has come to present a seemingly new model of authoritarian developmentalist capitalism embracing the state *and* market. Efforts have been made to maintain control of China from within, even with openness creating conditions conducive to domestic unrest, as are apparent in dramatically rising Gini indices, for example (Roberts 2011).[9] By the first decade of the 21st century, the rapid growth China's Gini coefficient had clearly set it apart from the other East Asian nations, threatening its stability and inducing leaders to use measures from coercion to extreme nationalism to show trials over corruption to maintain control. Thus, China has not succeeded in the growth

The rise of the qi ye ji tuan

with equity model of the recent past in the region, which was led by Japan in the 1960s and followed by Taiwan and the Republic of Korea (South Korea) in the 1970s, when the Gini coefficient fell or stayed low, thus giving some credence to the Asian 'miracle' literature (see Amsden 1989; Haggard 1990; Jayman 2004). China's deviation with a high Gini coefficient at the initial phase of industrialization drew attention to the region before the China model was recast in its present form, highlighting contradictions facing China's leaders.[10] As the income gap widened in China, by the 1990s the pattern of China's high Gini coefficient was set in place with the other Asian countries also beginning to develop high inequity (*The Economist* 2007).

In the context of authoritarian capitalism, China's role in the world has emerged as a concern for many, not least because China seems well positioned as a potential hegemon to offer an alternative to the Washington Consensus (Breslin 2011). In order to appreciate better China's current position and potential trajectory, however, it is essential to understand how capitalism has developed in this particular space to involve an authoritarian market system that is increasingly underpinned by *qi ye ji tuan*, or enterprise groups, which have been important in other capitalisms historically, but which have a distinct Chinese characteristic born of particular attempts at capitalist development within China. These enterprise groups are rapidly developing a global reach to obtain the necessary raw materials and markets to service diverse types of industries, which operate under models ranging from classic state enterprise systems to totally private firms. They are the backbone of any Chinese hegemonic epoch to come, and thus must be understood as far as possible, as the implications for post-colonial societies stand to be profound.

A potential Chinese hegemonic project arguably becomes real when the 'self-interest' of 'China' is being met, with Beijing pushing for its preferred organization of the world in order to facilitate this process. How much this may differ from classic Western hegemony is, however, not clear. Thus far, China's role has been controversial enough to elicit a backlash, as with the 1997 Asian economic crisis, when China was seen to undermine the region by redirecting investment to itself through a unilateral devaluation of its currency in 1994. With the growing role of *qi ye ji tuan* in Africa, there are problems that mirror those in Asia (Cheru and Obi 2010; Cheru and Modi 2013). While the focus on China itself has elicited feelings from admiration to alarm, the actions of the *qi ye ji tuan* merit particular scrutiny, especially within disciplines such as political science and international relations which readily mix the interests of nations with those of firms, or the interests of countries with the interests of the bourgeoisie.[11] While discourse about hegemony tends to be country specific, it is arguably the roles taken by firms that translate this into material reality, and so the interests of people and workers are often overlooked. Thus, attention to the development of China's *qi ye ji tuan*, and their interaction with the rest of the world, allows insight into the flavour of Chinese hegemonic potential against the background of the current US-centred hegemonic system of liberal capitalism that has served the West well for over

200 years. This also allows insight into the welfare of workers, whether in China or other places where workers are affected by Chinese firms.

THE EMERGENCE OF THE CHINESE AUTHORITARIAN MARKET SYSTEM AND THE *QI YE JI TUAN*

It is useful briefly to review the history of capitalism's development in the Chinese context—replete with successes and failures—in order to appreciate the specificity of this particular transformation compared to earlier capitalist transformations in Europe, as well as in the Asian powers of Japan and India. Historically, Chinese capitalism developed through a number of stages which effectively set the stage for China's contemporary position as a potential hegemon. Two of these are really important to note, before we can appreciate the present-day process.

First, what might be termed the 'organic' growth of capitalism ended in the Quing Dynasty, which crushed upstart social classes.[12] The crucial factor in this period of Chinese history was arguably the relative weakness of accumulation in terms of its slow growth and the easily identifiable upstart potential bourgeoisie class within a clearly stratified Chinese social system. In the end, social change that would have led to the rise of a bourgeoisie could not occur quickly enough to supersede the political economy of China, which at the time was run by dynastic politics in the face of territorial consolidation. As with other Asian nations, the internal focus left sea ways open for foreign capitalists to arrive from distant lands.

Second, following the imposition of unequal treaties on China in the middle of the 19th century, the West largely penetrated coastal China, reigniting China's entrepreneurs. This process accelerated in the 1920s when Europe was recovering from war and experiencing great demand for Asian goods. Capitalist development was, however, thwarted by war in China itself from the 1930s onwards and by the Japanese invasion, with Japan attempting to keep up with Western powers rather than be subjected to second-class status. Progress in this direction required the emergence of a strong party to draw China out of chaos and poverty. The strong party developed under Mao, leading to a triumphant Communist Party which provided the main resistance to the Imperial Japanese Army.

Capitalist transformation—which arguably we are now witnessing—finally came from within elements of the Chinese Communist Party itself under the influence of party elders at first, but increasingly under the nouvelle bourgeoisie unleashed from within the party and then joined by those bourgeoisie who are considered millionaire and billionaire outsiders. In this context, the apparent success of China's capitalist development today comes from what can be understood as the emergence of a Listian form of nationalist capitalism that places the state at the centre, but is best interpreted in terms of large firms emerging under state tutelage as parastatals, then moving into private hands, leading to corporate capitalism all without a liberal stage, but all interested in exploiting a ready-made proletariat educated and organized to function almost seamlessly in the primitive stages of capitalism.[13]

The rise of the *qi ye ji tuan* and the emergence of Chinese hegemony

The current authoritarian market system in China is being sustained by a nouvelle bourgeoisie that has its origins not in the historical development of society as in the Western Anglo-American liberal model, but rather in dominating the historical state via presence within the fractured Communist Party elite. Their enterprise, though, is concentrated in the political geographies of the main cities with their readily available proletariat as a source of labour, and beyond this in the easily accessible parts of coastal China, signifying the deeper roots of these spaces in early 20th-century capitalist development of the country, mentioned above. This contemporary elite has been purged of communists, leaving nationalists to become the core of the nouvelle bourgeoisie in organizing the nation. Via deliberate direction and controversial mechanisms, the nouvelle bourgeoisie has emerged from within the authoritarian state to dominate parastatals being privatized. A mix of capitalists, party members, bureaucrats and the military draws together the Chinese state and market in an authoritarian market system with increasingly global reach, which has the potential for an alternative Beijing Consensus that is beyond being merely discursive when considering the global reach of the *qi ye ji tuan*.[14]

The reforms initiated by Deng Xiao Peng have produced results predictable for those familiar with the vision of Alexander Hamilton and the scholarship of Friedrich List (1928 [1841]) on national systems of political economy, providing a developmentalist outcome. When considering the economy, these reforms have allowed China to regain the lost prominence of the 19th and 20th centuries. While China is behind the US economy at the beginning of the second decade of the 21st century, it is well on its way to becoming the largest economy by the end of it. The emerging 'China model' has evolved over time, opening the door to private entrepreneurs, who are now allowed to join the Chinese Communist Party (CCP). Indeed, the CCP might be more accurately described as the Chinese Capitalist Party. Signifying the wealth being captured in private hands, China has two stock exchanges, while Chinese firms, including firms owned by the government, raise funds in international capital markets. China's parastatals, or state-owned enterprises (SOEs), have restructured and continue to keep the course of being able to meet global auditing standards, with China's *qi ye ji tuan* beginning to number among the world's largest companies.

The enterprise group, or conglomerate, appeared in Asia in its first full formation in the early 20th century, though there are traces of it before this time. In its most successful incarnation it emerged as the *keiretsu*, successor to the more nationalistic *zaibatsu* of Japan. There are six such consortia in Japan: Mitsubishi, Mitsui, Sumitomo, Fuji, Sanwa and the Dai-Ichi Kangyo Bank. These consortia control the six consortia of banks, and through mergers and banking they were reorganized into three financial holding groups: Mizuho

Bank, Sumitomo Mitsui Bank of Tokyo-Mitsubishi, and UFJ Financial Group. The Korean form of conglomerate is the *chaebol*. There are five such consortia in South Korea: Samsung, Hyundai, SK, LG and Lotte. It is important to understand that these major consortia in Japan and South Korea, which operated within *Pax Americana*, were developed after World War II. This occurred during the Cold War under US hegemony and with the tacit co-operation of Washington, which was interested in the rapid recovery of Asia's front-line states against communism. This style of firm arguably came about as a result of bourgeois classes in Asia seeking foreign technology, markets and credit, all of which the US hegemon was willing and able to provide. Firms thus saw that it was essential to get the backing of the state and at the same time buttress it against societal and outside pressures with state-firm-union arrangements that were more co-operative, compared to the pre-World War II strife between labour and capital. Decades later, debates on these formations are ongoing in China, in the presence of an authoritarian state, so it is apparent that the firms themselves have emerged to be dominant in the context of China's particular history of capitalist transformation.[15] It is clear, though, that China has become the space in which rapid accumulation has finally arrived, as evidenced by the rise of the *qi ye ji tuan*.

It is important to keep in mind that the successes of Japan and South Korea in implementing the *zaibatsu* model as *keiretsu* and *chaebol* lie in statist foundations. Moreover, rapid post-war economic development in these two countries led to increases in national standards of living. After nearly 50 years of formation of these conglomerates under semi-authoritarian systems, the more democratically accommodating Japan of the 1960s began implementing the 'income doubling plan', which was realized in 1967, and then again in 1973. Essentially, the people's standard of living went hand in hand with the growth of the big enterprises, encouraging the Japanese public to support their growth and appreciate their power—and all this was possible in a country of around 100 million people which fortuitously managed to supply two wars in Korea and Viet Nam. In South Korea, with less than half of the Japanese population, a similar pattern to Japan emerged, and its path from authoritarianism to democracy also came on the back of massive exports to the hegemon's market which allowed rapid material gain for workers in the country and under the security blanket provided by the USA, while technology transfer came from the USA and Japan. The developmentalist model of growth with equity did not come to China, however, as the implementation of policies that favour all the people seems to be far more muted, with a rising Gini coefficient (Roberts 2011) and dissent from below (O'Brien and Li 2006: 117). Reductions in the price of houses and rent, tuition fees, medical expenses, etc., will likely be constrained and controlled by the *qi ye ji tuan* for self-interest and profits, as worsening income disparities suggest a sustained transfer of wealth from Chinese workers to firms both domestic and foreign, and perhaps the one element that keeps capitalists from China and those from the outside at peace with each other. Thus while China's *qi ye ji tuan* can be

The rise of the qi ye ji tuan

compared to Japan's *keiretsu* and South Korea's *chaebol*, the nature of these conglomerates and their particular place in the development of contemporary Chinese capitalism and hegemonic potential suggests they may have different implications, both contradictory and co-operative.

SOEs and the creation of the *qi ye ji tuan*

Like trees marked by growth rings, the *qi ye ji tuan* provide glimpses of the past through the complicated and non-linear histories of China's feudalism, communism and capitalism. The feudal system that both Marx and Weber underestimated—unlike in Europe or India—bequeaths to China a tradition of strong bureaucracy and central power essential for capital accumulation, as well as a history of inequity that was controlled from above with enough coercion to maintain control and enough consent to maintain performance legitimacy.[16] It is the stage of Chinese state ownership under communism and near-monopoly status at home, however, that has allowed *qi ye ji tuan* their formidable gains in economies of scale in the home market and networks that are now global. Today, it is not the Chinese military that coercively manages hegemony, but rather Chinese firms, in the form of *qi ye ji tuan*, whose ready access to world markets makes them the global face of China, Inc., whilst bringing home the middle-class foods and raw materials that allow some upward mobility to those fortunate enough to have steady work.[17] While they are crucial for sustaining the Chinese authoritarian model by affording the state performance legitimacy, it is the *qi ye ji tuan* that also establish China's mark on the 21st century, whether in hegemonic terms that suggest the possibility of a Beijing Consensus as an alternative to the Washington Consensus, or merely a discursive juncture in the way Japan's rising model was in the 1980s (see Murphy 1989; van Wolferen 1990).

The images now being established by Chinese firms are not accidental, and they rather set the specific Chinese context. Many Chinese firms have histories dating back into the 19th century, before the establishment of the People's Republic and the nationalization of firms that took place under Mao.[18] During the early days of the People's Republic, the commanding heights of the economy were nationalized, consistent with communist dogma that guided the Soviet planning system, which was seen by many post-colonial states in positive terms, and which underpins their current status. The nationalization of industry in China was considered essential, not only to forestall the emergence of a bourgeois takeover of power as witnessed in Western nations, but also in terms of organizing the economy for war, crucial in the Listian formation of the nation-state. Keeping firms in the hands of the 'people' was consistent with communist ideals. To thwart the '*comprador* class'—which Mao defined in 1926 as 'the Chinese managers or the senior Chinese employee in a foreign commercial establishment'[19]—from leading reactionaries against the revolution, nationalized industries included local firms and also subsidiaries of foreign firms. Following the Soviet model, authorities under Chairman Mao created ownership directly by the state and ownership by a collective of people. By 1958, the state sector accounted for 89.17% of industrial output, up from 32.69% in 1949 (Sun 1999). Some 30 years later, in 1978, the output value of SOEs accounted for 80.8% of total industrial output value in China, while the number of industrial SOEs accounted for 24% (Lin 1999: 6). The 'magic' of planning had not only grown the industrial output of SOEs to a target level, but had also left it in more or less the same place for three decades. State control 'magic' also meant targets rather than markets would guide production, stifling quality and innovation.[20]

In Mao's time politics firmly governed economics. Thus, during the 1960s and 1970s projecting Chinese hegemony meant that foreign relations were in the hands of bureaucrats in Beijing, in contrast to Western states where capitalists led the reaction against the Cuban revolution and inundated Congress with anti-Viet Nam sentiments. Thus, China developed close ties based on common values of workers and the ideology of post-colonialism, even if it kept out of the Non-Aligned Movement (NAM). Indeed, Beijing was active in fermenting revolution. China supported several people's movements to counter US hegemony or, as many in the Third World saw it, US imperialism. Yet Beijing's influence was not as strong as it might have been, and was largely limited to low-intensity conflict in Third World spaces which lacked staying power once revolutionary regimes lost. Thus, in Mao's time the ability of the People's Republic of China to project power abroad can be seen as centred in Beijing's bureaucracy and as relatively circumscribed within the context of the Cold War.

The death of Mao and the purging of hardliners brought epochal change. Following the open-door policy of Deng Xiao Peng in 1978, reform of the SOEs became increasingly important. For China to compete abroad effectively, it had to do so not on its terms, but rather on the terms of the world marketplace. In this context:

> A series of measures aiming at improving the efficiency of the SOEs and creating a mixed-ownership structure was adopted, including administrative decentralisation, liberalisation of the state material allocation system, profit retention and authority to invest and to import and export, as well as the introduction of Contract Responsibility System in SOEs. As a result, the SOEs were gradually deprived of their public administrative functions and the performance of quite a number of them has been greatly improved. Others were just closed down.
>
> (Lin 1999: 6)

The reforms of the open-door policy were important in building a market economy: *perestroika*, but while attempting to retain political control with less *glasnost*.[21] Labour market reform in the mid-1980s was followed by changes in the SOE Labour Contract System, which in turn was superseded by the Regulation on Unemployment Insurance for State Enterprise

The rise of the qi ye ji tuan

Employees in 1991, and the Labour Law of 1994. The Resolution on Unified Enterprise Basic Pension Insurance System of 1997 came into effect to terminate the permanent employment system in SOEs (Lin 1999: 6).[22]

In the last decade of the 20th century the reform of SOEs accelerated, leading to reorganizations, acquisitions, sell-offs, close-downs and bankruptcies, and ultimately to the shrivelling of the entire state sector in China. Consistent with the nationalist ideas of List and Mao, the SOEs left over were in strategic areas: largely in semi-protected industries or in monopoly positions in energy, telecommunications, steel and automobiles.[23] With favourable terms from the state—cheap capital and land especially—such areas remained profitable, forming the commanding heights of the economy. Reflecting an attempt to use global resources, including capital, some of these SOEs have since been listed on the stock market in China, and abroad for minority stakes. They do, however, remain under central control to deliver on national priorities (Nie 2005).

It appears that some SOEs have become increasingly profitable as they cut labour costs and increase automation, in essence having to keep up with productivity goals by squeezing labour, as Marxists would point out. Nie (2005) observes that government statistics show from 1998 to 2003 the number of state enterprises dropped by 40%, from 238,000 to 150,000, but the aggregate profits that these SOEs realized soared by 22.2 times, from an initial US$2.58 billion to $59.90 billion. Nie further notes that the total value of SOEs rose by around 60%, from $628.80 billion to $1.02 trillion, and in the first 10 months of 2004, the 181 central SOEs and their groups had gained overall profits of $50.6 billion, a 53% increase on the same period of 2003. It is not surprising that efficiencies would accrue rapidly once the most unprofitable units were shut down to abrogate the socialist contract by mass lay-offs of workers along with the attrition of older employees (Cai 2006: 17). Nonetheless, it is noteworthy that the competitiveness of SOEs has also been improving rapidly, according to Nie (2005). By the end of 2004, over 1,000 SOEs were listed in domestic and overseas stock markets, with a clear upgrading effect on their corporate governance and efficiency. By 2005 14 Chinese SOEs ranked among the top 500 enterprises in the world, compared to only five in 1998.

The conscious attempt at transformation mainly implemented by the State-Owned Asset Supervision and Administrative Commission (SASAC), which was basically to complete the restructuring procedure in the first decade of the 21st century by ensuring support for the best remaining SOEs, with thousands of others privatized or bankrupt. With the remaining SOEs the intention of the state through the SASAC was to build more internationally competitive enterprise groups, or *qi ye ji tuan*. This strategy of 'going global' was to ensure a more dynamic growth of exports, through use of *qi ye ji tuan* rather than the export of goods under foreign brands under the control of foreign firms with foreign technology. The medium-term goal was to have 50 Chinese enterprises among the world's top 500, yet by 2011, China had over 60 companies in the top 500 globally, and by 2013 the number had gone up to over 80 (CNNMoney 2011, 2013).

The shift in Global 500 rankings between 2011 and 2013 provides an important indicator of the growth in revenue of firms at a world level. It shows that China's most globally significant firms were in the key sectors of the global economy in keeping with national priorities, particularly considering their impact on the rest of the economy. For example, in energy, in 2013 Sinopec Group ranked fifth in Global 500 rankings, and it changed to fourth. China National Petroleum changed from sixth to fifth and State Grid stayed at seventh. In banking, Industrial & Commercial Bank of China improved from 77th to 29th, while China Construction Bank improved from 108th to 50th, and Agricultural Bank of China 127th to 64th. In insurance, China Life Insurance improved from 113th to 111th, while People's Insurance Co. of China improved from 289th to 256th and Ping An Insurance improved 328th to 181st. In communications, China Mobile Communications improved from 87th to 71st, China Telecommunications improved from 222nd to 182nd, and China United Network Communications improved from 371st to 258th. In transportation, China Railway Group moved from 95th to 102nd even while revenues improved, while China Railway Construction improved from 105th to 100th. In steel production, Baosteel Group ranked 212th, dropped to 222nd despite improved revenue, while HeBei Iron & Steel Group improved from 279th to 269th and Wuhan Iron & Steel improved from 341st to 328th. These key industries underline that China has developed powerful companies in the commanding heights of the economy, keeping to classical Listian prescriptions for developing a strong national economy.

Tensions between List's prescriptions, which have historically seen state-protected or state-guided industrialization in the USA, Germany and Japan on one hand, and Marx's critique that focuses on interests of workers on the other, are manifest in the Chinese case. This is particularly the case with respect to the objectives of profitability versus worker security, and thus has grave implications for China's hegemonic potential, and in this sense the insecurity for workers is not that different to that experienced in the West. However, these concerns are overshadowed in the transition to the market, with privatization of SOEs embodying a clash between the emergent bourgeoisie and the Listian nationalist state, leading not to a liberal democratic model that is palatable to the West, but rather an authoritarian one that is far more nationalist and capable of causing friction with the West, Japan and China's neighbours.[24] In terms of accumulation, the initial spurt of management buyouts had to be regulated, as the benefits of these fell to a few from the inside.[25] While SOEs were better managed, the appearance of these in the hands of insiders suggests accumulation resembling primitive forms. Indeed, the privatization of some of China's most famous companies, including Haier, Kelong and TCL, which occurred at a loss for the state, has led to intervention by the SASAC (Nie 2005).

The much-debated relationship between the state and capital is a longstanding one in critical scholarship. China's model may seem to offer a different path in navigating this relationship, an alternative to the Washington Consensus and the Soviet model. It is coloured by nationalism in the post-Mao era, with problems of that approach built in. Yet, the countering of the Washington Consensus began with the Japan, Inc. model of the 1980s, with its dominant role for the state in picking winners that emerged from the *keiretsu*, the successor to the *zaibatsu*. The pre-war Japanese model with the *zaibatsu* led the industrialization of Japan in the early 20th century, and was a model that was dissatisfied with the status quo and thus organized along Listian lines. Japan's economic crisis of the 1990s did lead to the assertion of the private sector over the state-led one, thus yielding to US hegemony, albeit still within the still robust *keiretsu* system. A global view and a close relationship with the West took Japan's firms abroad not just for the markets, but also for the production platform. This ensured their continued economic and political viability and global reach, making adaptation to neo-liberalism in the interests of Japan's bourgeoisie. In the Chinese case, much will depend on how China's particular nationalist model is tempered, particularly if Chinese firms are allowed the access that Japanese firms had. Beyond this, what will determine the response to China abroad depends on whether Chinese firms will also provide for the development of other countries by joint ventures, transfer of technology, etc., just as it demanded of foreign firms locating in China.

China's movement towards a significant global presence—perhaps even hegemony—has arrived via the specific way in which the Beijing model works and the discourse that has surrounded it. This has excited both those seeking an end to the Washington Consensus, and those seeking to identify a 'China threat'. Those seeking an alternative to Western hegemony are cautiously looking to China, as with Cheru and Obi (2010) and Cheru and Modi (2013). Those seeking to understand Chinese power as hostile to the USA are following a well-worn path, similar if not identical to that taken by those alarmed by Japan in the 1990s (see, for instance, Nester 1993; Prestowitz 1993). While developments are occurring in China, particularly with respect to the key vehicle linking it overseas, the *qi ye ji tuan*, the discourse is about a Beijing model. Yet the developments considered in this chapter suggest a more complex and fluid reality not well captured by static, state-centric models.

China's challenge to the Washington Consensus on free markets seems to be ongoing, yet ambiguous. The ruling CCP has not expressed an interest in becoming a bastion of free market capitalism. Officially, it stands against accumulation by bourgeois capital, as it is 'pursuing socialism with Chinese characteristics, which mandates a prominent role for state ownership' (Nie 2005). Yet to grasp early 21st-century capitalist transformation in China it is important to understand the combination of a growing population and its desire for resources, increasingly powerful segments of society difficult to control centrally, a greater interface with a world coveting cheap Chinese labour, and Chinese firms themselves looking overseas for cheap labour and resources. These factors help to explain why, after several failures, a bourgeoisie is taking hold today as an authoritarian market system is becoming entrenched in China, underpinned by *qi ye ji tuan* and their role in furthering China's hegemonic potential as an actor on the global stage.

As this system provides for unequal growth due to weak state intervention in outcomes, the need to maintain legitimacy has meant a dangerous popular nationalism at the expense of Japan and the West, India and even smaller South-East Asian countries. The desire to legitimate an alarmingly unequal society can only increase as the growing interests and priorities of the *qi ye ji tuan* can be seen to challenge the supposed tenant of 'socialism with Chinese characteristics', creating more tensions that have yet to be resolved. The rhetoric of socialism and Third World solidarity may make China's hegemony tolerable to post-colonial leaders and perhaps their societies also seeking rapid development, while alarming the Western bloc. Yet when exercised through the *qi ye ji tuan*, Chinese hegemony may not offer a true alternative to the Washington Consensus, but merely repeat what outside capitalist forces have always done to colonized or semi-colonized spaces.

Understanding class and the *qi ye ji tuan*

When we consider the matter of social class, it is difficult to find anything socially progressive in the 21st-century Chinese state, transformed with guidance from above rather than below. Without a social movement or genuine democracy, China's transition has been left to party officials at the centre and local levels. The emergence and success of *qi ye ji tuan* are based on exploitation of domestic and foreign labour and resources. In this context, China has become host to poor working conditions, reflected in a vast number of sweatshops in which domestic and global bourgeoisie exploit Chinese labour.[26] This exploitation has occurred mainly on the backs of rural migrants, who form the majority of the 'new' industrial working class, but consistent with historical patterns elsewhere. Such migrants, particularly women, can expect to work 12 hours a day or more for low wages in substandard factories, and are often kept under control in residences in which workers have been known to commit suicide. Developments over the past two decades in this regard suggest a gradual coalescing of US and Chinese hegemony, with workers literally worked to death to provide profits for a local and global bourgeoisie united in common purpose.

This profitable arrangement is sustained by flight from rural China, a phenomenon well known for its difficulty, with passes and restrictions in place in the country. Yet an estimated 70 million peasants have been removed from their land over the last two decades to make way for China's projects, from highways to railways, dams to factories, and luxury projects from massive shopping malls to golf courses.[27] With the legality of land acquisition in question, there is resistance as seen in Wukan, where officials have reportedly been expelled from the CCP over illegal land deals (BBC 2012). The private community development of town and village 'enterprises' parallels the privatization of SOEs, as insiders gain at the expense of the general population. This movement comes with great risks when the demand for labour falls, as in 2009, when an estimated 10 million migrant workers lost their jobs (Bowler

2009). This adds to pressure created by the millions of jobs lost during the privatizations of SOEs. While industrialization in some Asian countries has meant workers are only one or two generations removed from land, allowing some absorptive capacity, in China the problem is exacerbated by land being sold to businesses and developers. The availability of workers in the rural to urban migration over time has furthered the interests of capital from within China and from the outside seeking cheap labour.

The production structure in China is dependent on the repressive power of an authoritarian state, dominated by the CCP. With only token criticism from global quarters, the party is known to have crushed strikes and attempts to build free trade unions in mines and factories.[28] What is particularly noteworthy, however, is the extent to which party officials are personally involved in enterprises. A case highlighted in *The Guardian* is telling:

> The relationship between Zijin Mining and the Shanghang county government is set out in the company prospectus. In the last restructuring, Zijin Mining changed from a state-owned enterprise to a modern shareholder-owned enterprise. However, the largest shareholder is still the Shanghang county government. Many government officials have positions in Zijin Mining and these posts have been disclosed to the media. This mine was first set up in the 1990s and jointly operated by Sanxin Mining and Ronghe Mining. Their activities cut off groundwater supplies and some of the village farmland could not be irrigated. A government document shows that, at the beginning of 2007, this mine in Wuping County was transferred from Ronghe Mining directly to Zijin Mining by 'principle [sic] leaders of the county committee of the county government and under the efforts of the Land and Resources Bureau' and established as Wuping Zijin. Wuping Zijin became a subsidiary of Zijin Mining Group. According to a 2008 security bulletin published by the company, Zijin Mining owns 77.5% of Wuping Zijin. Wuping county is the second largest shareholder.
>
> (Chuanmin 2011)

The extent to which government officials are involved in profiting from Chinese firms provides insight deep into capitalist transformation in China. With the 'open-door' policy that president Hu Jintao describes as the 'cornerstone' of China's economic development, it is becoming increasingly clear that the upper echelons of the Chinese state, including the central government in Beijing, are becoming committed to integrating into the global capitalist system rather than providing a true alternative to the Washington Consensus. This move, contradictorily, leads to tensions between China and the West and concern about the availability of resources for China's continued growth as has been the case historically with capitalism. This has meant, for instance, war in resource-supplying nations such as Sudan, with other energy-supplying nations also being contested, as with Libya. To this extent, the Beijing

Consensus is oppositional to the Washington Consensus. However, both are against inculcating a socialist alternative, and neither have qualms about the pro-market approach characteristic of the Washington Consensus.

Open doors could indeed be shut were there a socialist alternative on offer by a hegemonic power. China is neither a communist country nor a socialist one. Besides, it is not clear that China's 'back door' is likely to be shut with Chinese capital now fully entrenched by also capturing the essence of nationalism that contests not only Japanese capitalism, but also US capitalism. Via nationalism, those within the state have become the leaders of the transition as they participate in a rapid accumulation process that is at once primitive and also reflective of more advanced stages of capitalist accumulation. Some of this new wealth is held in the increasing size of Class A shares on the Shanghai index, which is open to investors at home and select investors from abroad. The rapid accumulation process has been put in motion by those within the state itself and within the CCP, making resistance difficult. The aggressive purging of ideological communists is ongoing when they get in the way, as the party welcomes capitalists, demonstrating increasingly sophisticated ways of using cultural tools of domination by maintaining a 'CCP' image for the public while consorting with those who profit from elite positions in the state and market. Party officials are increasing their hold on the country's assets with interests in the privatization of Town and Village Enterprises (TVE) and SOE assets. The proliferation of private firms and the build up of personal wealth is proceeding apace. These reforms by the state and accrued profits have further spurred the privatization of banking, the growth of stock markets and the rapid expansion of credit, both essential for rapid accumulation of capital in all times and places. These instruments of capital have led the *qi ye ji tuan* to become increasingly prominent in China's economy.

Land in Chinese cities reflects rapid accumulation, with prices rapidly increasing. Indeed, the most obvious elements of the capitalist transition in China today are perhaps the rapidly rising land values and gleaming skyscrapers in cities that appear to spread in a systematic manner, erasing old neighbourhoods and their histories. This production of space is one of the most rapid and largest in the world, and an important source of wealth for a growing number of Chinese millionaires and billionaires.[29] The property boom in China, including in Hong Kong, has led to the creation of wealth now available to the new capitalist class, members of which have gone on to diversify into actual production of goods. Yet, with inflation running high, over 40% of the rural population has suffered an absolute decline in income, with the creation of a working class rapidly emerging via 'accumulation by dispossession', as Arrighi (2007: 68) observes, following Luxemburg by way of Harvey.[30] Arrighi (2007: 68) points to various forms that are now well known, including appropriations of public property, embezzlement of state funds and sales of land-use rights, which became the basis of huge fortunes. However, whilst such accumulation occurs, the more salient form is capturing labour power as there is much investment within China from local, regional and Western sources.

The rise of the qi ye ji tuan

Those such as Arrighi (2007) make the case that the new capitalist class has not yet seized 'control of the commanding heights' of economy, society and the state. Indeed, Arrighi (2007) finds that the CCP is still in power at the centre. This reading—which separates the 'new' capitalists who have emerged from real estate and the production of consumer goods, from state capitalists—is ultimately misleading. Simply put, it ignores private transactions between capitalists as each state enterprise is privatized at the local level, where local governments have continued the divesture of the state's assets, with many of these assets now in the hands of local officials-cum-investors. Local developers are able to acquire previously public space. Factories are created on formerly public land. Such developments are made possible with the co-operation of local authorities in control of the enforcement of laws. This form of rapid accumulation is indeed occurring by dispossession, but those taking advantage of it both outside *and* inside the state have a common interest in maintaining the system in order to exploit labour, with China now the world's factory and these emergent bourgeois classes either own parts of firms that are reliant on the *qi ye ji tuan*, or are within these themselves.

Marx identified the process of primitive accumulation as one stage of capitalism; however, it is clear that China's bourgeoisie has enjoyed a rapid ascent that has disturbed the usual order of things as understood in the West. The rise of China's *qi ye ji tuan*, large enterprise groups with increasingly global reach, is troubling to those unused to the new order. Are these *Chinese* conglomerates, or are they simply conglomerates? This type of question was never really addressed by List (1928 [1841]), in whose time the nation mattered much more. It remains to be seen whether nations continue to be the best unit of analysis in our globalizing world, when the fate of China's *qi ye ji tuan* rests on their ability to traverse the globe with an increasing share of their profits coming from overseas locations.

CONCLUSION: LIMITS OF CHINESE HEGEMONY AND THE RISE OF THE *QI YE JI TUAN*

In the Western historical experience capitalism has been sustained by the use of democracy to present a veneer of legitimacy to exploitation and accumulation, while in many other places where democracy is not practised, coercion has been used to sustain exploitation. It is thus that Dutch, and particularly British and US hegemony, was made palatable to the middle classes, allowing the notion of the 'end of history' deployed by Fukuyama (2006), but since abandoned. This chapter suggests that the present transition to capitalism in China is sustained by coercion but in the economic realm at home operationalized via firms in the hands of a *nouvelle* bourgeoisie who have acquired state-owned enterprises. At the national level it has provided a more Listian path to power, challenging Anglo-American hegemony of the 19th and 20th centuries. Chinese firms, along with SOEs in key sectors that support them, are likely to continue to reshape China's institutions to favour capitalism for the benefit of the Chinese bourgeoisie by holding onto the commanding heights of power of the state, which can only be done by eschewing the international and embracing the nationalist elements of capitalism, as List (1928 [1841]) advocated for dissatisfied powers.[31] The rise of the *qi ye ji tuan*, and the ability of these conglomerates to go abroad, signals the maturing of China's economic transition, while interactions of Chinese firms in the periphery of the world suggest China has emerged as a new centre of authoritarian capitalism.

Authoritarian capitalism has historically challenged so-called 'democratic' forms of capitalism now in the West and Japan which have contained dissent despite the extremes of neo-liberalism that led to the retrenchment of the welfare state from the 1970s, and then unemployment and underemployment that have only become worse since then. Faced with such challenges, questions and concerns about China's status as potential hegemon are thus cast: is Beijing capable and/or willing to replace US hegemony with its more efficient system of exploitation, but less sustainable political system?[32] Underlying the preoccupation with this question is angst about the fate of the 500-year emergence of global capitalism under a leading Western power, the 'hegemon' or leader of this historical cultural and economic bloc, and thus a fault line between capitalists of the East and West that lend themselves to contradictory ideas.

In considering the history of the growth of capitalism, economic historian Charles Kindleberger (1981, 1986) made the case that a hegemon must have the capability and the will to enforce the rules of the system, and a commitment to the system that is perceived as mutually beneficial to at least the major states. Moreover, capability means that the hegemon in question must have a dominant growing economy with leading technological or economic sectors, and most crucially it must have political power backed by military power that can be projected overseas. The rise of Chinese hegemony in the form of a challenge to the Washington Consensus seems clear at least in the discursive sense among the elite in policy circles concerned with democracy and capitalism. However, the material case against the Beijing Consensus comes from societies such as those in Sudan with harsh rule and human rights violations, but also from countries like Sri Lanka, where a 50-year democracy is being replaced by authoritarian tendencies—both backed by China. In the 21st century, the now visceral nationalism that Beijing deploys in its current phase of hegemonic extension of Chinese political economy to the global South makes its endurance limited. Viet Nam is directly confrontational, as is the Philippines, with both having drawn closer to the USA. Myanmar (Burma), long under the generals and seemingly in Beijing's camp, has also defected towards the West.

Overlooked in the Western discourse over hegemony is the inability of any form of capitalist hegemony to meet the needs of the periphery. The Washington Consensus and the emerging one from Beijing do not support the working classes. The Chinese state has discursively deployed much of its more legitimate historical, Cold War-era, counter-hegemonic relations with post-colonial societies in its attempt to legitimate its role in the 21st century vis-à-vis Africa, Asia and Latin America, in particular. However, with the nationalistic and

The rise of the qi ye ji tuan

military aspects of China's dominance already unwelcome at the 'Pacific Rim' level, the controversial transmission of Chinese hegemony as authoritarian capitalism has no space for people. Not unlike early imperialism, the extent of China's hegemony has fallen to the logical carrier: the transnational corporation in the form of the *qi ye ji tuan*. The Chinese firm is the key actor, not just in ensuring the transition to capitalism at home, but also in ensuring that China's market has new and deeper trading partnerships all over the world, including in the most vulnerable areas of the world that imperial powers exploited in the past. What happens to these states and societies is a matter of hope on one hand and history on the other. Yet, there is enough history to go on with respect to the *qi ye ji tuan*, so we can make some judgements now.

Capitalism in China has not surprisingly meant less and less power in the hands of the people and workers, whether in China or abroad, the total range of where the *qi ye ji tuan* operate. From the remote village-level concern with corruption to the rise of Shanghai billionaire capitalists holding real estate wealth, ordinary people are increasingly being left behind. This growing gap has come to weaken performance legitimacy and increasingly place that function on other means both cultural and political. The growth of Chinese popular nationalism with the tacit approval of the state is one element in this process. Such tendencies come with the historic shifts in class relations that guarantee corporate capitalism and the role of the firm. The demand remains as it has been: 'We're citizens. Return us our citizenship rights. We're not rural labor power even less are we slaves' (O'Brien and Li 2006: 117). Yet with communism gone, China is now in the hands of corporate capital, and unlikely to provide the social contract that rural and urban workers seek, whether within its borders or beyond them.

The separation of the Chinese state from its citizens in terms of economic security has meant the rapid emergence of a bourgeoisie that has managed to accumulate wealth consistent with primitive accumulation while acquiring a larger share of China's newly privatized firms. This well-travelled and sophisticated class has branched out of China to become part of the bourgeois classes that are now global in orientation with common material interests. They are thus likely to be part of a bourgeois class that would prefer to join the USA in helping to manage crises of capitalism. This emergent co-operation is already obvious in the manner in which elites of China and the USA have managed the economic crises of 2008. This is not, however, without tensions when activists from nationalist fronts undercut co-operation. Nonetheless, the bourgeoisie based in China and the USA is interested in an order that allows further accumulation by whatever means possible, and it would thus seem that the current crisis of US hegemony has more to do with discourses than material reality.

NOTES

1 The Chinese model is seen to be the antithesis of the Washington Consensus (Bergsten *et al.* 2009: 3). The role of informal institutions, where private entrepreneurs were far more

widespread even under the Communist Party, suggests the more plausible way to understand the transformation according to Tsai (2007).
2 This allusion is to Francis Fukuyama's (2006) well-known thesis. The alternative conception is said to be offered by China according to Stefan Halper (2010).
3 Contributions included paper, porcelain and gunpowder, to name only a few.
4 As presented by Asia for Educators (2009): 'Britain's troops had recently been toughened in the Napoleonic wars, and Britain could muster garrisons, warships, and provisions from its nearby colonies in Southeast Asia and India. The result was a disaster for the Chinese. By the summer of 1842 British ships were victorious and were even preparing to shell the old capital, Nanking (Nanjing), in central China. The emperor therefore had no choice but to accept the British demands and sign a peace agreement. This agreement, the first of the "unequal treaties", opened China to the West and marked the beginning of Western exploitation of the nation.'
5 Rosa Luxemburg (2003 [1951]: 367) notes: 'European civilisation, that is to say commodity exchange with European capital, made its first impact on China with the Opium Wars when she was compelled to buy the drug from Indian plantations in order to make money for British capitalists. In the seventeenth century, the East India Company had introduced the cultivation of poppies in Bengal; the use of the drug was disseminated in China by its Canton branch.'
6 For Marx the shift from localism and provincialism to the national context was essential in the formation of a bourgeoisie that controlled national politics via control of the state (Marx and Engels 1975: vol. VI, 486, 519; vol. VIII, 161).
7 This legacy of genocide is largely overlooked in present-day China's construction of nationalism. Dikötter (2010) suggests that while part of a 'quite forgotten' history in the official memory of the People's Republic of China, there was a 'staggering degree of violence' which was, remarkably, carefully catalogued in Public Security Bureau reports, which featured among the provincial archives he studied.
8 The restraint on US imperialism in the 1890s during the onset of the Gold Standard under Rutherford Hayes was only similar to the constraints on US power during the Bretton Woods era. Fouskas and Gökay (2012: 27) note 'the powerful drive of the open door imperialism since the 1970s, the role of US multinationals, massive retailers and off-shore business, which bring new dynamism to US domestic capitalism as they repatriate their profits and become inserted into the IRS (Inland Revenue System)'.
9 As Roberts (2011) explains, 'China's Gini coefficient, an income distribution gauge used by economists, worsened from below 0.3 a quarter-century ago to near 0.5 today ... Poverty researchers recognize anything above 0.4 as potentially socially destabilizing.'
10 This suggests that China's model is different from the developmental one offered by Chalmers Johnson (1982) on Japan.
11 International relations and to a lesser extent international political economy have tended to focus on nation-states as the unit of analysis. However, the actual impact of the strategies of firms affects working classes of the world and tends to get overlooked unless there is specific focus on issues such as poverty. Indeed, state-centric literature tends to assume that the interests of nations and the 'citizens' within are synonymous. Hence a critical analysis that focuses on states and firms immediately allows more focus on poor countries, but also workers wherever they are located.
12 Fear of independent traders rising above their station is not unique to China. This also occurred in nearby Japan, as with the treatment meted out to traders by the Samurai. Interestingly, the eventual failure in Japan's Meiji period of a closed country led to some Samurai joining the ranks of business. The Samurai occupy a place in the imagination of society even today.
13 Inspired by Alexander Hamilton, Friedrich List (1928 [1841]) was sanguine about the importance of production for power, while also learning the constitution of the

USA which allowed a Hamiltonian form of capitalism to rise in the fledgling USA via the marriage of agriculture and manufactures for rapid accumulation. Championing domestic capitalists was part and parcel of the task of the early 1800s with the national power that he prescribed essential to defend the fledgling republic from British jealousy.

14 Thus, rather than accept the notion that the idea of Chinese hegemony is more potent than its reality, as suggested by Breslin (2011), it is crucial to pay attention to the materiality of China's engagements as do, for example, Cheru and Obi (2010) when considering China's impact on Africa.

15 The debates seem to be centred on the legitimacy of the new capitalists. It is argued that about 3,000 individuals have accumulated their wealth through the privatization of public assets, and can be seen as stealing from the public. Yet this shift, while being noticed, seems widespread. Moreover, with shares also in the hands of the emerging middle class there is less resistance in reality. When the Shanghai index allows foreign ownership of class 'A' shares, as is planned, the chances are that China will be fully integrated into global capitalism.

16 Somewhat alluding to these specific historical circumstances in Eastern Asia there is a literature on 'performance legitimacy' (Stubbs 2001: 37–54). Also, terminology can be seen to highlight inequity, as He (2013) notes: 'Both online and off, Chinese have dusted off outdated vocabulary to describe their government and various social phenomena. Old fashioned phrases like guanfu "Official Mansion" and yamen "Official Gates" are used to refer to the authorities or the police, while tianchao "Celestial Dynasty" is used as a synonym for China in general.'

17 Stopford, Strange and Henley (1991) explore the matter of firms and diplomacy, suggesting that transnational corporations can exercise power. They show how global structural changes often impel governments to seek the co-operation of managers of multinational enterprises, but within the constraints of each country's economic resources, social structures and history.

18 The author's visits to Chinese firms that still rely on state funds suggest this history. As Foroohar (2013) notes, 'At the entrance of the 27-sq-km campus is a museum that documents the history of the company, beginning with its founding after the Qing dynasty's Opium Wars, when it was decided by the provincial governor that China should enhance its "learning of advanced technology from the West to resist the invasion of Western countries".'

19 It is useful to compare Mao's definition to others: 'The landlord class and the comprador class.[1] In economically backward and semi-colonial China the landlord class and the comprador class are wholly appendages of the international bourgeoisie, depending upon imperialism for their survival and growth. These classes represent the most backward and most reactionary relations of production in China and hinder the development of her productive forces. Their existence is utterly incompatible with the aims of the Chinese revolution. The big landlord and big comprador classes in particular always side with imperialism and constitute an extreme counterrevolutionary group. Their political representatives are the Étatistes and the right-wing of the Kuomintang.' In note [1], the *comprador* is defined as 'the Chinese managers or the senior Chinese employee in a foreign commercial establishment. The compradors served foreign economic interests and had close connection with imperialism and foreign capital'. The origin of this term is sometimes traced to Nicos Poulantzas (via Andre Gunder Frank) (Fouskas and Dimoulas 2013). For Poulantzas (1974: 71), the *comprador* 'is a fraction of the bourgeoisie which does not have its own base for capital accumulation, which acts in some way or other as a simple intermediary of foreign imperialist capital (which is why it is often taken to include the "bureaucratic bourgeoisie"), and which is thus triply subordinated—economically, politically, ideologically—to foreign capital'.

20 This is consistent with the dominant critique of Soviet communism as well.

21 By 1989 the Chinese model of gradual change was clearly the more successful path.
22 However, as Zengxian (1997) points out, the new labour contract system applied only to new employees. Until the first half of the 1990s, most employees in the SOEs retained lifetime employment.
23 It is not clear if there has been a formal deployment of the ideas of Friedrich List in China, as happened in Germany. The work of Deqiang (2000) suggests there is at least an awareness of Listian ideas. Breslin (2011) has been quick to ask the question of a China model, beyond List. Yet Breslin (2011: 1324) argues that 'it seems to be influenced, albeit indirectly, by one of the main critiques of Smith's ideas in the shape of Friedrich List's The National System of Political Economy'. What is clear is that there is a deliberate policy afoot that is informed by the literature and by historical lessons of which Chinese scholars, bureaucrats and members of the Communist Party are aware, rather than policy taking place in a vacuum or consisting of mere reactions to events.
24 Indeed, Sainsbury (2011) explains that in 2011 it was noted that the Chinese state sought to slow down the move to privatize the SOEs.
25 This refers to acquisitions of all or part of the equity capital of a company by its directors and senior executives.
26 Popular writers convey this with empathy. See, for instance, Klein (2010).
27 Writing in 2004, Yardley suggested that as many as 70 million peasants had lost their land.
28 It is well documented that the workplace in China is hazardous for workers. The capitalists running mines and factories do not adhere to the law systematically, leading to the idea that there is an understanding not to enforce the law. Areddy (2010) reports that an average of 187 workers die daily in mishaps.
29 There are more than a dozen property tycoons on a recent *Forbes* list of China's 40 top billionaires, whose gains have come from the private economy in China and on the back of its workers and by exploiting labour, land and resources. In 2011, China had 115 billionaires, behind only the USA, with 412 billionaires. This rapid accumulation of personal wealth has led to those such as thirty-something Yang Huiyan, now head of a Guangdong property empire, whose personal fortune inherited from her father was valued at $16.2 billion in 2007 (*Canadian Business* 2011).
30 Acknowledging Rosa Luxemburg's *The Accumulation of Capital*, Harvey (2003: 137–82) discusses 'accumulation by dispossession' as involving privatization and commodification of public goods, financialization, orchestration and manipulation of crises, and state involvement in redistributing wealth upward. This form of accumulation can be seen to concentrate wealth and power in the hands of the few through dispossessing the broader public.
31 There exists literature that attempts to capture the path of 'dissatisfied powers'. Carr (1993 [1939]: 188) has observed that just as the threat of class war by the proletariat is 'a natural cynical reaction to the sentimental and dishonest efforts of the privileged classes to obscure the conflict of interest between classes by a constant emphasis on the minimum interests which they have in common', so the warmongering of the dissatisfied powers was the 'natural, cynical reaction' to the sentimental and dishonest platitudinizing of the satisfied powers on the common interest in peace. Taking this a step further, Breslin (2010) finds China to be more responsible. Yet the Listian inspirations and the victims of China's wars around its borders challenge Breslin's thesis.
32 Strange (1987) discussed what she termed 'the persistent myth of lost hegemony'. More recently, Fouskas and Gökay (2012) discuss the fall of the US empire. While US military power remains supreme, its economic dominance over the world has clearly receded. The broader question, however, is whether there are willing followers of the USA or a desire for another leader when we consider the global bourgeoisie.

REFERENCES

Amsden, Alice (1989) *Asia's Next Giant: South Korea and Late Industrialization*, New York: Oxford University Press.

Areddy, James T. (2010) 'Accidents Plague China's Workplaces', *Wall Street Journal*, 28 July, online.wsj.com/article/SB10001424052748703977004575394262825550830.html (accessed 30 September 2012).

Arrighi, Giovanni (2007) *Adam Smith in Beijing: Lineages of the 21st Century*, London: Verso.

Asia for Educators (2009) 'The Opium War and Foreign Encroachment', afe.easia.columbia.edu/special/china_1750_opium.htm (accessed 30 September 2012).

BBC (2012) 'Ex-leaders of China Protest Village Wukan "Punished"', 24 April, www.bbc.co.uk/news/world-asia-china-17821844 (accessed 30 September 2012).

Bergsten, Fred C., Freeman, Charles, Lardy, Nicholas R. and Mitchell, Derek J. (2009) *China's Rise: Challenges and Opportunities*, Washington, DC: Peterson Institute for International Economics and Center for Strategic and International Studies.

Bowler, Tim (2009) 'China Warns of Unemployment Risk', BBC News, news.bbc.co.uk/2/hi/business/7915372.stm (accessed 30 September 2012).

Breslin, Shaun (2010) 'China's Emerging Global Role: Dissatisfied Responsible Great Power', *Politics* 30: 52–62.

——(2011) 'The China Model and the Global Crisis: From Friedrich List to a Chinese Mode of Governance?', *International Affairs* 87(6): 1323–43.

Cai, Yongshun (2006) *State and Laid-Off Workers in Reform China: The Silence and Collective Action of the Retrenched*, New York: Routledge.

Canadian Business (2011) Interactive Map: The Billionaires of the World, 6 October, www.canadianbusiness.com/article/48712-interactive-map-the-billionaires-of-the-world (accessed 30 September 2012).

Carr, E.H. (1993 [1939]) 'Carr', in H.L. Williams, M. Wright and T. Evans (eds) *A Reader in International Relations and Political Thought*, Vancouver: UBC Press, 179–91.

Cheru, Fantu and Modi, Renu (2013) *Agricultural Development and Food Security in Africa*, London: Zed Books.

Cheru, Fantu and Obi, Cyril (eds) (2010) *The Rise of China and India in Africa: Challenges, Opportunities and Critical Interventions*, London: Zed Books.

Chuanmin, Yang (2011) 'Toxic Mine Spill was Only Latest in Long History of Chinese Pollution', ChinaDialogue, guardian.co.uk, 14 April, www.guardian.co.uk/environment/2011/apr/14/toxic-mine-spill-chinese-pollution (accessed 30 September 2012).

CNNMoney (2011) 'Global 500: Our Annual Ranking of the World's Largest Corporations', money.cnn.com/magazines/fortune/global500/2011/countries/China.html (accessed 14 January 2014).

——(2013) 'Global 500: Our Annual Ranking of the World's Largest Corporations, 2013', money.cnn.com/magazines/fortune/global500/2013/full_list/ (accessed 9 March 2014).

Deqiang, Ha (2000) *Collision! The Globalization Trap and China's Real Choice*, Beijing: Economic Management Press.

Dikötter, Frank (2010) *Mao's Great Famine: The Story of China's Most Devastating Catastrophe*, London: Bloomsbury Publishing.

The Economist (2007) 'For Whosoever hath, to him Shall be Given, and he Shall have More. Income Inequality in Emerging Asia Heading Towards Latin American Levels', 9 August, www.economist.com/node/9616888 (accessed 30 September 2012).

——(2010) 'Hello America: China's Economy Overtakes Japan's in Real Terms', 16 August, www.economist.com/node/16834943 (accessed 30 September 2012).

——(2012) 'China in your Hand: A Brief Guide to Why China Grows so Fast', 25 May, www.economist.com/blogs/graphicdetail/2012/05/daily-chart-16 (accessed 30 September 2012).

Ferraro, Vincent (n.d.) 'The Theory of Hegemonic Stability, www.mtholyoke.edu/acad/intrel/pol116/hegemony.htm (accessed 30 September 2012).

Foroohar, Rana (2013) 'What China's Oldest Steel Factory Says About the Nation's Future', Time.com, business.time.com/2013/06/16/red-steel-city-what-chinas-oldest-steel-factory-says-about-the-nations-future/#ixzz2qVVPKIWd (accessed 14 January 2014).

Fouskas, Vassilis K. and Gökay, Bülent (2012) *The Fall of the US Empire: Global Faultlines and the Shifting Imperial Order*, London: Pluto Press.

Fouskas, Vassilis K. and Dimoulas, Constantine (2013) *Greece, Financialization and the EU. The Political Economy of Debt and Destruction*, London: Palgrave.

Fukuyama, Francis (2006) *The End of History and the Last Man*, New York: Avon Books.

Gilpin, Robert (1987) *Political Economy of International Relations*, Princeton, NJ: Princeton University Press.

Gulde, Anne Marie and Schulze-Ghattas, Marianne (1993) 'Purchasing Power Parity Based Weights for the World Economic Outlook', *Staff Studies for the World Economic Outlook*, Washington, DC: IMF.

Haggard, Stephan (1990) *Pathways from the Periphery: The Politics of Growth in Newly Industrializing Countries*, Ithaca, NY: Cornell University Press.

Halper, Stefan (2010) *The Beijing Consensus: Legitimizing Authoritarianism in Our Time*, New York: Basic Books.

Harvey, David (2003) *The New Imperialism*, New York: Oxford University Press.

He, Tang (2013) 'Feudalism Makes a Comeback in China: The Linguistic Quirks of a Bygone Era Signal the Inequalities of the Present', *The Atlantic*, www.theatlantic.com/china/archive/2013/08/feudalism-makes-a-comeback-in-china/278945/ (accessed 13 January 2014).

IMF (2012) 'GDP Based on PPP Share of World Total', *World Economic Outlook*.

Jansen, Marius B. (1954) *The Japanese and Sun Yat-Sen*, Stanford. CA: Stanford University Press.

Jayman, Jayantha (2004) *A Critical Understanding of Japan's Improved Late 20th Century Relations in Eastern Asia*, doctoral dissertation, London: London School of Economics.

Johnson, Chalmers (1982) *MITI and the Japanese Miracle*, Stanford, CA: Stanford University Press.

Kindleberger, Charles P. (1973) *The World in Depression, 1929–39*, Berkeley: University of California Press, 291.

——(1981) 'Dominance and Leadership in the International Economy: Exploitation, Public Goods, and Free Rides', *International Studies Quarterly* 25: 242–54.

——(1986) 'International Public Goods without International Government', *The American Economic Review* 76: 1–13.

Klein, Naomi (2010 [2000]) *No Logo*, revised edn, New York: Picador.

Lin, Justin Yifu (1999) 'Policy Burdens, Soft Budget Constraint and State-owned Enterprise Reform in China', Peking University and Hong Kong University of Science and Technology, www.bm.ust.hk/~ced/soereform.pdf (accessed 30 September 2012).

List, Friedrich (1928 [1841]) *The National System of Political Economy*, London: Longmans, Green & Co.

Luxemburg, Rosa (2003 [1951]) *The Accumulation of Capital*, New York: Routledge.

Marx, Karl and Engels, Friedrich (1975) *Collected Works*, London: University of Michigan Press.
Milner, Helen (1998) 'International Political Economy: Beyond Hegemonic Stability', *Foreign Policy* 110.
Murphy, M.R. Taggart (1989) 'Power without Purpose: The Crisis of Japan's Global Financial Dominance', *Harvard Business Review* 2 (March–April).
Nester, William R. (1993) *American Power, the New World Order and the Japanese Challenge*, New York: Palgrave Macmillan.
Nie, Stella (2005) 'Short History of Reforms Concerning Chinese State Owned Enterprises', Shanghai Flash, Commercial Section, Consulate General of Switzerland in Shanghai, No. 2, www.sinoptic.ch/shanghaiflash/2005/200502.htm (accessed 30 September 2012).
O'Brien, Kevin J. and Li, Lianjiang (2006 [1975]) *Rightful Resistance in Rural China*, New York and Cambridge: Cambridge University Press.
Poulantzas, Nicos (1974) Classes in Contemporary Capitalism, London: New Left Books.
Prestowitz, Clyde (1993) *Trading Places—How We are Giving Our Future to Japan and How to Reclaim it*, New York: Basic Books.
Roberts, Dexter (2011) 'China's Growing Income Gap', *Bloomburg Businessweek Magazine*, 27 January, www.businessweek.com/magazine/content/11_06/b4214013648109.htm (accessed 30 September 2012).
Sainsbury, Michael (2011) 'China Privatisation Machine into Reverse', *The Australian*, 27 January, www.theaustralian.com.au/business/china-privatisation-machine-into-reverse/story-e6frg8zx-1225995084947 (accessed 10 September 2012).
Stopford, John, Strange, Susan with Henley, John S. (1991) *Rival States, Rival Firms: Competition for World Market Shares*, Cambridge: Cambridge University Press.
Strange, Susan (1987) 'The Persistent Myth of Lost Hegemony', *International Organization* 41(4) (Autumn): 551–74.
Stubbs, Richard (2001) 'Performance Legitimacy and "Soft Authoritarianism"', in Amitav Acharya, B. Michael Frolic and Richard Stubbs (eds) *Democracy, Human Rights, and Civil Society in South East Asia*, Toronto: Joint Centre for Asia Pacific Studies, 37–54.
Sun, Jian (1999) 'Wage Reform, Soft Budget Constraints and Competition', Working papers No. 56, The United Nations University World Institute for Development Economics Research, February, www.wider.unu.edu/publications/working-papers/previous/en_GB/wp-156/_files/82530858957743082/default/wp156.pdf (accessed 30 September 2012).
Tsai, Kellee S. (2007) *Capitalism without Democracy: The Private Sector in Contemporary China*, Ithaca, NY: Cornell University Press.
Mao Tse-tung (1926) 'Analysis of the Classes in Chinese Society', in *Selected Works of Mao Tse-tung*, March, www.marxists.org/reference/archive/mao/selected-works/volume-1/mswv1_1.htm#bm1 (accessed 14 January 2014).
van Wolferen, Karel (1990) *The Enigma of Japanese Power: People and Politics in a Stateless Nation*, London: Vintage Books.
Yardley, Jim (2004) Farmers Being Moved Aside By China's Real Estate Boom, *The New York Times*, 8 December, query.nytimes.com/gst/fullpage.html?res= 9E0CE3D71231 F93BA35751C1A9629C8B63& pagewanted = all (accessed 30 September 2012).
Zengxian, Wu (1997) 'How Successful has State-owned Enterprise Reform been in China?' *Europe-Asia Studies* 49(7): 1237–62.

The global South
From dependency to convergence?

RAY KIELY

Recent years have seen impressive growth rates in countries like Brazil, India and the People's Republic of China, places previously regarded as being peripheral in the international order. Indeed, growth rates have been so impressive that some have argued that the so-called BRICs (Brazil, Russia, India and China, and as BRICS, perhaps South Africa) are transforming the international order, as new powers emerge to challenge declining US power. Moreover, it is not only the BRICs that have experienced high rates of growth, but other countries in the (former) global South, beneficiaries of a new order of trade taking place between Southern nations. Furthermore, many of these countries quickly recovered from the financial crisis of 2007–08, leading some to suggest that they have in effect 'decoupled' from dependence on the West. This is reinforced by China's growing international influence, and the rise of the Beijing Consensus which challenges the US-centred, neo-liberal Washington Consensus. Even some proponents of market liberalism see this as a possible state capitalist challenge to Western hegemony (*The Economist* 2012).

On the other hand, there is a paradox in all this, for equally it could be argued that the rise of these countries represents not so much a challenge to, but rather a triumph for, the West. The rise of these countries owes less to state capitalist deviations from neo-liberal prescriptions that originated in the West, and more to the embrace of globalization-friendly policies. Seen in this way, whatever the geopolitical implications might be, the rise of 'the rest' is a developmental triumph for the West, demonstrating the superiority of market-friendly policies that embrace the opportunities presented by globalization. Condemned to years of grinding poverty on the back of counter-productive policies, this interpretation sees great causes for celebration in the international order. The South is rising through the growth of manufacturing in some locations, commodity market booms caused in part by the rise of those same new manufacturing powerhouses, and with that a massive reduction in the number of people living in absolute poverty. This then is a tale of global convergence.

This chapter asks whether or not convergence is taking place and why this might (not) be the case. This question is addressed through an historical framework that traces the history of development since 1945, examining the questions asked by theories of development in that period, and why these still retain their relevance in the present. The issues are addressed in five sections:

Global South: dependency to convergence?

- an examination of development after 1945;
- the shift to neo-liberalism in the 1980s;
- the rise of globalization and emerging markets in the 1990s;
- the rise of East Asia and then the BRICs; and
- the limits of convergence in the current period.

DEVELOPMENT AFTER 1945

The post-war period saw significant changes in the international order. US hegemony was successful in promoting a more integrated, liberal international order in the capitalist world, with a long-term commitment to global integration, as opposed to the more fragmented (though still partly internationalized) national capitalisms of the period from the 1880s to 1945. This involved the promotion of international organizations, state sovereignty, open-door policies in terms of investment and trade, and aid such as the Marshall Plan. In practice, for the developing world, this meant that the international context favoured independence for former colonies, which were in any case undergoing substantial change in response to the rise of nationalist movements.

At the same time, this was also an era that saw an intensification of Cold War rivalries between the capitalist and state communist worlds, and this led to compromises in terms of the promotion of a liberal international order. First, the USA initially envisaged more or less market-based solutions to post-war reconstruction, in which capital would leave richer countries and flow to poorer ones, such as those in war-ravaged Europe. This was the basis of the Morgenthau Plan for post-war reconstruction, but this was abandoned and replaced by the Marshall Plan in 1948 as it became clear that capital was actually continuing to concentrate in the USA, and largely bypassing Europe. Marshall Aid was thus important in post-war reconstruction, and it was in part motivated by fear of communist expansion in Europe. Second, while creation of the United Nations (UN), the World Bank and the International Monetary Fund (IMF) showed a commitment to multilateralism, the USA retained significant power through vetoes (on the UN Security Council) and unequal voting rights (at the World Bank and IMF). Third, while the USA was committed to independence, in practice sovereignty was conditional and often the USA intervened in countries that it feared were moving in a communist direction, although actually communism and nationalism were often conflated.

On the other hand, the compromises of the liberal order did give some significant space for developing countries in terms of development. The USA was committed to the promotion of an international trade organization, but this was vetoed by Congress in 1948, and it was only in 1995 that the World Trade Organization (WTO) was created. In place of a formal organization, there was instead the more informal General Agreement on Tariffs and Trade (GATT), which was committed to long-term trade liberalization, but in practice allowed various exceptions to immediate liberalization. Moreover, countries could opt out of certain agreements, and for a time, GATT membership was low among developing countries. This allowed a certain degree of sovereignty in terms of development strategy (Williams 2011) and developing countries pursued an explicitly 'developmentalist' strategy in the period from the 1940s through to the late 1970s and early 1980s. What this strategy entailed was the promotion of industrialization policies through state protection, known as import-substitution industrialization. States planned for certain sectors to be developed, and allowed for these to be protected through various mechanisms, ranging from subsidies, tariffs on imports that might compete with these sectors, and import controls. This was not, however, incompatible with the promotion of capitalism, and states largely saw this as an opportunity to promote capitalism through state-guided policies (Wade 1990). This policy was also compatible with the US open-door policy of countries attracting foreign capital, though in some countries like India protectionism also meant restrictions on foreign capital investment, which sometimes caused conflict with the USA. Elsewhere, however, import-substitution industrialization (ISI) meant the promotion of capital investment within the home country, and this could be through either local or foreign capital, such as in Brazil. This was broadly compatible with US interests. These policies were promoted by developing countries as part of a process of catching up with the already developed world. Popular support existed for these policies as domestic populations were promised future increased living standards and the construction of powerful nations previously humiliated by colonial powers.

However, these policies also had an economic rationale which fed into wider debates around development theory. Dominant Western perspectives on development, bracketed together under the term modernization theory, suggested that all nation-states passed through similar stages of development on the path to modernity. Third World nations were at a lower stage of development but their pro-industrialization policies would aid this process of catch-up and convergence (Rostow 1960). It was important that poorer countries did catch up so that the threat of communism could be averted. Developmentalist policies were therefore not necessarily rejected by the USA, so long as they did not become too nationalist, anti-American and pro-communist. Indeed, the argument was made that contact with the West through open-door policies to investment could hasten the transition to modernity.

On the other hand, the case for industrialization was also made on different grounds, namely that it was necessary to alleviate the unequal position of developing countries in the international order. This was associated with the structuralist economics of Raul Prebisch (1959) and Hans Singer (1950), which argued that the developing world suffered from certain structured inequalities in the international economy. In particular, developing countries largely traded unfinished primary goods such as cocoa, coffee and rubber for finished manufactured goods produced in the developed world. This trade relationship was said to be unequal because there was a long-run tendency for the terms of trade to decline for primary goods producers as against manufactured goods producers. The prices of manufactured goods might fall, but they would not fall so rapidly as the price of primary products, Prebisch argued. He cited a number of reasons for this tendency, but the main one was that there were comparatively few manufactures and many primary goods producers, so intense competition in the case of the latter drove prices down further. For Prebisch and Singer, then, the root cause of structured hierarchy in the international economy was the division of labour in which poorer countries focused mainly on producing primary goods. This could be overcome by pro-industrialization policies, and ISI allowed this to happen. It was also a view promoted by the Third World through the Non-Aligned Movement (NAM) which developed out of the Bandung Conference of Third World nations in 1955, and the UN Conference on Trade and Development (UNCTAD), which was formed in 1964.

Both modernization theory and ISI then provided a rationalization for industrialization. Crucially, however, the former perspective regarded the West as part of the solution, while the latter saw the West (through the colonial legacy and the unequal international order) as part of the problem. This division was more intense with the development of a further branch of development theory, known as dependency theory. This was a very broad church of thinking (Frank 1969; Emmanuel 1972; Amin 1976; Cardoso and Faletto 1974), but what united it was the view that the developing world was in a dependent or subordinate position in the international order.

This, then, was the basis for the debate on development after 1945. On the one side was modernization theory, which argued that development was a process of catching up with the West, and that this involved industrialization but also pro-Western policies. The West was part of the solution. On the other side was dependency theory, which argued that development was hindered in some ways by the West, and so there needed to be some kind of break with the Western-dominated international order. In its mildest form, this meant protectionist policies, but some argued that there needed to be a more radical de-linking from the world economy. In the 1960s, for instance, Andre Gunder Frank (1969) argued that development and underdevelopment should be seen as two sides of the same coin, and that the development of the West was caused by the underdevelopment of the rest, and that the underdevelopment of the rest was caused by the development of the West.

It could be argued, however, that the post-war record suggests that *both* modernization theory, and the radical underdevelopment theory of Frank, were problematic. The developing world experienced quite high rates of growth in the post-war period. In the 1960s and 1970s, developing countries as a whole had an annual average per capita growth rate of 3%, higher than the averages for developed countries in the 19th century (Chang 2002: 132). Frank's argument that developing countries would stagnate if they remained a part of the world economy was thus problematic, as these growth rates were achieved without a full-scale de-linking from the world economy. However, was this development somehow dependent? The main point made by the idea of dependency was that capitalist development was taking place, but that it was somehow different from earlier, more 'normal' phases of capitalist development in the developed countries. This begged the question of what was 'normal' as opposed to 'dependent' capitalist development. On the other hand, it was too easy to assume, as did some orthodox (Rostow 1960) and Marxist (Warren 1980) development thinkers, that the growth taking place in the developing world was sufficiently great that it was indeed leading to a convergence between rich and poor countries around an assumed 'normal' capitalist development. Dependency theory too easily assumed a norm from which developing countries were deviating, while modernization theory assumed a norm to which all countries were converging (Gulalp 1986).

In contrast to these over-generalizations, what was occurring was significant levels of capitalist development, but on the whole this was not of a sufficient level to promote convergence between the First and Third Worlds. While all processes of capitalist development have been uneven, post-war capitalist development in most of the developing world was more uneven than previous national capitalist development processes. This could be seen both nationally and internationally. In the case of the former, the absorption of labour into formal employment, particularly in urban areas, was highly uneven and instead there was the massive growth of an urban, unemployed and underemployed informal sector, and with that the growth of a massive planet of slums (Davis 2004). Internationally, the tendency towards uneven development manifested itself most visibly in the nature and direction of capital flows and trade in the post-war international order. The internationalization of capital after 1945 was actually characterized by the increasing concentration of capital within the rich world, and most trade (measured in value terms) was between rich countries. This suggested that globally, uneven development was and is a cumulative process in which capital concentrates in certain locations, and relatively marginalizes other places. These processes existed in the post-war period, but it could be argued that they have intensified in recent years, as will be argued below.

We can conclude, then, that in the post-war period, capitalist development did take place across the Third World, but in most places it was acutely uneven and unequal, more so than in earlier periods. It also did not lead to convergence with the developed world, which enjoyed a golden age of high rates of growth, mass production and mass consumption.

THE SHIFT TO NEO-LIBERALISM

By the late 1960s and early 1970s, the post-war boom was coming to an end. The end of the post-war boom saw rising social conflict, revolution in the South, falling rates of profitability, growth and increasing unemployment and inflation, and the rise of possible challengers to US hegemony (Mandel 1975, 1980; Brenner 1998; and Chapter 3 in this volume). These developments all served to undermine the Bretton Woods order, which was based on fixed exchange rates and a gold-dollar standard (see Chapter 2 in this volume). In the late 1940s there was a dollar shortage, which was resolved by the USA exporting money through Marshall Aid and foreign investment. This enabled the USA's competitors, especially Japan and West Germany, to recover, but this was at the expense of the stability of the Bretton Woods system. This was because the value of the dollar was increasingly undermined, as the USA ran not only payments but trade deficits from the early 1960s. This reflected a key contradiction in the post-war international capitalist order—namely, that the dollar was not only an international currency, but was the USA's national currency too. Therefore, its value relative to other currencies ultimately depended on the competitiveness of the US economy. If this was undermined, then US gold reserves would erode, and it would therefore have to devalue, as the dollar would no longer be as 'good as gold'.

In 1971, the Nixon Administration took the decision to abandon gold convertibility and allow the dollar to float downwards. The end of dollar-gold convertibility was followed by a number of planned devaluations from 1971 onwards, which in turn led to an abandonment of the system of fixed exchange rates and its replacement by a 'managed floating' system from 1973, and other countries followed. This movement away from the fixed exchange rates and capital control system of Bretton Woods, to a new system of floating rates and freer capital movement, changed the context of domestic economic policy. In the case of the former, the domestic and the international were reconciled by policies that maintained the value of a domestic currency relative to gold or dollars, and promoted sufficient expansion to maintain full employment, at least in the 'advanced' capitalist countries. Thus, interest rates could be directly used to slow or increase investment and consumption. However, with the development of the Eurodollar market, followed by the end of fixed exchange rates, the context in which state monetary policy operated was increasingly internationalized. Policies designed to maintain growth and employment could now put pressure on the exchange rate and foreign exchange reserves, as financial speculators would sell local currency in favour of safer foreign currencies. The fall in reserves would have a deflationary effect on the economy. This shift represented the beginning of a shift to neo-liberal discipline in the developed countries.

The US government's decision to abandon the gold-dollar exchange standard and fixed exchange rates potentially gave the USA enormous financial power. In particular it eliminated the need for the USA to control its own balance of payments as the dollar remained the main source of international payment, and so (theoretically) unlimited amounts of dollars could be released into international circulation. However, this was at the cost of increasing inflation, and by the late 1970s it was clear that the expansionary policies of the Nixon, Ford and Carter presidencies could no longer hold. From the mid- to late 1970s, the USA ran record trade and current account deficits. At this point Saudi Arabia began to sell dollar reserves and leading

European countries made plans for developing a new currency, which could potentially become an alternative to the dollar. It was clear that there was a real threat of a crisis of confidence in the dollar, and therefore the international system that relied largely on this currency as a means of payment was under threat.

From 1979 onwards under Carter, and especially after the 1980 election of Reagan, there was a shift in policy in the USA. Any imposition of capital controls was rejected, and instead a new policy of controlling inflation was introduced. This was mainly implemented through increases in interest rates, which had the effect of squeezing domestic demand, at least in the early period of the Reagan years. It also had the effect of undermining the USA as a market for developing countries' exports, and increasing debt payment obligations in the developing world.

However, this tight monetary policy of controlling inflation and sustaining the dollar through high interest rates was accompanied by a growing 'military Keynesianism', in which demand was sustained by running massive budget deficits. These deficits occurred because the Reagan government massively increased military spending in the context of a renewed Cold War with the USSR (Halliday 1983), while at the same time promoting a policy of reducing taxation. Both trade and budget deficits were instead financed by attracting capital from overseas, including from the Eurodollar markets and from capital-starved Latin America, and this capital was initially attracted by high rates of interest. The high dollar therefore had the effect of keeping domestic prices low, which helped to keep inflation rates low. Thus, the USA went from being the largest creditor nation in the 1950s to the largest debtor and foreign capital recipient by the 1980s. These policies also had the side effect of lifting some other countries out of recession, as they stimulated demand for other countries' products. In 1980–85, external demand generated one-third of Japan's and three-quarters of West Germany's gross domestic product (GDP). In the case of Japan, this linkage was even more direct as around one-third of its total exports went to the USA (Schwartz 2000: 212, 216). Indeed, interdependence between the USA and Japan was great, as the latter partly funded the former's deficits, and so effectively Japanese financiers provided the credit needed by the US government that continued to subsidize the continued growth of Japanese exports (Brenner 1998: 184). By 1991, the USA's budget deficit stood at US$74 billion and the trade deficit at $4 trillion. The world's main creditor in the 1950s and 1960s had by the 1980s and 1990s become the world's largest debtor (Arrighi 1994: 316–17).

Meanwhile, in the developing world, a major 'debt crisis' emerged in 1982. In 1973–74 the price of oil quadrupled as a result of the cut in oil supplies by the Organization of the Petroleum Exporting Countries (OPEC) in response to the 1973 Arab–Israeli War. Oil exporters now needed to find an outlet for their windfall profits, and oil importers faced potentially devastating import bills. The oil exporting countries deposited their windfalls in European banks (or European affiliates of US banks) and these petro-dollars added to the already expanding Eurodollar market. Banks then loaned these dollars to a small number of countries, mainly located in Eastern Europe and especially Latin America (plus a few larger countries throughout the Third World). Thus, in the 1970s private bank lending became the major means by which some 'developing countries' gained access to capital, as opposed to official channels such as the IMF and World Bank, as was the case in the 1950s and 1960s.

Banks loaned money at low rates of interest and, in a competitive and 'unregulated' climate, often committed enormous sums to particular Latin American states—by 1982, the nine largest US banks had committed over twice their combined capital basis to a handful of developing countries. At this time, interest rates were low and repayment periods were relatively long term. However, from the late 1970s interest rates increased rapidly and repayment periods generally became shorter. The effect of the so-called 'Volcker shock' (named after the chair of the Federal Reserve, Paul Volcker) on developing country debtors was devastating, adding perhaps a further $41 billion to their debt (based on average interest rates from 1961–80). Moreover, high interest rates in the USA attracted capital from all over the world, including from high-debt and low-savings developing countries that needed this capital to help pay back debts. This combination of high interest rates and capital export from the indebted countries constituted a reversal of historic proportions.

In 1982, Mexico was the first country officially to default on its foreign debt, and when non-payment threatened to spread to Brazil, there was a real danger that Western banks—which had committed so much capital to Latin America—could fail. This was the start of the debt crisis. From the viewpoint of Western banks, they faced the prospect that a number of high-debt countries were in no position to pay back the interest on their loans. What was therefore needed was more money to be loaned to the high-debt countries, but with some guarantee that these countries could meet their debt obligations. However, while it may have been rational from the viewpoint of all the banks to lend more money, in the context of 'unregulated' competition, it made no sense for any one individual bank to carry out this task (as there were no guarantees that all the other banks would follow).

The debt crisis was effectively policed through granting limited access to new loans provided that they met with the approval of international finance, and particularly the IMF. The IMF therefore became a major agent in the international economy, effectively policing a whole series of economies that faced balance of payments difficulties throughout the 1980s. Thus, despite the relative lack of power given to the IMF in 1944, reflected mainly in terms of its small financial resources, it became a highly visible institution throughout the developing world, particularly after 1982. It received new (though still quite low) financial resources to help it carry out this task—and, alongside the conditions attached to its loans, this visibility led to massive protests against the institution from the 1980s onwards (Walton and Seddon 1994).

For the IMF, countries that faced severe balance of payments deficits, and therefore difficulties in meeting their interest payment obligations, were said to have adopted incorrect policies. What this amounted to was the idea that they were consuming more than they were producing, and importing more than they were exporting. This in turn was caused by too much government intervention in these economies. What was therefore needed was a set of policies that would encourage countries to re-adjust their economies, and start to export more than they imported, and produce more than they consumed, therefore enabling them to earn foreign exchange to meet their debt obligations. The USA advocated a policy of 'managed neo-liberalism' in which the IMF would play a key role in policing debtor nations, in terms of approving loans made either by the IMF itself or more indirectly the (increasingly diminishing) new loans from banks, subject to certain conditions. The burden of adjustment was placed solely in the hands of the debtor countries, rather than surplus countries, and this meant that in practice enormous policy changes had to be undertaken, such as privatization, state reform and liberalization of trade and investment policies. In effect, the developmentalism of the ISI period was replaced by the pro-market liberalism of the 1980s onwards.

The expectation that market-friendly policies would lead to high rates of growth was not, in the short term at least, realized, and the 1980s was the lost decade of development. For example, between 1980 and 2000, per capita income in sub-Saharan Africa fell by 9% (Chang 2012). For neo-liberal apologists, these disappointing results were less the result of market-friendly policies and more due to the poor policies that preceded the neo-liberal reforms (World Bank 1981, 1993). However, this argument ignored the 37% growth of per capita income that took place from 1960 to 1980 (Chang 2012), and downplayed the effects of higher interest rates, falling commodity prices, heightened import competition, and collapsing public infrastructure, education and skills which followed structural adjustment policies. The basic problem with the reforms that took place after 1982 was that they simplistically assumed that a developed and thriving private sector could simply replace the inefficient state sector, and that entrepreneurs freed from the shackles of the state could compete effectively in both their home markets and in export markets.

GLOBALIZATION AND EMERGING MARKETS FROM THE 1990S

By the 1990s, however, pessimism had given way to considerable optimism, with the argument that globalization was good for development. Globalization is a vague and slippery concept, but in this case, it essentially meant that developing economics should embrace the world economy through trade, investment and financial liberalization, and this would lead to growth and poverty reduction. An influential World Bank (2002) report argued that it was precisely those good globalizers that experienced growth and poverty reduction, in contrast to those low globalizers that were stagnating and still had high rates of poverty. The report claimed that there has been a decline in the number of people living in absolute poverty, from 1.4 to 1.2 billion (World Bank 2002: 30). At other times, the Bank and others have suggested slightly different figures, but on the whole the news is upbeat: the number of people living in absolute poverty is falling (Bhagwati 2004; Wolf 2004).

This argument would appear to be reinforced by the surge in foreign capital investment from the early 1990s onwards, including into the so-called periphery since the early 1990s. The total global amount of foreign direct investment (FDI) increased from $59 billion in 1982 to $202 billion in 1990, $1.2 trillion in 2000, down to $946 billion in 2005, and back up to $1.3 trillion in 2006 (UNCTAD 2002b: 3–5, 2007: 9). Developing countries generally accounted for around one-third of this total. This increase in FDI has also led to the growth of manufacturing in the developing world. In 1970, 18.5% of the total exports from the developing world were manufactured goods; by the end of the 1990s it was over 80% (UNCTAD 2002a: 5). For advocates of open policies, industrialization can occur through open investment policies which allow foreign (or national) companies to take advantage of low labour costs, and thus promote properly competitive industrialization rather than the high cost, white elephant approach associated with ISI. In the long run, competitive industrialization will lead to full employment, which in turn will lead to upgrading to a more developed kind of manufacturing, as occurred in the case of the earlier developers. Though this argument does not follow the rigid stages associated with modernization theory, the broad contentions certainly replicate this approach.

Moreover, with the growth of the likes of China, this has a favourable impact for the rest of the developing world, even if they have not industrialized at comparable levels. China has increasingly relied on the rising import of inputs, and the global export value of iron and steel, ores and minerals and non-ferrous metals increased by between 30% to 45% in 2004, which (in part) reflected rising demand from China, which is now the leading importer of many commodities (WTO 2005: 1–2). In 2004 Latin American exports expanded by 37%, much of which was accounted for by rising demand in East Asia, especially China (WTO 2005: 11). Some African countries, particularly Sudan and the Democratic Republic of Congo, have similarly boosted their sales in the Chinese market, as have some East Asian countries. These figures lead on to the argument that the rise of the BRICs is leading to a transformation of the international order, in which emerging powers take the lead in lifting the South as a whole out of poverty. This is addressed further in the final two sections.

THE RISE OF EAST ASIA AND THE BRICS

In recent years, the argument has been made that the growth of emerging markets has meant the rise of emerging powers. China is the most significant of these powers, but others have been identified such as Brazil, Russia and India, and perhaps even South Africa. These countries have been given the new label, the BRICs (or BRICS; Goldman Sachs 2001). These countries have experienced high rates of growth in recent years, and quickly recovered from the global economic slowdown in 2007–08. This has led some to conclude that we are witnessing a transformation of power in the international order as the USA experiences decline and new powers in the South rise (Khanna 2009). Moreover, the rise of the BRICs is an opportunity for other developing countries as they increasingly trade with these emerging powers and receive aid without conditions from China.

There are a number of issues at stake in the debate over the rise of the BRICs. It could be argued that their rise represents not only a geopolitical challenge to the West, but also a developmental challenge in which the neo-liberal Washington Consensus is replaced by the state-capitalist Beijing Consensus (Ramo 2004; Halper 2010; *The Economist* 2012; and Chapter 7 in this volume). On the other hand, it could be argued that the rise of the BRICs and growth in other parts of the South represents a triumph for Western, neo-liberal policies, and that these countries have developed precisely because they have adopted globalization or market-friendly policies (Yeyati and Williams 2012). This debate essentially repeats an earlier one over the rise of East Asia, and the first-tier newly industrializing countries (NICs) like the Republic of Korea (South Korea), Taiwan, Singapore and Hong Kong. On the one side of this debate is the neo-liberal position that the East Asian NICs developed via market-friendly policies, in contrast to the inefficient interventionist regimes in much of Africa and Latin America (Lal 1984; Pennington 2011). This view was challenged by those who argued that in fact the East Asian NICs saw very significant interventions which went against the grain of market forces. This was especially the case in Taiwan and South Korea, where from the 1950s through to the early 1990s there were many subsidies, tariffs and even import controls, as well as state-directed investment through five-year plans and controls on the movement of capital (Amsden 1989; Wade 1990). In this view, these countries developed through a series of developmental state interventions, specifically designed to draw selectively on the opportunities presented by the world market, but also limit the constraints that existed in the context of competition from already established overseas producers that could easily out-compete late developers. The neo-liberal response to the undoubted reality of developmental state interventions was to accept that intervention had taken place but to argue that development would have taken place anyway, thus rendering the interventions as irrelevant (World Bank 1993; Pennington 2011). The problem with this argument was that state intervention was in effect caught between a rock and a hard place, because it was either counter-productive and inefficient (as in Latin America and Africa), or, when rapid growth occurred, irrelevant (as in East Asia). That state intervention could never win said more about the ideological commitments of neo-liberals, both interventionist (World Bank 1993, 1997) and libertarian (Pennington 2011), than it did about the actual historical realities of capitalist development. Indeed, this point applied not only to East Asian capitalism, but also

Japan (Johnson 1982) and all historical cases of capitalist development (Chang 2002).

In terms of the BRICs, some argue that the rise of state capitalism in the BRICs represents both a geopolitical and developmental challenge to Western dominance, as China in particular becomes a new pole of attraction for developing countries. For some this is a cause for regret, as state capitalism is associated with authoritarian politics, neglect of human rights and ultimately the undermining of individual freedom (Bremmer 2008; *The Economist* 2012). Others welcome this development, suggesting that state capitalism represents a challenge to the market-friendly, neo-liberal policies that have undermined the development of the former Third World (Arrighi 2007). This perspective suggests that state capitalist policies are a rational response to the hierarchies generated by free trade and the free movement of capital, as competition in this scenario takes place less within a level playing field and more one where earlier developers have competitive advantages over later developers. The concentration of research and development, advanced technology, skills, infrastructure, and design and marketing means that higher-value production is similarly concentrated in the developed world, and parts of East Asia that have broken into high-value production through earlier periods of protectionist policies (Chang 2002). In stark contrast, and replicating the market-friendly intervention interpretation of East Asia, neo-liberals argue that state capitalism is an irrelevance and that the real reason for the rapid growth of the South is the adoption of market-friendly policies (World Bank 2002; Pennington 2011).

The point made about market-friendly intervention applied to East Asia can equally be applied to the BRICs. Neo-liberal explanations for the rise of East Asia and the BRICs are largely unconvincing, as they underestimate the rationale for state policies designed to deal with capitalist development, and especially late capitalist development. However, does this mean that state capitalism is a model for the developing world, a challenge to neo-liberal policies, and one that is promoting sustainable growth and convergence between the former South and rich North? The final section questions this assumption.

THE INTERNATIONAL CONTEXT AND THE LIMITS OF GLOBAL CONVERGENCE

Recent years have seen some significant shifts in the international political economy. The developed world's G-7 share of global GDP fell from 72% in 2000 to 53% in 2011; China's output per capita rose from 6% of the USA's in 1980, to 22% in 2008; the share of the South in world output increased from 23% to 33% between 2000 and 2009 (Wade 2011: 351). This is not only leading to convergence between the developed and developing worlds, but also a transformation of the international order and the possible end of US hegemony. One of the most compelling pieces of evidence for US decline is the massive trade deficits it has with the rest of the world. Developing countries as a whole moved from being deficit to surplus countries in 1996–2000 (Bernanke 2005), and much of this surplus is accounted for by the USA's deficit with East Asia, and China in particular (Thompson 2011). These imbalances were a central part of the global economic crisis that emerged in 2007–08, as US deficits were financed in part by Chinese savings, and investment by China in the USA took the form not only of investment in US Treasury bonds, but also more directly in the US housing market, and specifically in the (formerly) privately owned but government-backed wholesale mortgage lenders, Fannie Mae and Freddie Mac. When these institutions were nationalized in 2008, apparently under pressure from China, it was seen as a sign of a shift in power away from the USA and towards China, which in turn was indicative of a wider international transformation (Altman 2009).

This scenario should not be rejected out of hand, but this final section suggests some reasons why a more sceptical account of the rise of the BRICs, and the South more generally, might be necessary.

First, there is significant counter-evidence concerning both US decline and the rise of emerging powers in the South. Growing shares of world trade by the global South as a whole are concentrated in a few countries, and this reflects in part the import intensity of many Southern exports, and their growing (but subordinate) participation in global production networks led by multinational companies (UNCTAD 2002c; Kaplinsky 2005). Such participation has been associated with an increase in the flow of components and parts which are then assembled for export to the North—an argument that potentially reinterprets US trade deficits less as a weakening of hegemony and more reflective of its continued strength (Schwartz 2009; Kiely 2010). While there has been considerable growth in the South in recent years, including after the outbreak of the financial crisis, this has been based largely on demand for primary goods from China and not on diversification and industrialization. Seen in this way, it could be argued that the financial crisis that emerged in 2007–08 is not simply a crisis for US hegemony, but also for those emerging powers said to be challenging that hegemony (Kiely 2010; Nye 2010). The rapid recovery of the BRICs and much of the South since 2008 rests in part on unsustainable bubbles based on investment in real estate and property, particularly in China (Hung 2011; UNCTAD 2011), designed to replace lost markets in places like the USA. The implication is that decoupling from dependence on the West has not occurred, that current high rates of growth in much of the South rest on demand from China (and financial speculation in commodities), and that this demand is only being temporarily sustained by unsustainable bubbles within China. Thus, even if the US economy is likely to experience slow growth rates or even stagnation in the coming years (Palley 2012), this is less a story of the decline of the USA and the rise of the global South, and more one of uneven development and slower rates of growth for the world as a whole. Moreover, the rise of the BRICs should also be put into perspective: the combined outward FDI of Brazil, Russia, India and China in 2008 was less than that of the Netherlands.

China's foreign exchange reserves of $2.3 trillion in 2009 might have been the highest in the world, but this amount is actually less than the market capitalization of the top 10 US firms in the same year (Nolan and Zhang 2010: 101).

These observations apply not only to the BRICs as a whole, but to China itself. China is very dependent on foreign capital investment and sub-contracting agreements with Western firms. In 2003 the US retail company Wal-Mart imported $15 billion worth of products from China, which accounted for as much as 11% of all US imports from China (Kaplinsky 2005: 176). China has also successfully expanded its market share in labour-intensive sectors such as clothing, and this is likely to expand further as the effect of the phasing out of quotas takes hold. Thus, in clothing sectors where there have been quota removals, China's share has increased enormously. For instance, in 2002, the USA removed quotas in 29 categories of clothing, and China's share in these sectors rose from 9% to 65%, as prices fell by an average of 48% (Kaplinsky 2005: 176). Breslin (2005: 742–44) suggests that China's rise itself may be exaggerated, as its economic miracle cannot be divorced from its role in East Asian production networks. In particular, China specializes in completing the production of low-value, labour-intensive goods, and relies on technologies produced in other East Asian countries, with which it has a substantial trade deficit. Moreover, the East Asian region provided over 50% of total foreign investment into China for much of the 1990s. China has increased its exports to the European Union (EU) and the USA, while the rest of East Asia (excluding Japan) has seen its share of exports to the EU and the USA fall, while its export share to China has increased. Thus, China's percentage manufacturing exports to the USA increased from 9.1% in 1992 to 22.9% in 2000, and to the EU it increased from 9.5% to 16.7% during the same years. Over the same period, Thai export shares to the USA fell from 26.4% to 22.9% and to the EU from 21.3% to 17.7%, and South Korea's fell from 25.9% to 23.9% (USA), and although it showed a small increase in shares to the EU, the share of exports to the rest of East Asia was far larger. With some small variations, there has been a significant increase in shares by East Asian exporters to the rest of the region, while EU and US shares (either taken together or individually) have generally fallen or stagnated (Athukorala 2003: 40–41). Even more significant has been the increase in shares in parts and components rather than finished goods. Indeed, between 1992 and 2000, these accounted for 55% of the export growth of Indonesia, Thailand, Malaysia, Singapore, the Philippines and Viet Nam (Athukorala 2003: 33). There was no clearly identifiable pattern in the share of components and parts in trade to the USA or EU from East Asian countries, with some showing increases and some decreases, but generally the far bigger increases in shares of parts and components was in East Asian countries' trade with China. By 2000, the shares were 50.6% for Malaysia, 54.0% for Thailand, 50.3% for Singapore, 81.8% for the Philippines, 26.7% for South Korea, and 29.8% for Taiwan. At the same time, parts and components in China's share of exports to the USA (4.3% to 9.1%) and EU (2.9% to 10.9%) increased from 1992 to

2000, but from far lower bases and the total shares remained low (Athukorala 2003: 48–49). From 1992 to 2003, parts and components accounted for 52% (Taiwan), 44% (Malaysia), 70% (Philippines), 59% (Singapore) and 31% (Thailand) of the total manufacturing export growth for particular countries (Athukorala and Yamashita 2003: 33). For China, the figure was 17% (ibid.: 33) Taken together, these figures suggest that China has increased its role as a manufacturer of final goods produced within the East Asian region, which are exported to the EU and US (and Japanese) markets.

Does this necessarily matter? It could be argued that this breakdown and fragmentation of production is merely the latest stage in the increased specialization that exists in an increasingly efficient world economy. On the other hand, one could argue that China has developed a niche in manufacturing labour-intensive segments of particular value chains, which are limited in their capacity to generate high levels of value-added production. The Chinese state has attempted to develop national champions that concentrate on higher value-added activity, but their success in doing so has been limited. Where there has been more success is in labour-intensive but low value-added activity, either through FDI or through joint ventures, including with state-owned enterprises. In this respect, neo-liberals are correct to point to the limited successes of China's national champion policy, but this argument also ignores the reasons why the Chinese state has employed such a policy in the first place. The inequalities associated with unequal competition and buying practices alluded to above are reflected in the fact that firms 'focus on activities with low barriers to entry. Once the cost pressures become too intense, rather than moving upward into higher end activities or taking time to develop proprietary skills, the firms diversify into other low entry barrier markets' (Steinfeld 2004: 1976). Indeed, these tensions reflect a key contradiction in China's miracle, as the national champion policy is 'a story about a government claiming as its ultimate policy aim precisely the type of firms that its most high profile restructuring (and trade) policies militate against. In essence, the government is seeking to create the very firms that comparative advantage, not to mention global technological change, militate against' (Steinfeld 2004: 1980–81).

In addition, in regard to the US trade and budget deficits, it is predominantly Asian countries that finance US deficits, with China accounting for the largest amount ($727.4 billion in December 2008) of US Treasury securities. After the outbreak of the crisis, the Chinese Central Bank increased its purchase of US Treasury bonds, from $618 billion in September 2008 to $1,160 billion in December 2010 (Hung 2011: 234), and although increased purchases slowed down slightly in 2012, by September 2013 the figure had reached $1,293 billion (US Treasury 2013). The crisis has seen periodic expressions of concern by the Chinese leadership over US debt levels, but a Chinese diversification on a massive scale into other currencies would undermine the value of its dollar-denominated assets. Above all, a massive cut in domestic consumption by US consumers would hit Chinese exporters hard, and the Chinese economy is highly dependent on exports, and the USA is China's biggest export market (Hung 2009: 8–9; Breslin 2011). The notion that China can simply re-shift its priorities by focusing on the domestic economy underestimates the powerful vested interests in China supporting the export sector, and downplays the costs of moving out of dollar-denominated assets.

The discussion in this section suggests that we should be cautious in pointing both to a transformation of the international order and, related to that, a convergence between developed and developing countries. The rise of China and the other BRICs is easily exaggerated and even if it were not, we need to show considerable care in over-generalizing from the experience of some developing countries and falsely concluding a more widespread convergence. It may also be the case that China's rise is not necessarily such good news for other developing countries, an issue taken up in the conclusion.

CONCLUSION

This chapter has addressed the question of whether we are witnessing the emergence of the South as a global force in the current international order. More specifically, is it the case that the current crisis is giving rise to a new era in which the BRICs and Asia, and specifically China, are hegemonic challengers to the USA (Arrighi 2007; dos Santos 2011), or are we actually simply moving to a multi-polar world (NIC 2008), or even continued US hegemony located precisely in the ability of the USA to attract capital from overseas (Schwartz 2009)? The argument has been that parts of the South are emerging as more significant players, but that this is not so great as to amount to any significant challenge to US hegemony, at least in the short term.

Moreover, even if some countries are growing in significance in the international order, this does not mean that what is true for China is true for the South as a whole. Indeed, we could argue that at least some of the claims made for China's rise are less about a full analysis of changes in the international order, and more based on a normative commitment to rejection of both US hegemony and the neo-liberal (post-)Washington Consensus (Arrighi 2007). Indeed, from the opposite end of the political spectrum, this is precisely the *concern* of market liberals who see state capitalism as a challenge to Western hegemony.

However, a dichotomy between Washington and Beijing is problematic, and there is no good reason for suggesting that Chinese hegemony would be any more progressive than US hegemony. There are at least two reasons for this, first concerning relations between China and the rest of the South, and second concerning relations between different sections of society within the South itself. In the case of the former, China has expressed a long-held commitment to South-South solidarity, and while there may be specific examples where this might occur, we should also treat such claims with considerable scepticism. While much has been made of Chinese aid and trade with the developing world, we should also ask whether China's rise is a constraint for some developing countries which have suffered from deindustrialization due to competition from Chinese products, both in world markets and in their own domestic markets. Similarly, is aid dispersed less for reasons of solidarity and more for Chinese economic and strategic interests (Breslin 2010)?

Moreover, while rapid growth in parts of the global South has demonstrated tendencies towards convergence in some cases, there is also the issue of uneven development and inequality *within* these countries. In contrast to some popular accounts which suggest that the poor are increasingly being lifted out of poverty through economic growth (Collier 2008), one striking feature of the poorest 'bottom billion' is that a large proportion live not in the poorest, least-developed countries, but in the next tier, middle-income countries in the developing world (Sumner 2010). Some 900 million people (one in three workers) are unemployed and/or living in absolute poverty (based on the World Bank's purchasing power parity (PPP) $2-a-day definition), and it is estimated that the global economy will need to create 600 million new jobs over the next decade to meet the challenge of the global recession and incorporating new entrants into the labour market (ILO 2012). Seen in this way, the rise of emerging powers might be limited by domestic problems, including uneven development and inequality within these countries.

Having said that, growing inequality is hardly a problem restricted to the South, and inequality within the USA played a role in causing the financial crisis of 2007–08 (Galbraith 2012). Indebtedness in the context of stagnant real wages was used to maintain demand and thus growth in the USA, particularly in the context of the housing mortgage boom and subsequent crash. Seen in this way, uneven development and inequality are problems for all countries, hegemonic as well as emerging powers. However, given that continued levels of absolute poverty are much greater in the South, including among those middle-income emerging powers, it remains a greater problem there than in the USA. For this reason we may conclude that the overriding concern of dependency theories—the fact of structured hierarchies in the international economy—remains relevant. What is striking is that for all the talk of convergence in the international order, levels of inequality between people and countries remains enormous. Perhaps if there is convergence at all, it is one based on a convergence of contempt by elites, policy makers and ruling classes for those people left out of the benefits of growth—and these elites exist in all countries, both North and South.

REFERENCES

Altman, R. (2009) 'The Great Crash, 2008: A Geopolitical Setback for the West', *Foreign Affairs* 88(1): 2–14.
Amin, S. (1976) *Unequal Development*, New York: Monthly Review Press.
Amsden, A. (1989) *Asia's Next Giant*, Oxford: Oxford University Press.
Arrighi, G. (1994) *The Long Twentieth Century*, London: Verso.
——(2007) *Adam Smith in Beijing*, London: Verso.

Athukorala, P. (2003) *Product Fragmentation and Trade Integration: East Asia in a Global Context*, Australian National University Working Paper 2003/21, 1–67.

Athukorala, P. and Yamashita, N. (2003) *Product Fragmentation and Trade Integration: East Asia in a Global Context*, Australian National University paper, 1–41.

Bernanke, B. (2005) 'The Global Savings Glut and the US Current Account Deficit', www.federalreserve.gov/boarddocs/speeches/2005/2005-0414/default.htmer.

Bhagwati, J. (2004) *In Defence of Globalization*, Oxford: Oxford University Press.

Bremmer, I. (2008) 'The Return of State Capitalism', *Survival* 50(3): 55–64.

Brenner, R. (1998) 'The Economics of Global Turbulence', *New Left Review* I/229: 1–265.

Breslin, S. (2005) 'Power and Production: Rethinking China's Global Economic Role', *Review of International Studies* 31: 735–53.

——(2010) 'China's Emerging Global Role: Dissatisfied Responsible Great Power', *Politics* 30(S.1): 52–62.

——(2011) 'China and the Crisis: Global Power, Domestic Caution and Local Initiative', *Contemporary Politics* 17(2): 185–200.

Cardoso, F. and Faletto, E. (1974) *Dependency and Development in Latin America*, Berkeley, CA: University of California Press.

Chang, H.J. (2002) *Kicking Away the Ladder*, London: Anthem.

——(2012) 'Africa Needs an Active Industrial Policy to Sustain its Growth', *The Guardian*, 16 July.

Collier, P. (2008) *The Bottom Billion*, Oxford: Oxford University Press.

Davis, M. (2004) *Planet of Slums*, London: Verso.

dos Santos, T. (2011) 'Globalization, Emerging Powers and the Future of Capitalism', *Latin American Perspectives* 38(2): 45–57.

The Economist (2012) 'The Rise of State Capitalism—Special Report', 21 January: 3–18.

Emmanuel, A. (1972) *Unequal Exchange*, London: New Left Books.

Frank, A.G. (1969) *Capitalism and Underdevelopment in Latin America*, New York: Monthly Review Press.

Galbraith, J. (2012) *Inequality and Instability*, Oxford: Oxford University Press.

Goldman Sachs (2001) *Building Better Global Economic BRICs*, New York: Goldman Sachs Global Economic Group.

——(2007) *BRICs and Beyond*, New York: Goldman Sachs Global Economic Group.

Gulalp, H. (1986) 'Debate of Capitalism and Development: The Theories of Samir Amin and Bill Warren', *Capital and Class* 28: 39–59.

Halliday, F. (1983) *The Making of the Second Cold War*, London: Verso.

Halper, S. (2010) *The Beijing Consensus*, New York: Basic.

Hung, H.F. (2009) 'America's Head Servant', *New Left Review* II(60): 5–25.

——(2011) 'Sinomania: Global Crisis, China's Crisis?' in L. Panitch, C. Leys and G. Albo (eds) *The Socialist Register 2012*, London: Merlin, 217–34.

ILO (International Labour Organization) (2012) *Global Employment Trends 2012*, Geneva: ILO.

Johnson, C. (1982) *MITI and the Japanese Economic Miracle*, Stanford, CA: Stanford University Press.

Kaplinsky, R. (2005) *Globalization, Poverty and Inequality*, Cambridge: Polity.

Khanna, P. (2009) *The Second World*, Harmondsworth: Penguin.

Kiely, R. (2010) *Rethinking Imperialism*, Basingstoke: Palgrave.

Lal, D. (1984) *The Poverty of 'Development Economics'*, London: Institute of Economic Affairs.

Mandel, E. (1975) *Late Capitalism*, London: New Left Books.

—— (1980) *The Second Slump*, London: Verso.
NIC (2008) *Global Trends 2025*, Washington: National Intelligence Council.
Nolan, P. and Zhang, J. (2010) 'Global Competition after the Financial Crisis', *New Left Review* II(64): 97–108.
Nye, J. (2010) 'American and Chinese Power after the Financial Crisis', *Washington Quarterly* 33(4): 143–53.
Palley, T. (2012) *From Financial Crisis to Stagnation*, Cambridge: Cambridge University Press.
Pennington, M. (2011) *Robust Political Economy*, Cheltenham: Edward Elgar.
Prebisch, R. (1959) 'Commercial Policy in the Underdeveloped Countries', *American Economic Review* 44: 251–73.
Ramo, J. (2004) *The Beijing Consensus: Notes on the New Physics of Chinese Power*, London: Foreign Policy Centre.
Rostow, W. (1960) *The Stages of Economic Growth*, Cambridge: Cambridge University Press.
Schwartz, H. (2000) *States Against Markets*, London: Palgrave.
—— (2009) *Sub-Prime Nation*, Ithaca, NY: Cornell University Press.
Singer, H. (1950) 'The Distribution of Gains from Trade between Investing and Borrowing Countries', *American Economic Review* 40: 473–85.
Steinfeld, E. (2004) 'China's Shallow Integration: Networked Production and the New Challenges for Late Industrialisation', *World Development* 32(11): 1971–87.
Sumner, A. (2010) *Global Poverty and the New Bottom Billion*, Brighton: IDS Working Paper No. 349.
Thompson, H. (2011) *Mortgaging America's Future*, London: Palgrave.
UNCTAD (2002a) *World Investment Report 2002*, Geneva: UNCTAD.
—— (2002b) *Trade and Development Report 2002*, Geneva: UNCTAD.
—— (2002c) *The Least Developed Countries Report 2002*, Geneva: UNCTAD.
—— (2007) *World Investment Report 2007*, Geneva: UNCTAD.
—— (2011) *Trade and Development Report 2011*, Geneva: UNCTAD.
US Treasury (2013) 'Major Foreign Holders of US Treasuries', www.treasury.gov/resource-center/data-chart-center/tic/Documents/mfh.txt (accessed 8 January 2014).
Wade, R. (1990) *Governing the Market*, Princeton, NJ: Princeton University Press.
—— (2011) 'Emerging World Order? From Multipolarity to Multilateralism in the G20, the World Bank and the IMF', *Politics and Society* 39(3): 347–78.
Walton, J. and Seddon, D. (1994) *Free Markets and Food Riots*, Oxford: Blackwell.
Warren, B. (1980) *Imperialism: Pioneer of Capitalism*, London: Verso.
Williams, D. (2011) *International Development and Global Politics: History, Theory and Practice*, London: Routledge.
Wolf, M. (2004) *Why Globalization Works*, New Haven, CT: Yale University Press.
World Bank (1981) *Accelerated Development in sub-Saharan Africa*, Washington, DC: World Bank).
—— (1993) *The East Asian Miracle*, Oxford: Oxford University Press.
—— (1997) *World Development Report 1997*, Oxford: Oxford University Press.
—— (2002) *Globalization, Growth and Poverty*, Oxford: Oxford University Press.
WTO (2005) *International Trade Statistics*, Geneva: World Trade Organization.
Yeyati, E. and Williams, T. (2012) *Emerging Economies in the 2000s: Real Decoupling and Financial Recoupling*, Washington, DC: World Bank Policy Research Working Paper No. 5961.

The policy response to the great recession of 2008

Is it the 1930s all over again?

YIANNIS KITROMILIDES

INTRODUCTION

The recession of 2008 was the greatest economic crisis the world had faced since the Great Depression of the 1930s. It was preceded by the 'sub-prime' mortgage crisis, which originated in the USA and began in the summer of 2007, threatening the stability of the global financial system.

A recession is a period of reduced economic activity and economic prosperity. Formally in economics, the period of economic decline that constitutes a recession is defined as two or more consecutive quarters of negative economic growth in gross domestic product (GDP). In the narrow technical sense the great recession as a global phenomenon ended in mid-2009, although the recovery was anaemic and fragile and by 2011 a 'double-dip' recession had emerged in many countries. By contrast, during the Great Depression of the 1930s which started in 1929, recovery in the USA was not evident until 1933—about 16 consecutive quarters of negative growth. Of course, unemployment continued to be in double digits throughout the 1930s and full recovery was only achieved with the outbreak of World War II. Similarly, unemployment continued to be high even after the 'technical' end of the recent recession in terms of positive GDP growth.

Like the great recession of 2008, the 1930s Great Depression was also preceded by a financial disaster that originated in the USA: the Wall Street crash of 1929. Whenever there are similarities between historical events it is often asked whether it is possible for history to repeat itself. If indeed history can 'repeat itself', it is also natural to ask whether the 'lessons of history' have been learned. The great British historian A.J.P. Taylor, responding to the question of whether history teaches us any lessons, maintained that it was the other way round—that observing and understanding the follies of some current political decision making helps an historian to understand better historical events: 'the present enables us to understand the past, not the other way round' (Taylor 1957: 24). This chapter is predominantly concerned with two questions: to what extent was the great recession of 2008 a case of 'history repeating itself', and in responding to this crisis, have economic policy makers learned the 'lessons of history' and managed to avoid repeating past policy mistakes? Section two briefly examines the causes of the Great Depression of the 1930s and the policy response to the crisis. Section three does the same for the recession of 2008. In section four the two questions will be considered, and section five draws some conclusions.

THE GREAT DEPRESSION AND THE POLICY RESPONSE

The stock market crash of 'Black Tuesday', 29 October 1929, is generally considered to mark the beginning of the Great Depression in the USA, which quickly affected the rest of the world. The catastrophic effects of the stock market collapse were soon transmitted to the rest of the economy. The crash affected not only those who had bought securities with borrowed money, a practice known as buying stocks 'on margin', but also ordinary consumers who had bought houses and consumer durables on credit. Rising unemployment and falling incomes for those remaining in work meant falling aggregate demand in the economy and further rises in unemployment. For those households that had overextended credit commitments it meant foreclosure and repossession, which caused further weakening of aggregate demand in the economy. Declining aggregate demand meant a further fall in industrial production, leading to more business failures and more unemployment. The contraction of the economy was cumulative and long lasting. Between 1929 and 1933 real output in the USA declined by nearly 30%, the unemployment rate reached nearly 25%, while many of those who were employed worked part time. During this major contraction phase (1929–33) of the Great Depression there was sharp deflation, a situation of falling prices, which in the early 1930s ran at an annual rate of 10%. This exacerbated the fall in aggregate demand, as people postponed consumption to take advantage of falling prices. Another feature of this period which made a bad situation worse was the large number of bank failures. Between December 1930 and March 1933 the banking system in the USA shrank by half, with banks either closing down or merging with other banks. This produced a sharp reduction in the money supply, further aggravating the recession. Furthermore, in a period when there was no government guarantee of deposits, people started hoarding money, since a bank closure meant that depositors lost all their savings. On 6 March 1933 President Roosevelt declared a 'banking holiday', shutting down the entire US banking system. After the 'holiday' 2,500 banks never reopened. Those that survived, instead of making up for the lost deposits, retrenched sharply: then as now, banks reduced their lending to consumers and businesses which further added to the woes of the economy.

It was not only the industrial and financial sectors that were affected by the depression. American agriculture was already in dire difficulties because of the collapse of food prices, following the loss of the export market after World War I and prolonged drought conditions marked by devastating dust storms. As a result farmers' incomes were more than halved between 1929 and 1932, and many farmers lost their farms and equipment to foreclosures. In 1930 Congress passed the highly protectionist Hawley-Smoot Tariff, expecting to save American jobs. President Hoover signed the bill, despite advice in a letter from over 1,000 leading economists to veto it, and within a year 25 countries had retaliated by passing laws restricting US imports. The spread of protectionism and 'beggar-thy-neighbour' policies in the 1930s were counter-productive, creating an even deeper and longer-lasting global depression.

The traditional view of the global depression of the 1930s is that it began in the USA, then and now the world's largest economy, and once begun, it developed a momentum of its own, resulting in a vicious downward spiral that eventually spread throughout the world. In analysing the causes of the Great Depression, therefore, it was considered sufficient to study the origins by concentrating on the US experience. More recent studies have extended the geographic focus of the research on the causes of the Great Depression to include the experience of different national economies, and the role of the then prevailing international monetary system known as the Gold Standard (Bernanke 2004).

The traditional approach that focuses on the US experience stresses the importance of the policy response to the crisis: although the crisis was triggered by the 1929 Wall Street stock market crash, the depth and length of the depression was aggravated by government policy before and after the crash. These policy failures involved government action but also frequently government inaction. There are explanations that emphasize the failures of monetary policy and those that stress fiscal policy failures.

Pre-eminent among the studies that emphasize the role of monetary factors in the Great Depression and policy mistakes by the Federal Reserve Board before and after the crash of 1929 is that of Friedman and Schwartz (1963). In their book, *A Monetary History of the United States, 1867–1960*, they identify four causes of the Great Depression, each associated with a policy error by the monetary authorities in the USA. The first mistake by the Federal Reserve Board (FRB) was the tightening of monetary policy in 1928; second, the raising of interest rates in October 1931; third, the abandonment of open market operations in July 1932; and fourth, the general neglect of the collapsing banking system.

The justification for raising interest in 1928 was excessive speculation in Wall Street. Having failed to persuade the banks to limit lending to brokers and speculators in the stock market, the monetary authorities decided to curb speculative activity directly by raising the cost of borrowing. This tightening of monetary policy coincided with a slowdown in the economy in 1928, which contributed to the stock market crash in 1929. The FRB succeeded in curbing the speculative frenzy in Wall Street but it was a Pyrrhic victory. The same can be said of the second episode of monetary tightening identified by Friedman and Schwartz (1963): the sharp increase in interest rates in 1931. The rise was believed to be necessary in order to protect the dollar from currency speculation, following the exit of Great Britain from the Gold Standard. The dollar was in fact stabilized but given the depressed macroeconomic conditions of falling output, prices and employment, monetary tightening was the wrong policy.[1] Many officials in the FRB erroneously interpreted the prevailing low nominal interest rates as an indication of easy monetary policy. They were consequently reluctant to accede to pressure from the US Congress to ease monetary conditions by increasing the money supply through open market operations. Although under Congressional pressure the FRB conducted some open market operations between April and June 1932, as soon as Congress adjourned in July the policy was reversed. Thus despite low nominal interest rates, the real cost of borrowing was extremely high because with persistent deflation the value of loans that had to be repaid was appreciating. The monetary authorities in the USA, by refusing to engage in open market operations in order to expand the money supply, were making the extremely tight monetary conditions even more restrictive. To compound all these policy mistakes, the FRB bears a huge responsibility for allowing the banking crisis to develop into a full-scale banking collapse: it could and should have prevented the collapse of the US banking system, which was part of its mission. It failed to do so because the leadership of the FRB adhered to an economic theory that viewed the depression as a mechanism for purging the economic system of the financial excesses created during the boom of the 1920s. Many FRB officials believed that the collapse of the banking system was a harsh but necessary condition in order to 'cleanse' the system of its weak components.

These views were not confined to the FRB. The US Treasury, which had primary responsibility for economic and financial policy, concurred. In fact, the theory has come to be known as the 'liquidationist' thesis because of remarks attributed to Andrew Mellon, the incumbent US Treasury secretary in 1929, who, according to Galbraith (2009: 53), was a 'passionate advocate of inaction'. Mellon believed that the best policy to deal with the crisis was to 'liquidate labour, liquidate stocks, liquidate the farmers, liquidate real estate'. According to this philosophy, any active government policy to deal with the depression such as deficit spending and expansionary fiscal policy was futile. The prevailing economic orthodoxy maintained that any borrowing and spending by governments was ultimately ineffective because such spending would 'crowd out' private investment spending. In any case, any slowing down of the economic collapse would simply delay the necessary and inevitable adjustments in the economy. In other words, in 1929 US policy makers' view of a depression was not too dissimilar to their view of a hurricane or a storm: it was something to be weathered.

It soon became clear to President Hoover, who assumed office in 1929, that this depression was far worse than any previous depression and that the federal government had to act. He strongly believed, however, that any policy action by the federal government should not involve deficit spending. Hoover was a firm believer in fiscal rectitude, which meant balancing the government budget in a depression. In fact, during the election campaign of 1932 both the Republicans and the Democrats campaigned in favour of balanced budgets. The difference, of course, was that the newly elected President Roosevelt was prepared to abandon his pre-election promise to balance the budget and engaged in deficit spending in addition to reforming the banking system. With deficit spending the economy recovered, although not fully until the outbreak of World War II.

The combination of fiscal retrenchment and monetary contraction during a depression was a policy response to the economic crisis in the 1930s now widely acknowledged by economic historians to have made things decidedly worse: the depression was deeper and it lasted longer than necessary as a result of inappropriate policies. There is less agreement, however, with regard to the claim by Friedman and Schwartz (1963) that the Great Depression was caused predominantly by monetary factors. A big debate ensued for decades concerning the direction of causation between the money stock and the level of output in the economy: was the decline in the money supply in the 1930s the cause or the effect of the decline in output? The question of whether the underlying causes of the Great Depression were purely monetary remains controversial. What is beyond dispute is that the errors by policy makers in the FRB and the US Treasury sustained, aggravated and prolonged the Great Depression.

THE GREAT RECESSION OF 2008 AND THE POLICY RESPONSE[2]

In 1955 John Kenneth Galbraith published his book *The Great Crash 1929*, in which he provides the definitive account of the events leading to the Wall Street crash. On Tuesday 8 March 1955 Galbraith was invited by the Banking and Currency Committee of the US Congress to testify on the experience of the 1929 stock market crash. The committee was mainly concerned, in the light of the booming conditions in the markets, whether another 1929-style stock market crash was possible. In the introduction to the second edition of his book Galbraith (2009: 15) writes: 'Towards the end I suggested that history *could* repeat itself, although I successfully resisted all invitations to predict when.'

Throughout the book, as with his testimony to the Congressional committee, Galbraith did not make any forecast about the timing of the next crash, although in the final chapter of the book he ventured a prediction: a future (post-1955), 1929-style stock market 'adventure' and speculative collapse, although clearly to be avoided, would not cause the same kind of catastrophic effects on the US and global economy as in 1929. There were what Galbraith called significant 'reinforcements' in place in 1955 to make a repeat performance of the impact of the 1929 collapse on the US and global economy unlikely. These 'reinforcements', absent in 1929, included better financial regulation, less income inequality, more automatic stabilizers and also a 'modest accretion' of economic knowledge. The Glass-Steagall Act of 1933 meant that the banking system was better regulated and less prone to systemic collapse than in 1929, primarily because of the introduction of the Federal Deposit Insurance system and the strict separation of investment and retail banking.

Income inequality as measured by the proportion of income going to the top 1% of income recipients, including capital gains, declined significantly from the peak it reached just before 1929.[3] Taxes like progressive income tax and transfer payments such as unemployment and other welfare benefits were supposed to act automatically to reduce macroeconomic instability. Finally, in the 'modest accretion of economic knowledge', Galbraith was referring, of course, to the acceptance, unlike in 1929, of Keynesian ideas. His belief that this last 'reinforcement', the increase in economic knowledge of how to deal with depressions, would be utilized and applied by policy makers led Galbraith to conclude that 'A developing depression will not now be met with a fixed determination to make things worse ... Our determination to deal firmly and adequately with a serious depression is still to be tested. But there is a considerable difference between a failure to do enough that is right and a determination to do much that is wrong' (Galbraith 2009: 209). What Galbraith referred to in the quotation was, of course, the 'fixed determination' of policy makers on both sides of the Atlantic following the 1929 crash, to pursue the kind of policies discussed above, which had resulted in making the depression worse.

What Galbraith conceded in 1955 was a future possibility of indeterminate timing became a reality in 2008: a 1929-style global financial crisis, resulting from 1929-style speculative excesses combined with the proliferation of unregulated, 'exotic' but 'toxic' Wall Street financial innovations, resulted in a near-meltdown of the global financial system. Two of the 'reinforcements' identified by Galbraith in 1955 had long gone: the Glass-Steagall Act had been repealed in 1999 and income inequality in the USA had by 2007 reached pre-1929 levels. The third 'reinforcement'—the acceptance of Keynesian ideas—had given way to a new orthodoxy, known as New Consensus Macroeconomics (NCM), in which there was not much role and scope for traditional fiscal policy.[4] Automatic stabilizers were still in place but by themselves they were not considered adequate to prevent a major depression. Yet, the great recession of 2008 did not develop into a 1930s-style global depression, as Galbraith correctly predicted. In 2009, at the G-20 meeting in London, world leaders agreed to pursue a strategy of co-ordinated economic stimulus and fiscal expansion combined with a commitment to avoid protectionism in a deliberate attempt not to repeat the policy mistakes of the 1930s. There were not many loud voices demanding measures of savage austerity, balanced budgets and fiscal consolidation; nor were many doubts expressed by proponents of NCM about the effectiveness of fiscal policy and fiscal multipliers. For a brief moment the whole world became Keynesian again.

Not only in fiscal policy but also in monetary policy, policy makers were prepared to act in radically different ways from the 1930s. In both the USA and the UK the FRB and the Bank of England were ready to adopt measures that were 'unorthodox' and not adopted in the 1930s. They were not content, as in the 1930s, to consider the existence of near-zero interest rates as a sign of easy monetary conditions. They actively sought to expand the money supply through open market operations and the creation of 'electronic money', a policy known as 'quantitative easing'. At the same time, unlike in the 1930s, policy makers on both sides of the Atlantic were ready, following the collapse of Lehman Brothers, to provide unlimited support and effectively bail out the banking system in order to prevent the meltdown that occurred in the 1930s in the US banking system.

Future economic historians will no doubt debate and determine the relative importance of automatic stabilizers, Keynesian stimulus, quantitative easing, the absence of 'beggar-thy-neighbour' policies, the strength and robustness of emerging economies and other factors in preventing a global recession in 2008 from developing into a major global depression. Galbraith's optimism, however, that a global depression could be averted and that the policy-making system would not adopt pro-cyclical policies in the face of a developing depression that could make things worse, appears to have been vindicated: the 2008 global financial crisis did not develop into a global depression and a global recovery, albeit fragile, was soon under way in the second quarter of 2009.

By 2010, however, the policy-making environment radically changed in ways that Galbraith probably could not have expected: the 'fixed determination' to adopt policies that could make things worse was making a comeback. This was due primarily to the appearance of a force in economic policy making which, although not new, assumed critical power and influence in recent years due to globalization. This force was simply the concerns and apprehensions of liberalized international capital markets over ballooning government budget deficits and public indebtedness, unprecedented in peacetime. The reactions of international investors influenced by the opinions and pontifications of a small number of credit rating agencies began to play a decisive role in economic policy making during 2010. Increasingly, following the Greek bailout in May 2010, the dominant preoccupation of policy makers in economies struggling with the aftermath of the great recession of 2008 but with mounting debts was no longer how to prevent a recession developing into a depression, but how to prevent what had come to be known as a Greek-style tragedy. A 'Greek tragedy' in 2010 had come to be associated not with the works of the famous writers of tragedies in 5th-century BC Athens, but with the severe 'punishment' administered in successive stages by capital markets on an economy that failed to put in place a 'credible' plan for reducing indebtedness. The 'punishment' initially involved an increase in spreads of bond yields and a negative credit watch by credit rating agencies, followed by an actual credit downgrade. Typically the sequence of events leading to the downgrade makes it more expensive for a country to borrow in international capital markets, but ultimately, some would say inevitably, it makes it impossible for the country to refinance its maturing debts without some form of external assistance. In that case the country needs to be rescued by an international bailout, which in turn results in the imposition, in the case of European bailouts, of even more onerous austerity measures on the heavily indebted economies by international organizations like the International Monetary Fund (IMF), the European Commission (EC) and the European Central Bank (ECB). The 'punishment' by the markets, however, continues unabated even after the austerity measures are implemented: the austerity measures themselves become part of the problem, leading to further downgrades, higher spreads and more bailouts in a seemingly endless spiral towards an eventual default. The relentless message from the markets to policy makers in indebted economies is this: adopt tough austerity measures now in order to avoid having to adopt even tougher and more painful measures later. All this is deemed necessary, even though there is no guarantee that these policies, which force you to dig even deeper, will take you out of the hole. These, however, are precisely the kind of policy measures that Galbraith, in the light of the lessons from the experience of the 1930s and advances in our economic knowledge and understanding, thought would not be adopted by governments attempting to fight a developing depression. Yet since 2010, following a fragile and anaemic recovery from the worst global economic crisis since the 1930s, 'austerity mania' has swept through Europe and, to a lesser extent, the USA. Once again policy makers were pronouncing the arrival of the 'age of austerity' and demanding cuts and belt tightening—a policy response not too dissimilar to that following the 1929 crisis.

IS IT THE 1930S ALL OVER AGAIN?

There are two parts to this question. First, was history repeating itself in the 2008 great recession? Second, have the lessons from the policy mistakes of the 1930s been learned by policy makers dealing with the 2008 crisis?

With regard to the first part, there are at least three closely connected ways that in 2008 history was repeating itself. First, both crises were preceded by a period of 'speculative excesses', which in 1929 caused a US stock market crash, while in 2008 they caused a US house price collapse which created the threat of a near-meltdown in global banking and finance. Second, both periods preceding the crises were marked by some breathtaking financial innovations such as 'margin' buying of shares and investment trusts in the 1920s, and collateralized debt obligations and sub-prime mortgages in the 2000s—exotic innovations that turned out to be extremely 'toxic'. Third, during the build-up to both crises there was unwillingness by governments to regulate the financial sector properly. As James K. Galbraith points out in the foreword to the 2009 edition of his father's book, 'in both cases the American government knew what to do. Both times it declined to do it' (Galbraith 2009: v). In other words, public policy makers have failed to prevent history repeating itself. In responding to the crisis after 2010, they also appear to have forgotten the lessons of history.

The catalyst for this policy reversal was the 'debt crisis' in Europe, which broke out in May 2010 with the announcement by the newly elected Greek government that the country's debt situation was far worse than that shown by official statistics (Fouskas and Dimoulas 2012). This created a sovereign debt crisis in which affected countries were forced—either directly after a bailout by institutions like the IMF, EC or ECB, or indirectly through the threat of adverse market reaction and a credit downgrade—to adopt economic policies that could make things worse not only for the individual countries adopting austerity measures but also, through contagion, for the global economy. There is neither ambiguity nor much room for discretion on the nature of the measures deemed necessary or considered acceptable by markets for the purpose of deficit reduction: austerity, austerity and more austerity, combined with 'structural reform', which invariably means a massive attack on the public sector and the welfare system. This situation has been described by Krugman (2008) as 'policy perversity'.

It may of course be asked why it is considered 'perverse' to adopt austerity policies in countries with large budget deficits and total indebtedness, as prescribed and demanded by international creditors and credit rating agencies. These measures may be 'bitter', 'unpalatable' and 'painful' and the structural reforms long overdue, but in what sense can they be described as 'perverse'?

Austerity measures can be considered 'perverse' if they are contrary to what most economists would view as appropriate in dealing with a slowdown in the economy. In this sense, of course, Keynes's attack on economic policy in the 1930s was 'perverse' in terms of the prevailing standard economic doctrine and contrary to the established 'Treasury view' on deficit spending. A policy therefore can be 'perverse' in this sense, but not necessarily inappropriate: what may appear 'perverse' from one theoretical perspective may appear 'normal' from another perspective, and vice versa. Nevertheless, pro-cyclical and deflationary measures were proposed during the currency crises of Asia and Latin America in the 1990s even though the affected economies were experiencing significant economic slowdown. The same policies are now advocated to deal with the debt crisis in Europe and the USA in a situation when the global economy is making a fragile recovery from the great recession of 2008. These measures, therefore, can be considered 'perverse' because they are the exact opposite of the policies necessary to nurture a recovery and prevent a 'double-dip' recession, assuming of course that preventing a recession and a rise in unemployment is the overriding policy objective. Deficit reduction, however, demanded by the markets, might be considered a more urgent priority. In that case could austerity measures be considered 'perverse'? The austerity measures can still be considered 'perverse' if they produce the opposite *outcome* from the one intended. The declared primary objective of the current European fiscal austerity regime is to reduce ballooning public deficits. It would, therefore, be considered 'perverse' if austerity measures intended to achieve deficit reduction were to have no effect on the deficit or, in a worst case scenario, result in an increase in budget deficits.

Is this 'perverse' outcome, however, remotely possible? After all, an indebted household can reduce its deficit, the excess of expenditure over income, by adopting a reasonable austerity plan of cutting spending and increasing income through increased work effort. Why would the outcome be any different when the government attempts to reduce its indebtedness through tough austerity measures? The answer to this question is to be found in what Galbraith described as the 'modest accretion of economic knowledge' since the 1930s. The outcome of the process of restoring individual and national solvency might be different because, as Keynes taught us, at the macro level things tend to work out differently than at the micro level. This is known as the logical fallacy of composition: what is true for the part is not necessarily true for the whole. The so-called 'paradox of thrift' is a famous case in point. A similar paradox may be operating in connection to individual and national indebtedness: the austerity strategy will almost certainly work in reducing indebtedness at the individual level but not necessarily at the national level.[5] It is not inevitable, therefore, that savage austerity will result in a reduction in national indebtedness. If it has a big negative effect on growth, it may even produce 'perverse' outcomes. According to Amartya Sen, 'if the demands of financial appropriateness are linked too mechanically to immediate cuts, the result could be the killing of the goose that lays the golden egg of economic growth' (Sen 2011). Why then, given the obvious risks associated with this strategy, is there such a widespread endorsement and acceptance of this pre-Keynesian view that austerity will inexorably lead to public deficit reduction? The short answer is because financial markets demand it (Skidelsky 2009).

The theoretical argument, which has come to be known as 'expansionary fiscal contraction', is basically that austerity measures will not have a negative impact and may even stimulate economic growth. This is likely to happen because any deflationary effect of public sector cuts and tax increases will be offset by expansion of demand elsewhere in the economy. Demand in the private sector could rise because rational economic agents anticipating a reduction in taxes resulting from a reduction in the public deficit will start spending and investing more (Barro 1974). Measures to stimulate exports could also provide an additional source of extra demand, which could militate against the deflationary impact of austerity measures. Of course, how export growth is to be achieved simultaneously in several interconnected economies, especially when there is 'synchronized austerity', is never adequately explained. At the empirical level the austerity strategy is also supported by the Reinhart and Rogoff thesis that once a country's debt-to-GDP ratio exceeds 90%, economic growth is reduced by 1% (Reinhart and Rogoff 2009). The timely introduction of austerity measures therefore can promote growth by preventing the inevitable rise in interest rates that the crossing of the 90% 'debt intolerance' threshold will bring about. There is further support for the austerity strategy from a number of actual cases of individual countries that managed through tough austerity measures to eliminate big fiscal deficits in the past. Ireland and Canada in the late 1980s and early 1990s are often offered as such examples of successful fiscal consolidation. In both countries, however, this was achieved during a period when their main export

Policy response to the great recession of 2008

markets, the UK in the case of Ireland and the USA in the case of Canada, were experiencing boom conditions.

Despite the theoretical implausibility of the case supporting NCM (Arestis 2007, 2009) and despite the accumulating empirical evidence disputing the 'expansionary austerity' doctrine (Stiglitz 2010; Krugman 2010; Guajardo *et al.* 2011; IMF 2012), the austerity strategy is being adopted by country after country in Europe and strongly supported by 'deficit hawks' in the USA. Politicians and policy makers from different ideological backgrounds and political leanings are busy demanding from their electorate savage austerity and justifying the strategy, 1930s style, as the only way to end the crisis. Just as in the 1930s, fiscal contraction in a depression remains counter-productive. Nowhere is this 'policy perversity' more evident than in the eurozone periphery today, where synchronized savage austerity is imposed in the midst of the most serious global economic crisis since the 1930s, with the same consequences.

CONCLUDING COMMENTS

There are striking similarities but also significant differences in the policy response to the global economic crisis in the 1930s and in 2008. There are two main differences in the policy response. First, in terms of the actions of monetary authorities, the response in 2007–08 was dramatically different from the 1930s. There was decisive action to prevent the collapse of the banking and financial system and readiness to engage in 'unorthodox monetary policy' to ensure, through quantitative easing, that there was no catastrophic contraction of the money supply. Second, there was far greater willingness to employ Keynesian fiscal stimulus in 2008–10 than was the case in 1929–33. The emergence of ballooning public indebtedness in Europe and the USA, however, has radically altered the policy environment, elevating the role and influence of financial markets and international financial institutions in national policy making.

Galbraith predicted in his book, *The Great Crash 1929*, that a future 1929-style crisis would not be approached by policy makers with the same 'fixed determination to make things worse' as in the 1930s. In the immediate aftermath of the great recession of 2008, following the worst global financial crisis since 1929, Galbraith seemed to have been vindicated: austerity, fiscal contraction and protectionism, the trademark policies of the 1930s, were out. World leaders in their 2009 G-20 meeting in London agreed on a co-ordinated programme of fiscal expansion in a deliberate attempt to avoid the policy mistakes of the 1930s. This traditional Keynesian policy response was one of the 'reinforcements' that Galbraith thought were in place to prevent a 1929-style crisis from developing into a 1930s-style depression. Several 'rounds' of quantitative easing (QE1, QE2, QE3) took place in the USA and the UK (but significantly not by the ECB in the eurozone), in sharp contrast with the 1930s. Yet by 2010 there had been a radical reversal in fiscal policy. Galbraith's 'reinforcement' of the policy-making system was replaced, at least in

Europe and partially in the USA, by a pre-Keynesian obsession with deficit reduction. The catalyst for this policy reversal was not any solid economic knowledge or doctrine, but the naked, raw power of financial markets. Since 2010, therefore, national economic policy in large parts of Europe has been shaped not by the ideas, right or wrong, of economists as Keynes believed to be the case in the 1930s, but by the perceptions, right or wrong, of international capital markets and rating agencies. These perceptions are that savage austerity is the only means of reducing deficits and it ought to be implemented immediately. Even though there is accumulating evidence that the reality is that synchronized austerity, now as in the 1930s, is counter-productive, a reversal of the austerity strategy is nowhere in sight. Perhaps Taylor's pessimistic assessment on the question of 'learning the lessons of history' is more appropriate in this case than Galbraith's optimism that the policy-making system would not in the face of a 1929-style crisis persist with the same 'fixed determination' policies that make things worse.

NOTES

1 See Bernanke (2004) for a fuller discussion of the role of the Gold Standard system as a causal factor in the Great Depression.
2 The main themes in this and the next section of this chapter rely heavily on Kitromilides (2011, 2012).
3 The share was 22%–23% in 1929.
4 For a critique of NCM see Arestis (2007, 2009).
5 For a fuller discussion of this paradox see Kitromilides (2011).

REFERENCES

Arestis, P. (2007) 'What is the New Consensus in Macroeconomics?' in P. Arestis (ed.) *Is there a New Consensus in Macroeconomics?*, Houndsmills, Basingstoke: Palgrave Macmillan.
——(2009) 'Fiscal Policy within the New Consensus Macroeconomic Framework', in J. Creel and M. Sawyer (eds) *Current Thinking on Fiscal Policy*, Basingstoke: Palgrave Macmillan.
Barro, R.J. (1974) 'Are Government Bonds Net Worth', *Journal of Political Economy* 82(6): 109–17.
Bernanke, B. (2004) 'Money, Gold, and the Great Depression', www.federalreserve.gov/boarddocs/speeches/2004/200403022/default.htm.
Davidson, P. (2009) *The Keynes Solution: The Path to Global Economic Prosperity*, New York: Palgrave Macmillan.
Fouskas, V.K. and Dimoulas, C. (2012) 'The Greek Workshop of Debt and the Failure of the European Project', *Journal of Balkan and Near Eastern Studies* 14(1).
Friedman, M. and Schwartz, A.J. (1963) *A Monetary History of the United States, 1867–1960*, Princeton, NJ: Princeton University Press.
Galbraith, J.K. (2009 [1955]) *The Great Crash 1929*, London: Penguin Books.
Guajardo, J., Leigh, D. and Pescatori, A. (2011) 'Expansionary Austerity: New International Evidence', *IMF Working Paper* 11/158 (July).

IMF (2012) 'World Economic Outlook, October, 2012', Washington, DC: IMF Publication Services.
Keynes, J.M. (1936) *The General Theory of Employment, Interest, and Money*, New York: Harcourt Brace Jovanovich.
Kitromilides, Y. (2011) 'Deficit Reduction, the Age of Austerity and the Paradox of Insolvency', *Journal of Post-Keynesian Economics* (Spring).
——(2012) 'The 1929 Crash and the Great Recession of 2008', *Challenge* 55(1) (January–February).
Krugman, P. (2008) *The Return of Depression Economics*, London: Penguin Books.
——(2010) 'Fiscal Scare Tactics', *The New York Times*, 4 February, 25.
——(2012) *End this Depression Now*, New York: W.W. Norton.
Reinhart, C. and Rogoff, K. (2009) *This Time is Different. Eight Centuries of Financial Folly*, Princeton, NJ: Princeton University Press.
Rogoff, K. (2010) 'No Need for Panicked Fiscal Surge', *Financial Times*, 21 July, 13.
Sen, A. (2011) 'It Isn't the Euro. Europe's Democracy Itself is at Stake', *The Guardian*, 22 June, www.theguardian.com/commentisfree/2011/jun/22/euro-europes-democracy-rating-agencies.
Skidelsky, R. (2009) 'Why Market Sentiment has no Credibility', *Financial Times*, December, 22.
——(2010) *Keynes: The Return of the Master*, London: Penguin Group.
Stiglitz, J. (2010) 'To Choose Austerity is to Bet it all on the Confidence Fairy', *The Guardian*, October, 19.
Taylor, A.J.P. (1957) *The Trouble-Makers, Dissent over Foreign Policy 1792–1939*, London: Hamish Hamilton.

Understanding the global financial crisis

BÜLENT GÖKAY

On 15 September 2008, the supposedly safe, perpetually prosperous post-industrial global economic system blew itself up when Lehman Brothers filed for Chapter 11 bankruptcy. The 158-year-old iconic investment bank was forced into this extreme act when the collapse of the US sub-prime mortgage market turned the securitized mortgage-backed debt obligations into toxic assets. Initially, US$7.8 billion in mortgage-related bonds were considered worthless. The bank also admitted that it still had $54 billion of exposure to hard-to-value mortgage-backed securities (Gökay and Whitman 2009).

It is not often that we are faced with financial and economic turmoil so severe that the International Monetary Fund (IMF) calls it 'the largest financial crisis in the US since the Great Depression' (*The Guardian* 2008). Many observers portrayed the turmoil in financial markets in terms of a 'domino effect', claiming that 'the risk of a domino effect ... would be significant as many of the Emerging Europe region economies share the same vulnerabilities' (Fouskas and Gökay 2012). Others find metaphors drawn from chaos theory more suitable.

At the conclusion of his widely popular 1987 study of global political economics, *The Rise and Fall of the Great Powers*, English-born and Oxford-trained Yale historian Paul Kennedy observed, 'The task facing American statesmen over the next decades ... is to recognize that broad trends are under way, and that there is a need to "manage" affairs so that the *relative* erosion of the United States' position takes place slowly and smoothly' (Kennedy 1987: 534). In chronicling the decline of the USA as a global power, Kennedy compared measures of economic health of the USA, such as levels of industrialization and the growth of real gross national product (GNP), against those of Europe, Russia and Japan. What appeared from his analysis was a shift in the global political economy over the last 50 years which followed from underlying structural changes in the organization of the global financial and trading systems. In this chapter I shall argue that these shifts reflect fault lines in relationships between national economies that have been growing as a consequence of deep historical trends, with the People's Republic of China, India and Brazil now emerging as new centres of power, replacing the concentrations of power that developed in the post-World War II era. These shifts frame the present crisis as something more than an episodic and incidental spasm in the onward expansion of global capitalism, and argue that economics is much more driven by long-term, dynamic factors than is generally acknowledged.

Critical historical analysis requires definition of how it is critical, and identification of the spatial and temporal qualities in historical perspective. In this case, a critical analysis of the global political economy and its present crisis begins with understanding that this subject is structurally bounded by the political acts of governments because governments arguably determine the structural relationships within the global economy. This does not imply that ideology and cultural are not important—they are—but that government, acting as the institutional instrument of political elites, facilitates the way in which ideology and culture function through the structures that it authorizes. This varies from country to country according to the peculiar history and internal politics of each state, with internal political shifts inevitably rippling out to become shifts in the global political economy. In many cases, these internal shifts are prompted by national political elites, but occasionally, as in the present crisis, internal shifts appear quite beyond the control of national political elites, causing shifts in the global political economy that are similarly beyond the control of structures created by national governments. In the latter case, these global shifts illuminate fault lines in relationships between and among nations that have long historical trains. This discussion attempts to identify both the visible shifts and less visible fault lines that underlie the global political economy in crisis.

WHAT EXACTLY HAPPENED?

There seems to be a consensus that the immediate cause of the crisis lay in US sub-prime mortgage lending. During the last decade, a large number of people, previously considered a bad credit risk, were offered mortgages. Because house prices were rising and it seemed like they would continually increase, it was anticipated that if people could not keep up with their mortgage payments, their houses could be repossessed and sold at a generous profit. Indeed, it was such lending that pushed the very rises in the house prices upon which it relied. The greater and easier availability of mortgage funding predictably led to greater demand for housing. Sharp and consistent rises in house prices served to reinforce speculation, and the rise in house prices made the owners feel rich. The result was a consumption boom that has sustained the economy in recent years.

> The housing bubble had a double effect: it not only made American consumers feel confident that the value of their house was rising, enabling them to spend more; it was reinforced by a strong campaign from the banks, ... urging them to take out second mortgages and use the new money for consumption spending.
>
> (Gowan 2009: 25)

Those banks, mortgage lenders who lent the money, did not usually do so out of their own pockets. They went to others to borrow, and those others in turn would borrow from somewhere else. All major banks in the USA and in Europe were doing this, setting up special entities to borrow in order to lend. In this way, all kinds of different loans were packaged together into what came to be called 'financial instruments'. Financial instruments are simply defined as 'any contract that gives rise to both a financial asset of one enterprise and a financial liability or equity instrument of another enterprise'. More simple and straightforward financial instruments can be receivables, payables, loans, etc. There emerged, however, much more complex and complicated ones during the last decade, such as financial instruments involving derivatives, forward contracts and hedging activities. The finance market is composed of endless strings of bilateral transactions involving an incredibly diverse array of high-risk financial instruments. For a time all seemed to go well and provided enormous, almost effortless profits. There are limits, however, to how far economies can be sustained by debt that is not based on any real economic value created.

The first signs that all was not well were about four years ago. The eventual bursting of the housing bubble was inevitable once housing prices peaked in early 2006. Economic growth slowed in America, which ignited a sharp increase in the number of mortgage holders who could not afford the interest rates, and in the end there was a growing number of repossessions. Meanwhile, investors who had bought these mortgages through a range of schemes known as mortgage-backed securities, found out that the value of what they owned was sharply dropping. As a result, house prices fell quickly, and mortgage lenders discovered that they could not make enough from selling off roughly 1 million repossessed homes to pay back what they themselves had borrowed. The investment banks that had been so willing to lend money to mortgage lenders just as suddenly found out that they were facing losses of tens of billions of dollars. For some, the losses represented by various toxic securities simply diminished their reserves and brought them down. At that stage no one knew precisely how deep any particular bank's problems went, because the 'financial instruments' were incomprehensibly complicated.

As a result of all this, financial institutions right across the global economic system became afraid to lend each other money, in case they discovered that they could not get it back. Many banks stopped lending to one another, and lending practically stopped everywhere. This situation was called the 'credit crunch'. A credit crunch is, in simple terms, a crisis caused by a (sudden) reduction in the availability of liquidity in the financial markets. In the case of a credit crunch, banks hugely reduce their lending to each other because they are uncertain about how much money they have. These events led to a fundamental reassessment of the value of virtually every asset in the world.

Financial markets and credit institutions play a fundamental role in the modern economy, co-ordinating the production circuits and networks by directing capital to where it can make the maximum level of profit. They produce credit money and credit systems to smooth the payment of debt. Every modern economic activity depends for its day-to-day activities on continuous borrowing and lending. It would be quite appropriate, therefore, to compare a credit crunch to a heart attack. If it is not dealt with properly, the whole system immobilizes. This is why all the governments rushed to intervene, pouring billions of dollars into private banks, hoping that recipients would use the cash to start lending and borrowing again. The danger was that once a government had stepped in, nationalized the banks and taken on their entire debt, this debt could turn out to be greater than the whole gross domestic product (GDP) of the country. This is what happened in Iceland, while a number of other 'problem countries' came close to that point and asked the IMF for urgent help.

Many commentators in the media saw the story as ending there, and the only lesson they drew was the urgent need for more financial regulation. Most of the debate was centred on how much and what kind of regulation. Even a more critical and nuanced commentator, British anti-debt campaigner Ann Pettifor, explained the crisis in *openDemocracy* as 'the stupidity, poor economic analysis and sheer ignorance of those central bankers, politicians, auditors … ' (Pettifor 2008). Such an explanation, focusing on the blatant deceit and corruption of financial players, runs the risk of downplaying the structural features of the global economy in the 21st century, which indeed breeds such financial meltdowns.

Some commentators looked a little deeper. For example, Martin Wolf, chief economic commentator of the *Financial Times*, said: 'I now fear that the combination of the fragility of the financial system with the huge rewards it generates for insiders will destroy something even more important—the political legitimacy of the market economy itself—across the globe' (Wolf 2008). The same point was expressed by Ángel Gurría, secretary-general of the Organisation for Economic Co-operation and Development (OECD): 'the market system is in crisis' (Gurría 2008). Alan Greenspan, the former head of the Federal Reserve, called it the crisis that happens once in a century (Greenspan 2008). Other commentators pointed out that the main reason for the current crisis was that economic growth in the USA since the last recession seven years before had been to a large extent boosted by growing debt, both of consumers and of the US government (Wolf 2008).

For a healthy economy to function smoothly the wealth being produced throughout the system must be sold. If investment falls below savings, a gap opens up between what has been produced and what is being sold. Some producers cannot sell what they produce, and they have to scale down or even close, as a result of which their workers lose their jobs. This reduces still further what can be sold in the system. This did not happen until the recent crisis in the USA, because easy lending to US consumers had provided a domestic market and absorbed surplus production.

The credit crunch put a stop to this, because banks and mortgage lenders, fearing that they would be unable to meet their own financial obligations, stopped lending money to one another and to customers. Even when credit institutions recovered confidence (and capacity) in lending to each other, they were unlikely to start lending to people again soon with the same relaxed attitude. Credit would not start flowing just because banks could get hold of more liquidity. They would instead, most likely, use the funds to shore up their own finances, fix bad debts and build up their capital base in an attempt to become solvent.

THE REAL ROOTS OF THE CRISIS

The story told so far is not complete. We have not been told, for instance, why the rest of the world is so dependent on the US economy. Due to the highly complex, geographically extensive and transnational nature of production and trading networks, a crisis in one part of the system inevitably and directly affects the other parts. Furthermore, the size and strength of the US economy have made it the main determinant of the pace of expansion of the world economy as a whole. From the USA, the crisis spread to the rest of the world, which witnessed the first synchronized world recession since 1974. There were lots of proximate causes—the US housing bubble and the huge size of the American economy, persistent unresolved global imbalances, a lack of government regulation of the financial sector, lax and insufficient regulation that led to widespread underestimation of risk (Wolf 2009). However, all these are still symptoms. In order to make clear sense of this crisis, I would like to develop a broad picture here regarding the configuration of the world economy.

The recent crisis is an expression of the structural changes and deep-rooted contradictions that have occurred within the global system in the last 30 years. As a result, today's global economic system is marked by profound vulnerabilities. The explosive growth of the financial system during the last three decades relative to manufacturing and the economy as a whole, and the proliferation of speculative and destabilizing financial instruments of wealth accumulation are the direct result of this unbalanced situation.

The current economic system rests upon the search for profit and accumulation of capital. What stimulates investment, however, is not just the absolute level of profits, but the 'rate of profit', which is the ratio of profits to investment. Most observers of capitalism consider the rate of profit as one of the most important indicators of the health of the economic system. The rate of profit is an essential indicator that determines as well as exposes conditions of accumulation—in other words, the health of a particular economic body. For both classicals and neo-classicals, higher rates of profit mean greater investment, and higher growth rates are possible both because they provide greater sources of funds for investment, and because they generate higher expectations of future profits and through that a greater desire to invest. In the world economy, the rate of profit stayed more or less steady all through the late 1940s, the 1950s and the 1960s. As a result, these years witnessed steadily rising levels of investment and a continual boom. This era, from the end of World War II to the late 1960s, is generally referred to as 'the golden age of capitalism'. However, from the late 1960s until 1982, profit rates fell continuously, and the global economy witnessed real decline in the rate of global GDP increase. As a result, the mid-1970s and the early 1980s witnessed a number of deep economic recessions. Growth slowed, profits fell and serious levels of unemployment became a central feature of the system.

The response of governments to the economic recessions was to introduce a series of measures which later came to be known as neo-liberalism. Neo-liberal response(s) to the recession took the form of Reaganism in the USA and Thatcherism in Britain, and similar measures in most of the developed economies of the West. Under the pressure of the leading capitalist states (primarily the USA) and international monetary institutions (the IMF and World Bank), the developing economies adopted structural adjustment programmes along the same lines. As a result, global growth averaged 1.4% in the 1980s and 1.1% in the 1990s, compared to 3.5% in the 1960s and 2.4% in the 1970s (Harvey 2007: 154).

One essential element in this partial recovery of the rate of profit in the 1980s and 1990s was the increase in the share of total profits in total national incomes at the expense of wages. This meant that everywhere there was increased pressure for people to work harder and a wide range of attacks on and cuts in welfare services. It meant a fall in real wages and a massive increase in working hours. Almost everywhere in the world the proportion of the wealth produced that comes back to the workers has decreased since the 1970s.

As seen in the figures above, the profit rates never recovered more than about half their previous decline, and even the small booms of the neo-liberal era ran into serious trouble with a number of severe crises—most significantly, the stock exchange crash of October 1987, and the East Asian financial crisis of 1997 (and its contagious effects on the rest of the world economy). Both the US Federal Reserve and the Bank of England reacted on both occasions by cutting interest rates and encouraging lending. All this was made possible by an active process of 'deregulation'—in other words, the elimination of proper oversight of financial institutions and efforts. Such measures were able to encourage spending to some extent and thus to extend the booms, but in retrospect one can now conclude that they simply delayed recessions for a few years. After the recession of 2001–02, the US government cut taxes again, and the Federal Reserve slashed interest rates even further. All this encouraged even greater levels of, and riskier, borrowing than before, which pushed the housing bubble. Demand for assets such as homes increased, without a corresponding increase in new value being produced in the system. This caused the prices of these assets to rise even further. On paper, personal and business wealth increased, so it seemed that they now had the means to borrow more, and they became 'irrationally exuberant'. This led to a further increase in demand, and so on, and so forth. The 'demand' was largely fabricated by speculative mania on the part of developers and financiers who wanted to make great profits. In other words, many people were provided with mortgages (by relaxing income documentation requirements) to buy overpriced properties that they could not, in reality, afford. 'The housing bubble, associated with rising house prices and the attendant increases in home refinancing and spending, which has been developing for decades, was a major factor in allowing the economy to recover from the 2000 stock market meltdown and the recession in the following year' (Foster 2006). Under the euphemistic heading of 'financial innovation', a number of changes in institutional arrangements enabled banks and mortgage lenders to escape regulatory restrictions and expand their activities even further.

It seemed, for a time, that the economy was dragged out of recession, yet one can claim in retrospect that the same measures (i.e. the role finance played in resolving the recessions of the last decade with a 'cheap money, easy credit' strategy) laid the ground for the much more serious problems that the system came to face. Greater levels of risky borrowing led to speculative bubbles, which led to temporary prosperity, but which ultimately ended up in corporate collapse and in recession in the real economy.

The rise in profit rates was not enough to raise investment to its previous levels, but also rising profits at the expense of salaries had indeed cut the capacity of workers to buy consumer goods. From 2000 to 2005, the rise in after-tax income was barely one-third of the rise in home prices. Because the drain on wages was not and could not be used to invest more, extra profits were accumulated in the financial sector. As a result, a large amount of increased business profits was invested in various financial schemes. The value of financial wealth thus grew considerably, and the relations between productive capital and financial capital were profoundly modified, subordinating all other economic activity. The road to wealth accumulation was no longer manufacturing industry or the provision of financial services associated with manufacturing, but the buying and selling of assets using borrowed funds for profit. Until the recent crisis, there was a constant search for even further investment opportunities for this financial wealth. All this vast financial sector expansion over-accumulated financial capital, in other words 'the new centrality of the financial sector' greatly advanced speculation. This process, widely referred to as financialization, is defined as 'the increasing role of financial motives, financial markets, financial actors and financial institutions in the operations of the domestic and international economies' (Guttmann 2008). As a result of this complex structure, exceptionally high profits were achieved in the financial sector, but the whole system remained extremely vulnerable.

The share of financial services in the GDP of the USA surpassed that of industry in the mid-1990s. From 1973 to 2008 the portion of manufacturing in GDP fell from 25% to 12%. The share represented by financial services rose from 12% to 21%. In parallel to this, borrowing at all levels was encouraged by the new financial structures, which were reshaped and relaxed to allow high levels of risky borrowing. In the words of Peter Gowan, the last 20 years witnessed a 'structural transformation of the American financial system', as a result of which 'a New Wall Street System has emerged ... ,

Understanding the global financial crisis

producing new actors, new practices and new dynamics' (Gowan 2009: 6). The computerization of finance in the 1990s dramatically improved the system's ability to innovate, and a number of longstanding barriers to the reach and range of permissible activities were gradually undermined by various changes in the US financial services industry. In particular, the banking activity restrictions of the Depression-era Glass-Steagall Act which separated commercial and investment banking to control speculation and protect bank deposits, were repealed by the Financial Services Modernization Act of 1999, known as the Gramm-Leach-Bliley Act, as a result of which the financial system became increasingly volatile and unpredictable. By the end of the century, the level of personal borrowing in America rose to the record level of 9% of GDP. Mortgage refinancing and home equity loans (on the bubble-inflated values of their houses), in particular, enabled US households to cash in capital gains from rising housing prices without having to sell off their homes. There was no other way that all the goods and services produced within the system could be sold (Dicken 2007: 379–409).

The gap between stagnant or even declining wages and fast increasing consumer expenditure was closed by the accumulation of consumer debt. Consumer debt allowed many working families to maintain their standard of living to some extent. Today, US households spend more of their disposable income to pay off debts (14%) than to buy food (13%). In the USA, household indebtedness rose from 50% of GDP in 1980, to 71% in 2000, to 100% in 2007. Financial sector indebtedness was 21% of GDP in 1980, 83% in 2000, and 116% by 2007 (*Monthly Review* 2000; Foster 2006).

In Britain borrowing levels were even greater proportionally. Until the recent crisis, the housing boom was even crazier, with average house prices quadrupling in 12 years. The reason Britain is in so much trouble is that both its corporate debt and household debt are huge—a combination that makes the British economy such a credit liability. Michael Saunders from CitiGroup has calculated British 'external debt', which is what the country owes the rest of the world, as 400% of GDP, the highest in the G-7 by some margin. The next highest, France, is 176%. The USA is just 100%. Japan is about half that of the USA (*The Spectator* 2008; Gökay 2009).

Between mid-2000 and 2004, US households took on $3 trillion in mortgages (Dowling 2007: 51–56). Where did this money come from? During the same period, the US government, as well as the private sector, borrowed from the rest of the world $3 trillion. Between one-third and half of mortgages were financed with foreign money. The total US debt, which is the debt of individual households, private business and government, has doubled as a proportion of GDP since 1980, and was 350% of GDP even before the recent dramatic takeovers of new debt by the government. This is the result of 'financialization'—the enormous increase in debt of all kinds.

So, the current crisis—both the financial and 'real' economy crisis—was not simply owing to bankers' mistakes or greed, or a lack of government regulation of a hyperactive sector, or even bad financial technology, but instead those policies of the last three decades to use debt to overcome the stagnationist tendency of the economy. This is a structural issue. It is about an economy that cannot grow without resorting to a huge build up of debt and speculative financial asset investment. This crisis, which has engulfed the US economy and most of the Western world, has not come out of the blue. It is the outcome of processes stretching back more than three decades. What made it worse is the inter-relationship between continuing external and internal imbalances in the USA and the rest of the world economy. The USA and a number of other chronic deficit countries have a structurally deficient capacity to produce tradable goods and services. 'One of the most striking trends, since at least the 1960s but, especially since the 1970s, has been the disappearance of manufacturing jobs ... ' (Dicken 2007: 476). Indeed, the subprime crisis is actually a correction to years of debt-driven consumption in the USA, revealing the end of unstable economic growth based on 'spending tomorrow's income today'.

Therefore, the turmoil in global financial markets is the manifestation of not simply a conjunctural downturn, but rather a profound systemic disorder. It is the inevitable outcome of the progressive deregulation of financial markets, and colossal growth in the process of shifting investment from manufacturing to ever more exotic forms of financial speculation, the rise of the shadow banking system—the illusion of wealth—initiated by Wall Street and its 'back yard', the City of London. The current crisis points unambiguously to the conclusion that it is not possible to revive the level of consumption and investment by artificially boosting demand to fill the 'output gap' (Gowan 2009).

REFERENCES

Dicken, P. (2007) *Global Shift. Mapping the Changing Contours of the World Economy*, London: Sage, 379–409.

Dowling, W.A. (2007) 'Retirement Imperiled: The Case of HELOCs', *Journal of Business Case Studies* 3(4): 51–56.

Foster, J.B. (2006) 'The Household Debt Bubble', *Monthly Review* 58(1) (May), monthlyreview.org/0506jbf.htm (accessed January 2009).

Fouskas, V.K. and Gökay, B. (2012) *The Fall of the US Empire: Global Fault-Lines and the Shifting Imperial Order*, London: Pluto Press.

Gökay, B. (2009) 'Tectonic Shifts and Systemic Faultlines: A Global Perspective to Understand the 2008–9 World Economic Crisis', *Alternatives* 8(1) (Spring), www.alternativesjournal.net/volume8/number1/Gökay.pdf.

Gökay, B. and Whitman, D. (2009) 'Mapping the Faultlines: A Historical Perspective on the 2008–9 World Economic Crisis', *Cultural Logic*, clogic.eserver.org/2009/Gökay_Whitman.pdf.

Gowan, P. (2009) 'Crisis in the Heartland: Consequences of the New Wall Street System', Editorial of the *New Left Review* (January–February): 25.

Greenspan, A. (2008) 'Greenspan: Economy in "Once-in-a-Century" Crisis', CNNMoney.com, 14 September, money.cnn.com/2008/09/14/news/economy/greenspan/index.htm?cnn=yes (accessed October 2008).

The Guardian (2008) 'IMF Says US Crisis is "Largest Financial Shock since Great Depression"', Guardian.co.uk, 9 April, www.guardian.co.uk/business/2008/apr/09/useconomy.subprimecrisis (accessed October 2008).

Gurría, A. (2008) *OECD Observer*, October, www.oecdobserver.org/news/fullstory.php/aid/2753/ (accessed January 2009).

Guttmann, R. (2008) 'A Primer on Finance-Led Capitalism and its Crisis', *Revue de la régulation* 3/4(2), 15 November, regulation.revues.org/document5843.html (accessed February 2009).

Harvey, D. (2007) *A Brief History of Neoliberalism*, Oxford: Oxford University Press, 154.

Kennedy, P. (1987) *The Rise and Fall of the Great Powers: Economic Change and Military Conflict From 1500 to 2000*, London: Fontana Press.

Monthly Review (The Editors) (2000) 'Working Class Households and the Burden of Debt', *Monthly Review* 50(1) (May), monthlyreview.org/500editr.htm (accessed September 2008).

Pettifor, A. (2008) 'America's Financial Meltdown: Lessons and Prospects', openDemocracy, 16 September, www.opendemocracy.net/article/america-s-financial-meltdown-lessons-and-prospects (accessed January 2009).

The Spectator (2008) 'The True Extent of Britain's Debt', Spectator.co.uk, 10 December, www.spectator.co.uk/coffeehouse/3078296/the-true-extent-of-britains-debt.thtml (accessed January 2009).

Tabb, W.K. (2008) 'The Financial Crisis of U.S. Capitalism', *Monthly Review*, 10 October, www.monthlyreview.org/mrzine/tabb101008.html (accessed December 2008).

Wolf, M. (2008) 'Regulators Should Intervene in Bankers' Pay', FT.com, 15 January, www.ft.com/cms/s/0/73a891b4-c38d-11dc-b083-0000779fd2ac.html?nclick_check=1 (accessed January 2009).

——(2009) 'Choices made in 2009 will Shape the Globe's Destiny', *Financial Times*, 6 January, www.ft.com/cms/s/0/4f5c5ba2-dc22-11dd-b07e-000077b07658.html (accessed January 2009).

The political economy of the Arab uprisings

SHAMPA ROY-MUKHERJEE

INTRODUCTION

The current political turmoil in the Middle East and North Africa (MENA) region has brought 'democratization' and 'economic liberalization' to the forefront of political debate. The dramatic political developments since December 2010 have created uncertainty over future economic policy and reform in the MENA region (Khan 2012). Transitional governments in countries affected by the Arab Spring are working on a mandate to deliver greater political and economic accountability and transparency to ensure sustainable macroeconomic growth and political stability. There is still a considerable amount of uncertainty and debate as to whether the Arab nations that had embarked on market-driven economic reform in the 1990s, in line with the Washington Consensus, will continue on the same path or if the political transition triggered by the Arab Spring will force them to take an alternative route to economic growth. Furthermore, although the Arab Spring provides an unprecedented opportunity for political, economic and social reform in the long term, its immediate impact has been devastating, characterized by social unrest, sectarian violence, massive displacement of communities and deterioration of living standards in general (O'Sullivan *et al.* 2012: 1–4).

The countries belonging to the MENA region are hugely diverse at multiple levels such as history, population size, resources, policy and ideological orientation. However, they have several unifying characteristics (Malik and Awadallah 2013: 296–313). First, they all have similar demographic profiles characterized by a disproportionately large youth population—a 'youth bulge'. The median age in Arab countries is 25, the second lowest in the world, with only sub-Saharan African countries being younger (Springborg 2011b: 85–104). Second, all countries within the MENA region have a dominant public sector. Third, the main source of revenue for these countries comes from rents derived from oil and other hydrocarbons, international aid or remittances from abroad. Fourth, political power in these countries is peculiarly concentrated in the hands of few, inasmuch as a robust civil society is absent and Islam plays an important role in the articulation between the public and the private sphere. The Arab uprisings have had a very wide-ranging impact in the region, with some governments resorting to appeasement through increased subsidies and welfare and political reform, while in a handful of countries the political elite have taken an extreme hard-line stance to remain in power.

The political economy of the Arab uprisings

Over the past few decades, the economic development strategies adopted by the MENA countries follow a path similar to most developing countries. From the 1950s to the mid-1980s the development strategy comprised import-substitution industrialization (ISI) policies which included strict controls on international trade, overvalued exchange rates and government-controlled foreign exchange and credit markets (Dahi and Demir 2008: 522–35). The objective of such a strategy was to develop capital-intensive domestic industry producing goods and services in a highly protected business environment for domestic market consumption. This strategy resulted in the proliferation of large state-owned companies operating in uncompetitive and inefficient markets. The private sector benefited from government subsidies in the form of discounted prices of intermediate goods, cheap credit foreign exchange and import licences. Overall, the result was an economic system where the state was the dominant player and the private sector was virtually non-existent. During this period the economic performance across countries in this region was mainly influenced by volatile oil prices. The hike in oil prices in 1973 and 1979 led to rapid improvements in growth and development indicators within this region. The collapse of oil prices in the 1980s and 1990s has led to significant reversal in economic growth and prosperity. Since the 1990s many MENA countries have embraced market-led, outward-looking economic reform by adopting the structural adjustment programmes (SAPs) introduced by the International Monetary Fund (IMF) and World Bank. These reforms were based on the neo-liberal policies prescribed in the Washington Consensus which encouraged trade liberalization, fiscal discipline and private sector-driven growth.

The objective of the chapter is to review the recent economic developments and prospects of the MENA region in light of the policies outlined in the 'Washington Consensus' and the implications of the Arab uprising on short-term economic performance and policy. The chapter is divided into three sections. The first section defines the Washington Consensus, focusing on global impact of policy reforms and the 'post-Washington Consensus', which was an effort to address inadequacies of neo-liberal globalization innate in the term. The second section is a review of the economic performance and development of the MENA region before the Arab uprising in 2010 and how successfully countries within this region were able to adopt and implement the Washington Consensus policies. The third section links up the impact of reforms, driven by the neo-liberal policies of the Washington Consensus, upon social classes and categories, thus deciphering the causes of the Arab Spring in certain countries of the MENA region.

THE WASHINGTON CONSENSUS

The Washington Consensus was a set of economic policies following a term introduced by the English economist John Williamson in 1989, and in response to the Latin American experience during the 1980s and 1990s. Post-Allende

Chile, in fact, was the first country in the 1970s, and well before Thatcher's Britain, that experienced the key tenets of the Washington Consensus (privatizations, liberalization of financial and banking system, welfare cuts and so on). Latin American countries were struggling to overcome devastating debt crisis, triple-digit hyperinflation and balance of payments problems. Government spending was very high, monetary and fiscal policies were unstable and the weak central banks were unable to control unsustainable credit expansions (Feinberg 2008: 153–68). Export competitiveness was stifled by overvalued currencies and unsustainable exchange rate policies, leading to an ever-widening trade gap. The 1980s were the famous lost decade when Latin American countries experienced *stagflation* (high inflation accompanied by stagnation) and a decline in per capita income (Feinberg 2008: 153–68). In light of the Latin American crisis, a set of policies were formulated that were agreed by policy makers in Washington, DC, i.e. the US Treasury, the IMF and the World Bank as a policy basis for developing countries, given the experience in Chile and the relative success of neo-liberal policies in Britain and the USA under Thatcher and Reagan, respectively. The Consensus included a list of policy reforms, shown in Table 11.1.

Broadly speaking, the Washington Consensus advocated that governments should pursue economic reform through policies that: lead to macroeconomic stability through fiscal austerity and inflation control; encourage liberalization of trade and capital account; and promote privatization and deregulation of domestic markets (Gore 2000: 789–804). The Washington Consensus policies

Table 11.1 The original and augmented Washington Consensus

Original Washington Consensus	*Augmented Washington Consensus (original WC plus)*
Fiscal discipline	11. Corporate governance and institutional reform
Redirection of public expenditure toward broad–based public sector provision	12. Anti-corruption
Tax reform–broadening of tax base and cutting marginal tax rates	13. Flexible labor markets
Financial and interest rate liberalisation	14. WTO agreements
Competitive exchange rates	15. Financial codes and standards
Trade liberalisation	16. "Prudent" capital- account opening
Liberalisation of inward FDI	17. Non-intermediate exchange rate regimes
Privatisation of state enterprises	18. Independent central banks & inflation targeting
Deregulation	19. Social safety nets particularly for the socially excluded
Legal security for property rights targeting the informal sector	20. Targeted poverty reduction through efficient social mechanism for allocating resources

Source: Authors compilation of items from Rodrik (2006) and Williamson (2004).

inspired a wave of reforms that significantly transformed the policy landscape in many developing countries (Rodrik and Bank 2006: 973–87). These reforms were introduced and propagated through IMF and World Bank stabilization and SAPs and have become the prominent orthodoxy in development studies since the 1990s. This was a completely new approach to development and constituted a complete shift in paradigm.

The pre-Washington Consensus post-war development approach was primarily based on Keynesian economics, whereby the state had a key role to play in the management of aggregate demand. Various forms of central planning were considered the most efficient system of resource allocation not only in socialist economies but also in the developing economies of Asia, Africa and Latin America. Government control over domestic development was the underlying theme in most development models, during which time appeared Rostow's stages of growth hypothesis, Paul Rosentein-Rodan's big push industrialization hypothesis, the Harrod Domar growth model and the Gunnar Myrdal circular and cumulative causation model (Woo 2004: 9–43). Prescribed policies included import substitution, protection of domestic infant industry, direct involvement of the state in economic production and decision making, highly regulated financial and capital markets, and restrictive trade and foreign investment policy. This approach to development slowly died out in the late 1970s as a result of the poor economic performance of the countries that had embraced such state-controlled policies. The failure of state interventionism to promote effective and sustainable growth caused a significant shift in paradigm in favour of 'economic liberalization'. Economic liberalization focused on reducing the size and control of the state, promoting privatization and liberalizing foreign trade, especially trade of financial commodities (insurance, futures, etc.). These policy prescriptions have their foundations in neo-classical economics, which also forms the basis of the Washington Consensus. Thus the mantra of the Washington Consensus in line with neo-liberal orthodoxy was to 'stabilise, privatise and liberalise' (Nonneman 1996: 1–26; see also Chapter 3 in this volume).

Neo-liberal economists such as Lal, Little, Krueger and Bauer argued that market-led short-term efficiencies would lead to long-term growth. They believed that long-term economic growth was the only way to achieve the key development goals of poverty reduction and welfare enhancement and that growth could be achieved through market-driven economic policies by ensuring the most efficient allocation of resources. Empirical analysis reinforced the conviction that 'market failure' in itself did not justify government intervention and that 'bureaucratic failure', more likely to be prevalent in less developed economies, would only make matters worse. Lal proposed the slogan 'Get the prices right!' and ardently opposed economic policy that encouraged 'political pricing', most commonly manifested in developing countries with artificially maintained high exchange rates, government-controlled interest rates, subsidized agricultural products, and import tariffs on luxury and consumer goods (Lal 2012: 493–512).

The concept of 'poverty traps' based on the notion that poverty and stagnation were self-perpetuating and that foreign aid was the only way that the poorer economies could escape this trap was completely dismissed by Bauer and other neo-classical economists (World Bank 1997: 19–29). Implicit in the Washington Consensus was that a structural approach to poverty eradication should be based on increased returns on factor endowments and increased capital accumulation. The argument was based on Heckscher-Ohlin's (1933) Factor Price Equalization Theorem and Stopler-Samuelson Theorem that international trade liberalization would raise returns to an abundant factor, which in most poor countries is unskilled labour.

A comprehensive empirical study covering a period from 1970 to 2005 clearly indicates that countries that have embraced the trade liberalization policy prescription of the Washington Consensus by lowering the tariffs on capital and intermediate goods have shown a significantly higher rate of growth than those where trade barriers remain (Estevadeordal and Taylor 2013: 1669–90). The results validate the neo-classical growth model proposed by Robert Solow (1956), which states that a country starting off with a low per capita capital stock will experience a faster rate of growth of per capita income as it approaches the steady state and will ultimately converge with the developed economies. Theoretical models suggest a mechanism where lower tariffs will lead to cheaper capital and intermediate goods imports, resulting in accelerated growth rates in countries with low per capita capital stock.

The proponents of the Washington Consensus believed that economic development would lead to an inverse U-shaped pattern of inequality as proposed by Kuznets (1955: 1–28). Empirical studies conducted by Kuznets demonstrated that as a country developed, inequality would initially increase, then peak and eventually start to decrease. This is because industrialization initially would cause a significant urban-rural inequality gap. As more and more of the workforce moved away from low-paid jobs in rural areas in search of better job prospects in the urban areas, inequality was expected to decrease. This dual economy dynamics would eventually lead to fairer distribution of wealth. Many empirical studies have been conducted to test the validity of the Kuznets curve. Williamson carried out a study of wealth inequality in Britain between 1823 and 1915 and found that it followed a pattern consistent with the Kuznets curve (Lindert and Williamson 1985: 341–77). A similar trend for US wealth inequality data was found. Empirical studies investigating European countries show that data from France, Germany and Sweden are consistent with the Kuznets curve, but other countries such as Norway and the Netherlands demonstrate patterns of monotonically declining inequality from the mid-19th century (Acemoglu and Robinson 2010: 1–33). However, the pattern of inequality in most Latin American and South-East Asian countries does not seem to follow the inverted U-shape of the Kuznets curve. Empirical evidence seems to be inconclusive, highlighting the fact that not all development paths will be characterized by the Kuznets curve. These discrepancies may be due to the differing political factors and regional instabilities. In some cases, development induces increasing inequality, causing social unrest and forced democratization. These countries will be more likely to encourage institutional reform and redistribution of wealth. However, countries where development is linked to undemocratic paths show patterns inconsistent with Kuznets, either because development does not lead to rising inequality—the case of the 'East Asian miracle'—or because of low levels of political mobilization.

POST-WASHINGTON CONSENSUS

Although policy reforms propagated by the Washington Consensus were broadly embraced by Latin America, sub-Saharan Africa, the MENA region and East Asia, they were unable to produce the desired results in the majority of these countries. Per capita gross domestic product (GDP) growth in Latin America has been below expectations and short lived, rising from 0.06% in the period 1975–89, to 1.5% in 1990–2001 (Woo 2004: 9–43). During the same period the GDP per capita in Latin American has grown from -1.5% to -0.5% (Woo 2004: 9–43). Moreover, in 24 African countries the GDP per capita is below the 1975 level (Milanovic 2003: 345–65). Although the East Asian economies experienced high and sustained levels of per capita growth of 5.9% in the 1980s and 1990s, since the financial crisis in 1997–98 they have been widely condemned for their misguided economic policies (Stiglitz 1999: 94–120). Moreover, transitional economies that embraced the policy reforms of the Washington Consensus experienced significant reductions in their GDP. The phenomenal growth of India and the People's Republic of China since the 1990s highlights the fact that both followed development paths significantly different from those proposed by the Washington Consensus (Buckley 2009: 1–21).

Over the past decade the policy prescriptions proposed by the Washington Consensus have come under fire from many different quarters. Policy makers realized that the original list had a very narrow scope and focused predominantly on macro- and microeconomic policy reforms, and did not feature any institutional reform (Rodrik and Bank 2006: 973–87). This gave birth to the 'augmented Washington Consensus', which included a list of institutional reforms (Table 11.1). The realization was that the stabilization, liberalization and privatization policy reforms would not be sustainable if institutional conditions were poor. Strong governance, rule of law, political equality, social justice and economic efficiency were the key elements to long-term sustainable growth (Held 2005: 95–113).

Critics of the Washington Consensus proposed an alternative development path that had broader goals and objectives. This has been termed by many policy makers as the 'post-Washington Consensus'. Stiglitz, for example, argued that the new consensus should include the broader development objectives of 'sustainable development, egalitarian development and democratic development' (Stiglitz 1999: 94–120). However, the post-Washington

Consensus neither represents a clear departure from fundamental values of the Washington Consensus of neo-liberal globalization, nor does it attempt to reproduce the same neo-liberal policy regime (Ruckert 2006: 36–67). It is based on the concept of an 'inclusive neo-liberal development regime' in the global economy. It advocates that governments, and not the international financial institutions, should take the lead in both owning and directing the neo-liberal policies. Proponents of the new consensus believe that giving the recipient government ownership is more likely to result in a genuine commitment towards implementing the structural adjustment policies as well as wider participation from civil society. Inclusive neo-liberalism can only succeed if public institutions are transparent, accountable and responsive. It is argued that it is this kind of post-Washington Consensus path that should be the way forward in the Middle East.

THE MENA REGION: ECONOMIC PERFORMANCE AND CHALLENGES

Following the collapse of oil prices in the mid-1980s and the subsequent balance-of-payments crisis, some of the MENA countries adopted macroeconomic stabilization programmes promoted by the World Bank, IMF and other Western agencies (World Bank 2009). By the early 1990s nearly all MENA economies followed suit. These structural adjustment programmes included neo-liberal reforms that were in line with the Washington Consensus guidelines. The objective was to promote growth and prosperity in the region by opening up the political economies and integrating them into global markets (Naím 2000: 87–103). Pre-1990 development strategies had led to inward-looking, state-led economic systems that were unable to compete in the global market. The economic fortunes of this region were, and still are, heavily reliant on rents derived from fuel exports, international aid and remittances, resulting in volatile and unsustainable long-term growth. Reforms were introduced to dismantle the system of centralized bureaucratic control and to promote a market-driven economy with a strong private sector and an increased focus on international trade liberalization. This section of the chapter will be concentrating on the impact of these reforms on the economic performance of this region.

The MENA region may be characterized as one that holds massive hydrocarbon resources and yet suffers from low economic growth and development and high levels of unemployment (Dahi and Demir 2008: 522–35). Based on the availability of hydrocarbon resources and population size, the World Bank (2007) has classified the countries within this region into the following three groups:

- Resource-rich, labour-abundant countries (RRLA): this group includes countries that have high deposits of oil and natural gas and a large native population. Algeria, Iraq, Syria and Yemen fall into this category.
- Resource-rich, labour-importing countries (RRLI): the Gulf states of Bahrain, Qatar, Oman, Saudi Arabia, United Arab Emirates (UAE), Kuwait

The political economy of the Arab uprisings

and Libya fall into this group, and are characterized as countries that have large expatriate populations and high reserves of hydrocarbon resources.
* Resource-poor, labour-abundant countries (RPLA): this class includes small producers or importers of oil and natural gas. Egypt, Tunisia, Morocco, Jordan, Lebanon, Mauritania, Djibouti and the Palestinian autonomous area fall into this group.

Any analysis of the economic performance of this region will be done in the context of these three distinct groups in mind.

The economic performance in terms of GDP growth shows a positive trend in the MENA region, rising from 3.5% in the late 1990s to 6.3% in 2006 and 3.4% in 2011 (Table 11.2). Although there has been a significant improvement in the overall GDP growth in the region (pre-global recession 2007 and political turmoil in MENA 2010), the pattern of growth has been different for each of the separate groups. The major driver of growth has been oil revenues. The surge in GDP growth of the RRLI countries from approximately 3.3% in the late 1990s to nearly 7.5% in 2006 (see Figure 11.1) is due to soaring oil prices during this time period. RRLA countries also show a significant increase in GDP between 1996 and 2003, and then seem to have stagnated. The GDP of the RPLA countries dropped between 2000 and 2003; however, this group has shown signs of recovery since 2004, led mainly by Egypt. Egypt introduced a wave of new economic reforms in 2004 as part of a SAP steered by the IMF. This resulted in phenomenal 6.8% growth in GDP in Egypt in 2006. The Egyptian policy makers have focused on speeding up privatization in the manufacturing, construction and finance industries, contributing to the acceleration in industrial production to 3.4% in 2006 in the

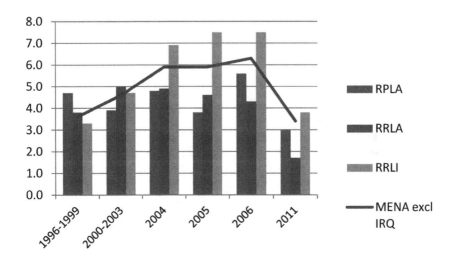

Figure 11.1 MENA GDP growth, 1996–2011

Table 11.2 MENA Region Statistics

Country	1996–99	2000–03	2004	2005	2006	2011
MENA Region (excluding Iraq)	average	average				
Real GDP growth (%)	3.6	4.6	5.9	5.9	6.3	3.4
CPI inflation (%)	4.2	2.8	4.1	5.5	5.3	12.3
fiscal balance (% GDP)	-2.8	1.5	6.8	11.8	14.5	2.1
current account balance (% GDP)	-0.1	7.1	11.0	16.9	20.7	11.0
foreign direct investment (% GDP)	1.0	0.9	0.9	1.5	1.7	1.4
Resource-poor, labour abundant (RPLA)						
real GDP growth	4.7	3.9	4.8	3.8	5.6	3.0
CPI inflation (%)	3.3	2.3	4.0	7	5.8	7.2
fiscal balance (% GDP)	-3.9	-5.8	-6	-6.7	-6	-8.4
current account balance (% GDP)	-4	-1.5	-0.6	-1.6	-1.7	-8.6
foreign direct investment (% GDP)	2.4	2.2	2.1	5.4	8.0	1.4
Resource-rich, labour abundant (RRLA)						
real GDP growth	3.8	5.0	4.9	4.6	4.3	1.7
CPI inflation (%)	12.6	9	10.5	9.4	8.7	10.5
fiscal balance (% GDP)	-0.9	1.8	2.5	4.6	3.1	-1.5
current account balance (% GDP)	1.7	7.3	4.7	11.0	10.6	6.5
foreign direct investment (% GDP)	0.2	0.5	0.6	0.5	0.9	0.5
Resource-rich, labour-importing (RRLI)						
real GDP growth	3.3	4.7	6.9	7.5	7.5	3.8
CPI inflation (%)	0.5	0.0	1.1	2.9	3.4	3.7
fiscal balance (% GDP)	-3.3	4.6	14.0	21.5	25.8	14.3
current account balance (% GDP)	1.1	11.0	19.0	25.9	32.0	14.8
foreign direct investment (% GDP)	0.7	0.5	0.7	0.7	0.3	1.9

Source: Authors calculations from World Bank database and DataStream.

RPLA group of countries. However, all groups have experienced significant reduction in GDP growth from 2007 onwards as a result of political unrest in the MENA region and the global economic downturn during that period.

The Egyptian government has also reduced import tariffs and income tax, thus boosting domestic consumption, which has been the main driving force behind Egypt's economic boom. Foreign direct investment (FDI) inflows rose

The political economy of the Arab uprisings

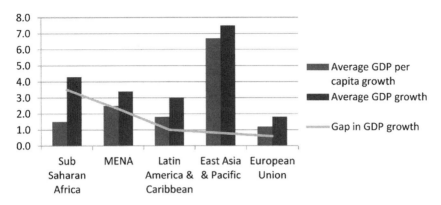

Figure 11.2 GDP and per capita GDP growth by region, 2012

from 0.3% of GDP in 2003 to 5.0% in 2006, which is significantly higher than any other country in this RPLA group. The main findings of the studies carried out by the World Bank demonstrate that GDP growth has been higher in those groups of countries, namely the RRPI and RPLA, where there has been strong evidence of implementation of reforms in order to achieve a better business environment (Nabli 2008). Yet, the inequality gap continued to increase, as the neo-liberal globalization of the Washington Consensus favoured certain social classes and groups at the expense of others.

Although the MENA region has experienced positive GDP growth rates since the mid-1990s, this has not been reflected in the GDP per capita growth rates in the region. This is not just because the population has grown faster in this region than GDP, but because of the class inequalities and increasing unemployment, especially among women and youth, caused by the neo-liberal reforms. Between 2000 and 2012 the annual average GDP growth rate was 4.0%; however, in the same period per capita GDP grew by only 2.5%.

The gap between GDP and per capita GDP in this region is very high, second only to the sub-Saharan African region. This gap varies amongst countries in the MENA region, the widest being in Iraq, Yemen and UAE, and the narrowest being in Morocco, Tunisia and Lebanon (World Bank data).

The overall fiscal position in the MENA region shows a vast improvement from a deficit of 2.8% of GDP in 1996 to a surplus of 14.5% of GDP in 2006, mainly due to the large revenues from oil exports. However, the surplus fell back to 14.3% in 2011.The growth in oil revenues from US$180 billion in 2002 to $620 billion in 2007 (Nabli 2008) has mainly been due to the rise in oil prices and has led to huge increases in capital account and fiscal balances. The main driver of positive increase in fiscal balances within the region has been the RRLI group with a fiscal balance of 25.8% in 2006. Kuwait, UAE and Saudi Arabia have reported the largest surpluses in this group. The RRLA saw their fiscal balance deteriorate from 4.6% in 2005 to 3.1% of GDP in 2006 and further fall to -1.5% in 2011. The RPLA have shown a

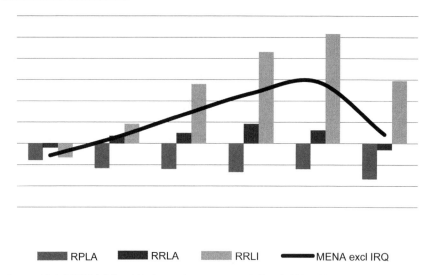

Figure 11.3 MENA Fiscal Balance (percentage of GDP) 1996–2011

slight improvement in fiscal deficit from -6.7% of GDP in 2005 to -6.0% in 2006 but fell back further to -8.4% in 2011. The high level of fiscal deficit in the RPLA countries was driven by weaker revenues and higher public spending. A reduction in import tariffs drove up import demand leading to high current account, thus further deteriorating the balance of payments.

There is no doubt that the most important factor in GDP growth and positive fiscal and current account balances in the MENA region has been the surge in oil revenues; however, there has also been a positive impact on the economic performance of the region as a result of the structural changes and reforms introduced since the mid-1990s. One of the most important areas of reform has been trade policy. Trade has increased due to the growing economic openness, setting up of free trade areas such as the Arab Maghreb Union (AMU), Gulf Cooperation Council (GCC) and Great Arab Free Trade Agreement (GAFTA), and the signing of free trade agreements with the European Union (EU) and USA. Nearly 85% of all exports in the MENA region are fuel and related exports, while manufactured exports constitute a very small part of total exports and are one of the lowest compared to other economic regions (Figure 11.4).

The RPLA countries have the highest proportion of manufactured exports within the region and the EU is their main export market. Intra-MENA trade is only a small fraction of the region's total trade. One of the reasons for poor intraregional trade is the lack of product complementarity. MENA region countries have not been able to diversify their product base, especially in manufacturing (Nabli 2008). However, surprisingly the intraregional trade pattern shows that the RRLI (mainly GCC) countries tend to trade amongst themselves, where lack of product complementarity is greatest, rather than

The political economy of the Arab uprisings

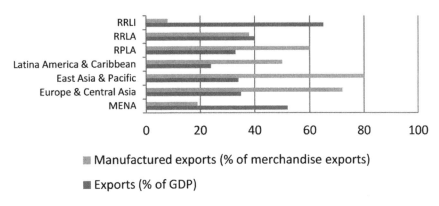

Figure 11.4 Manufactured exports as a percentage of total merchandise exports

with the Maghreb countries. High transportation and communication costs are an impediment to intraregional trade. The difficult terrain in the Arab regions and lack of infrastructure increase trade costs. Geographically the Maghreb countries are closer to Europe than other Arab countries, making it easier to trade with Europe.

Although there has been greater emphasis on trade reforms in recent years, tariff rates remain very high in the MENA region compared to anywhere else in the world (Nabli 2008).

Egypt, under pressure from the neo-liberal globalization policies of the Washington Consensus, introduced trade reforms in 2004 and 2007 to reduce tariffs from 17% to 6%. The strongest reformers in the region have been Egypt, Jordan, Lebanon, Yemen and Saudi Arabia. The difference in tariff rates within the region is one of the main reasons for poor intra-MENA trade.

There has been a significant increase in FDI in the MENA region over the past few decades, mainly due to increased investments in the energy sector. The majority of the inflows have been targeted towards the RRLI countries. In 2011 the region received approximately $64.5 billion of FDI, three-quarters of which went to the RRLI countries, with Saudi Arabia receiving 23% of the total inflow. The RPLA countries received a high proportion of the FDI inflows, with Egypt and Jordon being the main recipients. Although the RRLI countries received most of the FDI inflows in absolute terms, the RPLA countries did significantly better in relative terms. FDI inflows increased from 2.4% of GDP in the late 1990s to 8.0% of GDP in 2007. This is significantly higher than in the RRLI and RRLA countries. In order to attract more FDI, free economic zones have been set up in the region with the objective of providing financial, fiscal and regulatory incentives to investors.

The MENA region suffers from long-term structural unemployment, especially amongst youth, women and the educated. Long-term issues have been over-reliance on the public sector for job creation, along with labour market rigidities that have prevented private sector job creation (World Bank 2007).

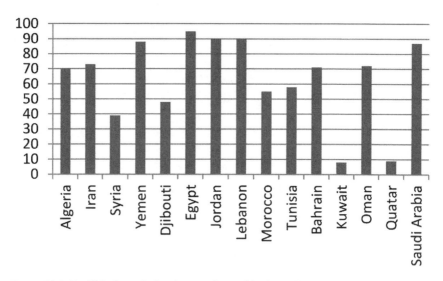

Figure 11.5 Tariff Reform Index (percentile ranking), 2000–07

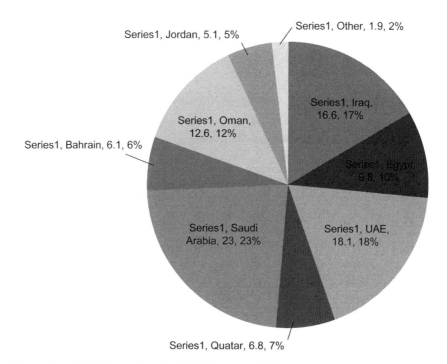

Figure 11.6 FDI inflows into the MENA region, 2011

In the absence of a robust civil society, i.e. a dynamic private sector able to create jobs and provide high wages, the state steps in as an employer of last resort, providing job security and generous benefits.

In general, public sector salaries are higher than the private sector salaries in this region. Unemployment rates vary across the MENA region, with the GCC countries having the lowest rates of unemployment. However, unemployment rates amongst GCC nationals are high as the states employ a high proportion of foreign nationals. The unemployment rates in Egypt, Tunisia and Morocco have been around 10% over the past decade, yet relative poverty and income inequalities have increased due to the retreat of the public sector and the implementation of neo-liberal reforms. Yemen, Algeria and the Palestinian autonomous area witnessed very high rates of unemployment over the past decade.

Unemployment figures in the MENA region can be slightly misleading, as a very large percentage of the population works in the informal sector where wages are low, jobs are insecure and working conditions are very poor. Demographic changes in the MENA region in conjunction with the neo-liberal reforms carried out under the banner of the Washington Consensus are the main cause of such high unemployment rates amongst the youth in the region.

The MENA region has vast endowments of human, financial and natural resources, making it an economically significant player in the global market. A review of recent developments and economic performance in the MENA countries shows that overall GDP growth in the region between 1996 and 2006 has been steadily increasing. However, the pattern of growth between RRLA, RRLI and RPLA countries varies significantly, with oil revenues being the main driver of economic growth. The strong economic acceleration in recent years has been matched by rapid increases in both total population and the labour force. As a result, the gap between GDP growth and GDP per capita growth has been increasing along with the unemployment rate and poverty levels. Unemployment is higher amongst graduates and women, and the region experiences large intra-regional labour movements, triggering substantial financial flows in the form of workers' remittances from abroad.

Oil and oil-related products account for three-quarters of the region's exports, with the EU being the region's most important trading partner. However, there is very limited intra-regional trade. This is mainly due to the poorly diversified export base of countries in this region. The region is also vulnerable to exogenous shocks—mainly oil price and commodity price shocks. Oil price shocks directly affect the government revenues of oil exporting countries. As the region is a net importer of food and other non-fuel primary goods, the recent rise in food and primary commodity prices has adversely affected the current account balance, fiscal balance and inflation rates of most MENA countries. A large proportion of government revenues are spent on subsidizing food and fuel prices. Further opening up of the region to foreign capital, especially financial capital, would have limited, if not negative, effects on real economic growth and job creation, thus perpetuating class inequalities.

CAUSES OF THE UPRISINGS

Social and political unrest still rumbles on in the Arab countries in transition (including Egypt, Jordan, Libya, Morocco, Tunisia, Syria and Yemen) four years after the Arab Spring uprisings started in December 2010 (Khandelwal and Roitman 2013). The political transition in these countries can be characterized by intense political and social unrest and unstable government formation. Political repression and income redistribution are instruments for bringing about discipline, order and social peace, but they do not always work if contradictions and social injustice run deep in the bones of society. In some countries within the MENA region political tensions remain high despite democratic transition. Although the patterns and demographics of the protests varied widely amongst the different countries, the unifying purpose was to achieve personal dignity, human rights and responsive government. However, there has also been a strong economic rationale for the uprisings. A recent survey conducted in Egypt revealed that two-thirds of the respondents identified either a lower level of inequality or provision of basic necessities for all citizens to be the essential characteristic of democracy (Desai 2011: 12–14). I argue that the Arab uprisings have been fuelled by poverty, inequality, unemployment and lack of economic opportunity, and if the transitional economies fail to address these concerns, democracy will fail. However, addressing this means reversing neo-liberal globalization and moving towards a political and economic regime that goes beyond the deficiencies of both the old, state-centric developmental model and that of neo-liberal globalization and the Washington Consensus.

Despite the neo-liberal reforms introduced in the 1990s, an arteriosclerotic state remains the most important economic player in the MENA region, stifling the scope for private sector-led sustainable economic growth. Most countries rely on the state for food and energy subsidies and for employment in the public sector. This has led to large fiscal burdens that the resource-rich Arab nations have managed to balance with rents derived from fuel exports, but resource-poor Arab nations are heavily reliant on foreign aid and remittances to balance fiscal outlays. The MENA region has operated the subsidy system for the past 40 years and current government spending on subsidies for the whole region is approximately $50 billion (World Bank 2011). This system, however, is inefficient and volatile, and does not encourage human resource development or entrepreneurship, or allow for poverty alleviation. The system perpetuates a social order that is preserved through repression and redistribution. However, the cost of redistribution has risen significantly due to escalating global food prices and the MENA region's massive reliance on food imports. Over 90% of food requirements of the GCC are imported (Malik and Awadallah 2013: 296–313). Volatile fuel prices have also led to fiscal instability and high levels of inflation in the region.

The state is still the largest employer across the region. Public sector employment ranges from 22% of the workforce in Tunisia to around 33%–35% in Jordan,

The political economy of the Arab uprisings

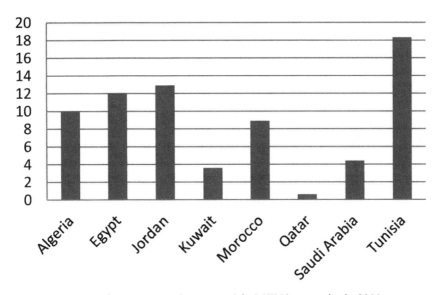

Figure 11.7 Unemployment rates (percentage) in MENA countries in 2011

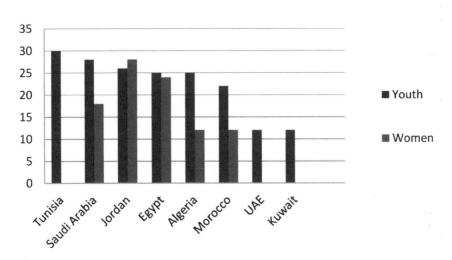

Figure 11.8 Unemployment in percentage among youth, women and educated in 2009

203

Egypt and Syria. People working in the public sector receive high salaries, job security and other benefits that the private sector is unable to deliver. Thus young graduates are attracted to public sector jobs where remuneration is not linked to skill or performance. This has resulted in a shortage of skilled workers in the private sector. There is also a massive gap in the skills acquired by graduates at university and the skills required by business. This complete mismatch of skills is a major source of unemployment in the MENA region. As the labour force in this region is growing at a much faster rate than jobs are created in the public sector the only way forward is to reform the welfare and subsidy system and promote private sector-led industrialization. This has led to a tremendous amount of discontent amongst the youth of this region. The state in the region is an agent of neo-liberal globalization, not an agent of self-reform. A study carried out by the World Bank on the quality of public administration in the MENA region measured the efficiency of the bureaucracy, rule of law, protection of property rights, the level of corruption, quality of regulations and mechanisms of internal accountability (World Bank 2003). The findings of the study showed that in terms of public sector accountability the region shows very high reform rankings, indicating a positive change in the attitude of public sector institutions. Public accountability measures transparency and openness of political institutions, public representation and participation, civil liberties and freedom of the press. This may be explained partly by the conditional ties imposed by aid donors to be more transparent and open and partly due to the pressures from international trading partners and investors.

The level of enterprise creation in the MENA region is significantly lower than that in Europe and other Organisation for Economic Co-operation and Development (OECD) countries. Research by O'Sullivan *et al.* (2012) shows that on an average, approximately two new firms are set up for every 1,000 working-age people in Europe. In the MENA region this figure is considerably lower at fewer than 1 per 1,000 working people. Time and again, this shows the level of weakness of civil society in the region, which can be attributed to the weak private economic sector and, as a consequence, to the problematic institutional articulation between it and the state.

CONCLUSION

This chapter has tried to show that economic success in the region has been mostly confined to the RRLI countries with vast reserves of hydrocarbon resources. These countries have been able to invest their fiscal reserves in infrastructure projects and in subsidizing fuel and food prices. This group of countries has also been able to attract considerable investment from abroad. Economic success in the RRLA countries has also been driven by foreign aid, fuel resources and remittances from abroad, making them highly susceptible to international oil price and labour market fluctuations. Tied in with aid and investment are conditions imposed by donor countries and institutions insisting on structural changes in goods, labour and capital markets. These conditions impose restrictions on the size and role of the governments in these countries. Evidence over the past couple of decades shows that these structural changes have been implemented in the MENA countries at different rates and with different degrees of success. The state still remains the dominant economic player in this region and the Arab population still regards it as the primary provider. The state has been able to hold on to its power by limiting the role of private enterprise and also by maintaining an exclusive nexus between the state and the few prominent private sector companies.

My research also shows that the Arab uprisings are linked to the inequalities created by the opening up of the Arab countries to foreign capital and financial agencies, a project commonly known as the Washington Consensus. This neo-liberal globalization programme has been highly diverse in its effectiveness throughout the MENA region. Although the wave of disillusionment and frustration amongst the Arab youth washed over the entire region with the same passion and propensity, the reaction of individual governments has been very varied. The RRLI and RRLA countries (with the exception of Libya and Syria), namely the GCC governments, followed the road of appeasement, promising more economic concessions in the form of more jobs, higher wages and lower food and fuel prices. It is interesting to see that negligible political concessions have been made. In the RPLA countries of Egypt and Tunisia the political change has been more radical and dramatic, with very few economic reforms. The resource-rich governments have been able to control the uprising through economic concessions and in some cases intimidation, whereas the resource-poor governments have not been able to make such economic promises and, despite military deployment, have fallen in the face of these uprisings.

The future of the region lies in how effectively and efficiently the interim or newly elected governments are able to implement the political and economic changes they promised in their election manifestos, and their ability to move their country beyond the pincers of on the one hand the Washington Consensus, and on the other the old, state-centric and inefficient developmental regime.

REFERENCES

Acemoglu, D. and Robinson, J. (2010) 'The Role of Institutions in Growth and Development', *Review of Economics and Institutions* 1(2): 1–33.

Achcar, G. (2012) 'Theses on the "Arab Spring"', Jadaliyy, Arab Studies Institute.

al-Atrash, H. and Yousef, T. (2000) 'Intra-Arab Trade: Is it too Little?', IMF Working Paper No. 00/10, Washington, DC.

Arestis, P. (2004) 'Washington Consensus and Financial Liberalization', *Journal of Post Keynesian Economics* 27(2): 251–71.

Assaad, R. and Roudi-Fahimi, F. (2007) *Youth in the Middle East and North Africa: Demographic Opportunity or Challenge?*, Washington, DC: Population Reference Bureau.

Breisinger, C., Ecker, O. and al-Riffai, P. (2011) *Economics of the Arab Awakening: From Revolution to Transformation and Food Security*, Washington, DC: International Food Policy Research Institute.

Brynen, R. (1992) 'Economic Crisis and Post-Rentier Democratization in the Arab World: The Case of Jordan', *Canadian Journal of Political Science/Revue canadienne de science politique* 25(1): 69–97.

Buckley, R. (2009) 'The Economic Policies of China, India and the Washington Consensus: An Enlightening Comparison', *UNSW Law Research Paper* series 22.

Campante, F.R. and Chor, D. (2012) 'Why was the Arab World Poised for Revolution? Schooling, Economic Opportunities, and the Arab Spring', *The Journal of Economic Perspectives* 26(2): 167–87.

Chaney, E., Akerlof, G.A. and Blaydes, L. (2012) 'Democratic Change in the Arab World, Past and Present [with Comments and Discussion]', *Brookings Papers on Economic Activity*, 363–414.

Dahi, O.S. and Demir, F. (2008) 'The Middle East and North Africa', *International Handbook of Development Economics* 2: 522–35.

Dalacoura, K. (2012) 'The 2011 Uprisings in the Arab Middle East: Political Change and Geopolitical Implications', *International Affairs (Royal Institute of International Affairs 1944-)* 88(1): 63–79.

Davidson, P. (2004) 'A Post Keynesian View of the Washington Consensus and How to Improve It', *Journal of Post Keynesian Economics* 27(2): 207–30.

Desai, R.M. (2011) 'The Economic Imperatives of the Arab Spring', *The G-20 Cannes Summit 2011: Is the Global Recovery Now in Danger*.

Estevadeordal, A. and Taylor, A.M. (2013) 'Is the Washington Consensus Dead? Growth, Openness, and the Great Liberalization, 1970s–2000s', *Review of Economics and Statistics* 95(5): 1669–90.

Feinberg, R. (2008) 'Competitiveness and Democracy', *Latin American Politics and Society* 50(1): 153–68.

Goldin, C. and Katz, L.F. (1999) *The Returns to Skill in the United States across the Twentieth Century*, Cambridge, MA: National Bureau of Economic Research.

Gore, C. (2000) 'The Rise and Fall of the Washington Consensus as a Paradigm for Developing Countries', *World Development* 28(5): 789–804.

Hakimian, H. (2011) 'The Economic Prospects of the "Arab Spring": A Bumpy Road Ahead', *CDPR Development ViewPoint* 63: 1–2.

Hassouna, H.A. (2001) 'Arab Democracy: The Hope', *World Policy Journal* 18(3): 49–52.

Held, D. (2005) 'At the Global Crossroads: The End of the Washington Consensus and the Rise of Global Social Democracy?' *Globalizations* 2(1): 95–113.

Joffé, G. (2011) 'The Arab Spring in North Africa: Origins and Prospects', *The Journal of North African Studies* 16(4): 507–32.

Khan, M. (2012) 'What Economic Model is Egypt Going to Adopt?' VoxEU.org, 8 November.

Khandelwal, P. and Roitman, A. (2013) 'The Economics of Political Transitions: Implications for the Arab Spring', *IMF Working Paper No. 13/69*.

Kuznets, S. (1955) 'Economic Growth and Income Inequality', *The American Economic Review* 45(1): 1–28.

Lal, D. (2012) 'Is the Washington Consensus Dead?' *Cato Journal* 32(3).

Lindert, P.H. and Williamson, J.G. (1985) 'Growth, Equality, and History', *Explorations in Economic History* 22(4): 341–77.

Malik, A. and Awadallah, B. (2013) 'The Economics of the Arab Spring', *World Development* 45(0): 296–313.

Milanovic, B. (2003) 'The Two Faces of Globalization: Against Globalization as we Know it', *World Development* 31(4): 667–83.

Moreno-Brid, J.C., Caldentey, E.P. and Nápoles, P.R. (2004) 'The Washington Consensus: A Latin American Perspective Fifteen Years Later', *Journal of Post Keynesian Economics* 27(2): 345–65.
Nabli, M.K. (2008) 'Middle East and North Africa: Recent Economic Developments and Prospects', IDB Lecture Series 2: Islamic Development Bank, Saudi Arabia.
Naím, M. (2000) 'Washington Consensus or Washington Confusion?' *Foreign Policy* 118: 87–103.
Nonneman, G. (1996) *Political and Economic Liberalization: Dynamics and Linkages in Comparative Perspective*, Boulder, CO: Lynne Rienner Publishers.
Ocampo, J.A. (2004) 'Beyond the Washington Consensus: What Do We Mean?' *Journal of Post Keynesian Economics* 27(2): 293–314.
Ohlin, B. (1933) *Interregional and International Trade*, Cambridge, MA: Harvard University Press.
O'Sullivan, A., Rey, M.-E. and Galvez, M. (2012) 'Opportunities and Challenges in the MENA Region', *The Arab World Competitiveness Report, 2011–2012*.
Rauch, J.E. and Kostyshak, S. (2009) 'The Three Arab Worlds', *The Journal of Economic Perspectives* 23(3): 165–88.
Rodrik, D. and Bank, W. (2006) 'Goodbye Washington Consensus, Hello Washington Confusion? A Review of the World Bank's "Economic Growth in the 1990s: Learning from a Decade of Reform"', *Journal of Economic Literature* 44(4): 973–87.
Ruckert, A. (2006) 'Towards an Inclusive-neoliberal Regime of Development: From the Washington to the Post-Washington Consensus', *Labour, Capital and Society* 39(1): 36–67.
Shafik, N. (1995) *Claiming the Future: Choosing Prosperity in the Middle East and North Africa: Summary*, Washington, DC: World Bank.
Smith, N. (2011) 'America's Global Implosion: From the Washington Consensus to the Arab Spring', *10 Years after September 11 A Social Science Research Council Essay Forum*.
Solow, R. (1956) 'A Contribution to the Theory of Economic Growth', *The Quarterly Journal of Economics* 70(1): 65–94.
Springborg, R. (2011a) 'The Political Economy of the Arab Spring', *Mediterranean Politics* 16(3): 427–33.
——(2011b) 'The Precarious Economics of Arab Springs', *Survival* 53(6): 85–104.
Stiglitz, J.E. (1999) 'More Instruments and Broader Goals: Moving Toward the Post-Washington Consensus', *Revista de Economia Política* 19(1): 94–120.
——(2002) *Globalization and its Discontents*, New York: W. W. Norton.
Tanoukhi, N. and Mazrui, A. (2011) 'Arab Spring and the Future of Leadership in North Africa', *Transition* 106: 148–62.
Williamson, J. (2000) 'What Should the World Bank Think about the Washington Consensus?' *The World Bank Research Observer* 15(2): 251–64.
——(2003) 'The Washington Consensus and Beyond', *Economic and Political Weekly* 38(15): 1475–81.
——(2004) 'The Strange History of the Washington Consensus', *Journal of Post Keynesian Economics* 27(2): 195–206.
——(2009) 'Short History of the Washington Consensus, A', *Law & Bus. Rev. Am.* 15: 7.
Woo, W.T. (2004) 'Serious Inadequacies of the Washington Consensus: Misunderstanding the Poor by the Brightest', *Diversity in Development: Reconsidering the Washington Consensus*, The Hague: FONDAD, 9–43.

World Bank (1997) *World Development Report 1997: The State in a Changing World*, Oxford: Oxford University Press.

——(2003) *Better Governance for Development in the MENA: Enhancing Exclusiveness and Accountability*, Washington, DC: World Bank.

——(2007) *Development Prospects in MENA*, Washington, DC: World Bank, web.worldbank.org/WBSITE/EXTERNAL/COUNTRIES/MENAEXT/DevelopmentProspectsinMENA2007.

——(2009) *MENA Development Report 2009: From Privilege to Competition, Unlocking Private-led Growth in the Middle East and North Africa*, Washington, DC: World Bank.

——(2011) *Doing Business Report 2011*, Washington, DC: World Bank, siteresources.worldbank.org/INTMENA/Resources/DoingBusiness2011.pdf.

Yom, S.L. (2005) 'Civil Society and Democratization in the Arab World', *Middle East* 9(4): 15, web.worldbank.org/WBSITE/EXTERNAL/COUNTRIES/MENAEXT/DevelopmentProspectsinMENA.

The politics and economics of the Greek debt crisis

CONSTANTINE DIMOULAS AND VASSILIS K. FOUSKAS

> The public debt becomes one of the most powerful levers of primitive accumulation. As with the stroke of an enchanter's wand, it endows unproductive money with the power of creation and thus turns it into capital, without forcing it to expose itself to the troubles and risks separable from its employment in industry or even usury. The state's creditors actually give nothing away, for the sum lent is transformed into public bonds, easily negotiable, which go on functioning in their hands just as so much hard cash would.
>
> (Marx 1976: 919)

No sooner had the ink dried on the *IMF Country Report on Greece* (February 2011), than a document outlining the 'strategy' the country had to pursue to pay back its debt was posted on the website of the Greek Ministry of Finance, instantly becoming an electronic bestseller: 'Greece: Medium-Term Fiscal Strategy 2012–15.' This was a follow-up. The year before (May 2010), the so-called 'troika' was established (the European Central Bank (ECB), International Monetary Fund (IMF) and the European Union (EU)), imposing on the country a *Memorandum of Understanding on Specific Economic Policy Conditionality*, pushing a virtually bankrupt state to implement untold austerity measures including, among others, wholesale liquidation of public assets. The reward? A loan of €110 billion, to be paid periodically in tranches on condition that Greece would register progress. Likewise, the *Memo* had become an electronic bestseller on all relevant governmental and non-governmental websites, inviting debate and political struggles of the sort Greece had not experienced at least since the advent of Andreas G. Papandreou's PASOK (Pan-Hellenic Socialist Movement) to power in 1981. This is one point to note, which should be seen alongside the fecundity of the notion of 'concatenation' put forth by Perry Anderson on the occasion of the Arab revolts (Anderson 2011). In fact, the whole of the Mediterranean and the Near Eastern area is in flames, the forms of struggle varying from country to country and from region to region, not to mention Ukraine and the new confrontation between Russia and the Euro-Atlantic powers.[1] However, there is also something else that should not go unnoticed in the case of Greece.

Never before in its post-war history, perhaps with the partial exception of the decade that followed the end of the bloody Civil War (1946–49), has the dependence of Greece on exogenous agencies been so conspicuous, total and complete: it is as if all Greek government officials, pundits, elites and *comprador* camaraderie are on the payroll of the IMF and the ECB. The IMF report of February 2011 asked Greece to impose additional austerity measures, so that a second loan of €109 billion would be secured. The PASOK government had a rough ride especially in summer 2011, as it was trying to convince trade unionist and PASOK rebels to approve the new 'troika' *diktat*. The bill for harsher austerity measures was eventually passed, turning the Greek state into a straightforward predator agency in the hands of the global financial usurers. Yet transparency has improved. It took some decades for historians to discover in declassified files of the State Department that most of the Greek colonels and other senior state personnel in the 1950s and 1960s who carried out the 1967 coup were on the payroll of the US Central Intelligence Agency (CIA)—something that the communist Left, as it were, had never doubted. However, in 2011, e-democracy solved such problems. Imaginative posters and graffiti on Athenian walls had already portrayed George A. Papandreou—the son of the founder of PASOK, Andreas G. Papandreou, and prime minister until the beginning of November 2011—as 'IMF employee of the year'.

The aim of this chapter is to trace the origins of the Greek debt crisis in its European context and by way of privileging agential, rather than structural, factors. Many writers draw inference on the basis of quantitative evidence available, thus failing to capture specific qualitative dimensions of the crisis linked to the complicated social stratification of Greece and its connection to the state. Intellectuals of the Left and post-Keynesian scholars and practitioners have provided the best analysis on the subject. So we start with them, but we also make references to liberal and social democratic views of the crisis. We then move on to provide a brief periodization of Greek economic and political history, followed by a more detailed focus on the 1974–89 period. We trace the profile of the Greek bourgeoisie of the period and follow its transformation in the 1990s and 2000s, which is when Greece enters completely the era of financialization under the monetary regime and discipline of the eurozone. Thus, we are able to examine the creation of the debt and its connection with the transformation of the dominant class, and without brushing aside quantitative evidence. Finally, we look at the disintegration of the middle classes of the 2010–13 period, which constitutes the basis for the reshuffling of the Greek political system. We conclude by outlining a specific policy proposal to deal with the debt crisis.

THE TWO LEFTS, AS ALWAYS

Mainstream liberal, and at times even social democratic, views explaining the Greek crisis today reduce the sources of debt to the inefficiency of a bloated state sector, periodically but constantly replenished through clientelistic-corporatist practices, patronage, cronyism and nepotism.[2] This, the account goes, has as a result a weak civil society bringing about administrative malaise to both private and public sectors, holding down rates of growth and suffocating the 'Greek entrepreneurial spirit'. From this viewpoint, institutions do not work, tax-collecting mechanisms are nonchalant with the huge state bureaucracy blocking development, modernization and supply-side economics, hence the origins of the debt. Overall, patronage, clientelism, tax evasion and a huge public sector, that is to say domestic factors alone, are responsible for Greece's plight today. The political solutions that stem from such an analysis are rather consequential. With a liberal solution, then these outstanding issues should be addressed via acts of bravery, such as an indiscriminate selling off of state assets accompanied by further cuts in real wages, pensions, the health system and education. With a social democratic solution, then the welfare state should be rebuilt via modernized mechanisms and practices of progressive taxation and in co-ordination with the broader European Left. Social democrats are indeed arguing for a centralized European state, with fiscal and financial powers to back the rickety structures of the euro—a world currency but one wholly dependent on the ECB, which cannot deal with matters of solvency, as this is the job of a ministry of finance.[3] For liberals and social democrats alike, a return to national currencies entails a step backwards to national self-sufficiency, thus spelling isolation and even authoritarianism and dictatorships à la 1930s. In this scenario, protectionism, authoritarianism and even war are just around the corner.

The second set of arguments, which is far more articulate and coherent, comes from the internationalist Left. As regards the origins of the Greek debt, the emphasis here is primarily, but not exclusively, on external state imbalances, namely on the balance of payments. One of the best expositions of this view comes from Costas Lapavitsas:

> Integration of peripheral countries into the eurozone has been precarious. This is apparent in their export performance, which is the mirror image of German performance. It is also apparent in the household financialisation, which has moved in the opposite direction to Germany. These structural contrasts lie at the root of the current crisis. The evidence also shows that it is fallacious to interpret the crisis as the result of inefficient peripheral economies being unable to deal with the efficient German economy. It is the size of the German economy and its export performance—which has very specific causes attached to the euro—that have allowed it to dominate the eurozone.
>
> (Lapavitsas *et al.* 2010: 386)

Thus, this view sees the debt of the European periphery trickling down from the core, especially Germany, a surplus state and enshrined in the balance of payments structure. All peripheral countries, including Greece, were forced to join the euro at high exchange rates, the ostensible purpose being to secure low inflation—that is, the traditional objective of Germany's central bank since the years of the Weimar Republic. The direct effect of this policy was to reduce the competitiveness of the periphery. Moreover, and as Germany was able to discipline its working class to accept low wages, in turn, making its economy even more internationally competitive thus boosting its trade surpluses, peripheral countries such as Greece began registering trade deficits. Thus, Greece became a 'hotbed for speculation', especially when government bonds and credit default swap (CDS) spreads between it and Germany widened.[4] From this perspective, the malaise of the Greek public sector and the problematic articulation between state and civil society mediated by parasitic rentier strata is seen as of secondary importance, because it is the current account deficit that has made worse an already problematic budget deficit. The political solution proposed? This current has quite consistently been arguing for some time now for a debtor-led default and exit from the euro and a return to the drachma. This should be done sooner rather than later. But why is this so? In this instance, Martin Wolf and Marxist scholarship are in agreement inasmuch as the obvious cannot be covered up.

'What is the case for persisting with lending ever more', writes Martin Wolf, 'taking a larger proportion of the liabilities of the Greek government on to public sector balance sheets?' He continues by listing the first and most important reason why this is happening:

> This strategy [of lending ever more] conceals the state of private lenders. It is far less embarrassing to state that one is helping Greece when one is in fact helping one's own banks. If private lenders have enough time, they can sell their loans to the public sector or write them off without capital infusions from states.
>
> (Wolf 2011)

Lapavitsas is even more straightforward:

> The response of the troika [EU, ECB, IMF] reveals systemic failure at the heart of the euro-zone. Greece will receive another large loan but must impose further austerity, including wage and pension cuts, perhaps 150,000 lost jobs in the civil service, more taxes, and sweeping privatisation. And what is likely to happen if the country accepts this? By the calculations of the troika, in 2015 sovereign debt will be 160% of GDP, servicing the debt will cost 10% of GDP, and the government deficit will be 8% of GDP. In short, Greece will still be bankrupt. What, then, is the point of the fresh bail-out? The answer is rescuing international bondholders and buying time for banks.
>
> (Lapavitsas 2011)

OUR ARGUMENT

We argue that there is merit in both perspectives, especially the second one, but we object to the way in which the complicated connection between the external and domestic environments of the state as the sources of the Greek debt is being thematized and understood. On the one hand, the liberal/social

Politics and economics of the Greek debt crisis

democratic perspective puts the cart before the horse, refusing to see that the budget deficit does not primarily originate from the corrupt and clientelistic practices of the Greek party system, or its inability to collect taxes, but from the practices/strategies of the ruling classes of that system. If the liberal argument were correct, Japan or, for that matter, the USA, two of the most clientelistic and corrupt regimes in the world, would never have experienced modernization and growth. On the other hand, the internationalist Left approach seems to downplay the domestic origins of the overall Greek debt, placing too much emphasis on current account and speculative attacks on Greek sovereign debt. However, empirical evidence suggests that new bourgeois *comprador* and rentier strata became very prominent in the Greek economy after the mid-1990s. Therefore, we need to amass a qualitative class analysis of Greek society in its articulation with the Greek governing elites and the internationalization/Europeanization of the state as whole in order to put forth a convincing explanation of the causes of the Greek crisis and the political solutions to it.

The classic definition of *comprador* bourgeoisie comes from Nicos Poulantzas (via Andre Gunder Frank): it is that 'fraction of the bourgeoisie which does not have its own base for capital accumulation, which acts in some way or other as a simple intermediary of foreign imperialist capital (which is why it is often taken to include the "bureaucratic bourgeoisie"), and which is thus triply subordinated—economically, politically, ideologically—to foreign capital' (Poulantzas 1975: 71). This bourgeoisie acts as a go-between for foreign companies in domestic and foreign trade and in money markets. We are set here to examine the peculiar profile this bourgeoisie assumed from the mid-1990s onwards, as it was only then that neo-liberalism and financialization (= globalization), as political programmes, made headway in Greece. Whereas the capitalisms of the Atlantic heartland in the 1970s and 1980s under the favourable post-1971 regime of free exchange rates and dollarization were experiencing the transformation of industrialists into financiers and speculators, Greek capitalists transformed themselves from petty industrialists to go-betweens and *comprador* financiers under state protection and tolerance, enjoying remarkable tax privileges, especially from the mid-1990s onwards. The peculiar fusion of *comprador* and financial/rentier capital with the Greek state apparatuses will be the *leitmotiv* of our analyses, especially when dealing with the post-1995 conjuncture.

In this respect, and given the gradual erosion of manufacturing in the Anglo-American core since the 1970s, Greece does not constitute an exceptional case—only the scale, size and forms of the creation of what Robert Brenner (2006) calls 'asset-price Keynesianism' are different. Greece was not dominated by a housing bubble, conjuring up the increased value of private assets (e.g. homes) to the growth of private consumption via re-mortgaging, equity capitalization, etc.[5] In the Greek case, the consumerist delirium had primarily been led by the local banking sector, which was dominated by offshore companies, with activities in the stock market, joint ventures in the

Balkans and the Near/Middle East, construction, defence and so on. However, in Greece, as elsewhere, this process was extremely internationalized and Europeanized, which meant extensive exposure to Greece's own 'asset price Keynesianism'. In turn, this boosted aggregate demand via all sorts of loans and credit card facilities offered to Greek consumers. Moreover, this type of 'asset price Keynesianism' was sustained by increasing the external borrowing requirement and, to a lesser degree, by direct structural funding from the EU, although this funding began withering away in the 2000s as new Central and Eastern European countries joined the EU. This 'new political economy' in Greece, which had been common almost everywhere in the West since the 1980s, coupled with an unusual inheritance structure due to Greece's historical problems in capital accumulation and the anti-communist policies of its elites. In short, this is what makes up our analytical framework for the understanding of the Greek debt problem today. It is through all these 'new practices' that Greece kept its business going after the gradual erosion of the real economy (agriculture, industry, retail) due to unequal exchange/trade relations. Obviously, that was not sustainable in times of global financial crisis, regardless of the run on Greece's sovereign debt in 2009–10, caused by speculation.

Our analyses adopt an historical and a political economy perspective. The Greek debt has structural/historical as well as conjunctural causes. 'In studying a structure', Gramsci argued, 'it is necessary to distinguish organic movements (relatively permanent) from movements which may be termed "conjunctural" (and which appear as occasional, immediate, almost accidental)' (Gramsci 1996: 177). In its modern history, Greece has officially defaulted on its debt obligations four times (1827, 1843, 1893 and 1932), which means that the country cannot out-compete core capitalisms regardless of whether or not it participates in a currency union. Capitalism develops in an uneven and combined way at all times, but the mode of dependency of the periphery on the core pertains to the way in which peripheral *comprador* and rentier strata have historically articulated their function inside and outside the power structures of the vassal state. This is a fundamental problem of the periphery that can be captured only with reference to *comprador* strata and their central position in the reproduction of social capital and the political system as a whole. Thus, we offer an interpretation of the causes of the Greek debt that draws on the articulation of external and domestic factors centred on the parasitic role of *comprador*/rentier-cum-financial capital. In this context, whereas Lapavitsas's position about a debtor-led exit from the eurozone stands tall, it has to be complemented and qualified with class analysis connecting the internal and external causes of debt, and with a political task that is of top priority: a democratic political alternative in Greece should seek, first and foremost, to eradicate this institutionalized alliance of *comprador*-cum-financial capital and ruling state elites, while renewing the productive capacity of the country, first and foremost, agriculture, industry and innovation (e.g. solar energy). From this perspective, our policy proposal for *socialist seisachtheia* includes not just exit from the euro, renegotiation of debt and cancellation of odious debt, but even more importantly, the smashing of the state machine, the result of the fusion between predator/*comprador*/financial capital and the political oligarchy of its corrupt party barons.

This is why we consider that the two main parties that have ruled Greece since the fall of the colonels in summer 1974, PASOK and New Democracy (ND), should go. These parties are as much responsible for the plight of the country as is global financial capital itself. Liberal and social democratic arguments about 'corruption', eradication of 'clientelism', 'populism', 'cronyism', 'nepotism' and so forth make sense only if placed in this class context. Liberals and social democrats see the problem in quantitative terms: too many civil servants employed on clientelistic grounds are the root cause of the deficit, so they should be sacked. We say, first, that this is not the root cause of the problem and, second, that the problem is qualitative: it has to do with the class composition of Greek society and the very political strategies of the ruling party elites in their effort to organize hegemony over a society in which a robust industrial base to absorb surplus labourers was missing. We long ago signalled that the propulsive force of the republic founded by Constantine Karamanlis in summer 1974 amid the Cyprus calamity and further consolidated by Andreas G. Papandreou's rule in the 1980s has been exhausted (Fouskas 1995). We were not heard, but the day of reckoning for those political elites has now arrived.

First, we dwell on the 1970s and 1980s, the formative years of a peculiar Keynesian type of corporatist-clientelistic establishment. This was born out of a convergence of the political elites of the ND and PASOK in their fusion with a 'state-fed' bourgeoisie and the banking sector under the pressure of social struggle. We will then move on to consider the origins of the present sovereign debt crisis and the transformation of the dominant factions of the bourgeoisie, also by way of evaluating a number of primary sources and statistical material carefully compiled and put together by a team of researchers at the Institute of Labour of the Confederation of the Greek Trade Unions in Athens (INE-GSEE). Statistics in Greece is a very sensitive issue. We should remember that the story of the Greek debt blew out of all proportion—and the downgrading of Greek sovereign bonds/debt began—when the PASOK government, once in office in October 2009, revealed that Greek gross domestic product (GDP) figures were fictional, and the deficit was double-digit, almost three times higher than the previous forecast.[6] We argue that not only the collapse of the eurozone, but also the entire globalization architecture built under what Peter Gowan called the Dollar-Wall Street Regime (DWSR), is in question. Arguably, Greece is a spent force. The question for the financial oligarchy today is how to save the euro, but one should go further. The global power centres seem to be on the move again, this time shifting away from the Atlantic core to the 'global East' (the People's Republic of China, India, Brazil, Russia, Indonesia, Turkey, South Africa). These are the thoughts we offer in our tentative conclusive section while summing up our policy proposal of *socialist seisachtheia*.

IMPERIAL CYCLES AND THE VASSAL

Greek social formation underwent three historically distinct phases of Western-led modernization and expansion. The first phase mirrors the political bipolarism between Charilaos Trikoupis and Theodoros Diligiannis during the second half of the 19th century and manifests the will of modernizer Trikoupis to promote both institutional reform and public works reproducing the Western pattern (for example, railways). Interestingly, and whereas Greece had re-entered international borrowing markets after having settled outstanding defaults in 1878, Trikoupis's government in 1893 had been forced to suspend payments on external debt, stating famously, *distichos eptocheusamen* ('we went bankrupt, unfortunately'). Excessive borrowing was needed to finance a large public sector and modernize the army, as Greece was still expanding against the Ottomans while wholly dependent, both politically and economically, on external powers (Britain, France and Russia). In 1898, foreign pressure led Greece to accept the creation of the International Committee for Greek Debt Management. This committee monitored the country's economic policy as well as the tax collection and management systems of Greece.

The second phase of Western-led modernization corresponds to the era of the liberal statesman, Eleftherios Venizelos, when the bourgeois breakthrough and agrarian reform were accomplished. Skilfully expanding the influence of Greece in the Balkans by employing the homogeneous nationalist discourse of *Megali Idea*—'Great Idea', meaning uniting all Greeks living in Ottoman and other territories in one greater Greek state—Venizelos expressed the interests of the Greek merchant and banking capital—a class extended across the arc of Near East-Constantinople-Smyrna-Macedonia—modernized the country, mobilized wide popular strata in politics and led the battle against the king and the old political class of *tzakia*. Yet his post-1917 foreign policy was mindless and adventurist, to say the least, as together with Lloyd George, he threw Greece into the quagmire of Asia Minor, suffering a catastrophic defeat at the hands of Turkish nationalists under Kemal Atatürk in August 1922. However, it was not just the Lloyd George-Venizelos gamble that was defeated at Sakarya river—Turkey was assisted by France, Italy and the Bolsheviks. From the perspective with which we look into the matter here, the greatest catastrophe was the destruction of the geography of Greek merchant and banking capital, which would have had all the historical possibilities and resources to create an independent and indigenous base of industrial capital accumulation. Had Britain's proxy war in the Near East been successful, then Greece would have had the capital and market base to be inserted into the orbit of the Western core on a more 'equal' basis, but Greece lost the war and it is now the only Western European state without a modern imperial past.

Having lost the war, Venizelos's inter-war period in politics was marred by an anti-communist stance and measures that tended to reproduce the privileges of a defeated state apparatus split between his faction and that led by General Ioannis Metaxas, his royalist opponent since 1915, who opposed the

Asia Minor campaign on solid strategic grounds.[7] Venizelos's second round of agrarian reforms aimed primarily at crushing the communist movement and turning the pauperized refugees from Asia Minor—an estimated 1,400,000 Christians left Asia Minor, whereas some 480,000 Muslims moved to Turkey—into petty land proprietors, thus keeping them away from communist influences. This deprived Greece of large-scale farming, damaging any international competitive advantage that Greek farming enjoyed (e.g. favourable weather conditions), a legacy with repercussions in the overall performance of the Greek economy that have reverberated since, especially after the entry of the country into the European Economic Community (EEC) in 1981. Time and again, and given the imperial contraction of the inter-war period and the credit crunch of 1929, Greece was one of the many countries defaulting on sovereign debt obligations. Venizelos's Greece imposed a moratorium on paying its outstanding foreign debt in 1932. This default lasted until 1964.

The third phase of capitalist modernization concerns the post-war economic boom of the 1950s and 1960s, corresponding to the international cycle of the so-called 'golden age'. Mass foreign direct investment (FDI), chiefly American, strengthened Greece's economic performance and advanced the contribution of manufacturing to GDP. Yet this was a rather 'passive revolution'. Post-Civil War Greece was an anti-communist state. Everything was vetted and watched over, not to mention appointments in the wider public sector. The Right-wing state of the Greek kingdom was the result of the defeat of the communist guerrillas in 1949, when it assumed the status of nearly a protectorate of the USA in the 1950s (Greece, along with Turkey, became a member of the North Atlantic Treaty Organization, NATO, in 1952 following its participation in the Korean war). However, as the modernizing impulse of the Western imperial core was extending its developmental spokes into the vassal, a certain independence of civil society began to manifest itself. A significant part of the population started to migrate not only abroad, but also within Greece proper, from agricultural zones into urban centres. As early as 1963, and despite the fact that the KKE (Communist Party of Greece) was outlawed, or because of this, the masses claimed political participation, an opening up of the existing limited democracy, forcefully expressing its opposition to the crown. This reformist movement was successfully represented by the party of the centre, under the leadership of elderly George Papandreou, who led the battle against the conservative bloc of Constantine Karamanlis and the king. However, everything came to a close with the military coup of 1967, followed by another 'passive revolution': during the period of the colonels (1967–74), Greece registered its highest rates of GDP growth, a developmental phase led by US investments, a massive construction boom especially in urban centres and tourist resorts, as well as emigrant remittances and other invisible earnings. The junta contained class struggle, while facilitating the partition of Cyprus—Turkey invaded the island in summer 1974, after Makarios, the Greek Cypriot leader, was deposed by the junta.

At this stage, an important remark has to be made. Whereas all three developmental phases of Greece corresponded to Western hegemonic cycles of expansion alongside the Braudelian/Arrighian bifurcation industry-cum-real economy/financialization, the vassal itself never managed to catch up with the Western cores, let alone the impending hegemon (first the UK, later the USA). As a consequence, the structures of political and economic dependence increased. In particular, under US supremacy as a NATO member since 1952, Greece became entirely a dependent spoke of Washington's hub, as was indeed the case with all NATO members, although the degree of political/military dependency varied according to the economic and geopolitical weight each state carried in the alliance, as well as the degree of social struggle registered within the NATO states proper. The key structural feature of the Greek social formation if compared with other core capitalisms is its extremely weak industrial base, which resulted historically in an increasingly bloated state apparatus, as it had to act strategically as an 'employer of last resort' containing social and class struggle.

THE FORMATION OF THE POST-1974 RULING CLASS: 1970S TO 1980S

The *stagflation* that hit the Euro-Atlantic core in the 1970s can surely be seen as a peculiar crisis of over-accumulation, what Robert Brenner calls 'over-capacity/overproduction', caused by 'uneven development'. Laggards, such as West Germany and Japan, managed to catch up with the USA, out-competing each other, the result being a fall in profitability from which the heartland has never managed to recover to date. Anglo-Saxon responses included, first, dollar devaluation, all the while getting rid of its gold fetter; second, petro-dollar recycling and replenishing of the US Treasury with wealth and paper produced by petro-states. Momentarily, the mantra going around was that the dollar was now pegged to petrol—'black gold'. The end of the fixed exchange rates system signalled the beginning of financialization/globalization, as speculators and investment banks began appearing one after the other, moving the global political economy from an M-C-M$'$ relation into an M-M$'$ one (M is money, C is commodity)—what Marx used to call 'money begetting money'. The Anglo-Saxon polities were on the move too. If the empirical categories of financialization/globalization apply primarily, but not exclusively, to the external environment of the state, then neo-liberalism/neo-conservatism applies primarily, but not exclusively, to the internal policy domain of the state. The 'freedom agendas' of Friedrich Hayek and Milton Friedman became incarnated in the programmes of Thatcher and Reagan in Britain and the USA, respectively, whereas Paul Volcker, chairman of the US Federal Reserve from 1979 to 1987, raised interest rates to a peak of 20% in June 1981 with the ostensible aim of fighting inflation, although his real objective was to 'smash', as Leo Panitch put it, 'working class power' (Panitch and Gindin 2005).

The Right against the Right

As the USA and Britain began implementing neo-liberalism and financialization in order to arrest the fall in profitability, especially in manufacturing, other states of the core had to adjust their policies to this twin programme. Greece, formally qualified as a member of the core since 1981, also had to start adopting a neo-liberal agenda, i.e. liberalization of the banking and financial system, welfare state retrenchment, wage cuts, deregulation of the labour market, and wide-ranging privatization of public utilities and business. None of this happened—in fact, quite the opposite—and Greece, after all, never really had a welfare state. The opening up of the post-1974 political system to the parties of the communist and socialist Left invited political participation and redistribution of wealth produced during Greece's 'golden age'. The real GDP growth in 1975 market prices was 9.9% in 1969, 8.9% in 1972, 7.3% in 1973, 6.0% in 1975, 3.4% in 1977 and 1.6% in 1980, just the year before PASOK assumed governmental power. This had been taking place in an economic environment in which the extended reproduction of the public sector pertained to minimal progress in real economy growth, especially in manufacturing, something that can be seen from the structure of GDP by economic sector (Table 12.1).

Two comments are necessary here. First, the increase in manufacturing did not reflect an increase in output or, even less so, in profitability heralding economies of scale; rather, as we shall see below, it represents the absorption by the state of a number of lame ducks in order to offset the falling rate of profit caused primarily by the global recession. The post-1974 Greek state began playing its role extensively as counter to the tendency of the rate of profit to fall, especially in the Greek manufacturing sector (since 1981 the EEC has offset some of the costs in the primary sector by subsidizing Greek agriculture). Second, manufacturing in Greece has always been dominated by small and medium-sized enterprises, which are extremely vulnerable to external competition and shocks. Thus, the state had to step in to solve profitability problems, a factor which, undeniably, contributed to the deterioration of public finances and an increase in the state's borrowing requirements, both internal and external. Just a year before the 'Volcker shock' in the USA and the advent of Thatcher to office in Britain, the governor of the National Bank of Greece in 1978, Angelos Angelopoulos, argued:

Table 12.1 Sectoral structure of GDP at factor costs as a percentage of total

Sector	1961	1971	1980
Agriculture	26.3	17.4	14.4
Industry	13.8	19.5	21.3
Services	48.7	49.9	53.0

Source: Our selective compilation of data from Andrew Freris, *The Greek Economy in the 20th Century,* New York, 1986, p. 156.

There are some private enterprises that are very important for the overall performance of the national economy. Nevertheless, due to internal and external factors, they encounter financial difficulties, which are bound to increase as Greece approaches the European Common Market. It would be wise, therefore, to increase the spending to them ... In essence, a new state organisation, helped by commercial banks, should be set up in order to subsidise or take over the management of those enterprises facing economic problems.

(Kalafatis *et al.* 1990: 35)

The Greek Right was somewhat set against the new international Right and its twin programme of neo-liberalism and globalization/financialization. From 1974 to 1981 a number of nationalizations took place in the banking sector, transport—including air transport—and shipyards. At some point in the early 1980s, the Greek state controlled almost 50% of the total fixed capital, participating, in one way or another, in almost every economic activity.[8] Thus, the wealth produced during Greece's 'golden age' began somewhat to be redistributed via a set of Keynesian policies, such as nationalization and an extension of the public sector via clientelistic recruitment—what the Greeks call *rousfeti*. In other words, the response of the Greek state to the international recession of the 1970s was not deregulation and financialization, but the unfolding of a peculiar type of Keynesian policy, all against the background of a ballooning trade deficit, which was only partially offset by invisible receipts (mainly migrants' and sailors' remittances).

These policies were undoubtedly partly linked to geopolitical reasoning, as the Cyprus crisis led the ruling elites to increase defence spending massively, a factor that has since been contributing to the state's budget deficit. Simply put, the Right-wing elites of the Greek state could not have contemplated any liberalization of public utilities and other industries, especially those with a strategic national dimension, such as telecommunications and energy. These sectors were considered directly relevant to the country's security. Papandreou's PASOK in the 1980s adhered to exactly the same policy schemes as those initiated by the Right of Karamanlis. As regards matters of foreign policy, Papandreou was even more 'radical'. When in opposition, his tactic was to argue against Greece's entry to the EEC and membership of NATO. Karamanlis, following the Cyprus debacle, withdrew Greece from the military structures of NATO and reversed Greece's military doctrine of considering

Table 12.2 Balance of payments deficit and invisible receipts (1960-80) in US$ millions current prices

	1961–65	1966–70	1971–75	1976–80
Trade deficit	481	836	2.319	4.908
Invisible receipts	330	679	1.488	3.426

Source: Our selective compilation of data from Freris, *The Greek Economy*, p. 188.

Politics and economics of the Greek debt crisis

the country's key enemy as being Greece's communist neighbours in the Balkans: Turkey was now the main enemy. However, Papandreou, catapulting the communists' anti-EEC and anti-NATO positions, argued for a complete withdrawal from NATO and the sinking of various Turkish exploration ships that were periodically appearing in the Aegean Sea in search of oil. Yet once he attained power, none of this became feasible or desirable. In this context, it is essential to point out that a new bipartisan political class, essentially Keynesian-corporatist-clientelistic, began emerging in post-authoritarian Greece, whose income distribution capabilities and power drew from the wealth produced during the previous decades of high growth rates (the 1950s and 1960s). Concomitantly, a genuinely specialized economic apparatus began to take shape at the core of public managerial activities, thus directly affecting its fiscal performance and contributing to the creation of unsustainable debt levels. It is this fusion of party political and local business elites and banks, all acting under the aegis of, and funded by, the state, that Papadreou's PASOK, being the ruling party, had to manage in the 1980s. Also worth mentioning in this respect is that whereas before it assumed office PASOK was proclaiming 'import-substitution' policies in order to strengthen Greece's industry and export capacity, none of this was really delivered after 1981.

Crisis of crisis management in the 1980s

Throughout the 1980s, the state, under PASOK's management, continued to expand forms of corporatist intervention, despite a worsening of public finance and a ballooning debt. Faithful to the ND programme, PASOK expanded the role of the state in the economy by nationalizing and even increasing employment in many firms that were facing economic/profitability problems: in the tourist sector (e.g. Xenia Hotels), in energy (e.g. Petrola Oil, SA), in transportation (e.g. OASA), in construction (e.g. Hercules General Cement Company, SA, the largest cement company in Europe), and in textiles (e.g. Peiraiki Patraiki, the largest textile manufacturer in Greece). PASOK's rescue operations employed a very specific method: the conversion of at least 50% of each company's outstanding debt into equity shares owned by the government via state-owned commercial banks that had initially issued the loans to these lame ducks. By 1985, some 40 companies with nearly 28,000 employees and with a total debt of 170 billion drachmas (US$6.9 billion) had been partially or entirely nationalized. This amalgamated business and banking capital under the aegis of PASOK's populist wing, headed by Papandreou himself. As a consequence, with gross capital formation being in the negative and with low labour productivity and capital output, the inflationary trend in the economy continued upwards. Worse, these policies failed to arrest unemployment, despite a flurry of clientelistic and nepotistic appointments in the public sector, including generous pension and holiday schemes and so on (Table 12.3).[9]

Table 12.3 Some key economic indicators, 1974–89

	1974–81	1982	1983	1984	1985	1982–85	1989	1985–89
GDP growth	3.1	0.4	0.39	2.7	3.1	1.6	2.5	2.08
Gross capital formation	-1.9	-1.9	-1.3	-5.7	5.2	-0.9	6.5	2.38
Inflation	16.8	20.7	18.1	17.9	17.9	18.3	14.3	16.8
Un/ment	2.3	5.8	9.0	9.3	9.3	8.7	8.5	8.4
Debt (% of GDP)	26.3	36.1	41.2	49.5	57.9	46.2	78.1	65.6

Sources: Our selective compilation of data from the European Commission, *European Economy: Annual Economic Report 1990–91*, Brussels, November 1990, p. 281.

This same populist wing expanded the public sector and created a universal health system, while maintaining wage rises in industry—most of which came under state control—around 30%, a real increase close to 6% annually.[10] PASOK did very little to reform public administration, while the setting up of an efficient tax-collecting machine was delayed, thus encouraging an underground economy and various illegal economic activities. Despite the 26% growth in real personal incomes during the 1980s, personal income tax receipts were still at the low level of 4.5% of GDP, which was less than half the OECD and European Community (EC) averages (OECD 1993). Under PASOK, the public sector became the dominant labour market in the Greek economy. Whereas before 1974 the state concentrated on recruiting personnel to police communism, the new political landscape after 1974 shifted the nature of the recruitment, adapting it to electoral cycles. According to the census for public employees by the Greek census agency conducted in 1956, civil servants, including army officers, accounted for 64,956 or 0.85% of the total population (7,632,801 at the time, according to the 1951 census). In 1961 the population was 8,388,553, the civil servants numbering 104,840 or 1.2%. Although there are no available data concerning public employment in the 1970s and 1980s, according to the 1991 census the total population was 10,259,900 but the number of civil servants in 1988 had risen to 589,386 or 5.7% of the total population.[11] We have a useful yardstick by moving forward some 20 years: in 2011 the total population of Greece was 10,787,690, yet the number of civil servants had soared to 768,009 (2010 census conducted by the Ministry of the Interior), or 7.1% of the total population. This represents an increase of 15.4% at a time when the official unemployment rate was 16.3% in the second quarter of 2011 (see Tables 12.10 and 12.11). Strong family ties, widespread petit bourgeois ownership that created strong inheritance structures, as well as a widespread sense of community, all of which was the result of past and present policies aiming at undercutting communist influence, backed the creation of a relatively prosperous yet highly unproductive societal

Politics and economics of the Greek debt crisis

structure.[12] Thus, despite the stagnation in private capital performance and growth ratio, people's income potential and purchasing power increased drastically. Funding coming from European programmes in the 1980s further buttressed the new managerial structures of income distribution (Table 12.4). In the event, agriculture and industry had all but disappeared by the late 1990s, making way for a recomposed, but always huge, public sector and new, small, private service sectors dominated by private banking capital, financial operators and a new *comprador* bourgeoisie, all phenomena we will explore in the next section.

Compared to its northern European partners or the USA, one could argue that Greece in the 1980s and early 1990s was a poor state with rich people. Arguably, therefore, PASOK pro-welfare policies of the 1980s and the Keynesian boosting of aggregate demand management—a trend that continued almost unabated halfway through the 1990s—was not the result of a 'rational choice' on the part of an independent entrepreneurial bourgeoisie in order to maintain and reproduce an extended subsumption of labour to capital with the state as the key class arbiter in disputes. It was something else.

The Greek welfare state was the product of a well-orchestrated political strategy formulated and practised by the ruling elites in order to establish their domination in the newly born political party democracy. We insist that this was a bipartisan (ND and PASOK) strategic intent, rather than a lack of an alternative due to the structural deficiencies of the Greek economy. With a tradition of civic culture lacking in Greece, PASOK's charismatic leader knew that all forms of clientelistic practices and political participation are in effect mechanisms for the acquisition of consensus, all the while undermining the electoral and political strength of the communist Left. At the same time he knew very well that this was economically problematic. *Thus, contrary to neoliberal—and at times even social democratic—orthodoxy, the fundamental problem that the ruling party elites of both ND and PASOK had to face and solve was not just how to rule in absence of a modern industrial sector, but how to modernize against the labour movement.*[13] This problem was solved with the same political recipe of the past, the difference being that post-1974 clientelistic and nepotistic practices assumed enormous proportion precisely because of

Table 12.4 EEC/EC transfers during PASOK's second term, 1985–89 (% change from previous year)

	1986	1987	1988	1989
Mediterranean Integrated Programmes		823	52.3	-53.3
Regional funds	421	-6.7	4.0	72.8
Agricultural subsidies	79	8.5	6.0	32.1

Source: Our compilation of data from Dimitrios Chalikias, *Annual Report of the Governor of the Bank of Greece for the Years 1987 and 1989,* Athens, 1988 and 1990 respectively, pp. 141–42.

the large amount of wealth available for redistribution and which had been produced during the 1950s and 1960s. It is in this sense that we argue that liberal and even social democratic arguments about 'clientelism' and 'populism', as phenomena hindering capitalist development and modernization, do not make sense.

All in all, our key argument in this section is that the two main parties, ND and PASOK, began building a post-authoritarian, post-1974 Greek state by way of pioneering inflationary, pro-Keynesian-cum-corporatist policies *ala-Greca*, at a time when similar practices were in retreat everywhere. There was no major drift towards neo-liberalism and financialization in the 1970s and 1980s, and indeed halfway through the 1990s, as was the case, for example, in François Mitterrand's France (the famous U-turn, 1982–83) or in Felipe González's Spain (especially from the second half of the 1980s onwards). Both the ND and PASOK, once in office, had to manage the disintegration of the industrial class, while dealing with societal demands for political participation and securing employment. There was little socialism in PASOK's rule, however defined. Predominately, what happened was the creation of a new bipartisan managerial class with the state apparatus and the two main parties at their epicentre managing public sector recruitment via internal and external borrowing, i.e. via management of national debt. PASOK's welfare state was primarily financed through borrowing, not taxation. Taxation was chiefly buttressing the lame ducks.

One could argue that this laggard position of Greece in the post-1971 international political economy and division of labour was what saved the country from defaulting on its ballooning domestic and external debt. Keynesianism *ala-Greca* arrived too late to do any good—for the time being. However, then one should consider certain geopolitical factors. Greece's entry to the EEC in 1981 and the collapse of 'really existing socialism' in the Balkans 10 years later, coupled with Greece's NATO membership, made Greece an ideal launching pad for financial and rentier penetration into the Balkans, with an experimental 'shock therapy' neo-liberal programme promulgated by a Harvard University professor, Jeffrey Sachs.[14] Greek rentier and financial interests would act as conduits of the big Western capital interests in this new scramble for the Balkans. This included involvement in straightforward geopolitical projects in direct competition with Russia, such as oil and gas pipelines. In any event, the case of Greece in the 1980s, a decade that ended with PASOK sinking in a series of financial scandals, could fit the perceptive term 'crisis of crisis management' coined by Claus Offe in his analysis on the crisis of the Keynesian state (Offe 1994).

To sum up: the post-1974 managerial class was an amalgamation, or fusion, of on the one hand, the various branches of the state apparatuses as they opened up to society via corporatist and clientelistic practices—this was happening at a 'low politics' level—and on the other, the state-financed business elites and banking capital—happening at a 'high politics' level. The 'high politics' level is far more important, especially if we want to locate the real sources of the national debt. It is this level that is primarily exposed to economic internationalization and shocks, and it is this level that incarnates issues of grand strategy and state military security. In addition, it is within this domain that large amounts of money become recycled and spent, without the Greek inland revenue services receiving a penny. Brenner's analyses and methodology indicate that the bourgeoisie can outflank class struggle from the bottom up, but it cannot outflank competition among its factions, whether these factions operate nationally, internationally or both. In other words, from an analytical point of view, competition among capitals and its factions are more important than conflicts between capital and labour. It is now important to consider the transformation of this managerial class in the 1990s and 2000s, as it is this, in conjunction with the international trends of financialization and European integration, that pushed Greece to bankruptcy in 2010–12.

THE ROAD TO BANKRUPTCY, 1990–2010

The strict monetarist criteria of the Maastricht Treaty—under negotiation since Delors's Single European Act in 1986—and later of the so-called 'Stability Pact', coupled with the end of authoritarian socialism over Greece's northern borders, undermined the political, economic and ideational bases of the peculiar bipartisan ruling class formed in the 1970s and 1980s. This unleashed all forces hitherto 'suppressed'. Deregulation of markets, privatizations and liberalization of banking and financial capital began pace slowly but steadily after 1991–92, while accelerating under the 'neo-revisionist PASOK' of Costas Simitis after 1996, when Simitis succeeded the ailing Papandreou.[15] At the time, the mantra in Greece was 'modernization' against Papandreou's 'populism'. Accordingly, from the mid-1990s onwards, the ruling class of the previous decades began transforming itself into a new agent adapting to, and taking advantage of, domestic and international circumstances. Increasingly, this class began assuming the features of a middle man between international/European financial capital on the one hand, and government on the other. Thus, whereas the formation of the ruling class in the 1970s and 1980s was primarily sourced from within the domestic environment of the state, the transformation of this class into a new hegemonic agent was primarily induced from without, owing to the new constraints imposed by the internationalization/Europeanization of the Greek state. In this respect, the structures of political and economic dependency of Greece, themselves made up of exogenous agents and structures, grew even deeper roots than hitherto. Simitis's vague 'modernization' agenda meant, above all, acceleration of the disintegrative tendencies of Greece's productive base (textiles, cement, agriculture, foodstuff, etc.). All in all, the structural asymmetries and faultlines between the European core—especially after Greece joined the eurozone in 2001—and its periphery, first and foremost Greece, became astoundingly pronounced.

The Greek workshop of debt and the profile of the new bourgeoisie

As we saw earlier, Greece did not simply have a problematic structure of public debt that appeared in the 1980s, something which was also true in the case of Italy, Belgium and other countries at the time. Greece had also tried to resist neo-liberalism and financialization, but all the while lacking robust export-orientated sectors to buttress sustainable levels of development, thus matching the rising trend of its debt structure and the borrowing requirement. As Greece was moving out of the domain of Keynesian policy, and entering the structures of neo-liberalism in the 1990s, a new policy framework of speculative and rentier activities became entrenched, contributing to making the domestic structures of debt more problematic, unsustainable and unmanageable by the ruling parties of PASOK and ND. This section is mostly committed to raising this dimension of the problem, which we believe is downplayed in the work of many scholars.

In the beginning it was asset capitalization, equity and profits through the share price index on the Athens Stock Exchange (ASE). The bubble of the ASE was largely buttressed by privatizations and the underground economy, as those positioning themselves in the ASE and buying and selling shares were not required to prove their income status, or where their income came from (Table 12.5).[16] The bubble burst in September 1999, never to reach that

Table 12.5 Athens Stock Exchange: Share price indices 1980–2010

Year	Share Price Indices	Annual change in price indices
1980	74.9	
1985	50.4	-24.5
1990	488.3	437.9
1995	914.15	425.85
1996	933.48	19.33
1997	1,479.63	546.15
1998	2,737.6	1,257.97
1999	5,535.1 (at 17.09.1999 was the peak 6,335)	2,797.5
2000	3,388.9	-2,146.2
2001	1748.4	-1,640.5
2002	2,263.6	515.2
2003	2,263.2	-0.4
2004	2,786.2	523
2005	3,663.9	877.7
2006	4,394.13	730.23
2007	5,178.83	784.7
2008	1,786.51	-3,392.32
2009	2,196.16	409.65
2010	1,413.94	-782.22
15.09.2011	864.98	-548.96

* Source: Our compilation of data from Concise Statistical Yearbooks for the respective years. Hellenic Statistical Agency (ELSTAT).

level again. As elsewhere in the West, the result of this speculative boom and bust cycle was to circulate paper assets and liquidity away from production, while concentrating wealth in the hands of very few speculators who 'cashed in and got out', switching the focus of their speculative activities elsewhere, mainly abroad. The loser, as usual, was the small investor—some 10% of Greeks had bought shares on the stock market, an apotheosis of Greek 'popular capitalism', what Tony Blair used to call 'stakeholder society'. European funds continued strengthening this fictitious liquidity by boosting the stock market with more than €3,500 million every year since 1988. This chorus of shares and paper assets increased in the 2000s as more businesses entered the market and ramified their activities in the banking, financial and other services. Large amounts of accumulated income on the part of middle and lower-middle classes were taken away, free of tax, from the financial capital through the ASE and without adding one iota to the competitiveness of the Greek economy. It is no accident that from the mid-1990s onwards hitherto unknown businessmen and companies appeared amassing a number of activities in Greece, the Balkans and the Near East, in the fields of banking, construction, defence equipment and procurement (including offset agreements), large-scale import-export, mass media, informatics and energy, all phenomena that should be seen in conjunction with the policies of privatization and deregulation—the essence of Simitis's 'modernization' agenda (Costas Simitis was prime minister from 1996 to 2004).

From 1994 to 1999 more than 100 companies had been privatized, the most important being AGET-Hercules, the cement company; Hellenic Shipyards; Peiraiki Patraiki (textiles); and a number of banks, including ETVA (Hellenic Industrial Development Bank). The privatization of Olympic Airways, the country's loss-making carrier, was blocked by its workers, but was eventually carried out in the late 2000s.[17] Given the small size of the country, an unusual number of new commercial banks sprang up, including European and international banks and their subsidiaries. In December 1996 cotton growers protested violently against the government for refusing to reschedule about $1.3 billion in debt owed to the state-controlled Agricultural Bank and to obtain reinstatement of a tax break on fuel. Strong protests also took place in Athens in 1998, when PASOK Finance Minister Yannos Papantoniou, in co-ordination with the managing directors of the Commercial Bank, announced the tendering of a majority stake in its Ionian subsidiary. In 1998, the drachma was devalued by 12.1% against the ECU (European Currency Unit), as the price of entry to the European Exchange Rate Mechanism (ERM). By the end of the millennium, Greek state authorities were presenting highly positive statistical data vis-à-vis the country's entry into the eurozone, which was scheduled for 1 January 2001, two years after the launch of the euro for the core of Europe: GDP was around 3.5%, one of the highest in Europe; inflation was down to 4.0% and the budget deficit had shrunk to 1.9% of GDP, well below the Maastricht convergence ceiling of 3%; the interest rate of the 12-month Treasury bill in 1997–98 ran at 9.5%, with the

European Monetary Union (EMU) fluctuation criterion being 7.8%. Meanwhile, international lenders began bidding for contracts with the Greek government in the run-up to the Athens Olympic Games of summer 2004, just as Greek rentier/financial capital penetration into the new Balkans assumed enormous proportions.

Companies such as the Alpha Group, Mytilineos SA, Bobolas SA, Intracom Holding SA, Marfin Bank, MIG and the Sfakianakis Group began dominating the new business environment. The Sfakianakis Group, for instance, which started in the early 1960s manufacturing buses, saw its profits declining in the 1980s and quickly diversified into *comprador* activities, becoming Greece's prime car importer from Germany, France, Italy and the USA. Greece's telecommunications operator, OTE, while under a programme of partial privatization, bought Romania's Rom Telecom, defeating Telecom Italia, the only other bidder (see Hope 1998: 2). US companies provided technology and other capital for further modernization. The Mytilineos business group bought Romanian SC Somerta Copsa Mica, a lead and zinc smelting company, with a view to expanding it into metal processing, boosting its supplies to Kosovo and Macedonia. Cement manufacturing Titan, in a joint venture with Holderbank of Switzerland, acquired Macedonia's plant Cementamica USJE. Latsis, a London-based shipping company, participated in equity ventures in Bulgaria and Romania through the 'Euro-merchant Balkan Fund, operated by Global Finance, a Greek venture capital fund manager' (Hope 1998: 2). Around the same time, Spiro Latsis set up Eurobank EFG in Greece, the third largest private bank in Greece, recycling paper and wealth stemming from oil trade and equity investment in, among others, Poland, the Ukraine, Turkey, Serbia, Romania and Bulgaria. In this delirium, divided Cyprus, an EU member state since 2004, was an offshore paradise and tax haven accommodating rentier and financial activities, whether of Greek, British, Russian, Serbian or Persian Gulf origin.[18] Thus, straight lines connect Dubai, Cyprus, London, Athens, Cairo, Sofia, Belgrade, Damascus and Moscow, reflecting the new geography of parasitic capital with no growth prospects in the baggage of its travellers. In this Eastern and Middle Eastern geographical architecture, Athens was a key pawn and conduit in the service of financialization and Jeffrey Sachs's 'shock therapy' programme. It should be noted that the amount of tax evasion of this new super-rich *comprador*-cum-financial class was enormous.[19]

None of the above activities was conducive to growth. Greek investments in the real economy involved small and medium-sized enterprises in the textile and brewing industries in Greece and the Balkans, but this could neither offset nor arrest the new domination by financial-cum-rentier/*comprador* capital.[20] Simitis's 'modernization' and 'anti-populist' programme co-constituted this new reality which, among others, penetrated deeply into Greece's social tissue, destroying the social mores and culture of working class and agrarian community. As organic produce became increasingly replaced by the imported genetically modified product of the core, the best local producers

Politics and economics of the Greek debt crisis

could do was to embrace the international domination of the market and become a petty *comprador*. Time and again, none of this brought any benefit to state finances. According to multiple announcements by the Ministry of Finance in September–October 2011, more than 6,000 individuals owed more than €150,000 each to the inland revenue. For the sake of comparison, the total amount these individuals owe to the tax authorities is in the region of €30 billion, while the annual spending of the Greek state for wages is less than €23 billion. It is no accident, therefore, that the public debt doubled from 2000 to 2009 (Table 12.6), and especially at the expense of the average Greek consumer. Yet this abrupt rise was not accompanied by an increase in the productive output of the economy, as the country's GDP presented a less dynamic structure.

It is interesting, in this respect, to factor in defence spending, which is justified purely on ideational rather than real grounds. One of the reasons why France, primarily, and Germany were the main holders of Greek debt is because Greek political elites, in their 'patriotic attempts' to move away from the USA's pro-Turkish grip, began using French and German arms suppliers. By exaggerating both the threat coming from Turkey and Greece's and Cyprus's own vulnerability, the 'realists' of the Greek cabinet could bid for high-tech expensive military gear: in 2009 defence expenditure in Greece was just below 4% of GDP, as opposed to 2.4% for France, 2.7% for Britain, 2.0% for Portugal, 1.4% for Germany, 1.3% for Spain and 4.7% for the USA. At the beginning of the full-fledged crisis of 2010, Greece bought six warships from France at a cost of €2.5 billion and six submarines from Germany at €5 billion. Between 2005 and 2009 Greece was one of the largest European

Table 12.6 Evolution of the Greek public debt and its relation to GDP in US$*

Year	Public debt	Annual change	% annual change of GDP*	Public debt per person	% annual change of public dept per person
2000	139,689,071,038	10,087,641,291	100	12,840.70	100
2001	149,776,712,329	28,884,931,507	107.2	13,701.68	106.7
2002	178,661,643,836	47,538,356,164	119.3	16,293.75	118.9
2003	226,200,000,000	47,538,356,164	126.6	20,602.64	126.4
2004	272,540,983,607	46,340,983,607	120.5	24,820.27	120.5
2005	271,193,150,685	-1,347,832,922	99.5	24,701.92	99.5
2006	287,170,808,219	15,977,657,534	105.9	26,211.64	106.1
2007	329,765,753,425	42,594,945,206	114.8	30,014.36	114.5
2008	346,575,409,836	16,809,656,411	105.1	31,555.10	105.1
2009	385,542,465,753	38,967,055,917	111.2	35,082.30	111.2
2010	378,241,095,890	-7,301,369,863	98.1	34,419.71	98.1
2011	375,772,602,740	-2,468,493,150	99.3	34,172.04	99.3
2012	393,420,821,918	17,648,219,178	104.7	35,741.33	103.8

Source: http://www.economist.com/content/global_debt_clock
* Our elaboration of data from the Hellenic Statistical Agency (ELSTAT) 2011.

importers of weaponry.[21] During that period, the purchase of 26 F-16s from the USA and 25 Mirage-2000s from France represented nearly 40% of the total import volume of the country. According to SIPRI (Stockholm International Peace Research Institute) data for 2006–10, Greece is the fifth highest arms importer in the world, with a global quota of 4%, about half that of India (9%), and two thirds of China's imports (6%)—it is worth noting that Chinese GDP is about 20 times bigger than Greece's nominal GDP.[22] Most of these transactions took place through the Greek state issuing debt. In Greece, there is no such thing as an 'industrial-military complex', but rather a *comprador-military complex*, a key faction within the wider financial/*comprador* oligarchy network, which is dominated by the Ministry of Defence, doing all sorts of wheeling and dealing under the radar of a liberal constitution and the taxpayer. In addition, this all means that the security of the country is a dependent spoke of the Atlantic core, whether American or Franco-German.

However, there is more to the affair than meets the eye. Not all defence deals were or are dealt with by issuing state bonds/debt. Offset regulation became part of the official Procurement Law, 3433/2006. The Greek Ministry of Defence is in charge through the department of the General Armaments Directorate (GAD), and the Division of Offsets (DO). Offsets and procurement are a complicated method of purchasing weapons and military technology, involving, among other things, barter agreements. This means that private interests in Greece can barter all sorts of assets, including land and infrastructure, on the altar of corrupt defence deals and hot money. The threshold for an offset request is €10 million. Much is done for the defence of Cyprus and the Aegean islands from the 'Turkish enemy': an Athens-based think tank dealing with offset and procurement *par excellence* is 'Epicos', with a very telling website.[23]

Having said this, the doubling of the Greek public debt from 2000 to 2009 (Table 12.6) should not be surprising. In addition, we can see from the table the increase of extra charges to the Greek taxpayer (fifth column) and all this has been happening without any corresponding increase in productivity and output, since the Greek GDP augments at a much slower pace than the debt (fourth column). This means an increasing inability on the part of the ruling parties of ND and PASOK to manage the debt obligations of the country. Moreover, the import/export ratio from 1994 to 2009 shrinks at the expense of exports and despite the significant growth registered (Table 12.7). Thus, the international competitive position of Greece worsened, the export-led manufacturing sector disintegrated further, and all this despite high borrowing and the rise in the share price index of the ASE (Table 12.9). Further, the structure of exports over imports (Table 12.7) shows the magnitude of the problem, caused by a combination of the uneven development between the core and the peripheral Greek state, and of the policies pursued by the new ruling economic and political party elites. From 1994 to 2009 the Greek economy lost almost 40% of its competitiveness, and this despite the fact that GDP growth remained relatively good (Table 12.6); domestic and external borrowing

Table 12.7 Exports over imports (%)

1994	43.9
1995	43
1996	41.4
1997	41
1998	35.9
1999	36.3
2000	35.1
2001	36.8
2002	31.5
2003	29.8
2004	29.1
2005	32
2006	32.4
2007	30.9
2008	28.6
2009	36.3
2010	28.7

* Source: Hellenic Statistical Agency (ELSTAT), Athens, 2011.

increased (Table 12.8); and the ASE's price index was doing quite well. In this respect—manipulation of statistics apart—the relatively wealthy picture of the Greek economy before the current crisis was not due to the improvement of the real economy, but due to the speculative, rentier and consumerist activities of the new business and middle classes. In other words, as elsewhere in the West, especially in the USA and the UK, the growth registered was debt driven, whereas the disintegration of the domestic economy from the mid-1990s onwards went hand in glove with the relative growth of *comprador*-cum financial elements—a substantial increase of imports and financialization through the ASE and external and domestic borrowing via banking mediation.

The borrowing requirement of the Greek state increased rapidly after 2001. This was due to further internationalization/Europeanization of the Greek state with the insertion of the country into this peculiar form of world money, the euro (Table 12.8). We see that whereas the initial loans were sourced domestically, this ceased to be the case after 2007, as the 2007–08 financial crisis wiped out the accumulated wealth of small paper-asset investors, while at the same time the Greek state was forced to pump money into the banks, degrading the structure of the budget deficit. This, in turn, could not have been offset by European funds, the volume of which was not sufficient (Table 12.8, column 4). It is clear that from 2007 onwards the Greek debt is split between national and international/European agencies and structures. Bank recapitalization that has been taking place since 2010 is carried out at the expense of the taxpayer, both Greek and European, leading mathematically to a creditor-led default, as initially pushed for by Germany. This eventually took place in February–March 2012. Greece is unable to service its debt or

Table 12.8 Annual loans of the Greek state, state receipts, receipts from EC and expenditures

Year	Domestic Loans	Foreign Loans	Receipts from EC	Receipts	Expenditures	Receipts-Expenditures
1998 (million drahmas)	9,609,693	1,344,888	98,202	9,521,604	21,378,017	-11,856,413
1999 (million drahmas)	8,365,025	1,272,140	114,189	10,626,457	21,253,001	-10,626,544
2000 (million drahmas)	5,454,921	1,695,821	119,077	12,186,488	21,602,748	-9,416,260
2001 (thousand euro)	14,990,301	1,773,632	2,658,226	41,021,321	60,443,281	-19,421,960
2002 (thousand euro)	29,956,909	379,321	1,371,316	37,437,431	69,144,977	-31,707,546
2003 (thousand euro)	35,934,079	2,034,098	1,052,393	37,866,221	76,952,341	-39,086,120
2004 (thousand euro)	40,165,350	9,882,539	2,810,607	39,859,803	92,781,544	-52,921,741
2005 (thousand euro)	39,416,790	5,379,852	2,623,819	42,969,056	90,437,198	-47,468,142
2006 (thousand euro)	27,439,833	9,715,000	3,563,523	47,363,182	88,122,280	-40,759,098
2007 (thousand euro)	35,822,354	25,544,219	4,810,946	49,962,035	116,178,904	-66,226,868
2008 (thousand euro)	34,906,408	34,754,244	4,668,300	52,530,042	126,912,696	-74,382,654

Source: Our own calculation based on data from the Concise Statistical Yearbooks of ELSTAT for the respective years, Hellenic Statistical Agency (ELSTAT).

Politics and economics of the Greek debt crisis

Table 12.9 Annual change of export over imports, the share prices in Athens Stock Exchange and gross domestic product in market prices

Year	% exports over imports	Share Price Indices	Annual change of gross domestic product in market prices
1994	43.9		no data available
1995	43	914.15	no data available
1996	41.4	933.8	107.4
1997	41	1,479.63	106.8
1998	35.9	2,737.6	105.2
1999	36.3	5,535.1	103
2000	35.1	3,388.9	103.4
2001	36.8	1,748.4	104.2
2002	31.5	2,263.6	103.4
2003	29.8	2,263.2	105.9
2004	29.1	2,786.2	104.4
2005	32	3,663.9	102.3
2006	32.4	4,394.13	105.2
2007	30.9	5,178.83	104.3
2008	28.6	1,786.51	101
2009	36.3	2,196.16	98
2010	28.7	1,413.94	95.5

Source: ELSTAT. The data about exports over imports, about the share price indices and about GDP in the years from 2001–10 have been compiled from the Concise Statistical Yearbooks. The GDP data for the years 1996–2000 have been compiled from the National Accounts of Greece.

ever pay back some of the principal since the actual and projected rate of growth from 2010 to 2014 ranges between -2.5% and -7.5%. Moreover, the European banking system seems to be unable to cope with the stress on its peripheral banks and pension funds inasmuch as the degree of leveraging takes on enormous proportions. Greek banks alone, for example, are dependent on ECB credit lines that amount to over €100 billion.[24] The new ruling classes of Greece, together with their Western masters, have failed spectacularly to deliver growth and sustainable development to the Greek population. What they have delivered, though, is a peculiar form of 'creative destruction', whereby the mechanism of national and international debt generates forms of primitive accumulation as Marx foresaw more than 150 years ago.

There is no doubt, therefore, that whereas the trade deficit is a substantial source of the overall Greek debt, numerous other factors, mainly of domestic origin, have to be factored into every calculation. Trade deficits are articulated in the current account, and especially in the structure of the unequal trade interaction between Greece and the European core, particularly Germany, Italy, France and the Netherlands. Some 70% of Greek imports come from Europe, while some 55% are from EU member states. Germany's share of total imports is 12%, Italy's 11% and France's 6%. Of the total of Greek exports, some 64% goes to EU member states (11.5% to Germany, 11.0% to Italy, 4.2% to France). On the surface, it appears that the import/export relation is in equilibrium, but this is not the case. In terms of absolute value, Greek exports to Germany are in the region of €1.9 billion, whereas the value of German exports to Greece is in the region of €7.2 billion.[25] There is also the dimension of the financial account. This can take various forms: FDI, portfolio flows and other flows driven by the financial sector. Recycling of German surpluses becomes clear from the overall composition of German exports over imports, thus accelerating the pace of concentration of the overall debt. In this context, the analysis by Lapavitsas *et al.* is meaningful:

> [I]nternational transactions of Euro-zone countries have been driven by the requirements and implications of monetary union. Peripheral countries have lost their competitiveness relative to Germany because of initially high exchange rates as well as because of the ability of German employers to squeeze workers harder. The result has been a structural current account surplus for Germany, mirrored by structural account deficits for peripheral countries. Consequently, German FDI and bank lending to the Euro-zone have increased significantly. 'Other' flows to peripheral countries rose rapidly in 2007–8 as the crisis unfolded, but then declined equally rapidly. That was the time when peripheral states were forced to appear in credit markets seeking funds.
> (Lapavitsas *et al.* 2010: 344)

Thus, the overall Greek debt today—about €340 billion outstanding, of which €100 billion was to matures by the end of 2014—stems both from domestic (private and public) and external (international and European) sources. It is the articulation and interaction of those two sources that should be considered carefully. However, uneven and combined development between the core and the periphery has its origins in the fault-lines developed in the *domestic* environment of the peripheral states, as it is the state form that condenses the manifestations of the international and social struggle. Moreover, these fault-lines pre-existed Greece's entry into the EMU. Greece has always been a peripheral country in relation to the Euro-Atlantic core and it is not its entry to the EMU that created a structural competitive disadvantage for the country.

Our main finding in this section is that the high growth rates of the post-1995 period in Greece are not due to the improvement of the real economy (productivity, output and valorization), but instead to the speculative and consumerist activities of middle to upper-middle classes and the *comprador*-cum-financial elements that have dominated the Greek social formation since then.[26] The ASE, offshore business interests escaping taxation, coupled with aggressive penetration of the Greek banking sector in the Balkans, which was basically used as a conduit for German and French financialization plans for the region, all constitute the form that 'asset price Keynesianism' assumed in

Greece. Alongside this picture one can draw the profile of the new, post-Keynesian, that is to say post-Constantine Karamanlis and post-Andreas G. Papandreou, bourgeoisie in Greece.

We can now turn to consider changes in the structure of the middle and lower-middle classes, which used to constitute the main electoral base of the two ruling parties—classes that Marx, in his analysis of Bonapartism in the *18th Brumaire* (1852), used to call 'classes-pillars of the regime'. We will argue that the current crisis has eroded key electoral constituencies of those parties, as delivery of clientelistic-cum-corporatist strategic undertakings of regime reproduction are no longer possible. Neither PASOK nor ND can manage the crisis, let alone provide a progressive exit from it.

The disintegration of the middle classes

Throughout the post-1995 period of neo-liberal pandemonium in Greece, and despite the high rates of growth—which, as we have seen, were debt driven—the Greek economy failed to create employment (Table 12.10). The economically active part of the population amounts to less than 60% of the total population, while unemployment remains high. The entry of migrants, especially Albanians, into the Greek labour market cannot be measured, as most are illegal and employed in the informal sector. During the 1990s and 2000s a major trend reversed, accentuating the fault-lines on which the Greek economy rests: from a migrant-exporting country in the 1950s and 1960s, Greece became a migrant-receiving one, eliminating one source of invisible earnings that had a positive effect on the balance of payments. In its stead, a large number of migrants from the Balkans, the Middle East and Central Asia poured into Greece after the collapse of 'really existing socialism', only to find themselves in a hostile and rather racist social environment, which was partly due to the inability of the formal Greek economy to create permanent employment and equal opportunities—something that is not unique across the Euro-Atlantic core.[27]

As we have seen, the structural and historical features of the Greek economy are shallow: nonchalant industrial and agricultural sectors that cannot compete with the core, and a large public sector all topped with the parasitic activities of *comprador* (import-exports) and micro-*comprador* (small local traders) capital in its fusion with the ruling political parties of PASOK and ND. However, the global financial crisis of 2007–08 caused things to boil over: an organized society, especially a capitalist one operating alongside a neo-liberal model and internationalized through financialization and Europeanization, cannot be viable if almost 50% of the population is idle or unemployed. Yet, the Greeks survived and even thrived, negotiating new social and political contracts with the ruling classes via electoral cycles. This was feasible for a number of reasons, of which two stand out: the strong inheritance structure of Greek society, coupled with strong family ties; and the large number of civil servants.

Table 12.10 Population over 15 years and employment in Greece in thousands, 1998–2010

Year	Population over 15 years	Labour force	% of population	Employees	Unemployed	% of labour force	Non-Active
1998	8,669.10	4,512.8	**59.1**	4,023.70	489.20	**10.80**	4,156.30
1999	8,754.70	4,583.7	**59.4**	4,040.40	543.30	**11.90**	4,171.00
2000	8,830.80	4,617.2	**52.3**	4,097.90	519.30	**11.20**	4,213.60
2001	8,898.50	4,581.6	**51.5**	4,103.20	478.4	**10.40**	4,316.90
2002	8,957.70	4,652.2	**51.9**	4,190.10	462.10	**9.90**	4,305.40
2003	9,008.90	4,728.40	**52.5**	4,286.60	441.80	**9.30**	4,280.50
2004	9,056.90	4,823.20	**53.3**	4,330.50	492.70	**10.20**	4,233.70
2005	9,102.60	4,848.80	**53.3**	4,381.90	466.90	**9.60**	4,253.90
2006	9,150.10	4,880.20	**53.3**	4,452.10	427.40	**8.80**	4,269.90
2007	9,206.70	4,917.90	**53.4**	4,519.90	398.00	**8.10**	4,288.80
2008	9,230.10	4,939.70	**53.5**	4,582.50	357.10	**7.20**	4,290.40
2009	9,262.40	4,974.50	**53.7**	4,531.90	442.60	**8.90**	4,287.90
2010	9,301.50	5,021.00	**54**	4,427.00	594.00	**11.80**	4,280.50

Source: Greek labour force surveys, 2nd quarter of each year, Athens, 2011 (our elaboration of data).

Politics and economics of the Greek debt crisis

Roughly speaking, from the late 1970s to the mid-1990s the middle and petit bourgeois class composition of Greek society remained structurally unaltered. Just as the ND and PASOK policies in the 1970s and 1980s failed to add an iota to the country's economic development prospects, so the new parasitic forms of capital accumulation and the shift to financialization caused neither widespread proletarianization nor a reduction in state personnel.

A key sociological feature of Greece, perceptively captured by the work of Constantine Tsoukalas in the 1980s and 1990s, is its large number of civil servants, micro-proprietors renting studio flats to tourists, petty merchants, shopkeepers, lawyers, doctors, taxi drivers, hoteliers, seasonal professions due to tourism, and builders and car engineers of all sorts. Underground economic activities are also thriving, with the size of the black economic sector estimated to be the same over the decades and as high as 45%–50%. The two ruling parties provided special regulations for the expansion and reproduction of those strata, and especially chemists/pharmacists, taxi drivers, judges, construction workers, public works contractors,[28] providers of social services and lawyers. This large middle—yet diversified—class constituted the key pillar of the two-party rule alternating in office since 1974—ND and PASOK. One would expect that a radical change in the structure of market and production would affect the class positions of those strata, yet nothing of the sort happened. As we have seen, neo-liberalism and the peculiar type of financialization introduced since at least the mid-1990s altered the profile of the Greek bourgeoisie, yet no substantial change can be detected in the composition of the middle and lower-middle classes, which is the largest voting bloc of both ruling parties.

According to Greek Labour Force Surveys (Table 12.11), the self-employed with employees (small business) amounted to 262,900 in 1991 and 354,900 in 2010, the petit bourgeoisie ('own account workers') decreased slightly from 1,095,200 in 1991 to 975,300 in 2010, and the number of unpaid family members remained almost unchanged. Importantly, salary and wage earners rose from 2,270,900 in 1991 to 2,660,100 in 2010, an increase due to the rise in the number of civil servants. In other words, the party-state machinery, despite all these projects of privatization and restructuring that took place under Europe's Stability Pact programme and Simitis's 'modernization', did not stop recruiting state personnel. Thus, no substantial change has occurred and no proletarianization has taken place. This is another way to see how the rates of growth achieved during the post-1995 period were debt driven. In fact, the accumulation of capital in Greece during that period took the form of external and domestic borrowing and speculation and boom and bust cycles in the ASE. *This is how Greece's new bourgeoisie, in its fusion with the two governing parties of ND and PASOK, retained its voting bloc and influence inside and outside the parliament and reproduced the consensus achieved under the old Papandreou and Karamanlis in the 1970s and 1980s.*

The expansionist reproductive ability, therefore, of the middle and lower-middle classes is remarkable: they adapted to the new economic environment by way of negotiating new clientelistic and corporatist contracts with the

Table 12.11 Employed according to their occupational status in thousands (1998–2010)*

Year	Self-employed with employees	Own account workers	Salary and wage earners	Unpaid family members
1991	262.9	1,095.20	2,270.90	231.3
1998	292.5	1,007.20	2,337.40	453.2
1999	305.8	991.6	2,370.70	405.6
2000	326.7	998.4	2,466.30	394.1
2001	336.3	954.3	2,545.30	346.3
2002	315	996.5	2,616.00	333.3
2003	310.2	1,018.5	2,746.20	341.9
2004	346.8	962.5	2,784.80	274.9
2005	352.2	967.5	2,834.10	277.5
2006	364.6	962.8	2,896.40	291.2
2007	369.7	963.4	2,974.80	290.4
2008	381.2	957.6	2,922.10	268.9
2009	384.9	961.2	2,853.90	263.7
2010	354.9	975.3	2,660.10	242.9

Source: Labour Force Survey, 2nd quarter of each year (our elaboration of data).

ruling parties. Apart from the state's traditional role as clientelistic recruiter, the regeneration and financialization of social economy allowed a high level of consumption via the domestic mechanisms of consumer debt creation (consumer loans, credit card facility, share buying, etc.). Money became cheap, and was recycled through the new private commercial banks, which wanted to take advantage of and capitalize on the consumer's modest wage or property ownership as collateral. In this respect, Greek society did not differ from other states of the Euro-Atlantic core. House mortgages played a role in the boom-bust cycle of 1995–2010, but not as significantly as in Spain, the UK or the USA. This is in large part due to the inheritance structure of Greek society—the result of reforms effected in the Venizelos era and the institution of a dowry which is still operational, especially in the countryside—and also due to the family culture. Owning at least one house in the countryside and one in the city, mainly Athens or Salonica, the average petit bourgeois Greek family would hoard money to buy their children a small flat in the city, but they would never encourage them to take out a mortgage. Athenian and other urban families would rather have their children live with them until they get married—although this is something we find extensively in other societies too, i.e. Italy—rather than pushing them to become independent and lead their own lives. Taking out a home mortgage is a new phenomenon in Greece. True, it began with the 'new economy' and became somewhat popular in the 2000s, but it never became a widespread consumer phenomenon threatening the balance sheets of the banks in case of a consumer default as a result of an increase in interest rates. Arguably, as elsewhere, all these activities, a mix of old and new attitudes in society, did anything but contribute to the productive output of the country as a whole.

Politics and economics of the Greek debt crisis

The above euphoria lasted until the new Papandreou government, elected in October 2009, announced that the statistics regarding debt and GDP growth had been manipulated. Greece immediately became a hotbed for speculation as its debt was due to mature by 2013–14. In 2009, Greece's growth crashed, unemployment rose, the public debt-to-GDP ratio was at 127% and the budget deficit at 15.4% of GDP. Turning to the IMF and the ECB for assistance spelled disaster. As known from the Latin American (1980s) and East-Central European (1990s) experiences, the IMF's expertise is not how to help poor nations in need to put them back on a path to growth, but how to exploit the debt mechanism to deplete the resources of those states and repatriate the much-needed cash to the treasuries of the core, especially the US Treasury. The ECB is no better. It does not accept state bonds, but lends out to commercial banks at 1% interest. These banks, in turn, multiply the interest rate to lend out to the European periphery states with debt problems. This is straightforward usury, creating conditions of primitive accumulation, inasmuch as the employees of financial capital, that is the political personnel of the vassal and beyond, are forced to implement policies that lead to pauperization. In the case of Greece, these policies were enshrined in the *Memorandum of Understanding* (May 2010) and *The IMF Country Report on Greece* (February 2011), and as time goes by the austerity measures become all the more unbearable, especially since the country's official creditor-led default of March 2012 and the new *Memorandum* imposed (Fouskas and Dimoulas 2013). The combined policies of the IMF and the ECB are leading the Atlantic economies as a whole into the abyss, not just the periphery.

The middle and lower-middle classes, especially the self-employed, are now faced with extraordinary policy measures. A reduction in social spending (health care, schools, universities) has already had a damaging effect, and the VAT for bars and restaurants has increased from 13% to 23%, threatening one of the mainstays of the Greek way of life. Some 150,000 jobs are to be cut in the public sector. Emergency taxation and extra property taxation, the latter as part of the electricity bill, have already been enforced. Cuts in pensions and salaries are to be as high as 50%. Unemployment stood at 27.5% in March 2014, and youth unemployment at 63%. Barter agreements have already appeared in working class and peasant communities, in urban centres and the countryside, and racism and xenophobia are on the rise. All major Greek cities, especially Athens, are war zones: no ordinary rule of 'rallies' or 'marches' applies and the country, being under constant threat of the 'troika' not releasing the next 'tranche' of money, is entirely paralyzed. Thus, with purchasing power constantly on the wane, GDP fell by a further 7.4% in the second quarter of 2011. This reversed all the gains made by the Greek labour and progressive socialist movement since 1974. In addition, the conditions of primitive accumulation that are being created demolish the very political constituency of the two-party ruling system. The policies imposed by the 'troika' and implemented by PASOK and ND undermine their very political existence. The 'classes-pillars' of the regime, as Marx put it, are ceasing to provide political and electoral support. PASOK and ND, as party formations, need a major overhaul by their masters if they want to play a political role in the future of Greece. In this context, it should be noted that the corporatist-clientelistic apparatus of the Greek political system is undergoing a profound crisis itself. The ruling classes are currently trying to hold onto power and contain their fall by forming 'emergency governments of national unity', but there is nothing that can save them if the labour movement manages to switch the alliance system from the corrupt party system to itself. However, if this is the case, then what kind of democratic alternatives are opening up for Greece? The concluding section of our chapter summarizes our key findings and attempts to provide an answer to that question.

CONCLUDING REMARKS AND POLITICAL PERSPECTIVES

The imperial chain develops in a combined and uneven way and Greece occupies a dependent/subaltern position in that chain. We have reviewed this by briefly recasting the developmental stages of modern Greece, showing the way in which the country has been historically and structurally inserted into the trajectory of core capitalisms since the 19th century. As a vassal in that chain, it followed and always lagged behind the core at every Braudelian/Arrighian stage of capitalist development, while always subjugating itself to the hegemon of the international system—first Britain, and the USA after World War II. The dependency relation developed over the decades is not geographic or quantitative; rather, it is deeply qualitative and constrains the action of political forces.

A member of NATO since 1952, Greece has always been part and parcel of the hub-and-spoke system of neo-imperial governance of the USA, and a key recipient of its 'open door' economic policy in the 1950s and 1960s—the decades of the 'golden age'. However, Greece experienced no welfare state and Keynesianism in those years, as the post-Civil War authoritarian consensus excluded large masses from politics, and with the communist Left being outlawed. When formal democracy was established in 1974, the two pro-establishment parties, PASOK and ND, faced a mass labour movement keen for change and democratic political participation. The bipartisan response was the implementation of pro-Keynesian reform policies 'Greek style', at a time when orthodox Keynesianism was in retreat everywhere. This national/international fault-line straddled the peculiarities of the very bipartisan strategy of the ruling parties. It also straddled the very structural deficiencies of Greek peripheral capitalism, composed of a weak and uncompetitive industrial sector and a huge tertiary one. As a consequence, social and class struggles after 1974 were marred by the recruitment policies of the two ruling parties alternating in power. Right across the spectrum of the state/civil society nexus, these policies took the form of clientelism-corporatism. However, it is wrong to see this, as liberals and even social democrats do, as the root cause of the debt problem. If anything, 'Greek-style' Keynesianism was able to recruit state personnel and govern by consensus precisely because it was able to redistribute the wealth produced during the 'golden age'. *It did so, therefore, not in absence of modernity but in order to modernize against the labour movement enhancing and aggravating the fault-lines upon which Greek capitalism was resting.*

If the 1974–81 period in Greece can be described as 'the Right against the Right'—meaning the diverging paths of the Greek and Western Right, with the former applying Keynesianism but the latter Reaganism/Thatcherism—the 1980s could well be presented under a 'crisis of crisis management' scenario. This description, first captured by Claus Offe, attributes well the PASOK rule and the exhaustion of the model of management, whereby almost 50% of the economy was regulated directly by the state. This type of development amalgamated a type of 'national bourgeoisie' wholly dependent on state subsidies and European structural funds—Greece entered the EEC in 1981, ahead of Portugal and Spains and this is because of geo-strategic and security considerations, rather than economic ones.

Many Left intellectuals and economists focus on the technical details of the Greek debt problem. In particular, they tend to emphasize the exogenous sources of the Greek debt (e.g. current account deficit) at the expense of domestic factors (e.g. budget deficit due to high defence spending); others consider the debt as being the result of the absence of a social democratic, pro-Keynesian government at the European level, whereby a progressive finance ministry would be in a position to sort out problems of insolvency in the troubled peripheral regions. We have benefited enormously from studying their work, but we have unearthed data showing that the issue of the Greek debt is far more complicated and sourced both in the domestic and the external environment of the state, hence it is a very political, rather than economic/technical issue. That is why we have argued that the class dimension of the problem is far more important, and class is viewed here as a dialectics of political and economic instances whereby the economic may determine in the 'first' but not in the 'last' analysis.

This is the method by which we have approached the historical formation of the new bourgeoisie in Greece from the mid-1990s onwards, the class primarily responsible for the creation of the debt. The structural process of transformation of the Greek economy from the 1990s onwards is the result of further internationalization/Europeanization of the Greek state (Maastricht Treaty, Stability Pact). External constraints became very pressing, imposing on the ruling parties of PASOK and ND a neo-liberal set of policies, encouraging financialization and extreme speculation. Under these conditions, a new type of businessperson appears, dominating Greece's social economy: the new bourgeois, without abandoning their manipulative relationship with the state, are not so much dependant on it; rather, they become increasingly dependent on debt creation via a deregulated banking sector and a vibrant stock market (the ASE), capitalized and mediated by key financial institutions of the core states. It is, therefore, a peculiar type of '*comprador* bourgeois', who are not just importing commodities (e.g. BMW cars from Germany), but financial commodities and instruments in order to dominate specific markets, whether in Greece or the Balkans. In this context, we have examined the role of offshore businesses and the importance of defence deals, especially of 'procurement and offset', which are also responsible for the creation of debt.

Just as neo-liberalism and financialization trickled down to Greece from the core, so did the immense financial crisis that hit the core in summer 2007. However, it does not mean that external factors of debt are more important than the domestic ones. Greece became a hotbed for speculation because the domestic class sources of debt—the new *comprador* ruling classes and their political party barons—could not produce a convincing and reliable strategy of money generation and real economic growth. For example, none of the large amounts of money and paper that had been recycled in Greece, the Balkans and the Near East during the 1990s and 2000s had been taxed or diverted into productive activities and investments in the real economy. The type of growth that dominated Greece after the mid-1990s was comprehensively debt driven, thus unsustainable, and based on what Robert Brenner called 'asset-price Keynesianism'. This is the way in which the structural process of uneven and combined development manifested itself not just in Greece but across the periphery of the eurozone. As a consequence, Greece has become the weakest link in the imperial chain today, although the first to see that, and capitalize upon it, was the bond holder, not any Greek Lenin.

Nothing of what we have described so far makes Greece stand out as a very special case. The specificity of the country has to do more with its geographical location, hence its geo-strategic and geopolitical importance, rather than its political and economic processes. What happened in Greece after the fall of the East (financialization, debt-driven growth, privatization, etc.) happened everywhere, albeit chaotically and definitely with delay—simply the forms were different and the magnitude of the whole picture. However, the travails of the eurozone itself are part of the broader crisis of the US-led hegemonic system, whose decline since the stagflation of the 1970s failed to be arrested by neo-liberalism and financialization/globalization. Overall, the crisis of both Greece and the eurozone should be placed in a global analytical framework that concentrates on a relative power shift from the Euro-Atlantic core to the 'global East' (China, India, Brazil, Russia, Indonesia, South Africa, Turkey). Every analysis of the Greek crisis that fails to factor in this dimension of the problem would be incomplete.

Greece's integration into the eurozone has been disastrous: it destroyed all the country's competitive advantages, especially in agriculture, and crushed the real economy and export capacity of the country. Simitis's 'modernization' agenda, the direct political expression of this process, has equally been disastrous. Greece defaulted within the eurozone in March 2012. However, this is not the only accomplishment of the new *comprador* bourgeoisie and their political representatives of PASOK and ND. One could even argue, quite rightly, that they are not solely responsible—the Euro-Atlantic core shares responsibility.

A key accomplishment of the new ruling classes has been to preserve the class and income structure of Greek society almost unaltered since the late 1970s, thus keeping the entire mechanism of bipartisan political consensus intact, i.e. clientelism, patronage, nepotism and cronyism. This time around, though, it was done not just by recruiting civil servants, but also by a partial transfer of the deficit from the state onto the consumer—cheap credit lines and money, consumer loans, credit card facilities and so on. This was enough to keep the 'fundamentals' of the regime going, that is to say to maintain the income levels of the middle and lower-middle classes, the 'classes-pillars' of the regime and every regime, as Marx put it.

In a way, the current crisis in Greece is cathartic: it disintegrates the corporatist-clientelistic links between the corrupt political system and civil society, and emancipates the societal from the pincers of the two-party state. The severe and untold austerity measures imposed on Greece by the 'troika' undermine the post-1974 social contract between society and the party system, causing disarray among party elites, pundits and interest groups. This is deeply significant: it increases political mobility and, potentially, strengthens the parties of the radical and progressive Left. At the same time, however, there are certain extreme Right-wing tendencies that should be carefully watched. Elites could exploit at any time, or even provoke, a Cyprus crisis, or manufacture a 'state of emergency' in the Aegean, thus catapulting the movement and transforming its class demand into a catastrophic nationalism buttressing authoritarianism at home and warmongering abroad.

If the above analysis is essentially correct, what policy should inform the action of the Greek and European Left? An ancient Athenian, Solon, did not simply legislate the abrogation of the debt of slaves with his 'seisachtheia laws', but also devalued the currency, the so-called 'mna', in order to facilitate payment of debt from ordinary citizens, and introduced new democratic institutions. However, as time goes by, a debtor-led default and exit from the eurozone, which would entail considerable devaluation of the new drachma, becomes very difficult. The immediate task of the labour movement should be to push for cancellation of the debt and also push for the destruction of the institutional and political connection between the corrupt *comprador*-cum-financial capital and the state administrative elites. A technical exit from the eurozone, or generous debt cancellation alone will not bring about the desired result—namely, boosting the industrial capacity of the country, increasing income from sources such as tourism, regeneration of the real economy, especially of agriculture, alternative energy projects, such as solar energy, etc. Abrogation of debt payment and debtor-led exit or cancellation of debt would mean nothing if unaccompanied by a radical domestic restructuring of the nexus between the real economy and the state under the leadership of productive social classes.

ACKNOWLEDGEMENT

A version of this chapter first appeared in the *Journal of Balkan and Near Eastern Studies* 14(1), March 2012.

NOTES

1 Even some *Financial Times* editorials seem to acknowledge that if the protesters around the capitalist world are not heard, then the preservation of liberal capitalism is in question: 'Capitalism and its Global Malcontents', FT Editorial, 24 October 2011.
2 For a terse version of this argument placing the blame entirely on Greece, see the Editorial of the *Financial Times*, 17 June 2011, p. 12. Media opinion, shared by mainstream political scientists and economists in Greece and abroad, has unfortunately subscribed to that misleading perspective. Read, for instance, Loukas Tsoukalis's op.-ed. in *The New York Times* (21 June 2011): 'The bailout by the European Union, with the participation of the International Monetary Fund, comes with strict conditions attached, conditions that the government has only partially met so far. The government has reduced the budget deficit to 10.5 percent of Greece's gross domestic product from more than 15 percent—no small achievement— and passed a bold pension reform plan. But it has been much more hesitant about structural reform of the economy and privatization of state-controlled enterprises, because of organized opposition by vested interests, resistance from within the party and from trade unions, and the snail's pace of Greek bureaucracy'. See also McDonald (2005). This liberal school of thought sees modernization and development as dependent variables of corruption and clientelism, as impediments to development and growth—which is totally false; if at all, the opposite is the truth. For the origins of this argument and a sustained critique of it, see Fouskas (1997).
3 See, among others, Husson (2011). Factions of PASOK and the non-PASOK Greek Left uphold similar analyses.
4 The 'spread' is the interest rate difference between bonds of two different countries, and CDSs are insurance taken out to protect bond dealers. In the case of Greece, the 'spread' is the difference between the interest rate the country borrows, and the interest rate Germany borrows. The latter borrows by issuing bonds at 3%, whereas the former at or above 10%. Thus, the 'spread' for the Greek bonds is 7%.
5 'Indeed', Brenner says, 'the strategy that he [Greenspan] evolved during the second half of the 1990s—and has continued to implement ever since—might usefully be called "stock market, or asset price, Keynesianism". In traditional Keynesian policy, demand is "subsidised" by means of the federal government's incurring of rising *public* deficits so as to spend more than it takes in taxes. By contrast, in Greenspan's version, demand is increased by means of corporations and wealthy households taking on rising *private* deficits so as to spend more than they make, encouraged to do so by the increased paper wealth that they effortlessly accrue by virtue of the appreciation of the value of their stocks, or other assets' (Brenner 2006: 293).
6 The first hints about false statistics came from the previous minister of finance, George Alogoskoufis, of the Right-wing ND party. All Eurostat, Organisation for Economic Co-operation and Development (OECD) and other statistics about Greece used by researchers across the world come from the National Statistical Services of Greece (ESYE), now re-named Hellenic Statistical Agency (ELSTAT) and placed under a new director, a former IMF employee, Andrew Georgiou. The Greek daily press are full of stories about the manipulation of statistics by the governments of Greece, most of which are true, especially since the country's political elites began struggling to enter the eurozone. The most famous such scandal was that under Costas Simitis's PASOK cabinet in the late 1990s, which paid Goldman Sachs €3 billion to manipulate Greek growth upwards and the Greek deficit downwards; see, among others, Tolios (2011: 56, passim); Hope (2011).
7 In two memos sent at the request of Venizelos's government in 1915, Metaxas argued that a possible Greek campaign in Asia Minor was destined to fail, rehearsing Napoleon's defeat in Russia. No militarily defensible frontiers in the

Politics and economics of the Greek debt crisis

sandjak of Smyrna existed and extension of communication lines, as the Greek army would have to pursue the enemy into the interior, would give enormous advantages to enemy forces, which could concentrate and choose the right moment to attack. So a military undertaking in Asia Minor on the part of Greece should be avoided at all costs, unless the allied armies were committed in practice to support Greece in this venture—which, of course, did not happen. Thus, everything happened as Metaxas had predicted. Instead of sending a Greek army to Smyrna, Metaxas suggested that Venizelos negotiate with the allies that Greece take Constantinople and Eastern Thrace, which would have provided the expanding/imperial Greek state with territorial continuity and control of the Dardanelles.

8 For a detailed account see, among others, Alexandropoulos (1990).
9 The generosity was especially pronounced for those working in public utilities and the Ministry of National Economy, but not for the average employee of the public sector, let alone the worker in the private sector or the majority of the elderly.
10 Papandreou did not hesitate to sack his then economy minister, Costas Simitis—and later successor prime minister employing Goldman Sachs to manipulate the statistics so Greece could join the eurozone in 2001—when the latter attempted to apply a package of austerity measures as projected by the pro-monetarist economic assessor of the Bank of Greece, and later governor, Nicos Garganas in 1985 (the so-called 'stabilization programme').
11 The national accounts published by the statistical service of Greece offers data about the level of wages the government pays but says nothing about the number of persons receiving salaries/wages, and what sort of wages, from the state.
12 Tsoukalas (1986) wrote marvellous essays on these issues. Tsoukalas's contribution is the introduction of the concept of 'polyvalence' in understanding employment structures in Greece, by which is meant the unassailable economic activities of all sorts of people making income from a number of professions, while at times even being employed by the state (e.g. a civil servant having 'rooms to let' to tourists on a Greek island).
13 Virtually, this is the concern of all bourgeoisies in the periphery and even in the core, although it takes on different forms in the latter. From Latin America and Africa, to the Balkans, Turkey and Eastern Europe, the list is endless. The best exposition of this argument can be found in the splendid work by Paggi and d'Angelillo (1986: 67), who refer to *trasformismo* as a key policy structure in the Italian polity, where the main problem was not 'how to govern in absence of modernity but how to modernise against the labour movement'.
14 The best critique of Sachs comes from Gowan (1995); also Gowan (1999: 187–247).
15 On the concept of neo-revisionism, see Sassoon (1996), who operates within a Bernsteinian framework according to which when capitalism changes itself the strategy of socialist parties should also adapt and change. In this respect, Jospin's, Blair's, Occhetto's and Shroeder's attempts to adjust to the new capitalism of financialization and free markets were, under certain conditions, welcomed as adaptation and survival strategies of the Left. The strength of this argument lies less in what these neo-revisionist parties ended up becoming in practice nowadays, and more in the fact that Sassoon sees socialist party renewal as a *conditio sine qua non* for the success of socialism. Socialism is thus an historical and structural project becoming a continuous historical reminder/threat and shadow of capitalist development per se. This is an aspect of his work that his reviewers world-wide have so far failed to grasp and analyse.
16 A not entirely insignificant role in the ASE's ascendance was played by the social security funds. Until the mid-1980s the goose with the golden eggs had been the stocks of social security funds locked into the Bank of Greece on an interest-free basis. In the main, these funds were used to provide cheap loans to the public and private sectors, the funds themselves receiving no significant returns. As these funds

matured and the number of pensioners increased rapidly in the 1990s—Greece has severe problems with population ageing—the ASE became an important outlet for capitalization and speculation (it should be noted, however, that social security funds cannot invest more than 20% of their funds in the stock market).

17 It should be noted that all the privatizations that occurred from 1991 to 2010 brought only €20 billion to the state, mainly used to sustain borrowing and the remaining lame ducks.

18 Greek shipping capital, a prime international force in world seaborne trade with no substantial base in Greece, should also be brought into the equation. A large part of the Greek merchant fleet is listed in the shipping register under flags of convenience, so no substantial tax income can be raised by the Greek state. This loss of income became even more significant in the 1990s and 2000s, as the world share of the Greek merchant fleet—under confirmed Greek ownership—which was 1% in 1947 and 12% in 1970, soared to 17.4% in 2000. Unlike other nationalities, Greek ship owners are under no legal compulsion to enter or remain on the Greek registry and they do so only during periods in which favourable tax regimes—such as laws 2687/1953, 89/1967 and 378/1968—come into force. Most Greek shipping is 'tramp', rather than 'liner' shipping. The former is conducted by vessels that move like taxis wherever chartered, with freight rates fixed in a free global market. The latter is conducted by vessels/liners that run like buses on regular schedules and according to predetermined routes and tariffs. Having said this, the only significant contribution of Greek shipping to the Greek economy is its net contribution to invisible earnings and employment. See, among others, Theotokas and Charlauti (2007: 33ff); Bredima (1991: 233–45).

19 An effort to estimate the size of tax evasion of the new bourgeoisie is made by Stathakis (2011: 193–205).

20 Even in the middle of the debt crisis in September 2011, Athens daily press reported that Mytilineos SA buys energy from the state electricity company, DEI (PPC SA), €41 per megawatt (MW), only to sell it back to DEI for €55 per MW. How is this possible? Mytilineos, which, among others, runs an aluminium business, received a licence from the Greek state to buy cheap electricity for the aluminium business. However, it set up a separate energy unit, selling back energy to DEI at a higher price. This type of domestic *comprador* activity against the very interests of the larger public is not just damaging state performance, it is insulting. None of the press reports has been denied or contradicted.

21 See, among others, Tolios (2011: 67–68).

22 www.sipri.org/databases/armstransfers.

23 See www.epicos.com/Portal/Top/ContactUs/Offices/Pages/default.aspx.

24 See Bank of Greece (2010); Hellenic Association of Banks (2011); Milne and Wiesmann (2011: 1). Despite the fact that the Report of the Governor, George Provopoulos, presents the banking system as a problem-free financial area, he does not fail to mention the degree of dependency of the Greek banks on eurozone capital (Bank of Greece 2010: esp. 171–200).

25 Similarly, the value of imports from France is €3.1 billion, while the value of Greek exports to France is down to €0.7 billion. For Italy, the numbers are €6.9 billion compared with €1.8 billion against Greece. See ELSTAT (2009: 168–72).

26 Herein lies our main disagreement with the analysis by Milios and Sotiropoulos (2010). Authors writing from a neo-liberal perspective also fail to identify the nature of growth rates in Greece from the mid-1990s to 2008 as a debt-led phenomenon; see, for instance, Pagoulatos and Triantopoulos (2009: 35–54).

27 Migrants in Greece from the former Ottoman and Soviet spaces number more than 1 million and, as expected, statistics fail to capture their employment record and impact on the social economy of the country. However, racist feelings in Greece have taken a disturbing turn over the last two years, as racist groups across the

country find easy scapegoats in the migrants, especially Albanians and Muslims. This is political raw material on which the extreme Right continues to build.

28 According to the Pan-Hellenic Union of Public Works (PESEDE), public works contractors number more than 6,200 businesses, half of which are run by one individual. Again, the fragmentation of the sector pertains to the clientelistic-corporatist nature of the party and state system, creating political clientele by contracting out public works to individuals of ambivalent technical ability and skill.

REFERENCES

Alexandropoulos, S. (1990) *Collective Action and Representation of Interests before and after 1974*, unpublished PhD dissertation, Athens: Panteion University, 26 June.

Anderson, P. (2011) 'On the Concatenation in the Arab World', *New Left Review* 68.

Bank of Greece (2010) *Report of the Governor of the Bank of Greece*, Athens: Bank of Greece.

Bredima, A.E. (1991) 'The Shipping Sector', in Speros Vryonis Jr (ed.) *Greece on the Road to Democracy: From the Junta to PASOK, 1974–1986*, New York: Aristide d Caratzas Publication, 233–45.

Brenner, R. (2006) *The Economics of Global Turbulence*, London: Verso.

Chalikias, D. (1988) *Annual Report of the Governor of the Bank of Greece for the Year 1987*, Athens: Bank of Greece.

——(1990) *Annual Report of the Governor of the Bank of Greece for the Year 1989*, Athens: Bank of Greece.

ELSTAT (Hellenic Statistical Services) (1979–2010) *Concise Statistical Yearbook*, Athens: ELSTAT.

European Commission (1990) *European Economy. Annual Economic Report 1990–91*, Brussels.

Financial Times (2011a) 'Editorial', 17 June.

——(2011b) 'Editorial', 24 October.

Fouskas, V.K. (1995) *Populism and Modernization. The Exhaustion of the Third Hellenic Republic, 1974–1994* (in Greek), Athens: Ideokinissi.

——(1997) 'The Left and the Crisis of the Third Hellenic Republic, 1989–97', in D. Sassoon (ed.) *Looking Left. European Socialism after the Cold War*, London: I.B. Tauris.

Fouskas, V.K. and Dimoulas, C. (2013) *Greece, Financialization and the EU. The Political Economy of Debt and Destruction*, London and New York: Palgrave-Macmillan.

Freris, A. (1986) *The Greek Economy in the 20th Century*, Athens: Croom Helm.

Gowan, P. (1995) 'Neo-liberal Theory and Practice for Eastern Europe', *New Left Review* 213.

——(1999) *The Global Gamble*, London: Verso.

Gramsci, A. (1996) *Selections from the Prison Notebooks*, London: n.p.

Hellenic Association of Banks (2011) *The Greek Banking System in 2010* (in Greek), Athens.

Hope, K. (1998) 'A Big Market Close to Home', *Financial Times*, Special Survey of Greece, 8 December.

——(2011) 'History of Statistics that Failed to Add Up', *Financial Times*, 30 September.

Husson, M. (2011) 'A European Strategy for the Left', *International Viewpoint*.

Kalafatis, S. *et al.* (1990) *Lame-Ducks in the Greek Economy* (in Greek), Athens: OAED.

Lapavitsas, C. (2011) 'Euro-exit Strategy Crucial for Greeks', *The Guardian*, 21 June.

Lapavitsas, C. et al. (2010) 'Euro-zone Crisis: Beggar Thyself and Thy Neighbour', *Journal of Balkan and Near Eastern Studies* 12(4) (December).
Marx, K. (1976) *Capital*, vol. 1, Harmondsworth: Penguin.
McDonald, R. (2005) *The Competitiveness of the Greek Economy*, Athens: Athens News Press.
Milios, J. and Sotiropoulos, D. (2010) 'Crisis of Greece or Crisis of the Euro? A View from the European "Periphery"', *Journal of Balkan and Near Eastern Studies* 12(3) (August).
Milne, R. and Wiesmann, G. (2011) 'ECB Ready to Reject Greek Downgrade', *Financial Times*, 5 July.
OECD (1993) *Economic Surveys of Greece for 1993*, Paris: Organisation for Economic Co-operation and Development.
Offe, C. (1994) *The Contradictions of the Welfare State*, Cambridge, MA: MIT Press.
Paggi, L. and d'Angelillo, M. (1986) *I comunisti Italiani e il riformismo*, Turin: Einaudi.
Pagoulatos, G. and Triantopoulos, C. (2009) 'The Return of the Greek Patient: Greece and the 2008 Global Financial Crisis', *South European Society and Politics*, 14 March.
Panitch, L. and Gindin, S. (2005) 'Finance and the American Empire', *Socialist Register*.
Poulantzas, N. (1975) *Classes in Contemporary Capitalism*, London: New Left Books.
Sassoon, D. (1996) *One Hundred Years of Socialism*, London: I.B. Tauris.
Stathakis, G. (2011) 'The Fiscal Crisis of the Greek Economy', in Scientific Association of Greek Political Economists, *Economic Crisis and Greece*, Athens: Gutenberg.
Theotokas, J. and Charlauti, G. (2007) *Greek Ship-owners and Maritime Business* (in Greek), Athens: Estia.
Tolios, J. (2011) *Crisis, 'Odious' Debt and Violation of Payments* (in Greek), Athens: Topos.
Tsoukalas, C. (1986) *State, Society, Labour in Post-war Greece* (in Greek), Athens: Themelio.
Wolf, M. (2011) 'Time for Common Sense on Greece', *Financial Times*, 22 June.

A–Z glossary

Key concepts in international political economy

Vassilis K. Fouskas

Absolute advantage

A country has an absolute advantage in trade in a specific good with another country if it can use fewer inputs and real resources in producing that good. This means that the costs of the commodity will be lower in terms of money. For example, certain countries in the world have an absolute advantage over France or Germany in producing bananas, simply because their climate is conducive to banana production. If you have one type of resource, then a producer with lower use of inputs has an absolute advantage.

Association of Southeast Asian Nations (ASEAN)

ASEAN is an organization composed of ten countries located in South-East Asia. The organization, originally formed on 8 August 1967 by the foreign ministers of Indonesia, Malaysia, the Philippines, Singapore and Thailand, has over time expanded to include Cambodia, Myanmar (Burma), Brunei, Laos and Viet Nam. As stated in the ASEAN Declaration, the core aims and purposes of this regional organization, among others, include accelerating economic growth, social progress and cultural development in the region, promoting overall peace and stability in the region, providing assistance to each other on matters of common interest, and collaborating effectively in order to strengthen the region's utilization of agriculture and industries. However, the members of this organization also abide by particular fundamental principles as set out in the 1976 Treaty of Amity and Cooperation in Southeast Asia. These principles include mutual respect for the independence, sovereignty, equality, territorial integrity and national identity of all nations. Moreover, the ASEAN member states vow to respect the internal affairs of one another and settle differences and disputes peacefully without any threat or use of force. One of ASEAN's most important economic agreements is the Asian Free Trade Area (AFTA) agreement, fronted by Malaysia, which is essentially a tool of neo-liberal globalization to help build up domestic firms and to attract foreign direct investment (FDI) to the region by using AFTA's tariff liberalization programme.

B

Balance of payments

The 'balance of payments' of a country is a summary of its economic transactions with the rest of the world over a specified period. Whereas any transaction resulting in a payment to another country is debited to the balance of payments account, any transaction resulting in a receipt from another country is entered as a credit to the balance of payments account. A country's balance of payments has two fundamental components: the *current account*, measuring trade in goods and services, and the *capital account*, measuring all asset transactions with other countries. Thus, if a country is running a deficit on its current account, a surplus in its capital account is necessary to ensure a balance of payments. A country can make various decisions to help attain this balance. For example, it can attract foreign direct investment (FDI) or offer attractive interest rates as a way of attracting short-term banking flows into its economic system. Balance of payments summaries are essential as they help demonstrate the competitive strengths and weaknesses of any given country in the international division of labour. A balance of payments crisis occurred in the **European Union** in the wake of the global financial crisis of 2007–08, the intermediary being the banking sector connecting paper assets and liabilities across the Atlantic.

Bank for International Settlements (BIS)

Established in 1930 to co-ordinate the payment of reparations by the German government to the Allies, the Bank for International Settlements, located in Basel, Switzerland, is the world's oldest intergovernmental institution. When its initial objective of facilitating Germany's reparation payments ended, the BIS took on a new role and focus as an international organization tasked with fostering international monetary and financial co-operation by concentrating on member central banks. In other words, the BIS took on the role of a bank for central banks. Thus, it does not serve individuals or corporate entities and its operations are typically confidential and unknown by the public. As stated in its mission statement, the main goals of the BIS are to serve its 60 **central bank** members in their pursuit of monetary and financial stability, and to foster international monetary and financial co-operation. However, BIS also seeks to promote information sharing and economic research. To do this, the BIS promotes discussion, facilitates collaboration, supports dialogue between central banks, conducts research on policy issues confronting central banks, and serves as a trustee in connection with particular international financial operations. Certainly in the service of post-**Bretton Woods** arrangements, the BIS has since 2004 published its accounts in terms of **Special Drawing Rights (SDRs)**. In March 2013, the bank had total assets of SDR 211,952.4 million. One SDR is equivalent to the sum of US $0.660, €0.423, ¥12.1 and £0.111. Included in that total is 404 tonnes (890,658 pounds) of fine gold.

Bretton Woods system

The Bretton Woods system refers to the liberal economic order established after World War II. It takes its name from the Bretton Woods conference held in 1944 in Bretton Woods, New Hampshire, USA. The conference was held to establish a new international financial system that would prevent another surge of the widespread economic turmoil that was witnessed during the inter-war period. Participants of the conference included the 44 Allied nations and Argentina. Despite this, the two most influential participants were without doubt the USA and United Kingdom. Both countries, represented by Harry Dexter White and John Maynard Keynes, respectively, had somewhat clashing views as to what the post-war international monetary system should look like. While the USA preferred a liberal system with low regulation, the British preferred a system that would restrict capital flows and establish strong international monetary institutions. Nevertheless, albeit considerably more similar to the international financial system White proposed, demonstrating the position of power the USA held in the international system at the end of World War II, a compromise was reached on how the new system would be structured. The Bretton Woods system that emerged was characterized by a number of new rules and procedures for the international community such as the establishment of a fixed exchange rate tied to the US dollar and the pegged rate currency regime, and quotas and subscriptions rooted in the **International Monetary Fund (IMF)** and the International Bank for Reconstruction and Development (IBRD) (the birth of the **World Bank Group (WBG)**). These two new institutions were created at the conference to help oversee the operation of the international financial system. These new rules, procedures and institutions that came out of the Bretton Woods conference essentially encouraged an open liberal economic system centred on the economic and political-military power of the USA.

C

Capital gain and capital gains tax

Capital gain represents a price increase in the value of an asset between the present time and the time the asset was purchased. During the creation of the housing bubble in the 2000s, capital gain has been a major vehicle for individual profiteering, especially by homeowners who could buy properties in order to let, thus covering mortgage payments, and then sell them when house market prices went up. A capital gains tax is usually collected upon the realization of sales by gain. Capital gains tax in the United Kingdom has been levied since 1965, although many forms of assets are excluded from United Kingdom capital gains tax. Significant common stock holdings are excluded from capital gains tax, usually on grounds of 'providing incentives to entrepreneurship'.

Capital markets (primary and secondary)

Financial capital could be defined as the accumulated wealth available to create further wealth, whether via financial/monetary means (e.g. currency speculation) or investing in real commodity production or infrastructure (e.g. manufacturing). The capital market refers to facilities and institutional arrangements through which funds, both debt and equity, are raised and invested. More specifically, as well as serving as a place where participants can manage and spread their risks, the capital market enables those who require additional funds to seek out others who wish to invest their excess. The capital market consists of development banks, commercial banks and stock exchanges. Unlike money markets, which are centred on short-term investments, capital markets enable companies and governments to raise long-term funds and are sometimes defined as markets in which money is provided for periods longer than a year. The capital market is characterized by primary and secondary markets. Primary markets facilitate the transfer of investable funds from savers to entrepreneurs seeking to establish new enterprises or to expand existing ones (typically via underwriting). The secondary market enables existing securities to be bought and sold among investors and traders. Interestingly, while capital markets were initially small physical spaces such as coffee houses, since the 1970s they have grown and are now located across different continents and conduct deals using advanced IT. Capital markets are a key aspect of **financialization/globalization**.

Carry trade

The term usually refers to currency trade by speculators in which borrowing in low-yielding currencies leads to high profits by lending (investing) in high-yielding currencies. Carry trade has proliferated since the collapse of the **Bretton Woods system**, when credit became available without major **exchange rate** restrictions. Speculators are usually blamed for sudden currency value depreciation and appreciation. George Soros, for example, has been blamed for the 1992 crisis of the British pound, which forced Britain out of the Exchange Rate Mechanism (ERM).

Cartel

A cartel is an informal and rather illegal agreement, often secret, verbal or informal, between a group of producers, either firms or countries, seeking to limit or completely eliminate competition among its members. Thus, to limit competition with each other, members of cartels rely on agreements made within the cartel. To do so, the members of cartels typically agree to restrict output to keep prices higher than they would normally be set at under competitive conditions. Additionally, cartel members may also generally agree on discounts, credit terms, which customers they will supply, which areas they will supply and who should win a contract. However, this does not incentivize members to provide better products at competitive prices, which results in consumers paying more for poor quality. Cartels are notoriously unstable because of the potential for producers to defect from the agreement and target larger markets by setting lower prices. Furthermore, organizations such as the European Commission provide incentives, such as the 'leniency policy', which encourage companies to hand over inside evidence of cartels; the first company to do so is exempt from any fines. Cartels are more likely to stay intact if they consist of fewer members. One of the most famous cartels in the world is OPEC, the Organization of the Petroleum Exporting Countries, although the USA has managed to manipulate its power in setting oil prices via **petro-dollar recycling**.

Central bank

A central bank is one of the most important financial institutions in every country as it occupies an extremely important place in the country's monetary and banking system. The central bank is principally tasked with administering national monetary policy, managing the supply of a country's money and the value of its currency on the foreign market, and acting as a bank to the government and to private banks. Essentially, the central bank is responsible for ensuring and maintaining the economic stability of a country and oversees the nation's financial system. It is also tasked with the issuing of notes, acting as a lender of last resort, and functioning as the custodian of the nation's reserves of foreign exchange. Notably, in the case of a developing nation, its central bank plays a pivotal role in the process of growth. The central bank of a country differs from commercial banks in that it does not have any direct link with the public, it is a state-owned institution and it controls and audits the entire banking system of a country. In a regional monetary union, such as the **European Union**, the central bank loses most of its powers by conceding them to a supranational central bank, the **European Central Bank (ECB)**.

Collateralized debt obligation (CDO) and credit default swap (CDS)

Collateralized debt obligations and credit default swaps are major instruments in the era of neo-liberal **financialization** that ushered in after the collapse of the **Bretton Woods system**. It is an asset-backed security that evolved to integrate mortgage-backed securities and other forms of debt. Thus, a piece of paper was created that included many forms of debt (slices) representing a promise to pay investors in a prescribed sequence, based on the cash flow the CDO collects from the pool of assets it owned. The assumption of financial engineers was that even if one slice of debt within a CDO goes bad, then other slices would keep doing well and the overall value of CDOs would not be affected and would keep making profits for the paper investors. To that, the exaggerating rating of those pieces of paper by the credit agencies came to be added. Instead of rating the debt by way of making as objective an assessment as possible, they began rating it higher than it should otherwise have been. This all proved to be the most serious miscalculation of the mathematical CDO model engineered in Wall Street. The financial crisis was triggered by subprime mortgage holders who, having lost their job or being unable to keep up with regular payments due to an increase in the interest rate, triggered an unprecedented crisis across the CDO financialization chain. The banking sector across the USA and Europe was the first to be affected. In theory, however, CDO investments were 'covered' by credit default swaps. In the unlikely case of a default, the financial engineers of Wall Street and the City of London argued, the CDS will pay out pre-specified amounts of money. Effectively, a CDS is the insurance on a CDO. However, there is a difference. Anyone could buy a CDS in the CDS market without necessarily owning a CDO and this is the difference between, say, house insurance (you need to own a house to have house insurance) and a CDS. Thus, when the crisis kicked in and it became evident that it could not be stopped easily, the CDO and CDS markets began disintegrating, causing havoc across the globalized financialization chain.

Common Agricultural Policy (CAP)

The Common Agricultural Policy refers to **European Union (EU)** regulations responsible for merging EU members' individual agricultural programmes. The CAP is principally responsible for stabilizing and elevating the prices of agricultural commodities by the use of variable levies and export subsidies. As stated by the EU Commission on Agriculture and Rural Development, the CAP is determined at EU level by governments of member states, operated by EU member states and is primarily aimed at supporting farmers' incomes while also encouraging them to produce high-quality products demanded by the market. The commission further notes that one of the core aims of the CAP is to encourage farmers to source new development opportunities such as renewable environmentally friendly energy sources. However, despite recent reform, it is important to note that the CAP concept faces substantial amounts of criticism, especially from the USA. It is regarded as a policy that contributes to unfair competition, artificially high food prices and environmental problems. It is also said to have a devastating effect on smaller farms. These issues are particularly prominent as the CAP accounts for nearly half of the EU's annual budget (€58 billion).

Comparative advantage

Relating to the trade patterns of countries, comparative advantage is the ability of one economic actor to produce a particular good or service at a lower opportunity cost than another actor. In other words, comparative advantage, a principle formulated by David Ricardo in 1817, refers to the special ability of a country to produce a certain product or service more cheaply than other products or services. For example, whereas the USA has a comparative advantage, and thus exports considerable amounts of chemicals, semiconductors, computers, jet aircraft and agricultural products, it has a comparative *dis*-advantage, and thus relies on the imports of goods such as coffee, raw silk, spices and natural rubber. There is no particular set of criteria that determines a country's comparative advantage. However, it is often determined by factors such as natural resources, climate, cost of labour, skills, capital and know-how, and sometimes government assistance.

Conditionality

A key concept in international political economy, conditionality describes the use of budgetary and policy conditions attached to debt relief, bilateral aid and loans given by countries, international financial institutions and organizations. Conditionality, usually employed by institutions such as the **International Monetary Fund (IMF)** and **World Bank**, essentially necessitates recipient countries to implement particular reforms as a *condition* of receiving assistance. In other words, conditionality is the term used to denote the policies that member countries which receive financial assistance are expected to follow within their own economies in order to remedy their financial troubles. Since the collapse of the **Bretton Woods system**, conditionality reforms are typically neo-liberal and supply-side undertakings, targeting public expenditure, wages, inflation, health and education. Thus, making general structural reforms, which target the management of the assisted economy, also become a necessary condition for the recipient country. Notably, in 1989, the British economist John Williamson coined the term **Washington Consensus**, which describes a set of 10 economic reforms that he regarded as representative of a typical set of conditions attached to loans sought by countries in debt crisis. This list comprised: fiscal discipline, redirection of spending priorities, lowering marginal tax rates, liberalizing interest rates, establishing a competitive exchange rate, liberalizing trade, liberalizing foreign direct investment inflows, privatization, deregulation and secure property rights. Although these conditions are highly controversial and opposed by **post-Keynesian**s and Marxists, organizations such as the IMF legitimize them by noting that they are essential in addressing the root causes of the financial problems in an economy.

Credit default swap (CDS)

See: Collateralized debt obligation (CDO) and credit default swap (CDS).

Credit rating agencies

Tasked with assessing the credit worthiness of corporations and governments, credit rating agencies are essential actors in the global economic and political arena. Contemporary financialized capitalism continues to rely on the ratings determined by bond rating agencies. Since the establishment of the first US-based bond rating agency in 1909 by John Moody, multiple other agencies such as Standard & Poor's and Fitch Ratings have also become dominant in the market. Collectively, these three agencies dominate 90%–95% of world market share. It has become particularly important for governments to pay attention to the judgement of these agencies, as a poor rating will influence the terms upon which they can access paper assets. Each agency has its own system of rating sovereign and corporate borrowers, as demonstrated by the different credit rating tiers they use. For example, while Standard & Poor's and Fitch Ratings use a letter sliding system (from 'AAA' to 'D'), Moody's uses its own ratings scale (from 'Aaa' to 'C'). A broad range of credit scores have been appointed by these agencies. Credit scores range from investment AAA-graded countries such as Australia, Canada, Denmark, Germany and Norway all the way to 'junk bond'-rated countries such as Belize ('CCC+') and, most recently, Greece, which has become the lowest-rated country in the world according to Standard & Poor's, with a rating of SD (selective default). Credit rating agencies are part and parcel of **financialization** and bear part of the blame for the 2008 crisis. For example, they used to give high ratings to debt that was extremely volatile as it included sub-prime titles.

Currencies (hard/reserve and soft)

Settling domestic transactions, within the border of individual countries, is relatively easy because the country's currency is accepted by all parties involved in the transaction. However, when more than one country is involved, a different system is necessary to settle transactions. In this system, currencies are divided into 'hard' and 'soft' currencies. This is an essential component in the international monetary system. Hard currencies are those currencies widely accepted around the world because they are the currencies of nations with large, stable markets. Hard currencies can therefore be used by more than one country in settling transactions, even if that particular currency is not the main currency of either country. Notably, between hard currencies there is typically a free and active market, making these currencies easy to acquire and dispose of in large quantities. Examples of hard currencies include the US dollar, British pound sterling, Japanese yen and the euro. Furthermore, hard currencies are freely convertible and can be used to finance international trade. On the other hand, soft currencies are not widely accepted in exchange for other currencies. Furthermore, they have the tendency to fluctuate or depreciate, are not freely convertible, easy to acquire or dispose of, and are not held as reserve currencies. Examples of soft currencies include the Zimbabwe dollar, Cuban peso and North Korean won. Thus, soft currencies are not widely accepted as a medium for settling international financial transactions.

Customs union

A customs union is an agreement between a group of countries that seeks to eliminate restrictive regulations of commerce between the members of the union by removing trade barriers to goods amongst themselves and adopting a common external tariff regime. Unlike a free trade area, a customs union imposes a common external tariff on imports from non-member countries. Furthermore, unlike a common market, a customs union does not allow free movement of capital and labour among member countries. Notably, a customs union is most often created as a means of increasing economic efficiency and establishing closer political and cultural ties between the member countries involved. For example, the **European Union (EU)** customs union means that no customs duties exist at internal borders between EU member states, common customs duties exist on imports from outside the EU, and a set of common rules of origin for products from outside the EU is in place.

D

Debt crisis

A debt crisis can be described as an event in which there is either a sovereign default, or secondary market bond spreads are higher than a critical threshold. Typically, this concept is tied to the international debt crisis of the 1980s, which was caused by the liberalization of capital markets, the interest rate hike introduced by the head of the US Federal Reserve, Paul Volcker, and poor decisions about interest rates made by developed states. More specifically, in the 1970s oil producers started investing large amounts of money in the Eurodollar markets. Thus, developed countries soon started receiving vast sums of money, for lending purposes, by oil producers because of the shift in wealth from oil consumers to oil producers. This money was quickly lent out by banks for profit to keen and eager states that had had internal economic problems and wanted to boost their economy via exports. However, this heavy borrowing, particularly by countries in Latin America, resulted in a prolonged financial crisis as it started to emerge that some debtor nations would not be able to make payments on their loans due to the increase in interest rates. Also, the 1970s **stagflation** blocked the export capacity of the global periphery creating a vicious cycle of debt creation. Typical here is the case of Yugoslavia, which borrowed large amounts of money from the **International Monetary Fund (IMF)** and the **World Bank** in the 1970s in order to finance growth via exports. The programme did not work due to the weakness of Western markets to absorb Yugoslav manufacturing produce, thus leading to a debt and fiscal crisis initiating the process of the country's disintegration. However, the hotbed of the debt crisis was Latin America, and was triggered in 1982 when Mexico, Brazil, Argentina and a number of other periphery states made it clear that they did not have the cash liquidity necessary to pay their creditors.

Deficit

A deficit can either occur in a country's **balance of payments** or in the budget of its government. In the balance of payments, the deficit is the sum of debits minus the sum of credits. More accurately, when exports and financial inflows from private and official transfers are worth less than the value of imports and transfer outflows, a deficit runs on the current account. This is what often triggers balance of payments crises. On the other hand, a government budget deficit occurs when a country's public spending exceeds government revenues. More precisely, the deficit is the excess of government expenditures over receipts from taxes. This is at the heart of a fiscal crisis of the state. Whereas surplus countries might encourage imports and restrict capital outflows, deficit countries might restrict imports and capital outflows.

Depression

As opposed to a business cycle **recession** that lasts no more than a year, a depression is a severe, long-term downturn with massive economic, social and political consequences. Typical characteristics of a depression are abnormally high unemployment; shrinking gross domestic product (GDP); and unavailability of credit and severe disruptions in inter-bank lending, including bank failures. Global trade contraction and domestic disinflation, accompanied by severe contraction in consumption, are also part and parcel of an economic depression. A typical period of depression was that which ushered in the financial crisis of 1929 and lasted until World War II.

Derivative (financial)

In general, a derivative is a piece of paper that establishes a future legal claim on some underlying asset. This asset can be a commodity, a currency or a security/bond. Derivatives can be used as a hedge in order to reduce risk, or as speculative tools on future movements of prices. A derivative can be a contract that satisfies the two parties involved, but it can also be a generic type of contract which can be traded freely on the market (futures). The former derivative is in fact an 'over-the-counter derivative', whereas the latter is a traded derivative. Over-the-counter derivatives are essentially banking instruments. In recent decades, derivatives were traded not so much on the basis of the underlying asset, but on the basis of a cash settlement freeing the participating parties from the legal obligation to deliver the underlying asset. Derivatives markets in the 2000s were in the region of over US$1,300 trillion. Having said this, one can understand the importance of banks in the process of extreme financial engineering that preceded the crisis of 2007–08 and thus the importance of the privatized banking system in financialization.

Devaluation

Devaluation is a monetary policy conducted by sovereign states with a pegged exchange rate regime lowering the value of the national currency relative to foreign currencies in order to address a balance of payments disequilibrium (debt caused by a balance of payments disequilibrium). Devaluation makes exports cheaper and thus attractive to other countries, but at the expense of increased import prices. Usually, countries that devalue also resort to capital controls and a high tariff policy in order to offset the negative aspects of devaluation. Devaluation is not possible in monetary unions, such as the European Monetary Union (EMU). Thus, as long as a country with a severe balance of payments problem does not default and exit the monetary union, then what remains as a solution to its debt woes is what can be termed 'internal devaluation', namely a severe retrenchment of the welfare state, wage and pension cuts, mass layoffs and an increase in taxation.

Dollarization

One of the consequences of the breakdown of the **Bretton Woods system** was that it brought the entire international political economy onto a dollar-standard regime, heralding the era of *fiat*, as opposed to *commodity*, money. More and more countries since 1971 have needed dollars in order to pursue their international transactions. Thus, dollarization refers to the official or unofficial reduction, or complete elimination, of a nation's national **currency** in favour of a foreign currency as legal tender for conducting transactions. Despite the name of this term, dollarization does *not* only refer to the adoption of the US dollar, as it can occur with various other currencies such as the euro. Dollarization typically occurs for one or two reasons and in one of two ways. It can occur because individuals and businesses have lost faith in their own currency because high inflation or repeated devaluation have led to asset substitution and the holding of what they perceive to be a safer currency. It can also occur to help ease trade relations with another, dominant economic partner. Furthermore, dollarization can take place in two ways: *de facto* and *de jure*. Whereas *de facto* means that while a national currency is still in existence, many people use another currency in *practice*, *de jure* dollarization refers to dollarization in law in which a national currency is legally replaced with another. There are various examples of dollarization. Most notably, in 2009 Zimbabwe experienced hyperinflation at a rate of approximately 89 sextillion % and the Zimbabwean dollar almost lost its complete value. Shortly following this upsurge, the Zimbabwean government essentially renounced its own currency and proclaimed that all domestic purchases could be made in foreign currencies.

Dumping (and anti-dumping)

In international trade, 'dumping' (often referred to as price discrimination) is a pricing practice that involves charging a lower price to foreign customers than to domestic customers. Although dumping is often associated with 'predatory pricing', it typically occurs because firms have less to fear from competitors in the domestic market, thus firms are led to charge higher prices to domestic consumers because they have greater security with them. Dumping can either be done lightly or heavily and this is typically determined by the **World Trade Organization (WTO)**. The WTO calculates dumping on the

Dumping (and anti-dumping)

basis of a 'fair comparison' between the price of the imported product in the 'ordinary course of trade' in the country of origin or export (normal value) and the price of the product in the country of import (export price). The WTO and other international financial institutions decry dumping particularly if it has the potential to damage the domestic industry or industries of the importing country. However, the WTO only goes as far as 'condemning' dumping and claims it cannot 'pass judgement'. Nevertheless, it is fair to concede that it does encourage countries to engage with the 'Anti-Dumping Agreement', an agreement allowing governments to act against dumping by imposing duties and tariffs in response to alleged dumping. Yet, many claim that this agreement simply does not go far enough to eliminate this potentially detrimental practice.

E

Economic interdependence

Economic interdependence refers to the extent to which economic performance, as measured by factors such as gross domestic product (GDP), inflation and unemployment in one country depends positively or negative on the performance of other countries. Liberal and globalization theorists believe that the world becomes more and more interdependent and the power of nation-states withers away as a result of increasing volumes of trade, foreign direct investment (FDI) and financial transactions. Physical and human capital, the transfer of technology and growing similarities in wages have narrowed the gap between core and periphery, leading to more and more convergence and diminishing the spectre of war. Realist/nationalist readings of international relations and international political economy contradict this approach by putting forward the role of the state in the driving of free market capitalism and even interdependence, whereas Marxist theorizing with its focus on class, imperialism and uneven and combined development, considers economic interdependence as a means for the uneven reproduction of social and regional hierarchies across the globe.

Economic sanctions

Economic sanctions, often used as important tools of a nation's foreign policy, can simply be defined as domestic penalties applied by one or more countries on another country. However, this concept is broad in its scope. Namely, economic sanctions can include economic penalties, such as prohibiting trade, stopping financial transactions, or barring economic and military assistance. Furthermore, sanctions can be imposed selectively, stopping only certain trade and financial transactions or aid programmes, or comprehensively, halting all economic relations with the target nations. Notably, economic sanctions are not only applied for economic purposes. For example, economic sanctions are also used when domestic pressure for action exists, to uphold international norms and to deter future offensive actions. It is important to note that the effectiveness of economic sanctions is often questioned. Although sanctions are typically regarded to be particularly effective when they are applied multilaterally and are supported by the greater international community, many argue that they do not end up achieving their goals and are often more detrimental than necessary. For example, experience shows that economic sanctions boost the cohesion of the regime and tend to rally large social segments round their authoritarian leadership. Operating under economic sanctions, authoritarian regimes tend thus to become even more authoritarian.

Euro-communism

See: **Gramsci, Antonio (1891–1937), Euro-communism and hegemony**

Eurocurrencies

Eurocurrencies are national, freely convertible currencies held in a banking system outside the country of origin of the currency. To contextualize this, US dollars deposited with a bank in London are referred to as 'Eurodollars'. Thus, the key point here is that the bank is located *outside* the country of the relevant currency. Although this term originally referred to dollars held outside the USA and Europe, it has come to refer to a wide series of financial transactions that take place in currencies other than the currency of the state in which the business is being conducted. Eurocurrency markets are typically free from most national controls and therefore serve as an outlet for deposits and a source of loans for major international corporations and for national governments.

European Central Bank (ECB)

This is the creation of the Treaty of Amsterdam of the **European Union (EU)** in 1997–98 and its main task is to co-ordinate and administer the monetary policy of the eurozone (18 member states). Having adopted the main tenets of the Deutsche Bank, its main aim is price stability, i.e. to keep inflation across the eurozone low. As opposed to the US Federal Reserve, the ECB is not the **central bank** of a (federal) state, because the EU is not a state. Thus, it cannot issue and buy debt pursuing activities such as 'quantitative easing'. What the ECB can do to regulate money supply and address debt issues across the eurozone is to negotiate repurchase agreements, or repos. These agreements represent a promise between the lender and the borrower that the securities sold will be bought back at a later date and at a higher price as interest accrued (the so-called 'repo rate'). However, in absence of a European-wide state with fiscal powers, repo liabilities are effectively paid by the taxpayers of Europe's periphery states, which, being unable to compete with the economies of the core, have accumulated large quantities of debt within the monetary union. More recently, the ECB won German support for a promise to buy sovereign bonds, but nobody knows what would happen if it had to start delivering on the promise.

European Union (EU)

Founded in 1957 with the Treaty of Rome as the European Economic Community (EEC), the EU represents the most advanced form of regional co-operation in the world. It has created a common market among member countries, a customs union, and a currency union was launched in 1999 (Greece entered in 2001). The EU developed by way of a number of expansion waves. As of 2014, it numbered 28 members, of which 18 are members of the eurozone. Whereas economic integration is quite advanced, the EU enjoys only some forms of political integration. It has developed a number of specialized institutions, legal and auditing bodies, and is enforcing legislation and common policies among its members. There are members of European Parliament (MEPs), who are elected from each country during EU-wide elections. However, the EU falls short of being a federal state with central political and economic powers. Rather, it is a loose co-federation with a very small central budget and is unable to issue debt via its Central Bank (see **European Central Bank**). Thus, when the eurozone crisis broke out in 2009–10, the euro area was in danger of complete disintegration. It is commonly accepted that the state benefiting most from the so-called 'process of European integration' is Germany, the strongest economic power in Europe.

Exchange rates (fixed and floating)

An exchange rate is the rate at which one currency can be exchanged for another. In other words, it is the value of one country's currency compared to that of another country. When the currency of one country is used as a medium of settlement for an international transaction, its value has to be fixed against the currency of the other country; this fixing is known as the determination of the exchange rate. There are two ways of determining the price of a currency against another. A fixed exchange rate is a system under which currencies are fixed, or pegged, at a set price relative to each other. In fact, under such a regime government intervention is necessary to ensure that market rates are close to the official rates. Under a floating exchange rate regime the value of a currency is determined by the foreign exchange market. To contextualize these different exchange rate regimes, while the USA allows its currency to float, Germany, France and other members of the eurozone have effectively set a fixed exchange rate across Europe. Thus, the overarching policy of a government toward the exchange rate, to allow it to float or instead fix or peg its value to another currency, is called an exchange rate regime. In international political economy, exchange rates are of vast importance. For example, the dollar's exchange rate against the euro is one of the world's most important prices, with potentially huge economic consequences in the international arena. In the era of **financialization/globalization** that was ushered in after the end of the **Bretton Woods system** in 1971, speculators make large profits in the money markets by moving their funds around, taking advantage of the diverse interest rate and exchange rate regimes.

Export-oriented industrialization (EOI)

Export-oriented industrialization is a strategy to achieve economic growth through the expansion of export-oriented industries. This is a particularly important concept in international political economy because over the past few decades, a number of developing countries, such as the **newly industrialized countries (NICs)** and the Asian Tigers, have used this model to achieve rapid gains in economic growth and industrial production. In essence, EOI is industrialization in which consumer goods are manufactured to be exported to the vast market of industrialized countries. In order to achieve EOI, a state can carry out various measures. It can maintain a weak currency to promote export, support export industries by grants and loans at preferable interest rates, establish 'free trade zones' to attract multinationals wanting to produce for export, and/or use cheap labour to export low value-added products. Advocates of this mode of industrialization note that it enables a path to the creation of jobs, a decline in unemployment levels, the training of a skilled industrial labour force and an increase in foreign exchange inflows (this in turn eases balance of payments issues). However, critics of EOI shed light on some of the fundamental flaws of this mode of industrialization. They maintain that EOI actually creates minimum employment at very low wages and leads to a lack of product diversity as nations pursue their comparative advantage. However, there are modes of rapid economic development, such as that of Italy during the so-called 'golden age of capitalism' (1950–70), which do not fit into either perspective described above. In Italy, rapid industrialization and economic improvement occurred by pursuing a Fordist regime of high wages domestically and an export-oriented strategy.

Export processing zone (EPZ)

An export processing zone (EPZ) is an industrial zone producing goods for export in which prevailing labour regulations and taxation laws do not normally apply. In an EPZ a set of incentives is used to attract foreign companies to invest in operations whereby imported materials undergo some degree of processing before being re-exported. EPZs are dominated by the principles of free trade, foreign investment and an export-driven ethos. They are particularly attractive to transnational corporations because they offer low-wage labour with minimal external costs. There is a lot of praise for EPZs. Some say that they provide a link to global markets, contribute to employment and income generation, boost the export sector, raise the quality and performance standards of local industry, attract important technologies and earn foreign exchange. However, critics say they are exploitative enclaves that increase dependency on external agents and fail to produce the hoped-for benefits they set out. EPZs are also said to have become notorious for low wages and poor working conditions.

Export subsidy

An export subsidy is a payment made by a government to encourage the export of specific products and discourage the sale of goods on the domestic market. In other words, it is an attempt by governments to interfere with the free flow of exports by paying firms or individuals for shipping a good abroad. These subsidies are similar to taxes in that they can come in the form of a fixed sum per unit or as a proportion of the value exported. Types of export subsidies include direct payments, the granting of tax relief, the granting of low-interest loans, disposal of government stocks at below-market prices, subsidies financed by producers of processors as a result of government actions, transportation and freight subsidies, and marketing subsidies. Essentially, because export subsidies reduce the price paid by foreign importers, domestic consumers are punished and end up paying more than foreign importers. The justification for the implementation of export subsidies varies. However, the use of export subsidies is typically linked to promoting self-sufficiency or for national security reasons. Export subsidies are particularly important in any discussion of international political economy because they shift patterns of trade away from production based on comparative advantage. This in turn disrupts trade flows and has the potential to undermine globalization. In fact, they are viewed as among the most disruptive impediments to the operation of international markets because they punish domestic consumers and taxpayers. Institutions such as the **World Trade Organization** particularly place high importance on containing and eradicating the use of export subsidies.

F

Fair trade

There is no unanimously agreed upon definition of 'fair trade', yet it remains a key concept in global political economy. Advocates of fair trade argue that the current global trading system is profoundly biased against the developing world. Thus, as its name suggests, the 'fair trade' initiative seeks to initiate a more just system of international trade. In order for a more just trading order to materialize, proponents of fair trade typically argue two points. They maintain that more equitable prices need to be paid to producers and labourers in the developing world. Furthermore, they argue that labour standards and the well-being of workers in the developing world are in desperate need of reform. Thus, 'fair trade' is trade in which fair payment is made to the producers of the goods and, by paying a little bit extra, consumers get a product they know has been ethically produced. This approach to international trade, which seeks to contribute to sustainable development, is supported by a number of 'fair trade organizations' which heavily engage in raising awareness and campaigning for the support of marginalized producers and workers. However, it is also quite a complex issue that raises various questions such as 'who gets fair trade?', 'who decides what is fair payment?' and 'shouldn't all trade be fair?'

Financialization/globalization and financial crisis

Financialization and globalization are considered here as consubstantial processes that have their roots in capitalist modernity, which began many centuries ago and took different forms in Asia, Western Europe and the Americas. If the paramount visible unit of a capitalist economy is the 'commodity', then commodities travel both nationally and internationally, potentially creating a global political economy. However, commodities of any kind are financed in every instance of their production, circulation and consumption. Thus, financialization, globalization and political economy are strictly interlinked in modern history. However, finance did not play the same role, nor did it have the same significance in various historical periods. Historians and political economists influenced by Fernand Braudel see the dominance of finance as a period that commences when real economy (agriculture, manufacturing and trade) declines and merchants and capital owners seek new profitable investments away from declining manufacturing units. At the same time, Braudel observed, a transition period opens leading from one form of imperial hegemony to another. In most recent periods, finance and banking began to play a very important role after the first serious economic crisis of capitalist accumulation in the 1890s, leading to the financial and banking crisis of 1929. After that, finance began playing again an important role after the **stagflation** of the 1970s and the collapse of the fixed exchange rates system of **Bretton Woods**. However, this time around, finance has been articulated across the power of the dollar as world money and as fiat money. This is important, because the only anchor of the global economy becomes the currency of a particular state, that of the USA, attributing enormous privileges to the US Treasury. In the contemporary debates on financialization, the term came to signify an increasing independence of the banking and financial sector from material production as opposed to the first decades of the 20th century in which finance was in fact an amalgamation of banking and industrial capital, one of the main characteristics of imperialism. The financial crisis that erupted in 2008 was precisely the result of the extreme forms of financialization (sub-prime and irresponsible lending, debt packaging and selling across the world, securitization and futures, collateralized debt obligations, etc.) adopted first by the USA and Britain and then spread across the world's banking and financial system (financialization chain). Financialization, in many respects, can be seen as a strategy adopted by the main capitalist centres in response to the stagflation of the 1970s and the falling rates of profits in the industrial sector. Financialization is a regime of capital accumulation stimulated by domestic neo-liberal reforms (privatization of state enterprises, welfare retrenchment and liberalization of markets). If financialization applies primarily to the external environment of the state, neo-liberal reforms apply primarily to the domestic environment of it. Obviously, these two policy forms feed each other. Thus, many analysts use the term 'neo-liberal globalization' or 'neo-liberal financialization'. At the one, starting end of the process has been the USA and its financial centre, Wall Street, followed by the City of London. At the other, receiving end have been countries of the periphery and semi-periphery, forced to open up their markets and industry to the post-Bretton Woods, neo-liberal era of US-led financialization.

Foreign direct investment (FDI)

Foreign direct investment is a form of investment typically made by a transnational corporation, which brings control over physical assets by a firm into a foreign country. In other words, FDI is the process whereby investment is made outside the host country of the investing company for the purpose of controlling the production, distribution and other activities of a firm inside the source country. According to the International Monetary Fund's *Balance of Payments Manual*, FDI is made to acquire a lasting interest in an enterprise operating in an economy other than that of the investor, the investor's purpose being to have an effective voice in the management of the enterprise. FDI consists of a package of assets and intermediate goods such as capital, technology, management skills, access to markets and entrepreneurship. One of the key features of FDI, which distinguishes it from 'portfolio investment', is that a 10% shareholding typically allows the foreign firm to exert significant controlling influence over the key policies of the underlying project. Thus, one of the distinguishing features of FDI is the element of control the foreign firm has over management policy and decisions. Recently, developing, transitioning and emerging economies have increasingly viewed FDI as a source of economic development and modernization. As a result, many countries have liberalized their FDI regimes. If FDI takes the form of 'portfolio investment', then it means that the investor is solely interested in financial profiteering (passive investment in securities/shares) and not in real development projects.

Founder's profit (or promotional profit)

This is an original form of profit generated from the trading of financial assets. It is appropriated by the founders of a capitalist joint-stock company and represents the difference between the sum obtained from the sale of stock and the sum that is actually invested in the company. The profit is appropriated by the founders of the company when the stock is issued for an amount that significantly exceeds the amount invested in the company. The concept is credited to Rudolf Hilferding (1877–1941), a Marxist political economist, and found its best elaboration in his book *Finance Capital* (1910).

Free trade/free trade agreement (FTA)

Free trade exists when the international exchange of goods is neither restricted nor encouraged by government-imposed trade barriers. Therefore, it occurs when goods and services are bought and sold between countries without restrictions such as tariffs or quotas. The determination of the distribution and level of international trade is left to the operation of market forces. Building upon this, a free trade agreement (FTA) is a legally binding agreement between two or more countries which significantly reduces or eliminates tariffs and trade barriers. FTAs aim to remove barriers to trade and investment by creating a free flow of goods, services, investment and people; they also cover protection of intellectual property rights, government procurement and dispute settlement. Essentially, FTAs represent the liberalization of trade and the bringing about of closer economic integration. These agreements allow capitalist states to focus on their competitive advantage and freely trade for the goods they lack the experience to produce. Interestingly, producers and exporters whose products qualify for preferential tariffs benefit from FTAs because their products become more competitive due to lower tariffs.

G

General Agreement on Tariffs and Trade (GATT)

GATT was the main institutional focus of the international trade regime in 1947–94. With the failed attempt of the USA to create the International Trade Organization (ITO) (Congress blocked the effort), GATT served as a framework for gradually liberalizing trade. GATT was primarily established to break down trade barriers and to ensure a smooth flow of commodities and capital by reducing tariffs, quotas and subsidies. Furthermore, GATT was premised on the key principle of non-discrimination and reciprocity. While non-discrimination ensured that countries could not restrict or promote imports of certain goods from one given country and not another, reciprocity ensured that countries equally shared preferential treatment to each other. Thus, the goods of one country cannot be treated differently from the same goods produced locally. Although GATT was very successful in lowering tariffs and other major trade barriers as well as finding success in many multilateral trade negotiations, it became clear by the 1980s that it was no longer as relevant to the realities of world trade as it had been in the 1940s. Trade had become substantially more complex, globalization began changing the international economy and international investment was exploding. Thus, the institutional structure of GATT began struggling to keep up with the changing nature of international trade. GATT provided a solid foundation for its successor, the **World Trade Organization (WTO)**.

Global division of labour

The concept of 'division of labour' in modern times first appeared in Adam Smith's *The Wealth of Nations* (1776) and simply refers to the process of assigning different tasks to different people in a society. Thus, quite simply, the term division of labour refers to how different people fit into the production process and how particular tasks are assigned to different people with different skills. Periodic bouts of technological innovation and the training that follows restructure the social/technical division of labour and increase the importance of intellectual labour in the production and distribution process. The division of labour becomes more and more global, also in the sense of population movements on the ground, i.e. of massive migratory waves from the global periphery/South/East to the core and vice versa. Spurred on by neo-liberal globalization and deepening interdependence and uneven development, the concept of division of labour has become central to any discussion of international political economy. The key aspect of the global division of labour is that production is no longer confined to national economies but production processes are relocated to different parts of the world through the so-called global production networks (GPNs). However, it is important to mention that many groups, such as women, migrants and unskilled workers, have been disfavoured in the global division of labour.

Global fault-lines

This is a new concept in international relations and international political economy literature introduced by Vassilis K. Fouskas and Bülent Gökay in their joint work, *The Fall of the US Empire. Global Fault-lines and the Shifting Imperial Order* (2013). The argument is that the concept of *uneven and combined development*, first launched by Leon Trotsky and further elaborated by George Novack, Ernest Mandel and Justin Rosenberg, has partial heuristic and explanatory powers. Although it is extremely useful in capturing global capitalist developments, it abstracts from global geopolitical, societal, cultural and ideational structures upon which such developments rest. It attributes primacy to (uneven and combined) economic development as if unable to get rid of the 'determination in the last analysis by the economic instance'. Moreover, historically, it seems that it was developed as a concept having its point of departure in British capitalism, which then spreads in an uneven and combined developmental way around the globe. In other words, it reads as a Euro-centric concept. Accordingly, the world is divided into 'the West' and 'the Rest', and a system of knowledge is constructed around a series of binary hierarchies with Europe unfailingly occupying the higher position. Even Trotsky, the most brilliant mind of the Bolshevik Revolution, could not escape Euro-centric bias.

It is also claimed that 'global fault-lines' are inspired by Gunder Frank's work, in particular his *Re-Orient* (1998). It is viewed as a non-Euro-centric vision of global history. Capitalism is defined both as a mode of production, a concept that abstracts from large-scale industry first developed in Britain/Europe, and as the commodity mode of production, forms of which we find in a number of Middle Eastern and Asian empires that pre-existed Britain's industrial breakthrough. If the uneven development of the elements of the totality (economic, political, ideational, cultural, the dominant structures and impositions of empires on their vassals, etc.) is extreme, then this leads to severe disruptions, crises and even wars, whether local (conflict over a pipeline project in Chechnya), regional (the eight-years war between Iran and Iraq), or global (World Wars I and II). Just like the movements in the tectonic plates originating in Earth's radioactive, solid iron inner core, the vast shifts in the structures of the international system are the outcome of changes that have been taking place beneath the surface of social life for decades, if not centuries and millennia. In historical periods when the elements of the totality are in a kind of symbiosis, then there is relative peace and the totality balances out, yet without undoing the system's fault-lines.

Globalization

See: **Financialization/globalization and financial crisis**

Global production networks (GPNs)

This is a global circuit of capital, which includes all the phases of production, circulation and consumption of commodities and services. More than a chain, it is a circuit in which a number of factors contribute, such as technology, energy, finance, logistics, services and regulatory systems. GPNs characterize inter-firm relationships. They are complex networks and structures forming multilateral and intricate lattices of economic activity. These production networks and complex markets are primarily co-ordinated and regulated by global firms, which are called **multinational corporations** (or transnational corporations).

Gold Standard

The Gold Standard characterizes an international monetary system in which the value of a currency is equal in value to and exchangeable for a specified amount of gold. The Gold Standard replaced the bimetallic standard as an international financial system and lasted from its introduction in 1880 until the outbreak of World War I in 1914. The main characteristic of the Gold Standard was that exchange rates of different countries were fixed, and the parities were set in relation to gold. Thus, if a government's currency was on the Gold Standard, it automatically agreed to convert it to gold at a pre-established price. By doing so, a self-regulating mechanism was created for adjusting the balance of payments, since disequilibria could be remedied by inflows and outflows of gold. Notably, there are various benefits to having a gold standard. For example, it ensures a relatively low level of inflation. Additionally, economies on the Gold Standard are less able to avoid or offset either monetary or real shocks, making real output more variable. However, the important element here is that the state must be in a position to impose on society automatic deflation in order to offset imbalances in the current account, but this required politically inept populations where the poor were shut out of decision making. This was feasible in pre-World War II Britain, for example, when only a minority of the population was eligible to vote. Mass democracies after 1945 were not conducive to these forms of authoritarian discipline.

Gramsci, Antonio (1891–1937), Euro-communism and hegemony

Antonio Gramsci was a Italian Marxist theorist whose writings dwelled on understanding 'why the socialist revolution in the West has failed', as opposed to the success of Lenin's Bolsheviks in Russia in 1917. In an article entitled 'The Revolution against *Capital*', Gramsci claimed that the October Revolution in Russia had invalidated the idea that the revolution had to await the full development of capitalism. He thus sets himself apart from the evolutionistic tendencies of some German Marxists, such as Karl Kautski and Edward Bernstein, who argued that the revolution is the result of the full development of productive forces (workers, technological innovation and advanced technology production) in a given country. In his *Prison Notebooks*, Gramsci explained that Western societies have a robust civil society which, coupled with advanced methods of political governance combining coercion and consent, can deter revolution and arrest the development of working-class movement. After the death of Gramsci, his successor in the lead of the Italian Communist Party (PCI), Palmiro Togliatti, attempted to move the Marxist discourse in Europe beyond the two consolidated social and economic systems of the Cold War, the capitalist, incarnated in the USA, and the communist, incarnated in the USSR, pioneering a 'third way' to socialism with democracy and civil liberties. This strategy required that the Left achieves hegemony in civil society which would allow it to dethrone the bourgeoisie from its ruling position in the state. Hegemony implies a situation in which the working class prevails within the wider bloc of subaltern classes in a given national formation, that is to say, the middle classes recognize its primacy in the struggle against the ruling bloc. Arguably, however, this discourse, later epitomized as 'Euro-communism', failed to provide a realistic alternative beyond European social democracy and the ossified model of the Soviet Union.

H

Heavily Indebted Poor Countries (HIPC) initiative

The HIPC initiative is the first international debt relief scheme targeted at reducing the debt burdens of the poorest and most heavily indebted countries. The HIPC initiative was launched by the **International Monetary Fund** and the **World Bank** in 1996 and, shortly thereafter, in 1998–99 was expanded and became the Enhanced HIPC initiative. The HIPC initiative currently identifies 39 countries, most of these located in sub-Saharan Africa, as eligible to receive debt relief. Under this initiative, countries that qualify for debt relief have their debt reduced in return for meeting certain performance criteria. The enhanced version of the initiative changed in that it lowered the debt-burden thresholds, which enabled a broader group of countries to qualify for larger volumes of debt relief. Along with this, a 'floating completion point' was established to provide incentives to speed up reforms and increase country ownership. Despite the widespread international recognition of this initiative, it has faced its fair share of criticism. Many argue that this initiative focuses too much on the repayment of debt and usury, and not enough on reducing poverty or improving prospects of long-term economic growth and sustainable development.

Hyperinflation

See: **Inflation and hyperinflation**

I

Imperialism

The classic definition of imperialism is the export of capital from one country to another in order to appropriate that country's resources. Imperialism came to prominence as an answer to the crisis of capitalism in the 1890s, which promoted the amalgamation of banking and industrial capital, forming the basis of finance capital. In contemporary international political economy, imperialism is, by and large, appropriation of international value via international firms and production networks, or use of financial instruments and profiteering circuits of financial capital. However, the economics of imperialism should not be seen separately from its hegemonic politics and imperial geopolitics. In the past, modern imperialism was more formal, in the sense that imperial states that were after the conquest of global markets in the periphery, such as Britain and France, were in the business of setting up colonies in those peripheries, imposing on them direct colonial rule. However, post-1945 imperialism, especially after the success of de-colonization in the 1950s and 1960s, and this time dominated by the USA, was more informal. The USA sought influence and global hegemony via monetary, economic, ideological and military instruments. The USA is not interested, for example, in ruling Afghanistan or Saudi Arabia directly. All it wants is a subservient government that can be the result of a few US military bases on the desert. The **Bretton Woods system**, for example, and the primacy of the dollar in global trade that resulted after the end of the system in 1971, characterize aspects of monetary and economic primacy of the USA, whereas the foundation of the North Atlantic Treaty Organization (NATO) and various bilateral security arrangements with Japan and Australia characterize political aspects of USA primacy. Overall, imperialism has strong political connotations which do not go away during the era of **financialization/globalization** and the primacy of the USA in the international order.

Import-substitution industrialization (ISI)

Import-substitution industrialization is the strategy of achieving economic growth by restricting imports and promoting domestic industry. ISI became the dominant strategy in the developing world during the 1960s after being recommended as an industrialization model by the Economic Commission for

Latin America and the Caribbean (ECLAC) in the 1950s. Essentially, ISI is a strategy based on the protection of local infant industries from international competition. This protection enables local industries to acquire the experience and skills necessary to reach a level of development necessary for them to compete in the global market. In order to carry out ISI, a nation can adopt numerous measures. It can promote the development of export industries at home with the use of export subsidies, implement various foreign exchange controls, offer preferential rates for foreign exchange to selective importers of key goods, establish legal measures requiring the obtainment of a licence to import particular goods and offer a number of industrial incentives. Proponents of ISI maintain that it increases domestic employment and pliability in the face of global economic shocks. They also claim that it is more environmentally efficient as it eliminates the need for long-distance transportation of goods. However, critics of this mode of industrialization state that the local industries it supports become obsolete because they are not exposed to internationally competitive industries, and thus lag behind in technology and know-how.

Inflation and hyperinflation

Inflation, typically measured by the consumer price index (CPI) or by the implicit price deflator, refers to the increase in the overall price level of an economy. Inflation typically signifies an upward movement in the general price of goods and services which ordinarily results in a decline of the purchasing power of a nation's currency. If inflation results from a government attempt to stimulate the economy, it is referred to as 'reflation'. Inflation occurs for various reasons. It can materialize because of an increase in demand at a time when the supply of labour is tight and industrial capacity is fully utilized. It can also occur because of a lack of congruence between increases in wage rates and increases in productivity. Additionally, a sharp decline in the sources of supply can cause inflation. 'Hyperinflation', as its name suggests, refers to a rapidly accelerating rate of inflation. Hyperinflation is detrimental to any economy because it undermines the ability of its currency to perform its traditional functions. Under capitalism, capitalists are frequently forced by the very nature of developments and social struggle to raise commodity prices in order to offset losses in profitability.

Intellectual property rights

Intellectual property rights are rights granted to creators of inventions or ideas embodied in products or production technologies, for the purpose of promoting creativity in the arts and innovation in the economy. These rights come in numerous forms such as patents, copyright, trademarks and semiconductor chip designs. Furthermore, these property rights generally give the creator exclusive rights over the use of his or her creation for a certain period of time.

This allows holders to fix whatever price they deem adequate compensation for their creative efforts. Notably, the **World Trade Organization's (WTO)** Agreement on Trade-Related Aspects of Intellectual Property Rights (TRIPS) is one of the most important intellectual property rights agreements in the international arena. According to its mandate, it covers how basic principles of the trading system and other international intellectual property agreements should be applied, how to give adequate protection to intellectual property rights, how countries should enforce those rights adequately in their own territories, and how to settle disputes on intellectual property between members of the WTO.

International commodity agreement (ICA)

An international commodity agreement is an agreement amongst producing and consuming countries to improve the functioning of the global market for a particular commodity. More accurately, it is an agreement between a group of nations to help stabilize trade, supplies and prices of a commodity for the benefit of participating countries. These agreements can include mechanisms to influence market prices by adjusting export quotas and production when market prices reach certain trigger price levels. Furthermore, ICAs can employ buffer stocks which release stocks of commodities onto the market when prices rise to a certain level and build them up when they fall.

International Monetary Fund (IMF)

The IMF is an international organization initially attached to the United Nations. It was founded at the **Bretton Woods** Conference in 1944, is headquartered in Washington, DC, and consists of 188 member countries. Although the IMF started its life as a specialized agency of the United Nations, it has its own charter, governing structure and financial framework in place. This global organization is tasked with helping oversee a healthy global financial system and to provide assistance and guidance to any member country in need; it is often referred to as a 'lender of last resort'. It has established a quota system for member representation that is based on relative size in the global economy. The IMF clearly sets out its particular goals: to promote international monetary co-operation and exchange rate stability, facilitate the balanced growth of international trade and provide resources to help members in balance of payments difficulties or to assist with poverty reduction. Yet, like many other organizations, the IMF is faced with controversy and criticism. Many argue that the IMF does not take into account local economic conditions and cultures in the countries it assists, that its neo-liberal policies are not always suitable for the situation of particular countries, that the institution lacks transparency, and that it often supports military dictatorships and has no consideration of human rights. One of the most astute criticisms of the IMF has been that it essentially acts as an agent of the US Treasury Department.

International Swaps and Derivatives Association (ISDA)

Initially created in 1985 under the name 'International Swap Dealers Association', ISDA is essentially a trade organization sponsored by major banks to facilitate over-the-counter **derivatives**. Its headquarters are in New York and it has created a contract facilitating derivative transactions. Thus, in the post-**Bretton Woods** era, banks came to be increasingly involved in **financialization** processes, speculative arbitrage and easy profiteering.

L

London Interbank Offered Rate (LIBOR)

The LIBOR is a rate of interest estimated by leading London banks, which they use for transactions with each other. A key function of the LIBOR is to value financial **derivatives**. However, the banks that set the interest rate for the LIBOR are also the same banks that dominate derivatives trading, thus the LIBOR rate tends to be manipulated by banks to generate easy profiteering through derivatives transactions, leading to corruption scandals.

M

Monopoly

A monopoly, typically caused by barriers to entry, occurs when one firm or country is the sole supplier of a commodity or service. The simplest way for a monopoly to arise is for a single firm to own a key resource. A notable example of a market power arising from the ownership of a key resource is the South African diamond company, DeBeers. The company, at times, has controlled up to 80% of production from the world's diamond mines. Monopoly control results in closing entry into the industry to other potential competitors. This confers power upon the monopoly holder and may lead to abuse of power because the seller usually has complete control over the quantity of goods released into the market and the ability to set the price at which they are sold. Because of this, a lower level of production and a higher price of the commodity or service than would normally occur in a more competitive market will typically be set. A monopoly will remain the only seller in its market because other firms cannot enter the market and compete with it. Liberal economists argue that a monopoly is an example of market failure that leads to economic inefficiency. Marxist-Leninists see this as an opportunity offered by the historical tendency of the system to concentrate economic power in fewer hands, thus preparing the transition to state capitalism and socialism.

Most favoured nation (MFN) status

Most noted for being a cornerstone of **General Agreement on Tariffs and Trade (GATT)/World Trade Organization (WTO)** trade law and a key concept in the liberalization of international trade, most favoured nation status is a principle stipulating that countries extend to every other country the same degree of preferential treatment. Thus, any country recipient of MFN treatment must receive equal trade advantages by any given country granting such treatment. The main aim of MFN status is to prevent discriminatory treatment among members of an international trading organization. In the exact words of the GATT agreement, MFN is: 'any advantage, favour, privilege or immunity granted by any contracting party to any product originating in or destined for any other country shall be accorded immediately and unconditionally to the like product originating in or destined for the territories of all other contracting parties.' It is a guarantee of non-discrimination or equal treatment in trade relations. There are various prominent advantages to having MFN status but these advantages concern primarily the developed states of the core. Critics argue that developing countries of the global South have not been accommodated. The United Nations Conference on Trade and Development (UNCTAD), founded in 1964, has sought to extend MFN status to developing countries, but this has proven very difficult in practice.

Multinational corporation (MNC)

There is no formal definition for a multinational corporation, although different definitions have been proposed using different criteria. However, a multinational corporation is commonly regarded as a business enterprise that retains direct investment overseas and maintains value-added holdings in more than one country. It is driven by profit making. Typically, an MNC sends abroad a package of capital, technology, managerial talent and marketing skills to carry out production in foreign countries. Furthermore, many note that the key aspect of an MNC is that although it carries out operations in a number of other countries, its managerial headquarters are located in one country only. However, some argue that a truly global multinational corporation is one that looks to every market in the world as a potential market and allocates resources without regard for the location of its home country. MNCs have become extremely important actors in the international arena as the globalization of international markets continues. More firms have realized that the key to their future success depends on increasing their business activities in developing countries, such as the People's Republic of China, India, Brazil, South Africa and South-East Asian states.

N

Neo-liberalism

This is a set of state policies aiming at reversing the achievements of the Keynesian period of Western growth. It aims, in addition, to disarticulate the links between heavy industry and the state, giving way to financial and banking capital as primary agents of the economic sphere. As such, neo-liberalism means welfare and wage retrenchment, privatization and strict monetary policies in order to curb inflation. First implemented in Chile by a group of policy makers trained at the University of Chicago in the 1960s, neo-liberalism achieved prominence in the West with the policies of Margaret Thatcher in Britain, who became prime minister in 1979, and Ronald Reagan in the USA, who became president in 1981.

New International Economic Order (NIEO)

The New International Economic Order refers to the co-ordinated demands put forward by developing countries in the 1970s for reform of the international economic order. These multilateral policy options, proposed during the United Nations Conference on Trade and Development (UNCTAD), aimed to improve the position of developing nations in the world economy after the end of the **Bretton Woods** system. The general principles of the NIEO include preferential treatment, self-determination, non-interference, non-discrimination, transfer of technology to developing countries and economic gain by the beneficiary.

Newly industrialized countries (NICs)

The term newly industrialized countries refers to a socioeconomic classification applied to various countries around the world with economies that have not yet reached First World status but have, in a macroeconomic sense, outplaced their developing counterparts. In other words, NICs are countries that have a high level of economic growth and export expansion, outpacing the less-developed countries but not the industrialized and developed world. Because of this, NICs can be considered countries undergoing rapid economic growth. Examples of NICs include Brazil and Mexico, the four Asian Tigers (Hong Kong, Singapore, the Republic of Korea (South Korea) and Taiwan), Turkey, Malaysia, the People's Republic of China and India. NICs are typically characterized by countries that target industries and promote them through import protection, tax incentives and subsidies.

P

Petro-dollar recycling

From the 1960s onwards, the states of the Organization of the Petroleum Exporting Countries (OPEC) began accumulating large surpluses of dollars from petroleum trading. In the early 1970s, the USA managed to strike an agreement with Saudi Arabia, the key oil power in OPEC and the country with the largest oil reserves in the world, according to which surpluses produced from petroleum trade will be invested in US paper (Treasury bills, securities, etc.). This provided petro-states with secure investments and high returns, while at the same time helping the USA to refinance its current account and budget deficits. Many other countries have since imitated OPEC, without necessarily being oil or gas producers. Today, for example, Japan and the People's Republic of China are two of the largest holders of US debt, helping the USA to refinance its twin deficits (budget deficit and current account deficit).

Post-Keynesianism

Post-Keynesianism in political economy draws from John Maynard Keynes's main work, *The General Theory* (1936). The theoretical foundation of post-Keynesian economics is the principle of *effective demand*. This principle postulates that demand matters in the long as well as the short run, so that a competitive market economy has no natural or automatic tendency towards full employment. Michal Kalecki, Hyman Minsky and Joan Robinson are some key post-Keynesian thinkers. Some post-Keynesian thinkers, such as Michal Kalecki, or the political economists writing for the journal *Monthly Review*, combine Marxist and Keynesian analyses, achieving remarkable research outputs.

Post-Marxism

Post-Marxism is a theoretical body of work in social sciences that attempts to extrapolate from Marxist political, economic and social theory elements and postulations that are relevant to the analysis of contemporary capitalism. It is often combined with neo-Marxist streams of thought (e.g. the work of Nicos Poulantzas, Elmar Altvater, Göran Therborn and Christian Palloix), and also with other social theorists, such as the work of Max Weber and Alexis de Tocqueville. Post-Marxists are thus not 'orthodox Marxists', although many post-Marxists, such as David Harvey, remain faithful to Marx's key analyses on capitalist exploitation. Post-Marxists have significantly advanced social theory and Marx's own work.

Promotional profit

See: **Founder's profit (or promotional profit)**

Purchasing power parity (PPP)

This is a computation method to measure the value of different currencies. Instead of having government or the market itself providing the exchange rate of various currencies, PPP rests on determining domestic purchasing power by calculating the price of a basket of goods in given countries in their local currencies. PPP exchange rates help to avoid misleading comparisons that can arise with the use of exchange rates determined either by the market or the government. PPP exchange rates tend to represent a more accurate comparison in terms of standards of living across countries.

Q

Quota

A quota is a government-imposed restriction that limits the quantity of goods and services that can be imported or exported over a specified period of time. Quotas are typically used in international trade to help with the regulation of the volume of trade between countries. Quotas can be used for different reasons. For example, they can be used to increase domestic production by reducing imports as a means of helping protect domestic production. They can also be used as coercive economic weapons. Quotas are different to tariffs in that they are typically more effective in restricting trade. They are the most widely used method of restricting quantity, volume or value-based imports into a country. They may be unilateral according to commodity, or they can be selective on a country or regional basis. An extreme type of quota is an embargo, which prohibits all trade between countries. A less common type is the voluntary entry restriction, in which foreign countries agree to restrict their exports to a country, but are actually forced into compliance through the use of direct or subtle political pressure by major trading partners.

R

Recession

A recession is an economic contraction lasting for at least three consecutive quarters of a fiscal year. A recession is a short-term decline in national business activity. It is a downturn in the business cycle during which real gross domestic product (GDP) declines, business profits fall, unemployment rises and production capacity is underutilized. Thus, during a recession, a nation's economy recedes, or pulls back, from its normal buying and selling patterns and people hold back from spending as much money as they normally would, or demand fewer goods and services. Recessions typically come about when there is a widespread drop in spending, which is brought on by a supply shock or the bursting of a financial bubble. They are characterized by rising unemployment rates and falling rates of production, capital investment and economic growth. One of the most dangerous aspects of national recessions is that they have the potential to spread (commonly referred to as the domino effect). This can pose severe problems for the global economy because while each nation has its own financial system which is managed independently, those systems are also interdependent: they rely upon each other for their well-being and smooth functioning (often referred to as economic globalization). Global recessions can therefore lead to a decline in the gross world product (GWP, or the amount of all goods and services produced around the world added together). Notably, recession is different from **depression** in that these falling rates are not as severe or persistent.

Reserve currency (world money)

Reserve **currencies** or world monies are held by governments and institutions outside the country of issue and are used to finance international economic transactions. Reserve currencies are held in vast quantities by governments and institutions as part of their foreign exchange reserves and tend to be the international pricing currency for products traded on a global market such as oil and gold. The dollar is the prime global reserve currency, followed by the euro, the British pound sterling and the Chinese renminbi. The People's Republic of China had its currency pegged to the US dollar until July 2005, but after that the peg was lifted, only to resume, under intense pressure by the USA, in 2008 due to the financial crisis.

S

Special Drawing Rights (SDRs)

This is an international reserve asset created by the **International Monetary Fund (IMF)** in 1969 and at the behest of the US Treasury in order to prop up the declining US dollar. It is not a currency but a claim to currency held by the IMF and its member countries. SDRs become important when the global **reserve currency**, namely the US dollar, is weak and countries cannot use it as a means to trade and make other transactions. SDRs can be exchanged for US dollars, Japanese yen, euros and British pounds sterling.

Stability and Growth Pact (SGP)

According to the European Commission, the Stability and Growth Pact is a rule-based framework for the co-ordination of fiscal policies across the **European Union (EU)** member states. It was the result of an agreement outlined by a resolution and two European Council regulations in July 1997 in the context of the Treaty of Amsterdam, which envisaged an 'ever closer union'. The SGP contains two main frameworks: the preventive framework and the corrective framework. The preventive framework outlines and ensures that fiscal policy is conducted in a sustainable manner, while the corrective framework regards action in the case of an excessive deficit. Critics say that the SGP is an attempt by the core powers of the EU to impose their neo-liberal austerity policies across Europe. If a member state finds itself in breach of the SGP, then it enters into a regime of surveillance and even sanctions, the result being extreme forms of austerity and social upheaval.

Stagflation

Stagflation refers to a serious economic downturn experienced by a country or countries characterized by the simultaneous existence of stagnation and insistent and obstinate inflation. One of the most important features of stagflation is the fall in the rate of profit across the real economic sector. This induces capitalists to diversify their activities and move into *haute finance*, where profits are made through speculation and financial engineering. A typical historical period of stagflation is that of the 1970s in Europe, Japan and the USA.

T

Tobin Tax

The Tobin Tax is a transaction tax that has been put forward by Nobel Laureate economist James Tobin in response to growing consensus, particularly by social democratic critics of the liberal global financial system. The intention was to restrain capital mobility and reduce the risk of sudden withdrawals of speculative funds, which cause interest rate hikes. It aimed to secure greater stability by slowing down extreme speculative activity in financial markets. It essentially proposes that a currency transaction tax is necessary to manage exchange rate volatility. Tobin has discussed at length the ability for currency exchanges to transmit disturbances in international financial markets. Thus, by levying a charge on foreign exchange dealings, the Tobin Tax would discourage people from trading currencies simply to make money, yet it would not deter foreign exchange transactions for purposes such as buying imports or tourism and other medium- to long-term investments. A similar 'financial transaction tax' idea can be found in Keynes's *General Theory*.

Trade barriers (tariff and non-tariff barriers)

A trade barrier is a government or public authority restriction on the free import or export of goods or services. Trade barriers grow in significance because of globalization and **financialization**. These barriers typically include tariff and non-tariff barriers, which attempt to protect selected domestic industries from international competition. Tariff barriers are taxes imposed on commodity imports based either on the value of the good or on a fixed price per unit, and are typically levied by a national government when imports cross its customs boundaries. Tariff barriers are attempts to shelter selected domestic industries by restricting the quantity and raising the price of competing imports. Non-tariff barriers provide effective restraints on trade. Non-tariff barriers to trade include import licences, export licences, import **quota**s (e.g. 'voluntary export restraint', 'orderly market agreements'), subsidies, anti-dumping measures (see **Dumping**), **exchange rate** manipulation, local content requirements, and health and safety regulations. Thus, whereas tariffs are taxes levied on the value of imports which increase the price to the domestic consumer making imported goods less competitive, non-tariff barriers are more diversified and

Trade barriers (tariff and non-tariff barriers)

technical. Non-tariff measures are used as a means of discriminating against imports without levying taxes directly on merchandise, or to offer assistance to exports. However, non-tariff barriers have become a controversial topic in the era of globalization. They are often viewed with concern because they are not traditional methods of discouraging imports through the application of duties. It is therefore thought that they are hampering and undermining globalization by the 'back door'.

Washington Consensus

This term, coined by John Williamson in 1989 in his essay 'What Washington Means by Policy Reform', referred initially to the dominant views of the 1980s and early 1990s, namely that the developed industrial countries can and must impose on the periphery—beset by a debt crisis, especially in Latin America—a set of policy measures, such as budgetary discipline, deregulation of financial and banking sectors, welfare retrenchment, trade liberalization, etc. Later on, the term came to encapsulate the wider policy agenda of **neo-liberalism** and neo-liberal **financialization**, manifested through the explosion of **derivatives** and securities trading, **collateralized debt obligations (CDOs) and credit default swaps (CDSs)**, etc.

World Bank Group (WBG)

The WBG is the world's leading multilateral development agency and consists of five institutions: the International Bank for Reconstruction and Development (IBRD), the International Development Association (IDA), the International Finance Corporation (IFC), the Multilateral Investment Guarantee Agency (MIGA) and the International Centre for Settlement of Investment Disputes (ICSID). The central organization, the IBRD, was created at the **Bretton Woods** conference. These five organizations are dedicated to providing financial and technical assistance and guidance to developing countries around the world. The World Bank promotes a liberal economic framework and its establishment was fundamental in the construction of a global capitalist order revolving around liberal economic values. The WBG sets out to satisfy three main goals: provide loans to countries, develop international norms and resolve disputes. As set out in its articles of agreement, with an official goal of reducing poverty, the WBG must make decisions guided by a commitment to promoting foreign investment, international trade and facilitate capital investment. However, despite its prominence in the international arena, the role of the World Bank, particularly since the beginning of the 1980s, has faced its fair share of scrutiny and controversy. This can be attributed to various factors—most notably, the devastating neo-liberal structural adjustment policies it imposed on struggling countries in the 1980s, the continuing conditions it attaches to its loans, and the negative impact of its policies upon the environment. Despite aims to eliminate a repeat of the past and a shift from adjustment to 'sustainable development lending', the WBG remains a controversial organization. Namely, critics maintain that the agency focuses on profits rather than people, has distorted the concept of development and cares about money rather than the improvement of lives in developing countries.

World Trade Organization (WTO)

The WTO is the officially recognized institutional structure of the international trade regime. It was originally set up under the **General Agreement on Tariffs and Trade (GATT)** and was formally created in 1995 as a result of the Uruguay Round of trade negotiations. Composed of a series of agreements incorporating principles from GATT as well as newer topics such as **intellectual property rights**, investment, services, telecommunications and banking, the WTO is an institution aimed at ensuring the efficiency, predictability and freedom of international trade flows. It does this by dealing with the regulation of trade between its 146 member countries. The WTO offers a dispute settlement process that seeks to ensure its members' adherence to WTO agreements and provides a platform for members to negotiate and formalize trade agreements. Although the WTO is composed of 146 countries and is negotiated and signed by governments, rather than serving governments in particular, it seeks to help producers of goods and services, exporters and importers carry out their business. The WTO is currently attempting to complete negotiations on the Doha Development Round, which began in 2001 as the international community recognized the necessity of focusing on developing nations. Not surprisingly, the WTO has faced incredulity and distrust as a key actor in international political economy. It is often argued that the WTO is not impartial and favours the wealthier countries and **multinational corporation**s which have greater negotiation authority. Furthermore, many critics maintain that environmental and labour issues are ignored by the WTO, which effectively acts as the main agent of globalization driven by the USA. As such, the WTO is widening income inequalities across the global periphery, undermining social welfare and progress.

Select bibliography

Abbott, A. (2001) *Chaos of Disciplines*, Chicago, IL: University of Chicago Press.
Acemoglu, D. and Robinson, J. (2010) 'The Role of Institutions in Growth and Development', *Review of Economics and Institutions* 1(2): 1–33.
Achcar, G. (2012) 'Theses on the "Arab Spring"', Jadaliyy, Arab Studies Institute.
Akyüz, Y. (1998) 'The East Asian Financial Crisis: Back to the Future', in K.S. Jomo (ed.) *Tigers in Trouble: Financial Governance, Liberalisation and Crises in East Asia*, London: Zed Books, 33–43.
al-Atrash, H. and Yousef, T. (2000) 'Intra-Arab Trade: Is it too Little?' *IMF Working Paper* No. 00/10, Washington, DC.
Alexandropoulos, S. (1990) *Collective Action and Representation of Interests before and after 1974*, unpublished PhD dissertation, Athens: Panteion University, 26 June.
Allen, F. and Gale, D. (1999) 'The Asian Crisis and the Process of Financial Contagion', *Journal of Financial Regulation and Compliance* 7(3): 243–49.
Altman, R. (2009) 'The Great Crash, 2008: A Geopolitical Setback for the West', *Foreign Affairs* 88(1): 2–14.
Amin, S. (1973) *Le développement inégal. Essai sur les formations sociales du capitalisme périphérique*, Paris: Minuit.
——(1976) *Unequal Development*, New York: Monthly Review Press.
Amsden, A. (1989) *Asia's Next Giant: South Korea and Late Industrialization*, New York: Oxford University Press.
——(1993) 'Asia's Industrial Revolution: "Late Industrialisation" on the Rim', *Dissent* 40(Summer): 324–32.
Anderson, P. (2011) 'On the Concatenation in the Arab World', *New Left Review* 68.
Applebaum, R. and Henderson, J. (eds) (1992) *State and Development in the Asian Pacific Rim*, Newbury Park, CA: Sage Publications, 33–70.
Areddy, J.T. (2010) 'Accidents Plague China's Workplaces', *Wall Street Journal*, 28 July, online.wsj.com/article/SB10001424052748703977004575394262825550830.html (accessed 30 September 2012).
Arestis, P. (2004) 'Washington Consensus and Financial Liberalization', *Journal of Post Keynesian Economics* 27(2): 251–71.
——(2007) 'What is the New Consensus in Macroeconomics?', in P. Arestis (ed.) *Is there a New Consensus in Macroeconomics?*, Basingstoke: Palgrave Macmillan.
——(2009) 'Fiscal Policy within the New Consensus Macroeconomic Framework', in J. Creel and M. Sawyer (eds) *Current Thinking on Fiscal Policy*, Basingstoke: Palgrave Macmillan.
Arrighi, G. (1994) *The Long Twentieth Century*, London: Verso.
——(2007) *Adam Smith in Beijing: Lineages of the 21st Century*, London: Verso.
Asia for Educators (2009) 'The Opium War and Foreign Encroachment', afe.easia.columbia.edu/special/china_1750_opium.htm (accessed 30 September 2012).

SELECT BIBLIOGRAPHY

Assaad, R. and Roudi-Fahimi, F. (2007) *Youth in the Middle East and North Africa: Demographic Opportunity or Challenge?* Washington, DC: Population Reference Bureau.

Athukorala, P. (2003) *Product Fragmentation and Trade Integration: East Asia in a Global Context*, Australian National University Working Paper 2003/21, 1–67.

Athukorala, P. and Yamashita, N. (2003) *Product Fragmentation and Trade Integration: East Asia in a Global Context*, Australian National University paper, 1–41.

Ba, A.D. (2009) 'A New History: The Structure and Process of Southeast Asia's Relations with a Rising China', in M. Beeson (ed.) *Contemporary Southeast Asia*, Aldershot: Palgrave Macmillan, 192–207.

Bacevich, A. (2002) *American Empire*, Cambridge, MA: Harvard University Press.

Bank of Greece (2010) *Report of the Governor of the Bank of Greece*, Athens: Bank of Greece.

Barro, R.J. (1974) 'Are Government Bonds Net Worth', *Journal of Political Economy* 82(6): 109–17.

Barrow, C.W. (1990) *Universities and the Capitalist State. Corporate Liberalism and the Reconstruction of American Higher Education, 1894–1928*, Madison, WI: University of Wisconsin Press.

BBC (2012) 'Ex-leaders of China Protest Village Wukan "Punished"', 24 April, www.bbc.co.uk/news/world-asia-china-17821844 (accessed 30 September 2012).

Beeson, M.K. (2007) *Regionalism and Globalization in East Asia: Politics, Security, and Economic Development*, Basingstoke: Palgrave Macmillan.

Beeson, M.K. and Bell, S. (2000) 'Australia in the Shadow of the Asian Crisis', in Richard Robison *et al.* (eds) *Politics and Markets in the Wake of the Asian Crisis*, London: Routledge, 297–312.

Beeson, M.K. and Robison, R. (2000) 'Introduction: Interpreting the Crisis', in Richard Robison *et al.* (eds) *Politics and Markets in the Wake of the Asian Crisis*, London: Routledge, 3–24.

Bello, W. (2010) 'States and Markets, States Versus Markets: The Developmental State Debate as the Distinctive East Asian Contribution to International Political Economy', in M. Blyth (ed.) *Routledge Handbook of International Political Economy (IPE): IPE as a Global Conversation*, Abingdon: Routledge, 180–200.

Bergson, A. (1992) 'Communist Economic Efficiency Revisited', *The American Economic Review* 82(2): 27–30.

Bergsten, F.C., Freeman, C., Lardy, N.R. and Mitchell, D.J. (2009) *China's Rise: Challenges and Opportunities*, Washington, DC: Peterson Institute for International Economics and Center for Strategic and International Studies.

Bernal, J.D. (1969 [1954]) *Science in History*, 4 vols, Harmondsworth: Penguin.

Bernanke, B. (2004) 'Money, Gold, and the Great Depression', www.federalreserve.gov/boarddocs/speeches/2004/200403022/default.htm.

——(2005) 'The Global Savings Glut and the US Current Account Deficit', www.federalreserve.gov/boarddocs/speeches/2005/2005-0414/default.htmer.

Bhagwati, J. (2004) *In Defence of Globalization*, Oxford: Oxford University Press.

Black, W. (2005) *The Best Way to Rob a Bank*, Austin, TX: University of Texas.

Borchardt, K. and Buchheim, C. (1992) 'The Marshall Plan and Key Economic Sectors: A Microeconomic Perspective', in C.S. Maier and G. Bischof (eds) *The Marshall Plan and Germany*, Oxford: Berg, 410–51.

Bordo, M. (1993) 'The Bretton Woods International Monetary System: A Historical Overview', in M.D. Bordo and B. Eichengreen (eds) *A Retrospective on the Bretton*

Select bibliography

Woods System: Lessons for International Monetary Reform, 3-108, Chicago, IL: University of Chicago Press.
Bowler, T. (2009) 'China Warns of Unemployment Risk', BBC News, news.bbc.co.uk/2/hi/business/7915372.stm (accessed 30 September 2012).
Bredima, A.E. (1991) 'The Shipping Sector', in Speros Vryonis Jr (ed.) *Greece on the Road to Democracy: From the Junta to PASOK, 1974–1986*, New York: Aristide d Caratzas Publications, 233–45.
Breisinger, C., Ecker, O. and al-Riffai, P. (2011) *Economics of the Arab Awakening: From Revolution to Transformation and Food Security*, Washington, DC: International Food Policy Research Institute.
Bremmer, I. (2008) 'The Return of State Capitalism', *Survival* 50(3): 55–64.
Brenner, R. (1998) 'The Economics of Global Turbulence', *New Left Review* I/229: 1–265.
——(2002) *The Boom and the Bubble: The US in the World Economy*, London: Verso.
——(2006) *The Economics of Global Turbulence: The Advanced Capitalist Economies from Long Boom to Long Downturn, 1945–2005*, London: Verso.
Breslin, S. (2005) 'Power and Production: Rethinking China's Global Economic Role', *Review of International Studies* 31: 735–53.
——(2010) 'China's Emerging Global Role: Dissatisfied Responsible Great Power', *Politics* 30(S.1): 52–62.
——(2011a) 'China and the Crisis: Global Power, Domestic Caution and Local Initiative', *Contemporary Politics* 17(2): 185–200.
——(2011b) 'The China Model and the Global Crisis: From Friedrich List to a Chinese Mode of Governance?' *International Affairs* 87(6): 1323–43.
Brick, H. (2006) *Transcending Capitalism. Visions of a New Society in Modern American Thought*, Ithaca, NY: Cornell University Press.
Bryan, D. and Rafferty, M. (2006) *Capitalism with Derivatives. A Political Economy of Financial Derivatives, Capital and Class*, New York/London: Palgrave Macmillan.
Brynen, R. (1992) 'Economic Crisis and Post-Rentier Democratization in the Arab World: The Case of Jordan', *Canadian Journal of Political Science/Revue canadienne de science politique* 25(1): 69–97.
Buckley, R. (2009) 'The Economic Policies of China, India and the Washington Consensus: An Enlightening Comparison', *UNSW Law Research Paper* series 22.
Buiter, W.H., Corsetti, G. and Pesenti, P.A. (1998) *Financial Markets and European Monetary Cooperation: The Lessons of the 1992–93 Exchange Rate Mechanism Crisis*, New York: Cambridge University Press.
Burch, P.H., Jr (1980) *Elites in American History*, three vols, New York: Holmes & Meier.
Burke, E. (1790) *Reflections on the Revolution in France*, London: Dodsley.
——(1934) *Reflections on the Revolution in France* [1790] and *Thoughts on French Affairs* [1791], Vol. IV of the *Works of Edmund Burke*, Oxford: Oxford University Press; London: Humphrey Milford.
Busch, K. (1974) *Die multinationalen Konzerne. Zur Analyse der Weltmarktbewegung des Kapitals*, Frankfurt: Suhrkamp.
Cafruny, A.W. (2010) 'The Global Financial Crisis and the Crisis of European Neoliberalism', in L.S. Talani (ed.) *The Global Crash: Towards a New Global Financial Regime?* London: Palgrave, 121–39.
Cai, Y. (2006) *State and Laid-Off Workers in Reform China: The Silence and Collective Action of the Retrenched*, New York: Routledge.

Calderisi, R. (2006) *The Trouble with Africa: Why Foreign Aid is Not Working*, New York: Palgrave Macmillan.

Calvo, G.A. and Talvi, E. (2008) 'Sudden Stop, Financial Factors, and Economic Collapse in Latin America: Learning from Chile and Argentina', in N. Serra and J. E. Stiglitz (eds) *The Washington Consensus Reconsidered: Towards a New Global Governance: Towards a New Global Governance*, Oxford: Oxford University Press, 119–49.

Camdessus, M. (1996) 'Is the New Bretton Woods Conceivable', Address to the Société d'Economie Politique, Paris, 19 January, Washington, DC: International Monetary Fund.

——(1997) 'The Agenda for Global Financial Cooperation', Address to the Association of Japanese Business Studies, Washington, DC, 13 June, Washington, DC: International Monetary Fund.

——(1998) 'The IMF and Good Governance', Address at Transparency International, Paris, France, 21 January, Washington, DC: International Monetary Fund.

——(1999a) 'Looking Beyond Today's Financial Crisis: Moving Forward with International Financial Reform', Remarks to the Foreign Policy Association, New York, 24 February, Washington, DC: International Monetary Fund.

——(1999b) 'Governments and Economic Development in a Globalized World', Remarks at the 32nd International General Meeting of the Pacific Basin Economic Council, Hong Kong, 17 May, Washington, DC: International Monetary Fund.

Cameron, R. and Neal, L. (2003) *A Concise Economic History of the World*, New York: Oxford University Press.

Campante, F.R. and Chor, D. (2012) 'Why was the Arab World Poised for Revolution? Schooling, Economic Opportunities, and the Arab Spring', *The Journal of Economic Perspectives* 26(2): 167–87.

Canadian Business (2011) Interactive Map: The Billionaires of the World, 6 October, www.canadianbusiness.com/article/48712-interactive-map-the-billionaires-of-the-world (accessed 30 September 2012).

Cardoso, F. and Faletto, E. (1974) *Dependency and Development in Latin America*, Berkeley, CA: University of California Press.

Carr, E.H. (1993 [1939]) 'Carr', in H.L. Williams, M. Wright and T. Evans (eds) *A Reader in International Relations and Political Thought*, Vancouver: UBC Press, 179–91.

Carroll, T. (2010) *Delusions of Development: The World Bank and the Post-Washington Consensus in Southeast Asia*, New York: Palgrave Macmillan.

Case, W. (2009) 'The Evolution of Democratic Politics', in M. Beeson (ed.) *Contemporary Southeast Asia*, Aldershot: Palgrave Macmillan, 91–110.

Cesarano, F. (2006) *International Monetary Theory*, Leiden: Cambridge University Press.

Chalikias, D. (1988) *Annual Report of the Governor of the Bank of Greece for the Year 1987*, Athens: Bank of Greece.

——(1990) *Annual Report of the Governor of the Bank of Greece for the Year 1989*, Athens: Bank of Greece.

Chaney, E., Akerlof, G.A. and Blaydes, L. (2012) 'Democratic Change in the Arab World, Past and Present [with Comments and Discussion]', *Brookings Papers on Economic Activity*, 363–414.

Chang, H.-J. (1998) 'South Korea: The Misunderstood Crisis', in K.S. Jomo (ed.) *Tigers in Trouble: Financial Governance, Liberalisation and Crises in East Asia*, London: Zed Books, 222–31.

Select bibliography

——(2002) *Kicking Away the Ladder*, London: Anthem.
——(2006) *The East Asian Development Experience: The Miracle, the Crisis and the Future*, London: Zed Books.
——(2012) 'Africa Needs an Active Industrial Policy to Sustain its Growth', *The Guardian*, 16 July.
Cheru, F. and Modi, R. (2013) *Agricultural Development and Food Security in Africa*, London: Zed Books.
Cheru, F. and Obi, C. (eds) (2010) *The Rise of China and India in Africa: Challenges, Opportunities and Critical Interventions*, London: Zed Books.
Chiodo, A.J. and Owyang, M.T. (2002) 'A Case Study of a Currency Crisis: The Russian Default of 1998', *Federal Reserve Bank of St. Louis Review* (November/December): 7–18.
Chuanmin, Y. (2011) 'Toxic Mine Spill was Only Latest in Long History of Chinese Pollution', ChinaDialogue, guardian.co.uk, 14 April, www.guardian.co.uk/environment/2011/apr/14/toxic-mine-spill-chinese-pollution (accessed 30 September 2012).
CIA (2012) *The World Factbook*, Washington, DC: CIA.
Clark, I. (1997) *Globalization and Fragmentation*, New York: Oxford University Press.
CNNMoney (2011) 'Global 500: Our Annual Ranking of the World's Largest Corporations', money.cnn.com/magazines/fortune/global500/2011/countries/China.html (accessed 14 January 2014).
——(2013) 'Global 500: Our Annual Ranking of the World's Largest Corporations, 2013', money.cnn.com/magazines/fortune/global500/2013/full_list/ (accessed 9 March 2014).
Collier, P. (2008) *The Bottom Billion*, Oxford: Oxford University Press.
Collins, R. (1998) *The Sociology of Philosophies. A Global Theory of Intellectual Change*, Cambridge, MA: Harvard University Press.
Cox, R.W. (1993 [1983]) 'Gramsci, Hegemony and International Relations: An Essay in Method', in Stephen Gill (ed.) *Gramsci, Historical Materialism, and International Relations*, Cambridge: Cambridge University Press.
Dahi, O.S. and Demir, F. (2008) 'The Middle East and North Africa', *International Handbook of Development Economics* 2: 522–35.
Dalacoura, K. (2012) 'The 2011 Uprisings in the Arab Middle East: Political Change and Geopolitical Implications', *International Affairs (Royal Institute of International Affairs 1944–)* 88(1): 63–79.
Dalrymple, R. (1998) 'Indonesia and the IMF: The Evolving Consequences of a Reforming Mission', *Australian Journal of Political Science* 52(3): 233–39.
Davidson, P. (2004) 'A Post Keynesian View of the Washington Consensus and How to Improve It', *Journal of Post Keynesian Economics* 27(2): 207–30.
——(2009) *The Keynes Solution: The Path to Global Economic Prosperity*, New York: Palgrave Macmillan.
Davis, M. (1980) 'Why the US Working Class is Different', *New Left Review* I(123): 3–16.
——(2002) *Late Victorian Holocausts. El Niño Famines and the Making of the Third World*, London: Verso.
——(2004) *Planet of Slums*, London: Verso.
de Grauwe, P. (1996) *International Money*, New York: Oxford University Press.
de Long, J.B. and Eichengreen, B. (1993) 'The Marshall Plan: History's Most Successful Structural Adjustment Program', in R. Dornbusch, W. Nolling and R. Layard (eds) *Postwar Economic Reconstruction and Lessons for the East Today*, Cambridge, MA: MIT Press, 189–230.

de Vries, M.G. (1995a) 'The Bretton Woods Conference and the Birth of the International Monetary Fund', in O. Kirschner (ed.) *The Bretton Woods-GATT System: Retrospect and Prospect After 50 Years*, New York: M.E Sharpe, 3–18.

——(1995b) 'Bretton Woods 50 Years Later', in O. Kirschner (ed.) *The Bretton Woods-GATT System: Retrospect and Prospect After 50 Years*, New York: M.E Sharpe, 128–42.

Denisova, I. (2012) *Income Distribution and Poverty in Russia*, OECD Social Employment and Migration Working Papers, No. 132, Paris: OECD Publishing.

Deqiang, H. (2000) *Collision! The Globalization Trap and China's Real Choice*, Beijing: Economic Management Press.

Desai, R.M. (2011) 'The Economic Imperatives of the Arab Spring', *The G-20 Cannes Summit 2011: Is the Global Recovery Now in Danger*.

Despres, E., Kindleberger, C. and Salant, W. (1966) 'The Dollar and World Liquidity: a Minority View'. *The Economist* 218 (5 February): 526–29.

Dicken, P. (2007) *Global Shift. Mapping the Changing Contours of the World Economy*, London: Sage, 379–409 (6th edn, 2011).

Dikötter, F. (2010) *Mao's Great Famine: The Story of China's Most Devastating Catastrophe*, London: Bloomsbury Publishing.

Djankov, S. and Murrell, P. (2002) 'Enterprise Restructuring in Transition: A Quantitative Survey', *Journal of Economic Literature* 40(3): 739–92.

Dore, R. (1987) *Taking Japan Seriously—A Confucian Perspective on Leading Economic Issues*, London: The Athlone Press.

dos Santos, T. (2011) 'Globalization, Emerging Powers and the Future of Capitalism', *Latin American Perspectives* 38(2): 45–57.

Dowling, W.A. (2007) 'Retirement Imperiled: The Case of HELOCs', *Journal of Business Case Studies* 3(4): 51–56.

Durkheim, E. (1964 [1933, 1893]) *The Division of Labor in Society*, 5th edn, trans. G. Simpson, New York: Free Press; London: Collier-Macmillan.

Easley, D., López de Prado, M.M. and O'Hara, M. (2012) 'The Volume Clock: Insights into the High Frequency Paradigm', working paper, ssrn.com/abstract=2034858.

EBRD (2007) *Transition Report 2007: People in Transition*, London: European Bank for Reconstruction and Development.

——(2011) *Transition Report 2011: Crisis and Transition. The People's Perspective*, London: European Bank for Reconstruction and Development.

Eckstein, A. (ed.) (1971) *Comparison of Economic Systems: Theoretical and Methodological Approaches*, Berkeley: University of California Press.

The Economist (2007) 'For Whosoever hath, to him Shall be Given, and he Shall have More. Income Inequality in Emerging Asia Heading Towards Latin American Levels', 9 August, www.economist.com/node/9616888 (accessed 30 September 2012).

——(2010) 'Hello America: China's Economy Overtakes Japan's in Real Terms', 16 August, www.economist.com/node/16834943 (accessed 30 September 2012).

——(2012a) 'China in your Hand: A Brief Guide to Why China Grows so Fast', 25 May, www.economist.com/blogs/graphicdetail/2012/05/daily-chart-16 (accessed 30 September 2012).

——(2012b) 'The Rise of State Capitalism—Special Report', 21 January: 3–18.

Edison, H.J., Luangaram, P. and Miller, M. (1998) 'Asset Bubbles, Domino Effects and "Lifeboats": Elements of the East Asian Crisis', *CEPR Discussion Paper No. 1866*, London: Centre for Economic Policy Research.

Select bibliography

Ee, K.H. and Zheng, K.W. (2009) 'Ten Years From the Financial Crisis: Managing the Challenges Posed by Capital Flows', in R.W. Carney (ed.) *Lessons from the Asian Financial Crisis*, New York: Routledge, 84–111.
Eggertsson, T. (2004) *Economic Behaviour and Institutions*, Cambridge: Cambridge University Press.
Eichengreen, B. (1993) *Reconstructing Europe's Trade and Payments: The European Payments System*, Manchester: Manchester University Press.
——(1996) 'Institutions and Economic Growth: Europe after World War II', in N. Crafts and G. Toniolo (eds) *Economic Growth in Europe since 1945*, Cambridge: Cambridge University Press, 38–70.
——(2000) 'The EMS Crisis in Retrospect', *NBER Working Papers*, no. 8035, www.nber.org/papers/w8035.
——(2007) *The European Economy Since 1945*, Princeton, NJ and Oxford: Princeton University Press.
——(2008) *Globalizing Capital*, London: Princeton University Press.
ELSTAT (Hellenic Statistical Services) (1979–2010) *Concise Statistical Yearbook*, Athens: ELSTAT.
Elsthain, J.B. (2001) 'Why Public Intellectuals?' *The Wilson Quarterly* 45(4): 43–50.
Emmanuel, A. (1972) *Unequal Exchange*, London: New Left Books.
Estevadeordal, A. and Taylor, A.M. (2013) 'Is the Washington Consensus Dead? Growth, Openness, and the Great Liberalization, 1970s–2000s', *Review of Economics and Statistics* 95(5): 1669–90.
Estrin, S., Hanousek, J., Kocenka, E. and Svejnar, J. (2009) 'The Effects of Privatisation and Ownership in Transition Economies', *Journal of Economic Literature* 47(2): 699–728.
European Commission (1990) *European Economy. Annual Economic Report 1990–91*, Brussels.
Evangelist, M. and Sathe, V. (2006) 'Brazil's 1998–99 Currency Crisis', unpublished paper.
Evans, P.B. (1995) *Embedded Autonomy: States and Industrial Transformation*, Princeton, NJ: Princeton University Press.
Fazio, G. (2010) 'Emerging Markets and the Global Financial Crisis', in L.S. Talani (ed.) *The Global Crash: Towards a New Global Financial Regime?* London: Palgrave, 100–20.
Feinberg, R. (2008) 'Competitiveness and Democracy', *Latin American Politics and Society* 50(1): 153–68.
Felker, G. (2009) 'The Political Economy of Southeast Asia', in M. Beeson (ed.) *Contemporary Southeast Asia*, Aldershot: Palgrave Macmillan, 46–73.
Feridun, M. (2004) 'Russian Financial Crisis of 1998: An Econometric Investigation', *International Journal of Applied Econometrics and Quantitative Studies* 1(4): 113–22.
Ferraro, V. (n.d.) 'The Theory of Hegemonic Stability, www.mtholyoke.edu/acad/intrel/pol116/hegemony.htm (accessed 30 September 2012).
Financial Times (2011a) 'Editorial', 17 June.
——(2011b) 'Editorial', 24 October.
Fischer, S. (1987) 'British Monetary Policy', in R. Dornbusch and R. Layard (eds) *The Performance of the British Economy*, Oxford: Oxford University Press.
Foley, D.K. (2007) 'The Economic-Historical Roots of U.S. Foreign Policy', New York University series—*Critical Issues in Global Affairs*, 18 November.
Foroohar, R. (2013) 'What China's Oldest Steel Factory Says About the Nation's Future', Time.com, business.time.com/2013/06/16/red-steel-city-what-chinas-oldest-

steel-factory-says-about-the-nations-future/#ixzz2qVVPKIWd (accessed 14 January 2014).
Foster, J.B. (2006) 'The Household Debt Bubble', *Monthly Review* 58(1) (May), monthlyreview.org/0506jbf.htm (accessed January 2009).
Foster, J.B. and Magdoff, F. (2009) *The Great Financial Crisis: Causes and Consequences*, New York: NYU Press.
Fouskas, V.K. (1995) *Populism and Modernization. The Exhaustion of the Third Hellenic Republic, 1974–1994* (in Greek), Athens: Ideokinissi.
——(1997) 'The Left and the Crisis of the Third Hellenic Republic, 1989–97', in D. Sassoon (ed.) *Looking Left. European Socialism after the Cold War*, London: I.B. Tauris.
——(2003) *Zones of Conflict*, London: Pluto Press.
Fouskas, V.K. and Dimoulas, C. (2012) 'The Greek Workshop of Debt and the Failure of the European Project', *Journal of Balkan and Near Eastern Studies* 14(1).
——(2013) *Greece, Financialization and the EU. The Political Economy of Debt and Destruction*, London and New York: Palgrave-Macmillan.
Fouskas, V.K. and Gökay, B. (2005) *The New American Imperialism*, Westport, CT: Praeger.
——(2012) *The Fall of the US Empire, Global Fault-Lines and Shifting Imperial Orders*, London: Pluto Press.
Frank, A.G. (1971 [1965]) *Capitalism and Underdevelopment in Latin America. Historical Studies of Chile and Brazil*, rev. edn, Harmondsworth: Penguin.
Freris, A. (1986) *The Greek Economy in the 20th Century*, Athens: Croom Helm.
Friedman, M. and Schwartz, A.J. (1963) *A Monetary History of the United States, 1867–1960*, Princeton, NJ: Princeton University Press.
Fukuyama, F. (2006) *The End of History and the Last Man*, New York: Avon Books.
Fülberth, G. (1991) *Sieben Anstrengungen, den vorläufigen Endsieg des Kapitalismus zu begreifen*, Hamburg: Konkret.
Galbraith, J.K. (1967) *The New Industrial State*, Harmondsworth: Penguin.
——(2009 [1955]) *The Great Crash 1929*, London: Penguin Books.
——(2012) *Inequality and Instability*, Oxford: Oxford University Press.
Garber, P.M. (1993) 'The Collapse of the Bretton Woods Fixed Exchange Rate System', in M.D. Bordo and B. Eichengreen (eds) *A Retrospective on the Bretton Woods System: Lessons for International Monetary Reform*, Chicago, IL: University of Chicago Press, 461–94.
——(1998) 'Notes on the Role of Target in a Stage III Crisis', *NBER Working Paper Series*, no. 6619, www.nber.org/papers/w6619.
Germain, R. (2010) *Global Politics and Financial Governance*, Palgrave Macmillan.
Giavazzi, F. and Giovannini, A. (1989) *Limiting Exchange Rate Flexibility: The European Monetary System*, Cambridge, MA: MIT Press.
Gilbert, M. (2000) *The Second World War*, London: Phoenix.
Gilpin, R. (1987) *Political Economy of International Relations*, Princeton, NJ: Princeton University Press.
Gimbel, J. (1976) *The Origins of the Marshall Plan*, Stanford, CA: Stanford University Press.
Glynn, A. (2007) *Capitalism Unleashed*, Oxford: Oxford University Press.
Gökay, B. (ed.) (2006) *The Politics of Oil*, Abingdon: Routledge.
——(2009) 'Tectonic Shifts and Systemic Faultlines: A Global Perspective to Understand the 2008–9 World Economic Crisis', *Alternatives* 8(1) (Spring), www.alternativesjournal.net/volume8/number1/Gökay.pdf.

Select bibliography

Gökay, B. and Whitman, D. (2009) 'Mapping the Faultlines: A Historical Perspective on the 2008–9 World Economic Crisis', *Cultural Logic*, clogic.eserver.org/2009/Gökay_Whitman.pdf.

Goldin, C. and Katz, L.F. (1999) *The Returns to Skill in the United States across the Twentieth Century*, Cambridge, MA: National Bureau of Economic Research.

Goldman Sachs (2001) *Building Better Global Economic BRICs*, New York: Goldman Sachs Global Economic Group.

——(2007) *BRICs and Beyond*, New York: Goldman Sachs Global Economic Group.

Goodhart, C. (1998) 'The Two Concepts of Money: Implications for the Analysis of Optimal Currency Areas', *European Journal of Political Economy* 14: 407–32.

Gore, C. (2000) 'The Rise and Fall of the Washington Consensus as a Paradigm for Developing Countries', *World Development* 28(5): 789–804.

Gowa, J. (1983) *Closing the Gold Window*, Ithaca, NY: Cornell University Press.

Gowan, P. (1995) 'The Theory of and Practice of Neo-liberalism for Eastern Europe', *New Left Review* 213: 1.

——(1999) *The Global Gamble*, London: Verso.

——(2009) 'Crisis in the Heartland: Consequences of the New Wall Street System', Editorial of the *New Left Review* (January–February): 25.

——(2010) *A Calculus of Power*, London: Verso.

Gramsci, A. (1971) *Selections from the Prison Notebooks*, trans. and ed. Q. Hoare and G.N. Smith, New York: International Publishers (written 1929–35).

Gray, J. (1999) 'IMF Suddenly Hears the Poor', *The Australian Financial Review*, 4 October.

Greenspan, A. (2008) 'Greenspan: Economy in "Once-in-a-Century" Crisis', CNNMoney.com, 14 September, money.cnn.com/2008/09/14/news/economy/greenspan/index.htm?cnn=yes (accessed October 2008).

Greider, W. (1989) *The Secrets of the Temple*, New York: Touchstone.

Grenville, S. (2009) 'Ten Years After the Asian Crisis: Is the IMF Ready for "Next Time"?', in R.W. Carney (ed.) *Lessons From the Asian Financial Crisis*, New York: Routledge, 198–221.

Gros, D. and Thygesen, N. (1998) *European Monetary Integration*, Harlow: Addison Wesley Longman.

Grubel, H. (1977) *The International Monetary System*, Harmondsworth: Penguin.

Guajardo, J., Leigh, D. and Pescatori, A. (2011) 'Expansionary Austerity: New International Evidence', *IMF Working Paper* 11/158 (July).

The Guardian (2008) 'IMF Says US Crisis is "Largest Financial Shock since Great Depression"', Guardian.co.uk, 9 April, www.guardian.co.uk/business/2008/apr/09/useconomy.subprimecrisis (accessed October 2008).

Gulalp, H. (1986) 'Debate of Capitalism and Development: The Theories of Samir Amin and Bill Warren', *Capital and Class* 28: 39–59.

Gulde, A.M. and Schulze-Ghattas, M. (1993) 'Purchasing Power Parity Based Weights for the World Economic Outlook', *Staff Studies for the World Economic Outlook*, Washington, DC: IMF.

Gurría, A. (2008) 'OECD Observer', October, www.oecdobserver.org/news/fullstory.php/aid/2753/ (accessed January 2009).

Guttmann, R. (2008) 'A Primer on Finance-Led Capitalism and its Crisis', Revue de la régulation 3/4(2), 15 November, regulation.revues.org/document5843.html (accessed February 2009).

Gyntelberg, J. and Schrimpf, A. (2011) 'FX Strategies in Periods of Distress', *BIS Quarterly Review*, December issue.
Haggard, S. (1990) *Pathways from the Periphery: The Politics of Growth in Newly Industrializing Countries*, Ithaca, NY: Cornell University Press.
Hakimian, H. (2011) 'The Economic Prospects of the "Arab Spring": A Bumpy Road Ahead', *CDPR Development ViewPoint* 63: 1–2.
Hale, D.D. (1998) 'The IMF, Now More than Ever: The Case for Financial Peacekeeping', *Foreign Affairs* 77(6): 7–13.
Halliday, F. (1983) *The Making of the Second Cold War*, London: Verso.
Halper, S. (2010) *The Beijing Consensus: Legitimizing Authoritarianism in Our Time*, New York: Basic Books.
Harberler, G. (1953) 'Reflections of the Future of the Bretton Woods System', *American Economic Review* 43(2): 81–95.
Harvey, D. (2003) *The New Imperialism*, New York: Oxford University Press.
——(2005) *A Brief History of Neo-liberalism*, Oxford: Oxford University Press.
Hassouna, H.A. (2001) 'Arab Democracy: The Hope', *World Policy Journal* 18(3): 49–52.
Hayek, F.A. (1935) *Collectivist Economic Planning*, London: Routledge.
——(1945) 'The Use of Knowledge in Society', *American Economic Review* 25(4): 519–30.
——(1979) *Law, Legislation and Liberty Vol. 3: The Political Order of a Free People*, Chicago: University of Chicago Press.
He, T. (2013) 'Feudalism Makes a Comeback in China: The Linguistic Quirks of a Bygone Era Signal the Inequalities of the Present', *The Atlantic*, www.theatlantic.com/china/archive/2013/08/feudalism-makes-a-comeback-in-china/278945/ (accessed 13 January 2014).
Held, D. (2005) 'At the Global Crossroads: The End of the Washington Consensus and the Rise of Global Social Democracy?' *Globalizations* 2(1): 95–113.
Hellenic Association of Banks (2011) *The Greek Banking System in 2010* (in Greek), Athens.
Hewison, K. (2000) 'Thailand's Capitalism Before and After the Economic Crisis', in Richard Robison *et al.* (eds) *Politics and Markets in the Wake of the Asian Crisis*, London: Routledge, 192–211.
Higgott, R. (2000) 'The International Relations of the Asian Economic Crisis: A Study in the Politics of Resentment', in Richard Robison *et al.* (eds) *Politics and Markets in the Wake of the Asian Crisis*, London: Routledge, 261–82.
Hilferding, R. (1973 [1910]) *Das Finanzkapital*, Frankfurt: Europäische Verlagsanstalt.
Hogan, M.J. (1987) *The Marshall Plan, Britain, and the Reconstruction of Western Europe, 1947–1952*, Cambridge: Cambridge University Press.
Holbig, H. and Gilley, B. (2010) 'Reclaiming Legitimacy in China', *Politics & Policy* 38(3): 395–422.
Hope, K. (1998) 'A Big Market Close to Home', *Financial Times,* Special Survey of Greece, 8 December.
——(2011) 'History of Statistics that Failed to Add Up', *Financial Times*, 30 September.
Hudson, M. (2003) *Super-Imperialism*, London: Pluto Press.
Hughes, H.S. (1958) *Consciousness and Society. The Reorientation of European Social Thought 1890–1930*, New York: Vintage.
Hung, H.F. (2009) 'America's Head Servant', *New Left Review* II(60): 5–25.
——(2011) 'Sinomania: Global Crisis, China's Crisis?' in L. Panitch, C. Leys and G. Albo (eds) *The Socialist Register 2012*, London: Merlin, 217–34.

Select bibliography

Husson, M. (2011) 'A European Strategy for the Left', *International Viewpoint*.
Ikenberry, J.G. (1993) 'The Political Origins of Bretton Woods', in M.D. Bordo and B. Eichengreen (eds) *A Retrospective on the Bretton Woods System: Lessons for International Monetary Reform*, Chicago, IL: University of Chicago Press, 155–82.
ILO (International Labour Organization) (2012a) 'ILOStats: Statistics and Databases', ilo.org/global/statistics-and-databases/lang-en/index.htm.
——(2012b) *Global Employment Trends 2012*, Geneva: ILO.
IMF (International Monetary Fund) (1990) *Annual Report 1990*, Washington, DC: IMF.
——(1994) *Annual Report 1994*, Washington, DC: IMF.
——(1997a) *Annual Report 1997*, Washington, DC: IMF.
——(1997b) *Good Governance: The IMF's Role*, Washington, DC: IMF.
——(1998) *Annual Report 1998*, Washington, DC: IMF.
——(1999) *Annual Report 1999*, Washington, DC: IMF.
——(2010) *Balance of Payments and International Investment Position Manual*.
——(2012a) 'GDP Based on PPP Share of World Total', *World Economic Outlook*.
——(2012b) 'World Economic Outlook, October, 2012', Washington, DC: IMF Publication Services.
——(2013) *World Economic Outlook Database*, www.imf.org/external/pubs/ft/weo/2013/02/weodata/index.aspx.
Irwin, D. (1995) 'The GATT's Contribution to Economic Recovery in Post-War Western Europe', in B. Eichengreen (ed.) *Europe's Postwar Recovery*, Cambridge: Cambridge University Press.
Ito, T. (2007) 'Asian Currency Crisis and the International Monetary Fund, 10 Years Later: Overview', *Asian Economic Policy Review* 2(1): 16–49.
Jalée, P. (1973) *L'impérialisme en 1970*, Paris: Maspero.
Jansen, M.B. (1954) *The Japanese and Sun Yat-Sen*, Stanford, CA: Stanford University Press.
Jayasuriya, K. (2000) 'Authoritarian Liberalism, Governance and the Emergence of the Regulatory State in Post-Crisis East Asia', in Richard Robison *et al.* (eds) *Politics and Markets in the Wake of the Asian Crisis*, London: Routledge, 315–30.
Jayman, J. (2004) *A Critical Understanding of Japan's Improved Late 20th Century Relations in Eastern Asia*, doctoral dissertation, London: London School of Economics.
Jenkins, R. (1991) 'The Political Economy of Industrialisation: A Comparison of Latin America and East Asian Newly Industrializing Countries', *Development and Change* 22: 197–231.
Jessop, B. and Sum, N.-L. (2001) 'Pre-disciplinary and Post-disciplinary Perspectives', *New Political Economy* 6(1): 89–101.
Joffé, G. (2011) 'The Arab Spring in North Africa: Origins and Prospects', *The Journal of North African Studies* 16(4): 507–32.
Johnson, C. (1982) *MITI and the Japanese Miracle: The Growth of Industrial Policy, 1925–1975*, Stanford, CA: Stanford University Press.
Jomo, K.S. (1998) 'Introduction: Financial Governance, Liberalisation and Crises in East Asia', in K.S. Jomo (ed.) *Tigers in Trouble: Financial Governance, Liberalisation and Crises in East Asia*, London: Zed Books, 1–32.
——(2000) 'Comment: Crisis and the Developmental State in East Asia', in Richard Robison *et al.* (eds) *Politics and Markets in the Wake of the Asian Crisis*, London: Routledge, 25–33.

——(2009) 'Causes of the 1997/1998 East Asian Crises and Obstacles to Implementing Lessons', in R.W. Carney (ed.) *Lessons from the Asian Financial Crisis*, New York: Routledge, 33–64.
Jorion, P. (2000) 'Risk Management Lessons from Long-Term Capital Management', *European Financial Management* 6(3): 277–300.
Kahn, R.F. (1950) 'The European Payments Union', *Economica* 17(67): 306–16.
Kalafatis, S. *et al.* (1990) *Lame-Ducks in the Greek Economy* (in Greek), Athens: OAED.
Kaplinsky, R. (2005) *Globalization, Poverty and Inequality*, Cambridge: Polity.
Katzenstein, P.J. (1997) 'Introduction: Asian Regionalism in Comparative Perspective', in P.J. Katzenstein (ed.) *Network Power: Japan and Asia*, New York: Cornell University Press, 1–45.
Kautsky, K. (1914) 'Der Imperialismus', *Die Neue Zeit*, 1913–14, 2. Band: 908–22.
Keating, M.F. (1999) 'Divergence and Convergence between the IMF and the World Bank's Conceptions of Development during the 1990s', in *Proceedings of the 1999 Conference of the Australasian Political Studies Association*, Volume II: Refereed Papers, Sydney: University of Sydney, 429–38.
Keating, M.F., Kuzemko, C., Belyi, A.V. and Goldthau, A. (2012) 'Introduction: Bringing Energy into International Political Economy', in C. Kuzemko, A.V. Belyi, A. Goldthau and M.F. Keating (eds) *Dynamics of Energy Governance in Europe and Russia*, Basingstoke: Palgrave Macmillan, 1–22.
Kennedy, P. (1987) *The Rise and Fall of the Great Powers: Economic Change and Military Conflict From 1500 to 2000*, Fontana Press.
Kennen, P.B. (ed.) (1994) *Managing the World Economy*, Washington, DC: Institute for International Economics.
Kenwood, G. and Lougheed, A. (1992) *The Growth of the International Economy, 1820–2000*, London: Routledge.
Keohane, R. and Nye, J. (1977) *Power and Interdependence: World Politics in Transition*, Boston, MA: Little, Brown.
Keynes, J.M. (1936) *The General Theory of Employment, Interest, and Money*, New York: Harcourt Brace Jovanovich.
——(2011 [1921]) *A Treatise on Probability*, La Vergne, TN: Lightning Source.
Khan, M. (2012) 'What Economic Model is Egypt Going to Adopt?' VoxEU.org, 8 November.
Khandelwal, P. and Roitman, A. (2013) 'The Economics of Political Transitions: Implications for the Arab Spring', *IMF Working Paper No. 13/69*.
Khanna, P. (2009) *The Second World*, Harmondsworth: Penguin.
Khor, M. (2008) 'The Malaysian Experience in Financial-Economic Crisis Management: An Alternative to the IMF-Style Approach', in J.A. Ocampo and J.E. Stiglitz (eds) *Capital Market Liberalization and Development*, Oxford: Oxford University Press, 205–25.
Kiely, R. (2010) *Rethinking Imperialism*, Basingstoke: Palgrave.
Kindleberger, C.P. (1973) *The World in Depression, 1929–39*, Berkeley, CA: University of California Press, 291.
——(1981) 'Dominance and Leadership in the International Economy: Exploitation, Public Goods, and Free Rides', *International Studies Quarterly* 25: 242–54.
——(1986) 'International Public Goods without International Government', *The American Economic Review* 76: 1–13.

Select bibliography

Kitromilides, Y. (2011) 'Deficit Reduction, the Age of Austerity and the Paradox of Insolvency', *Journal of Post-Keynesian Economics* (Spring).
——(2012) 'The 1929 Crash and the Great Recession of 2008', *Challenge* 55(1) (January–February).
Klein, N. (2010 [2000]) *No Logo*, revised edn, New York: Picador.
Koopmans, T.C. and Montias, J.M. (1973) 'On the Description and Comparison of Economic Systems', in A. Eckstein (ed.) *Comparison of Economic Systems: Theoretical and Methodological Approaches*, Berkeley: University of California Press.
Kornai, J. (1990) *The Road to a Free Economy. Shifting from a Socialist System: The Example of Hungary*, New York: W.W. Norton.
Krippendorff, E. (1982 [1975]) *International Relations as a Social Science*, Brighton: Harvester.
Krugman, P. (1979) 'A Model of Balance-of-Payments Crises', *Journal of Money, Credit, and Banking* 11(3): 311–25.
——(1991a) *Geography and Trade*, Cambridge, MA: MIT Press.
——(1991b) 'Increasing Returns and Economic Geography', *Journal of Political Economy* 99: 483–99.
——(1995) 'Growing World Trade: Causes and Consequences', *Brookings Papers on Economic Activity* 1: 327–62.
——(2000) *The Return of Depression Economics*, London: W.W. Norton & Co.
——(2008) *The Return of Depression Economics and the Crisis of 2008*, Harmondsworth: Penguin Books.
——(2010) 'Fiscal Scare Tactics', *The New York Times*, 4 February, 25.
——(2012) *End this Depression Now*, New York: W.W. Norton.
Krugman, P. and Obstfeld, M. (2008) *International Economics*, New York: Pearson.
Kuczynski, J. (1977) *Gesellschaftswissenschaftliche Schulen*, Vol. 7 of *Studien zu einer Geschichte der Gesellschaftswissenschaften*, Berlin: Akademie-Verlag.
Kuznets, S. (1955) 'Economic Growth and Income Inequality', *The American Economic Review* 45(1): 1–28.
Labriola, A. (1908 [1896]) *Essays on the Materialistic Conception of History*, trans. C. H. Kerr, Chicago, IL: Charles H. Kerr & Co.
Lal, D. (1983) *The Poverty of Development Economics*, London: The Institute of Economic Affairs.
——(1999) *Renewing the Miracle: Economic Development and Asia*, Melbourne, Victoria: Institute of Public Affairs.
——(2012) 'Is the Washington Consensus Dead?' *Cato Journal* 32(3).
Lapavitsas, C. (2011) 'Euro-exit Strategy Crucial for Greeks', *The Guardian*, 21 June.
——(2013) *Profiting without Producing*, London: Verso.
Lapavitsas, C. et al. (2010) 'Euro-zone Crisis: Beggar Thyself and Thy Neighbour', *Journal of Balkan and Near Eastern Studies* 12(4) (December).
Lasswell, H. (1997) *Essays on the Garrison State*, New Brunswick, NJ: Transaction Publishers.
Lauridsen, L.S. (1998) 'Thailand: Causes, Conduct, Consequences', in K.S. Jomo (ed.) *Tigers in Trouble: Financial Governance, Liberalisation and Crises in East Asia*, London: Zed Books, 137–61.
Layne, C. (2006) *The Peace of Illusions*, Ithaca, NY: Cornell University Press.
Leftwich, A. (2000) *States of Development: On the Primacy of Politics in Development*, Cambridge: Polity.

Lenin, V.I. (1917) *Imperialism, the Highest Stage of Capitalism*, in *Collected Works*, vol. XXII, Moscow: Progress.

Lin, J.Y. (1999) 'Policy Burdens, Soft Budget Constraint and State-owned Enterprise Reform in China', Peking University and Hong Kong University of Science and Technology, www.bm.ust.hk/~ced/soereform.pdf (accessed 30 September 2012).

Lindert, P.H. and Williamson, J.G. (1985) 'Growth, Equality, and History', *Explorations in Economic History* 22(4): 341–77.

Lippmann, W. (2010 [1922]) *Public Opinion*, n.p.: BNPublishing.com.

Lipton, D. and Sachs, J. (1990) 'Privatisation in Eastern Europe: The Case of Poland', *Brookings Papers on Economic Activity* 2: 293–341.

List, F. (1928 [1841]) *The National System of Political Economy*, London: Longmans, Green & Co.

Locke, J. (1993 [1690]) *An Essay Concerning Human Understanding*, abridged and ed. J.W. Yolton, London: Dent; Vermont: Tuttle.

Luxemburg, R. (1966 [1913]) *Die Akkumulation des Kapitals. Ein Beitrag zur Ökonomischen Erklärung des Imperialismus*, Frankfurt: Neue Kritik.

——(2003 [1951]) *The Accumulation of Capital*, New York: Routledge.

MacIntyre, A. (ed.) (1994) *Business and Government in Industrialising Asia*, St Leonards: Allen and Unwin.

Magdoff, H. (1969) *The Age of Imperialism. The Economics of U.S. Foreign Policy*, New York: Monthly Review Press.

Malik, A. and Awadallah, B. (2013) 'The Economics of the Arab Spring', *World Development* 45(0): 296–313.

Mandel, E. (1969) 'Where is America Going?' *New Left Review* 54.

——(1975) *Late Capitalism*, London: New Left Books.

——(1980) *The Second Slump*, London: Verso.

Mankiw, N.G. (2012) *Macroeconomics*, New York: Worth.

Mao T. (1926) 'Analysis of the Classes in Chinese Society', in *Selected Works of Mao Tse-tung*, March, www.marxists.org/reference/archive/mao/selected-works/volume-1/mswv1_1.htm#bm1 (accessed 14 January 2014).

Marx, K. (1976) *Capital*, vol. 1, Harmondsworth: Penguin.

Marx, K. and Engels, F. (1956–71) *Marx-Engels Werke*, 35 vols, Berlin: Dietz. Vols. 23–25 contain *Capital*, I–III.

McDonald, R. (2005) *The Competitiveness of the Greek Economy*, Athens: Athens News Press.

Meek, R. (1972 [1956]) 'The Marginal Revolution and its Aftermath', in E.K. Hunt and Jesse G. Schwartz (eds) *A Critique of Economic Theory*, Harmondsworth: Penguin.

Mikesell, R.F. (1994) 'The Bretton Woods Debates: A Memoir', *Essays in International Finance*, No. 192, Princeton, NJ: International Finance Section.

——(1995) 'Some Issues in the Bretton Woods Debates', in O. Kirschner (ed.) *The Bretton Woods-GATT System: Retrospect and Prospect After 50 Years*, New York: M.E Sharpe, 19–29.

Mikesell, R.F. and Furth, J.H. (1974) 'The Behavior of Foreign Dollar Holdings', in R.F. Mikesell and J.H. Furth (eds) *Foreign Dollar Balances and the International Role of the Dollar*, Cambridge, MA: NBER, 58–84.

Milanovic, B. (2003) 'The Two Faces of Globalization: Against Globalization as we Know it', *World Development* 31(4): 667–83.

Select bibliography

Milios, J. and Sotiropoulos, D.P. (2009) *Rethinking Imperialism: A Study of Capitalist Rule*, London and New York: Palgrave Macmillan.
——(2010) 'Crisis of Greece or Crisis of Euro? A View from the European "Periphery"', *Journal of Balkan and Near Eastern Studies* 12(3): 223–40.
Milne, R. and Wiesmann, G. (2011) 'ECB Ready to Reject Greek Downgrade', *Financial Times*, 5 July.
Milner, H. (1998) 'International Political Economy: Beyond Hegemonic Stability', *Foreign Policy* 110.
Milward, A.S. (1984) *The Reconstruction of Western Europe, 1945–1951*, London: Methuen.
Monthly Review (The Editors) (2000) 'Working Class Households and the Burden of Debt', *Monthly Review* 50(1) (May), monthlyreview.org/500editr.htm (accessed September 2008).
Moreno-Brid, J.C., Caldentey, E.P. and Nápoles, P.R. (2004) 'The Washington Consensus: A Latin American Perspective Fifteen Years Later', *Journal of Post Keynesian Economics* 27(2): 345–65.
Moschella, M. (2010) *Governing Risk: The IMF and Global Financial Crises*, Hampshire: Palgrave Macmillan.
Mosley, L. and Singer, D.A. (2011) 'The Global Financial Crisis: Lessons and Opportunities for International Political Economy', in N. Phillips and C. Weaver (eds) *International Political Economy: Debating the Past, Present and Future*, Abingdon: Routledge, 223–30.
Mundell, R. (1961) 'A Theory of Optimal Currency Areas', *American Economic Review* 51 (September): 657–65.
Murphy, M.R. Taggart (1989) 'Power without Purpose: The Crisis of Japan's Global Financial Dominance', *Harvard Business Review* 2 (March–April).
Myrdal, D. (1969) *Objectivity in Social Research*, London: Pantheon Books.
Nabli, M.K. (2008) 'Middle East and North Africa: Recent Economic Developments and Prospects', IDB Lecture Series 2: Islamic Development Bank, Saudi Arabia.
Naím, M. (2000) 'Washington Consensus or Washington Confusion?' *Foreign Policy* 118: 87–103.
Neiss, H. (2009) 'Conclusions', in R.W. Carney (ed.) *Lessons from the Asian Financial Crisis*, New York: Routledge, 249–56.
Nester, W.R. (1993) *American Power, the New World Order and the Japanese Challenge*, New York: Palgrave Macmillan.
Nesvetailova, A. (2010) *Financial Alchemy in Crisis: The Great Liquidity Illusion*, London: Pluto Press.
Newton, C. (1984) 'The Sterling Crisis of 1947 and the British Response to the Marshall Plan', *The Economic History Review*, New Series, 37(3): 391–408.
NIC (2008) *Global Trends 2025*, Washington: National Intelligence Council.
Nie, S. (2005) 'Short History of Reforms Concerning Chinese State Owned Enterprises', Shanghai Flash, Commercial Section, Consulate General of Switzerland in Shanghai, No. 2, www.sinoptic.ch/shanghaiflash/2005/200502.htm (accessed 30 September 2012).
Nitzan, J. and Bichler, S. (2002) *The Global Political Economy of Israel*, London: Pluto Press.
Nolan, P. and Zhang, J. (2010) 'Global Competition after the Financial Crisis', *New Left Review* II(64): 97–108.

Nonneman, G. (1996) *Political and Economic Liberalization: Dynamics and Linkages in Comparative Perspective*, Boukder, CO: Lynne Rienner Publishers.

North, D. (1990) *Institutions, Institutional Change and Economic Performance*, Cambridge: Cambridge University Press.

Nye, J. (2010) 'American and Chinese Power after the Financial Crisis', *Washington Quarterly* 33(4): 143–53.

O'Brien, K.J. and Li, L. (2006 [1975]) *Rightful Resistance in Rural China*, New York and Cambridge: Cambridge University Press.

Obstfeld, M. (1993) 'The Adjustment Mechanism', in M.D. Bordo and B. Eichengreen (eds) *A Retrospective on the Bretton Woods System: Lessons for International Monetary Reform*, Chicago, IL: University of Chicago Press, 201–56.

Obstfeld, M., Shambaugh, J.C. and Taylor, A.M. (2008) 'Financial Stability, the Trilemma, and International Reserves', emlab.berkeley.edu/~obstfeld/OSTreserves.pdf.

Ocampo, J.A. (2004) 'Beyond the Washington Consensus: What Do We Mean?' *Journal of Post Keynesian Economics* 27(2): 293–314.

Ocampo, J.A., Spiegel, S. and Stiglitz, J.E. (2008) 'Capital Market Liberalization and Development', in J.A. Ocampo and J.E. Stiglitz (eds) *Capital Market Liberalization and Development*, Oxford: Oxford University Press, 1–47.

OECD (Organisation for Economic Co-operation and Development) (1993) *Economic Surveys of Greece for 1993*, Paris: Organisation for Economic Co-operation and Development.

——(2003) *Privatising State-Owned Enterprises. An Overview of Policies and Practices in OECD Countries*, Paris: OECD.

Offe, C. (1994) *The Contradictions of the Welfare State*, Cambridge, MA: MIT Press.

Ohlin, B. (1933) *Interregional and International Trade*, Cambridge, MA: Harvard University Press.

Okfen, N. (2003) 'Towards an East Asian Community? What ASEM and APEC Can Tell Us', *CSGR Working Paper No. 117/03* University of Warwick, Centre for the Study of Globalisation and Regionalisation, June.

O'Sullivan, A., Rey, M.-E. and Galvez, M. (2012) 'Opportunities and Challenges in the MENA Region', *The Arab World Competitiveness Report, 2011–2012*.

Overbeek, H. (2000) 'Transnational Historical Materialism', in R. Palan (ed.) *Contemporary Theories in Global Political Economy*, London: Routledge.

Paggi, L. and d'Angelillo, M. (1986) *I comunisti italiani e il riformismo*, Turin: Einaudi.

Pagoulatos, G. and Triantopoulos, C. (2009) 'The Return of the Greek Patient: Greece and the 2008 Global Financial Crisis', *South European Society and Politics*, 14 March.

Palley, T. (2012) *From Financial Crisis to Stagnation*, Cambridge: Cambridge University Press.

Palloix, C. (1973) *Les firmes multinationales et le procès d'internationalisation*, Paris: Maspero.

Panitch, L. (2012) *The Making of Modern Capitalism*, London: Verso.

Panitch, L. and Gindin, S. (2005) 'Finance and the American Empire', *Socialist Register*.

Parmar, I. (2012) *Foundations of the American Century. The Ford, Carnegie and Rockefeller Foundations in the Rise of American Power*, New York: Columbia University Press.

Pauly, L.W. (1994) 'Promoting a Global Economy: The Normative Role of the International Monetary Fund', in Richard Stubbs and Geoffrey Underhill (eds) *Political Economy and the Changing Global Order*, London: MacMillan.

Pennington, M. (2011) *Robust Political Economy*, Cheltenham: Edward Elgar.

Select bibliography

Perotti, E. (2002) 'Lessons from the Russian Meltdown: The Economics of Soft Legal Constraints', *International Finance* 5(3): 359–99.
Pettifor, A. (2008) 'America's Financial Meltdown: Lessons and Prospects', openDemocracy, 16 September, www.opendemocracy.net/article/america-s-financial-meltdown-lessons-and-prospects (accessed January 2009).
Pineda, J. and Rodriguez, F. (2006) 'The Political Economy of Investment in Human Capital', *Economics of Governance* 7(2): 167–93.
Pinto, B. and Ulatov, S. (2010) 'Financial Globalization and the Russian Crisis of 1998', *Policy Research Working Paper Series No.5312*, Washington, DC: World Bank.
Polanyi, K. (2001 [1944]) *The Great Transformation: The Political and Economic Origins of Our Time*, Boston, MA: Beacon Press.
Poliakov, L. and Wulf, J. (eds) (1989 [1959]) *Das Dritte Reich und seine Denker*, Wiesbaden: Fourier.
Pollard, S. (1997) *The International Economy*, London: Routledge.
Polterovich, V. (2012) *Institutional Reform Design*, paper presented at ESHET Conference, St Petersburg, 19 May.
Popper, K. (1973) *The Open Society and its Enemies*, London: Routledge & Kegan Paul.
Poulantzas, N. (1971) *Pouvoir politique et classes sociales*, 2 vols, Paris: Maspero.
——(1974a [1970]) *Fascisme et dictature*, 2nd edn, Paris: Le Seuil/Maspero.
——(1974b) *Les classes sociales dans le capitalism aujourd'hui*, Paris: Maspero.
——(1975) *Classes in Contemporary Capitalism*, London: New Left Books.
——(2008 [1973]) 'Internationalization of Capitalist Relations and the Nation-state', in J. Martin (ed.) *The Poulantzas Reader. Marxism, Law, and the State*, London: Verso.
Prasad, E., Rogoff, K., Wei, S.J. and Kose, M.A. (2003) 'Effects of Financial Globalisation on Developing Countries: Some Empirical Evidence', *IMF occasional Paper No. 220*, Washington, DC: International Monetary Fund.
Prebisch, R. (1959) 'Commercial Policy in the Underdeveloped Countries', *American Economic Review* 44: 251–73.
Prestowitz, C. (1993) *Trading Places—How We are Giving Our Future to Japan and How to Reclaim it*, New York: Basic Books.
Ramo, J. (2004) *The Beijing Consensus: Notes on the New Physics of Chinese Power*, London: Foreign Policy Centre.
Rauch, J.E. and Kostyshak, S. (2009) 'The Three Arab Worlds', *The Journal of Economic Perspectives* 23(3): 165–88.
Ravenhill, J. (2009) 'From Miracle to Misadventure: The Political Economy of the 1997–98 Crises', in R.W. Carney (ed.) *Lessons from the Asian Financial Crisis*, New York: Routledge, 15–32.
Rehmann, J. (1998) *Max Weber: Modernisierung als passive Revolution: Kontextstudien zu Politik, Philosophie und Religion im Übergang zum Fordismus*, Berlin: Argument Verlag.
Reinhart, C. and Rogoff, K. (2002) 'The Modern History of Exchange Rate Arrangements: A Reinterpretation', *NBER Working Paper*, No. 8963.
——(2009) *This Time is Different. Eight Centuries of Financial Folly*, Princeton, NJ: Princeton University Press.
Roberts, D. (2011) 'China's Growing Income Gap', *Bloomburg Businessweek Magazine*, 27 January, www.businessweek.com/magazine/content/11_06/b4214013648109.htm (accessed 30 September 2012).

SELECT BIBLIOGRAPHY

Robertson, J. (2007) 'Reconsidering American Interests in Emerging Market Crises: An Unanticipated Outcome to the Asian Financial Crisis', *Review of International Political Economy* 14(2): 276–305.

——(2008) *Power and Politics after Financial Crises: Rethinking Foreign Opportunism in Emerging Markets*, Palgrave Macmillan.

Robison, R. and Rosser, A. (2000) 'Surviving the Meltdown: Liberal Reform and Political Oligarchy in Indonesia', in Richard Robison *et al.* (eds) *Politics and Markets in the Wake of the Asian Crisis*, London: Routledge, 171–91.

Rodrik, D. (1998) 'Who Needs Capital Account Convertibility?' in S. Fischer *et al.* (eds) *Should the IMF Pursue Capital Account Convertibility?* Essays in International Finance No. 207, Princeton, NJ: Princeton University Press.

Rodrik, D. and Bank, W. (2006) 'Goodbye Washington Consensus, Hello Washington Confusion? A Review of the World Bank's "Economic Growth in the 1990s: Learning from a Decade of Reform"', *Journal of Economic Literature* 44(4): 973–87.

Rogoff, K. (2010) 'No Need for Panicked Fiscal Surge', *Financial Times*, 21 July, 13.

Rose, A.K. (1991) 'Why Has Trade Grown Faster than Income?' *The Canadian Journal of Economics* 24: 417–27.

Ross, D. (1991) *The Origins of American Social Science*, Cambridge: Cambridge University Press.

Rostow, W. (1960) *The Stages of Economic Growth*, Cambridge: Cambridge University Press.

Ruckert, A. (2006) 'Towards an Inclusive-neoliberal Regime of Development: From the Washington to the Post-Washington Consensus', *Labour, Capital and Society* 39 (1): 36–67.

Sachs, J. (1993) *Poland's Jump to the Market Economy*, Cambridge: MIT.

——(2005) *The End of Poverty*, London: Penguin,

Sachs, J.D. and Woo, W.T. (1999) 'Executive Summary: The Asian Financial Crisis: What Happened, and What is to Be Done', *World Economic Forum (Asia Competitiveness Report 1999)*.

Sainsbury, M. (2011) 'China Privatisation Machine into Reverse', *The Australian*, 27 January, www.theaustralian.com.au/business/china-privatisation-machine-into-revers e/story-e6frg8zx-1225995084947 (accessed 10 September 2012).

Sassoon, D. (1996) *One Hundred Years of Socialism*, London: I.B. Tauris.

Schenk, C.R. (2010) *The Decline of Sterling: Managing the Retreat of an International Currency, 1945–1992*, Cambridge: Cambridge University Press.

——(2011) *International Economic Relations Since 1945*, Abingdon: Routledge.

Schwartz, H. (2000) *States Against Markets*, London: Palgrave.

——(2009) *Sub-Prime Nation*, Ithaca, NY: Cornell University Press.

Seabrook, L. (2001) *US Power in International Finance*, London: Palgrave.

Sen, A. (2010) *The Idea of Justice*, London: Allen Lane.

——(2011) 'It Isn't the Euro. Europe's Democracy Itself is at Stake', *The Guardian*, 22 June, www.theguardian.com/commentisfree/2011/jun/22/euro-europes-democracy-rat ing-agencies.

Shafik, N. (1995) *Claiming the Future: Choosing Prosperity in the Middle East and North Africa: Summary*, World Bank.

Singer, H. (1950) 'The Distribution of Gains from Trade between Investing and Borrowing Countries', *American Economic Review* 40: 473–85.

Skidelsky, R. (2009) 'Why Market Sentiment has no Credibility', *Financial Times*, December, 22.

Select bibliography

——(2010) *Keynes: The Return of the Master*, London: Penguin Group.
Smith, A.L. (2001) 'Indonesia: Transforming the Leviathan', in J. Funston (ed.) *Government and Politics in Southeast Asia*, London: Zed Books, 74–119.
Smith, N. (2011) 'America's Global Implosion: From the Washington Consensus to the Arab Spring', *10 Years after September 11 A Social Science Research Council Essay Forum*.
Solomon, R. (1977) *The International Monetary System, 1945–1976: An Insider's View*, New York: Harper and Row.
Solow, R. (1956) 'A Contribution to the Theory of Economic Growth', *The Quarterly Journal of Economics* 70(1): 65–94.
Spangenberg, S. (1998) *The Institutionalised Transformation of the East German Economy*, Heidelberg: Physica Verlag.
The Spectator (2008) 'The True Extent of Britain's Debt', Spectator.co.uk, 10 December, www.spectator.co.uk/coffeehouse/3078296/the-true-extent-of-britains-debt.thtml (accessed January 2009).
Springborg, R. (2011a) 'The Political Economy of the Arab Spring', *Mediterranean Politics* 16(3): 427–33.
——(2011b) 'The Precarious Economics of Arab Springs', *Survival* 53(6): 85–104.
Stathakis, G. (2011) 'The Fiscal Crisis of the Greek Economy', in Scientific Association of Greek Political Economists, *Economic Crisis and Greece*, Athens: Gutenberg.
Steinfeld, E. (2004) 'China's Shallow Integration: Networked Production and the New Challenges for Late Industrialisation', *World Development* 32(11): 1971–87.
Steinherr, A. (2000) *Derivatives: The Wild Beast of Finance. A Path to Effective Globalization*. Chichester: John Wiley and Sons Ltd.
Stiglitz, J.E. (1998a) 'The Role of International Financial Institutions in the Current Global Economy', Address to the Chicago Council on Foreign Relations, Chicago, 27 February, Washington, DC: The World Bank.
——(1998b) 'Sound Finance and Sustainable Development in Asia', Keynote Address to the Asia Development Forum, Manila, 12 March, Washington, DC: The World Bank.
——(1999) 'More Instruments and Broader Goals: Moving Toward the Post-Washington Consensus', *Revista de Economia Política* 19(1): 94–120.
——(2000) 'Capital Market Liberalization, Economic Growth, and Instability', *World Development* 28(6): 1075–86.
——(2002) *Globalization and its Discontents*, London: Penguin.
——(2010) 'To Choose Austerity is to Bet it all on the Confidence Fairy', *The Guardian*, October, 19.
Stopford, J., Strange, S., with Henley, J.S. (1991) *Rival States, Rival Firms: Competition for World Market Shares*, Cambridge: Cambridge University Press.
Strange, S. (1987) 'The Persistent Myth of Lost Hegemony', *International Organization* 41(4) (Autumn): 551–74.
Stubbs, R. (2001) 'Performance Legitimacy and "Soft Authoritarianism"', in Amitav Acharya, B. Michael Frolic and Richard Stubbs (eds) *Democracy, Human Rights, and Civil Society in South East Asia*, Toronto: Joint Centre for Asia Pacific Studies, 37–54.
——(2005) *Rethinking Asia's Economic Miracle: The Political Economy of War, Prosperity and Crisis*, New York: Palgrave Macmillan.
Sumner, A. (2010) *Global Poverty and the New Bottom Billion*, Brighton: IDS Working Paper no. 349.

SELECT BIBLIOGRAPHY

Sun, J. (1999) 'Wage Reform, Soft Budget Constraints and Competition', Working papers No. 56, The United Nations University World Institute for Development Economics Research, February, www.wider.unu.edu/publications/working-papers/previous/en_GB/wp-156/_files/82530858957743082/default/wp156.pdf (accessed 30 September 2012).

Svensson, L.E.O. (1992) 'The Foreign Exchange Risk Premium in a Target Zone with Devaluation Risk', *Journal of International Economics* 33: 21–40.

Tabb, W.K. (2008) 'The Financial Crisis of U.S. Capitalism', *Monthly Review*, 10 October, www.monthlyreview.org/mrzine/tabb101008.html (accessed December 2008).

Tanoukhi, N. and Mazrui, A. (2011) 'Arab Spring and the Future of Leadership in North Africa', *Transition* 106: 148–62.

Taylor, A.J.P. (1957) *The Trouble-Makers, Dissent over Foreign Policy 1792–1939*, London: Hamish Hamilton.

Taylor, L. (1997) 'The Revival of the Liberal Creed—the IMF and the World Bank in a Globalized Economy', *World Development* 25(2): 145–52.

Terborgh, A.G. (2003) 'The Post-War Rise of World Trade: Does the Bretton Woods System Deserve Credit?', LSE Working Paper No. 78/03.

Theotokas, J. and Charlauti, G. (2007) *Greek Ship-owners and Maritime Business* (in Greek), Athens: Estia.

Therborn, G. (1976) *Science, Class and Society. On the Formation of Sociology and Historical Materialism*, London: Verso.

Thompson, E.P. (1968 [1963]) *The Making of the English Working Class*, Harmondsworth: Penguin.

Thompson, H. (2011) *Mortgaging America's Future*, London: Palgrave.

Tiek, K.B. (2000) 'Economic Nationalism and its Discontents: Malaysian Political Economy after July 1997', in Richard Robison et al. (eds) *Politics and Markets in the Wake of the Asian Crisis*, London: Routledge, 212–37.

——(2003) *Beyond Mahathir: Malaysian Politics and its Discontents*, London: Zed Books.

Tinbergen, J. (1952) *On the Theory of Economic Policy*, Amsterdam: North-Holland.

Tolios, J. (2011) *Crisis, 'Odious' Debt and Violation of Payments* (in Greek), Athens: Topos.

Triffin, R. (1961) *Gold and the Dollar Crisis*, Yale, CT: Yale University Press.

Tsai, K.S. (2007) *Capitalism without Democracy: The Private Sector in Contemporary China*, Ithaca, NY: Cornell University Press.

Tsoukalas, C. (1986) *State, Society, Labour in Post-war Greece* (in Greek), Athens: Themelio.

UNCTAD (2002a) *World Investment Report 2002*, Geneva: UNCTAD.

——(2002b) *Trade and Development Report 2002*, Geneva: UNCTAD.

——(2002c) *The Least Developed Countries Report 2002*, Geneva: UNCTAD.

——(2007) *World Investment Report 2007*, Geneva: UNCTAD.

——(2011) *Trade and Development Report 2011*, Geneva: UNCTAD.

UNDP (2010) *Human Development Report*, Washington, DC: World Bank.

——(2012) *Human Development Indicators*, Washington, DC: UNDP.

US Treasury (2013) 'Major Foreign Holders of US Treasuries', www.treasury.gov/resource-center/data-chart-center/tic/Documents/mfh.txt (accessed 8 January 2014).

van der Pijl, K. (2009) *A Survey of Global Political Economy*, PDF web-textbook, version 2.1. www.sussex.ac.uk/ir/research/gpe/gpesurvey.

——(2014) *The Discipline of Western Supremacy*, vol. III of *Modes of Foreign Relations and Political Economy*, London: Pluto.

Select bibliography

van Wolferen, K. (1990) *The Enigma of Japanese Power: People and Politics in a Stateless Nation*, London: Vintage Books.
Varoufakis, Y. (2013) *The Global Minotaur*, London and New York: Zed Books.
Vatikiotis, M. (1998) *Indonesian Politics Under Suharto: The Rise and Fall of the New Order*, third edn, New York: Routledge.
Veblen, T. (1994 [1899]) *The Theory of the Leisure Class*, New York: Penguin.
Volcker, P. and Gyohten, T. (1992) *Changing Fortunes*, New York: Times Books.
Volz, U. (2006) 'On the Feasibility of a Regional Exchange Rate System for East Asia: Lessons of the 1992/93 ERM Crisis', Working Paper: The Whitney and Betty MacMillan Center for International and Area Studies at Yale.
Wade, R. (1990) *Governing the Market: Economic Theory and the Role of Government in East Asian Industrialisation*, Princeton, NJ: Princeton University Press.
——(1998a) 'From "Miracle" to "Cronyism": Explaining the Great Asian Slump', *Cambridge Journal of Economics* 22: 693–706.
——(1998b) 'The Asian Debt-and-Development Crisis of 1997–? Causes and Consequences', *World Development* 26(8): 1535–53.
——(2011) 'Emerging World Order? From Multipolarity to Multilateralism in the G20, the World Bank and the IMF', *Politics and Society* 39(3): 347–78.
Wallerstein, I. (2001 [1991]) *Unthinking Social Science. The Limits of Nineteeh-Century Paradigms*, 2nd edn, Philadelphia, PA: Temple University Press.
Walton, J. and Seddon, D. (1994) *Free Markets and Food Riots*, Oxford: Blackwell.
Warren, B. (1980) *Imperialism: Pioneer of Capitalism*, London: Verso.
Watson, M. (2005) *Foundations of International Political Economy*, Basingstoke: Palgrave Macmillan.
Weber, M. (1947) *The Theory of Social and Economic Organisation*, London: Free Press.
Weiss, L. and Hobson, J.M. (2000) 'State Power and Economic Strength Revisited: What's So Special about the Asian Crisis', in Richard Robison *et al.* (eds) *Politics and Markets in the Wake of the Asian Crisis*, London: Routledge, 53–74.
Williams, D. (2011) *International Development and Global Politics: History, Theory and Practice*, London: Routledge.
Williams, W.A. (1972 [1959]) *The Tragedy of American Diplomacy*, New York: W.W. Norton.
Williamson, J. (1990) 'What Washington Means by Policy Reform', in J. Williamson, *Latin American Adjustment: How Much has Happened?* Washington, DC: Peterson Institute for International Economics.
——(1993) 'Democracy and the "Washington Consensus"', *World Development* 21(8): 1329–36.
——(2000) 'What Should the World Bank Think about the Washington Consensus?' *The World Bank Research Observer* 15(2): 251–64.
——(2003) 'The Washington Consensus and Beyond', *Economic and Political Weekly* 38(15): 1475–81.
——(2004) 'The Strange History of the Washington Consensus', *Journal of Post Keynesian Economics* 27(2): 195–206.
——(2009) 'Short History of the Washington Consensus, A', *Law & Bus. Rev. Am.* 15: 7.
Winters, J.A. (2000) 'The Financial Crisis in Southeast Asia', in Richard Robison *et al.* (eds) *Politics and Markets in the Wake of the Asian Crisis*, London: Routledge, 34–52.
Wolf, M. (2004) *Why Globalization Works*, New Haven, CT: Yale University Press.

——(2008) 'Regulators Should Intervene in Bankers' Pay', FT.com, 15 January, www.ft.com/cms/s/0/73a891b4-c38d-11dc-b083-0000779fd2ac.html?nclick_check=1 (accessed January 2009).

——(2009) 'Choices made in 2009 will Shape the Globe's Destiny', *Financial Times*, 6 January, www.ft.com/cms/s/0/4f5c5ba2-dc22-11dd-b07e-000077b07658.html (accessed January 2009).

——(2010) 'The IMF's Foolish Praise for Austerity', *Financial Times*, 30 September.

——(2011) 'Time for Common Sense on Greece', *Financial Times*, 22 June.

Wolfensohn, J.D. (1999) 'Remarks at the International Conference on Democracy, Market Economy and Development', Seoul, 26 February, Washington, DC: The World Bank.

Woo, W.T. (2004) 'Serious Inadequacies of the Washington Consensus: Misunderstanding the Poor by the Brightest', *Diversity in Development: Reconsidering the Washington Consensus*, The Hague: FONDAD, 9–43.

Woods, N. (2006) *The Globalizers: The IMF, the World Bank and their Borrowers*, New York: Cornell University Press.

World Bank (1981) *Accelerated Development in sub-Saharan Africa*, Washington, DC: World Bank).

——(1991) *World Development Report 1991: The Challenge of Development*, New York: Oxford University Press.

——(1993) *The East Asian Miracle: Economic Growth and Public Policy*, Oxford: Oxford University Press.

——(1997) *World Development Report 1997: The State in a Changing World*, New York: Oxford University Press.

——(1998) *East Asia: The Road to Recovery*, Washington, DC: The World Bank.

——(1999) *World Development Report 1998–9: Knowledge for Development*, New York: Oxford University Press.

——(2002) *Globalization, Growth and Poverty*, Oxford: Oxford University Press.

——(2003) *Better Governance for Development in the MENA: Enhancing Exclusiveness and Accountability*, Washington, DC: World Bank.

——(2007) *Development Prospects in MENA*, Washington, DC: World Bank, web.worldbank.org/WBSITE/EXTERNAL/COUNTRIES/MENAEXT/DevelopmentProspectsinMENA2007.

——(2009) *MENA Development Report 2009: From Privilege to Competition, Unlocking Private-led Growth in the Middle East and North Africa*, Washington, DC: World Bank.

——(2011) *Doing Business Report 2011*, Washington, DC: World Bank, siteresources.worldbank.org/INTMENA/Resources/DoingBusiness2011.pdf.

——(n.d.) *Data and Statistics*, various years, web.worldbank.org.

WTO (World Trade Organization) (2005) *International Trade Statistics*, Geneva: World Trade Organization.

Yardley, J. (2004) Farmers Being Moved Aside By China's Real Estate Boom, *The New York Times*, 8 December, query.nytimes.com/gst/fullpage.html?res=9E0CE3D71231F93BA35751C1A9629C8B63&pagewanted=all (accessed 30 September 2012).

Yeyati, E. and Williams, T. (2012) *Emerging Economies in the 2000s: Real Decoupling and Financial Recoupling*, Washington, DC: World Bank Policy Research Working Paper no. 5961.

Yom, S.L. (2005) 'Civil Society and Democratization in the Arab World', *Middle East* 9(4): 15, web.worldbank.org/WBSITE/EXTERNAL/COUNTRIES/MENAEXT/DevelopmentProspectsinMENA.

Zeisel, H. (1975 [1933]) 'Zur Geschichte der Soziographie', in M. Jahoda, P.F. Lazarsfeld and H. Zeisel, *Die Arbeitslosen von Mariehal. Ein soziographischer Versuch*, Frankfurt: Suhrkamp.

Zengxian, W. (1997) 'How Successful has State-owned Enterprise Reform been in China?' *Europe-Asia Studies* 49(7): 1237–62.

eBooks
from Taylor & Francis
Helping you to choose the right eBooks for your Library

Add to your library's digital collection today with Taylor & Francis eBooks. We have over 45,000 eBooks in the Humanities, Social Sciences, Behavioural Sciences, Built Environment and Law, from leading imprints, including Routledge, Focal Press and Psychology Press.

Choose from a range of subject packages or create your own!

Benefits for you
- Free MARC records
- COUNTER-compliant usage statistics
- Flexible purchase and pricing options
- 70% approx of our eBooks are now DRM-free.

Benefits for your user
- Off-site, anytime access via Athens or referring URL
- Print or copy pages or chapters
- Full content search
- Bookmark, highlight and annotate text
- Access to thousands of pages of quality research at the click of a button.

ORDER YOUR FREE INSTITUTIONAL TRIAL TODAY

Free Trials Available

We offer free trials to qualifying academic, corporate and government customers.

eCollections
Choose from 20 different subject eCollections, including:

- Asian Studies
- Economics
- Health Studies
- Law
- Middle East Studies

eFocus
We have 16 cutting-edge interdisciplinary collections, including:

- Development Studies
- The Environment
- Islam
- Korea
- Urban Studies

For more information, pricing enquiries or to order a free trial, please contact your local sales team:

UK/Rest of World: **online.sales@tandf.co.uk**
USA/Canada/Latin America: **e-reference@taylorandfrancis.com**
East/Southeast Asia: **martin.jack@tandf.com.sg**
India: **journalsales@tandfindia.com**

www.tandfebooks.com